CANADA

ST. LAWRENCE

LAKE ONTARIO

ADAMS

NEW YORK

ROME • WESTERN

ERIE CANAL

ONEIDA

ALBANY

LAKE CHAMPLAIN

VERMONT

NEW HAMPSHIRE

PORTLAND

MASSACHUSETTS

BOSTON

HUDSON R.

CONNECTICUT

NEW HAVEN

PROVIDENCE

RHODE ISLAND

NEW YORK CITY

NEWARK

SOUND

LONG ISLAND

PENNSYLVANIA

SUSQUEHANNA R.

PRINCETON

PHILADELPHIA

NEW JERSEY

DELAWARE

ATLANTIC OCEAN

MARYLAND

MD.

VIRGINIA

JAMES R.

HANOVER

(CHESAPEAKE BAY)

HAMPDEN SYDNEY

WILLIAMSBURG

MTS.

CAROLINA

REVIVAL AND REVIVALISM

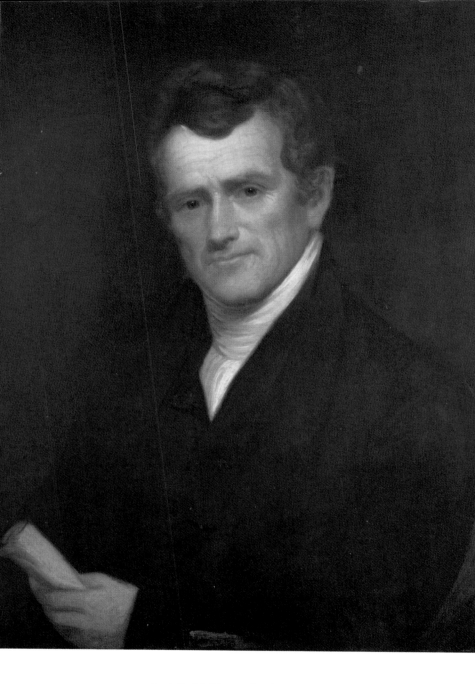

Archibald Alexander (1772–1851)
A portrait by John Neagle.
Reproduced by courtesy of
Princeton Theological Seminary,
New Jersey.

REVIVAL AND REVIVALISM

THE MAKING AND MARRING OF AMERICAN EVANGELICALISM

1750–1858

Iain H. Murray

THE BANNER OF TRUTH TRUST

THE BANNER OF TRUTH TRUST
3 Murrayfield Road, Edinburgh EH12 6EL
PO Box 621, Carlisle, Pennsylvania 17013, USA

*

© Iain H. Murray 1994
First published 1994
Reprinted 1996
Reprinted 2002
ISBN 0 85151 660 2

*

Typeset at The Spartan Press Limited, Lymington, Hants
and printed and bound at The Bath Press, Bath

TO
JEAN ANN
ON THE
FORTIETH ANNIVERSARY
OF OUR ENGAGEMENT

CONTENTS

[vii]

ILLUSTRATIONS

PREFACE

Two feelings are uppermost as I see this book go to press. First, thankfulness for the opportunity to have lived with such a theme and with those who, though long dead, speak to us still. Second, indebtedness to so many for the help which has made it possible.

My interest in American church history goes back to the 1950s but it was invitations to speak on the subject of revivals in the United States at the Family Conference of Grace Baptist Church, Carlisle, Pennsylvania, and at the Pensacola Theological Institute, Florida, in the summer of 1973, which laid the groundwork for this volume. I shall be ever grateful to the sponsors of those conferences and to the many present whose kindness opened a new world of friendships. As a family we learned why George Whitefield could say, 'The Americans are the most hospitable people under heaven'. The summer of 1973 also provided an opportunity to visit a few of the places connected with this history and this deepened the desire to pursue the subject further. It was not, however, until the late 1980s, when living in Australia, that it was possible to do more serious research and to commence writing. In that location I had the surprise of finding great spoils in the private library of the Rev Robert O. Evans at Hazelbrook in the Blue Mountains of New South Wales. Mr Evans has long specialised in American revival history and no one could have been more generous in his aid.

Other sources to which I owe particular thanks are the libraries of the University of Sydney; Dickinson College, Carlisle, Pennsylvania; New College, Edinburgh; together with the Evangelical Library and Dr Williams's Library, London. Miss Grace Mullen, the Archivist of Westminster Theological Seminary, Philadelphia, went to great lengths in obtaining for me copies of three rare and essential pamphlets from the 1820s. The list of friends who have helped me find particular books is so long that I will not attempt to name them but I do sincerely thank them all. Special thanks are due to Mr Daniel

[xi]

K.Tennant, and to the Rev Thomas T. Ellis for opening up Southern Presbyterian history to me. My friends, Mrs Robyn Phillips, Dr John R. de Witt and Dr Sinclair B. Ferguson, have all contributed much by way of aid and advice in bringing these pages to completion. As usual, my colleagues in the work of the Banner of Truth Trust on both sides of the Atlantic have given much encouragement and have transformed my copy into the book now in the reader's hands.

In working on this subject I have often thought of the words of Archibald Alexander, written in 1845: 'Many pious people among us are not aware that the ground on which they tread has, as it were, been hallowed by the footsteps of the Almighty. And who knows but that prayers offered in faith remain yet to be answered.'

IAIN H. MURRAY
Edinburgh, 13 July 1993

INTRODUCTION

Freehold Presbyterian Church,
New Jersey, a centre of evangelical
influence in the colonial period

The whole theory of revivals is involved in these two facts; viz., that the influence of the Holy Spirit is concerned in every instance of sound conversion, and that this influence is granted in more copious measure and in greater power at some times than at others. When these facts concur, there is a revival of religion.

Joel Hawes in Edward A. Lawrence, *The Life of Joel Hawes* (Hartford, Conn., 1871), p. 113.

It was a striking proof of the determination of heaven to spread the gospel through the world, that Jerusalem should have been selected as the place, and the day of Pentecost as the season, for the first great out-pouring of the Spirit: because a blow then and there struck could not fail to tell with emphasis on all the surrounding nations. So, in our own day, it is a signal from heaven, of no ordinary import, that the Spirit is actually descending in power on several of our large cities and towns, as well as on colleges and seminaries of learning. The consequence of which is that men of wealth and extended influence are brought to 'count all things but loss for Christ'; and champions of truth and heralds of salvation are thus multiplied. At the same time, the missionary channels, which are daily opening, and the religious publications, which are circulating by thousands and tens of thousands, afford facilities of communication altogether unparalleled in the history of Christ's kingdom.

Baxter Dickinson, *The National Preacher* (New York, January 1827), pp. 126–8.

[xiv]

I have somewhere met the remark, that 'the chariot of the gospel never has free course, but the devil tries to be charioteer'. There is nothing he is so much afraid of as the power of the Holy Ghost. Where he cannot arrest the showers of blessing, it has ever been one of his devices to dilute or poison the streams . . . With the obvious signs of the times in view, who does not see that this artful foe would enjoy his malignant triumph, if he could prejudice the minds of good men against all *revivals of religion*? This he does, not so much by opposing them, as by counterfeiting the genuine coin, and by *getting up* revivals that are spurious and to his liking. Revivals are always spurious when they are *got up* by man's device, and not *brought down* by the Spirit of God.

> Gardiner Spring, *Personal Reminiscences of the Life and Times of Gardiner Spring* (New York, 1866), vol. 1, pp. 217–8.

An impression prevails that Presbyterians of the Old School, do not believe in revivals of religion, but this is erroneous. The differences between them and the New School are not as to the fact of revivals, but as to the evidences of their genuineness.

> Lewis Cheeseman, *Differences Between Old and New School Presbyterians* (Rochester, N.Y., 1848), p. 150.

By 1854, a corrrespondent of the *Independent* could write jovially, 'Brethren, if you will follow the above directions for *two months*, and do not enjoy a revival of religion of the *old stamp*, you may tell me and the public, that I am no prophet.'

. . . If salvation was available for the asking, then a revival was a matter of getting the greatest possible number to ask – a matter of salesmanship. As theology grew simpler, technique became predominant.

> Bernard A. Weisberger, *They Gathered at the River: The Story of the Great Revivalists and Their Impact upon Religion in America* (Boston, 1958), pp. 147, 271.

I do not desire, I do not advise a bustling, artificial effort to get up a revival, nor the construction of any man-devised machinery . . . I want God's work, not man's . . . I want no revivalist preachers.

> John Angell James, *Discourses Addressed to the Churches* (London, 1861), pp. 544–5, 551.

There is one grace you cannot counterfeit . . . the grace of *perseverance*.

Gardiner Spring, *The Life and Times of Gardiner Spring*
(New York, 1866) vol. 1, p. 51.

Things are allowed to be said and done at revivals which nobody could defend . . . If, for a moment, our improvements seem to produce a larger result than the old gospel, it will be the growth of mushrooms, it may even be of toadstools; but it is not the growth of trees of the Lord.

C. H. Spurgeon, *An All-Round Ministry*
(London, 1900: Banner of Truth repr. 1965), pp. 375–6.

I would affirm that much of the modern approach to evangelism, with its techniques and methods, is unnecessary if we *really* believe in the doctrine of the Holy Spirit and His application of God's message . . . Should we not concentrate more, as the church has done through the centuries, upon praying for, and laying the basis of Christian instruction for, revival as it is described in the Bible?

D. M. Lloyd-Jones, 'Conversions:
Psychological and Spiritual', *Knowing the Times*
(Banner of Truth, 1989), pp. 88–9.

The understanding of the subject of revival has passed through several distinct phases in American history. In the first phase, from the 1620s to about 1858 (the year which marked the last general religious awakening in North America), revival was understood to refer to 'some special seasons wherein God doth in a remarkable manner revive religion among his people'. The words are those of Solomon Stoddard in 1712[1] but they might have been drawn from any one of a multitude of preachers and authors. From the time of the first settlers in New England, the phenomenon was regarded as a 'surprising work of God', to use the later phrase of Jonathan Edwards. Looking back on history, Joel Hawes, minister of the First Congregational Church of Hartford, Connecticut, could write in 1832: 'The church of which I am pastor, like most of the early churches of New England, was planted in the spirit of revivals . . . Revivals of religion have always been held in high estimation by the church.'[2] Abel Stevens was reflecting exactly the same standpoint when he attributed the success of American Methodism to 'one chief source', namely, 'this "power from on high", this "unction from the Holy One".'[3]

[1] From his chapter 'The Benefit of the Gospel' in *The Efficacy of the Fear of Hell, to Restrain Men from Sin* (Boston, 1713), quoted by Michael J. Crawford, *Seasons of Grace: Colonial New England's Revival Tradition in Its British Context* (New York: Oxford University Press, 1991), p. 110.

[2] Letter 6, in the Appendix to W. B. Sprague, *Lectures on Revivals of Religion* (1832; Banner of Truth, 1959).

[3] Abel Stevens, *A Compendious History of American Methodism* (New York, 1867), p. 582.

Although the ideas for it were born earlier, it was not until the last forty years of the nineteenth century that a new view of revival came generally to displace the old, and a distinctly different phase in the understanding of the subject began. A shift in vocabulary was a pointer to the nature of the change. Seasons of revival became 'revival meetings'. Instead of being 'surprising' they might now be even announced in advance, and whereas no one in the previous century had known of ways to secure a revival, a system was now popularised by 'revivalists' which came near to guaranteeing results. But instead of revival and revivalism being recognized as two different things, the remarkable fact is that the promoters of the new view, whose books came to govern evangelical thought, appeared to believe that they represented the authentic thought of American Christian history. This phase of understanding ran its course in the opening decades of the twentieth century. Despite its alleged evangelistic success, the organised 'revival' inevitably brought the very word into disrepute. The opinion became widespread that such revivals did more harm to the churches than they did good. In the outcome, revival was for many years a discredited subject and the study of it fell into abeyance.

Yet another phase began in 1958–59 with the publication of the books of Bernard Weisberger and William McLoughlin.[1] These authors pleaded for a serious and what they thought of as a scientific re-examination of the whole subject. McLoughlin opened his Preface with the words, 'History has not dealt fairly with American revivals'. Weisberger wrote: 'There are numerous histories of revivals in the United States written by devout ministers or worshippers in the evangelical denominations. They are, almost without exception, useless as history.'[2]

The work of these two writers, and of others who followed them, is valuable in its analysis of the character of revivalism. A mass of evidence has been produced to show that the idea behind the revivalist methods of 'the call to the altar', that is,

---

[1] Bernard A. Weisberger, *They Gathered at the River: The Story of the Great Revivalists and Their Impact upon Religion in America* (Boston: Little, Brown and Co., 1958); William G. McLoughlin, *Modern Revivalism: Charles Grandison Finney to Billy Graham* (New York: Ronald Press Co., 1959).

[2] *They Gathered at the River*, p. 275.

Introduction

the public invitation to come forward 'to receive Christ', was 'to separate the penitents – those actively seeking salvation – from the rest of the congregation so that they could be made more easily and more intensely subject to the psychological and social pressures of the minister and of the community of the converted'.[1] Or, as another writer says, 'American revivalism began as a method of obtaining (at least in appearance) the external signs of conviction, repentance and rebirth'.[2] But while these modern authors are able to show why revivalism is discredited, they fail to recognize the all-important distinction between religious excitements, deliberately organized to secure converts, and the phenomenon of authentic spiritual awakening which is the work of the living God. The two things are treated as essentially the same. They are aware, of course, that orthodox Christianity at an earlier date protested that revival and revivalism – far from being of the same genus – are actually opposed; but they never take that case seriously and it does not enter into their understanding of history. If revivalism can be explained in purely human terms, so, they think, can revival. Thus they follow the authors of the second phase in using the terms interchangeably, even when writing of eras long before preachers ever thought of trying to organise revivals or of securing mass conversions. In other words, these modern writers on revival endorse the erroneous idea that revivalism constituted no real departure from the revival tradition which had formerly existed in all the Protestant denominations. But while they agree on this point with the authors sympathetic to revivalism in the later nineteenth century, they disagree with them profoundly on something more basic. Whereas those authors regarded both revival and revivalism as supernatural, the more recent writers see the power of God in neither. Thus Weisberger tells us frankly: 'I want to emphasise that this is a book about religion, and not a religious book. In the past, most histories of revivalism looked no further for explanation than the sovereign pleasure of God. As a historian, I have tried to

---

[1] Richard Carwardine, *Transatlantic Revivalism: Popular Evangelicalism in Britain and America, 1790–1865* (Westport, Conn.: Greenwood Press, 1978), p. 13.

[2] John Kent, *Holding The Fort, Studies in Victorian Revivalism* (London: Epworth Press, 1978), p. 367.

interpret revivals in purely secular terms.' This is tantamount to saying that if God is in history at all that fact lies outside the bounds of serious historical discussion. Such a standpoint seeks to open a door into the meaning of history when the key to its significance has already been discarded.

My thesis in this book is that in the period of our study, American history was shaped by the Spirit of God in revivals of the same kind as launched the early church into a pagan world. Until 1858, innumerable authors understood events which they had themselves seen in this way. For the most part I try to let these witnesses speak for themselves. They belonged to various denominations. Some were comparatively untrained 'saddle-bags' frontier preachers, others were leaders and scholars at such institutions as Yale and Princeton, Dartmouth and Andover. What they had in common was the conviction that God is always faithful to his Word, that Christ is risen and that the Holy Spirit has been given to ensure the advancement of his kingdom. But it may come as a surprise to find that these men were equally opposed to what was merely emotional, contrived or manipulated. They believed that strict adherence to Scripture is the only guard against what may be wrongly claimed as the work of God's Spirit. They foresaw the danger of revivalism long before it became a respected part of evangelicalism, and they would have had no problem in agreeing with the criticism which has since discredited it.

What is needed now is to get back to the authors of the eras *before* the whole meaning of revival was confused. This is not easy to do. For reasons which will appear later in these pages, practically all the potted evangelical histories of American revivals produced since the 1860s have treated revival in the framework of revivalistic belief. There is scarcely a mention of the extent of the difference between the old and the new. It is generally books published before 1860 that will help us. In that connection the recent bibliography produced by Richard Owen Roberts is a major asset in the discovery of older titles,[1] a few of which have also been republished by Mr Roberts in a 'Revival Library' series. I hope that these pages will also lead

[1] Richard Owen Roberts, *Revival Literature; An Annotated Bibliography, with Biographical and Historical Notices* (Wheaton, Ill.: Roberts Publishers, 1987).

many readers to sources which they can explore for themselves.

The reason for beginning this book in the 1750s with Samuel Davies is practical rather than historical. Davies constituted no new starting point, for his thinking on this subject was identical with his predecessors. But to have started earlier, in the seventeenth century or with the Great Awakening of the 1740s, would have meant a book of unmanageable size, and much is already available on the Great Awakening. The Second Great Awakening is far less known.

I have included a lengthy appendix on 'Revivalism in Britain' in part because it is a reminder of how closely Britain and the United States are related. Bismark, the German leader, regarded the fact that the British and the Americans spoke the same language as the most important fact of the nineteeth century. J. W. Alexander of New York called his hearers to consider 'what Providence has done in regard to the diffusion of the English language . . . From no language of the earth could there be collected a more able, extensive and complete exposition and defence of the truth, against infidelity on one hand and Romanism on the other, than from our own.'[1] This communion of language would never have possessed the influence which it did had evangelical Christianity not brought so many of the people of the two nations to read the same Bible and to worship the same triune God. At one of the darkest hours in the Second World War, Harry Hopkins, President Roosevelt's closest adviser and confidant, met with Winston Churchill and Tom Johnston (Secretary of State for Scotland) in a Glasgow hotel. At the conclusion of anxious discussion, Lord Moran recalled, Hopkins said to the British Prime Minister: 'I suppose you wish to know what I am going to say to President Roosevelt on my return. Well, I'm going to quote you one verse from that Book of Books in the truth of which Mr Johnston's mother and my own Scottish mother were brought up: "Whither thou goest, I will go; and where thou lodgest, I will lodge: thy people shall be my people, and

---

[1] 'A Thanksgiving Sermon on the English Language' in the *Presbyterian Magazine*, Ed. C. Van Rensselaer (Philadelphia, 1857), pp. 251, 255.

thy God my God". Then he added very quietly: "Even to the end".[1] Just over twenty years later, when Churchill left Idlewild (now Kennedy) Airport, in New York, for the last time, he said, 'As long as the United States and Great Britain are united, the future is one of high hope, both for ourselves and for the free world'.

Today both nations are drifting fast from a common spiritual heritage. It is no coincidence that the old unity, which went deeper than ancestral roots, has weakened just as adherence to Protestant and evangelical Christianity has been weakened. The kingdom of Christ will survive any wreck of nations, but we believe that, under God, the unity of prayer and faith of Christians on both sides of the Atlantic is still vitally related to the cause of Christ world-wide. Literature in the English language is still the literature which schools the greater part of the Christian church. As in the past, a true awakening in either country is sure to affect the other, as well as nations far beyond. This book has been written in the hope that it may strengthen faith and encourage prayer for another great outpouring of the Spirit of God.

[1] Lord Moran, *Winston Churchill; The Struggle for Survival, 1940–1965* (London: Constable, 1966), p. 6. Moran, who was present, adds, 'I was surprised to find the P.M. in tears'. One day, perhaps, someone will write a book on the effect of Christianity on the joint destinies of America and Britain. In the 1750s Samuel Davies spoke of 'a union of hearts which cannot bear, without pain, the intervention of the huge Atlantic', and in the 1880s C. H. Spurgeon would commonly pray for 'the sister country across the flood'.

I

SAMUEL DAVIES AND THE MEANING OF 'REVIVAL'

Nassau Hall, Princeton

I

Short in its duration, Samuel Davies' ministry cast a shadow far beyond his own day. It endured as a force among his contemporaries who outlived him by forty or more years into the early nineteenth century. Thereafter, through his published sermons and the all-too-brief records of his life, a common tradition of what Davies was survived on both sides of the Atlantic. 'In accomplishing the great objects contemplated in the Christian Ministry,' wrote a Methodist in 1842, 'few men . . . in any age have been more honored than Davies.'[1] John Angell James in his classic on the Christian ministry first published in 1847, explained how he came to see more clearly the significance of earnest, awakening preaching through reading Davies' sermons, and from that time, he said, 'I have made the conversion of the impenitent *the* great end of my ministry.'[2] Speaking at Westminster Theological Seminary in 1967, Martyn Lloyd-Jones urged upon students for the ministry the reading of those same sermons and called Davies 'the greatest preacher you have ever produced in this country'.[3]

[1] R.W.A., 'Review, *Sermons on Important Subjects* (1842)', p. 138, quoted in G. W. Pilcher, *Samuel Davies: Apostle of Dissent in Colonial Virginia* (Knoxville, Tenn.: University of Tennessee Press, 1971), p. 87.

[2] J. A. James, *An Earnest Ministry the Want of the Times*, 4th ed. (London, 1858), p. 20.

[3] D. M. Lloyd-Jones, *Knowing the Times: Addresses Delivered on Various Occasions 1942–1977* (Edinburgh: Banner of Truth, 1989), p. 263. Ashbel Green, a successor to Davies in the presidency of Princeton College, wrote: 'President Davies, from what I have heard of him, was probably the most accomplished preacher that our country has produced'. Joseph H. Jones, *Life of Ashbel Green* (New York, 1849), p. 251.

The known facts of Davies' early life are fragmentary in the extreme. A note in his own hand in his Bible records, 'Born in New-Castle County Pennsilvania Nov. 3, 1723'. The counties of Delaware (of which New Castle was one) were at this time attached to Pennsylvania and, with New York and New Jersey, made up 'the Middle Colonies'. These four colonies together had an immigrant population of some 65,000 at the beginning of the eighteenth century. Although of Welsh parentage, Davies usually designated himself and his hearers in later years as 'free-born Britons'.

Samuel was the only son of a godly mother and his early education was under their Baptist pastor, Abel Morgan. By the time he was eleven his mother had become attached to the Presbyterians, which may have been the reason for his removal to another school 'some distance from home'. We know that at some point in his teenage years he was a pupil at the small classical school of the Englishman William Robinson. It was probably around the same time as Robinson left school-mastering for the work of the ministry in 1740, or soon after, that Davies removed to the 'log college' of the Rev. Samuel Blair at Fagg's Manor. In this rural location in Chester County, Pennsylvania (north of New Castle), Blair had settled among a Presbyterian people in 1739. He was not impressed by their spiritual condition:

The nature and necessity of the new birth was but little known or thought of. The necessity of a conviction of sin and misery by the Holy Spirit opening and applying the law to the conscience, in order to a saving closure with Christ, was hardly known at all to the most . . . There was scarcely any suspicion at all, in general, of any danger of depending upon self-righteousness, and not upon the righteousness of Christ alone for salvation. Papists and Quakers would be readily acknowledged guilty of this crime, but hardly any professed Presbyterian.[1]

Both at Fagg's Manor and much further afield, these spiritual conditions were to undergo such a change in 1740 that the

[1] Letter of Blair, printed in Archibald Alexander, *Biographical sketches of the founder, and principal alumni of the Log College, together with an account of the revivals of religion under their ministry*: (Princeton, N.J., 1845; London: Banner of Truth, 1968), pp. 156–57.

whole future history of the nation was to be affected by it. Recalling that time later in his life when he was preaching in Virginia in 1757, Davies said:

About sixteen years ago, in the northern colonies, when all religious concern was much out of fashion, and the generality lay in a dead sleep in sin, having at best but the form of godliness, but nothing of the power; when the country was in peace and prosperity, free from the calamities of war, and epidemical sickness; when, in short, there were no extraordinary calls to repentance; suddenly a deep, general concern about eternal things spread through the country; sinners started out of their slumbers, broke off from their vices, began to cry out, What shall we do to be saved? and made it the great business of their life to prepare for the world to come. Then the gospel seemed almighty, and carried all before it. It pierced the very hearts of men with an irresistible power. I have seen thousands at once melted down under it; all eager to hear as for life, and hardly a dry eye to be seen among them. Many have since backslidden, and all their religion is come to nothing, or dwindled away into mere formality. But, blessed be God, thousands still remain shining monuments of the power of divine grace in that glorious day.[1]

Davies was a Christian before the Great Awakening. At the age of fifteen he had assurance that he had passed from death to life and was already committed to a life in the ministry of the gospel. But under Blair at Fagg's Manor he would have gained a conception of preaching that would never leave him. In later years he recalled the experience he shared with fellow students:

When, all attention, eager to admit
The flowing knowledge, at his reverend feet
Raptured we sat . . .
Oh, Blair! whom all the tenderest names commend –
My father, tutor, pastor, brother, friend!

The Awakening was heralded by a new kind of preaching, which was authoritative, fervent, and heart-searching, and one of its most conspicuous results was the multiplication of the number of preachers in the same mould.[2] William Robinson,

---

[1] Samuel Davies, *Sermons on Important Subjects* (London, 1824), vol. 4, pp. 49–50 (hereafter Davies).
[2] The change in preaching is discussed in my *Jonathan Edwards: A New Biography* (Edinburgh: Banner of Truth, 1987), pp. 124–33.

Davies' former teacher, was among the first. Ordained in August 1741 by the New Brunswick Presbytery (the centre of evangelical influence in New Jersey and Pennsylvania), he became 'a bright meteor . . . blazing in the light of God wherever he went'. 'Love to God and souls as an irresistible impulse bore him on over every possible infirmity and obstacle.' Declining a call to succeed William Tennent at Neshaminy Creek, Robinson chose to travel far and wide in the sparsely settled, unevangelized regions to the west and south. His was the first voice for the gospel which many were to hear down the great Valley of Virginia, across the Blue Ridge Mountains and into the small towns of North Carolina. Archibald Alexander, a shrewd judge of American church history, wrote in the 1840s: 'Probably Mr Robinson during the short period of his life was the instrument in the conversion of as many souls as any minister who ever lived in this country.'[1]

Of particular relevance to our story is Robinson's arrival at Hanover in Hanover County, Virginia, where he preached for four days in July 1743. The place, twelve miles from Richmond, and in a comparatively prosperous district, was one of the first populated after Virginia's settlement in the early seventeenth century. The people were not unchurched for, in a special sense, the Church of England was established by law in the Old Dominion. All Virginians paid tithes to the clergy, and the Book of Common Prayer held undisputed sway, since some 1,000 people of Puritan conviction had removed north in the 1640s. But when George Whitefield, one of their own clergy, preached at Williamsburg, the capital of the colony, in 1739, there were Anglicans who found his message strangely new.[2] Four years later a book of Whitefield's sermons reached Hanover County, fifty miles from Williamsburg; and a group led by Samuel Morris, convicted by what they read, stopped attending the formal service of the established Church to gather

---

[1] Alexander, *Log College*, p. 209.

[2] Writing of Virginia to Joseph Bellamy in 1751, Davies observed: 'The Clergy universally, as far as my Intelligence extends, have embraced the modish System of Arminian Divinity, (tho' I allow myself the Pleasure to hope there are sundry conscientious Persons among them) and the Calvinistic, or rather Pauline Articles of their own Church are counted horrendous and insufferable.'

instead at what they called a 'Reading Room' where they 'heard' Puritan preachers of the previous century like Bolton, Baxter, Flavel, and Bunyan. Such were the circumstances when Robinson came in July 1743, and the effect of four days of preaching in Hanover was immense. 'Few in the numerous assemblies on these four days appeared unaffected,' wrote Morris. 'They returned alarmed with apprehensions of their dangerous condition, convinced of their former entire ignorance of religion, and anxiously inquiring what they should do to be saved. And there is reason to believe there was as much good done by these four sermons as by all the sermons preached in these parts before or since.'[1]

Before Robinson left Hanover he was pressed by the people to receive a generous financial gift. He persisted in his refusal, but found the money securely hidden in his heavier-than-usual saddle-bags on the morning of his departure. With a smile he accepted it and assured them of a good use to which it would be put: 'There is a young man of my acquaintance, of promising talents and piety, who is now studying with a view to the ministry; but his circumstances are embarrassing; he has not funds to support and carry him on without much difficulty; this money will relieve him.'

The 'young man' towards whom Robinson had a special regard was Samuel Davies. It was to Davies that he also bequeathed his library on his death in 1746. The short years of Robinson's ministry had followed rather than coincided with the Great Awakening, but his labours proved that there could be powerful local revivals – as at Hanover in 1743 – when the conditions no longer prevailed elsewhere. It was probably Robinson who called on Davies to help him in another such revival which broke out in Somerset County, Maryland in 1745, the year before Robinson's death. Davies remembered that time as 'the most glorious display of divine grace in Maryland':

I was there about two months, when the work was at its height, and I never saw such deep and spreading concern; the assemblies were numerous, though in the extremity of a cold winter, and unwearied in attending the word; and frequently there were very few among them

---

[1] Alexander, *Log College*, pp. 199–200.

that did not give some plain indications of distress or joy. Oh! these were the happiest days that ever my eyes saw.[1]

Not surprisingly, given the demands afforded by such opportunities, together with the hard study that preceded his being licensed to preach the gospel, in 1747 Davies' health was in a precarious state. On 19 February of that year the New Castle Presbytery ordained him as an evangelist and directed his attention to Virginia. This brought him, about two months later, to preach to the worshippers at the Reading Room in Hanover. He had heard of the need there from Robinson and others, but, he wrote, 'I had no more thoughts of it, as my pastoral charge, than of the remotest corner of the world.'[2] For both people and preacher it proved to be a joyful visit: 'Though the fervour of the late work was considerably abated, and my labours were not blessed with success equal to that of my brethren, yet I have reason to hope they were of service in several instances.' The eagerness of Davies' scattered hearers carried him into adjacent counties, and it was soon apparent that the people who would make up any charge were spread over a district of some sixty miles.

Oppressed by a sense of his 'rawness and inexperience', Davies' health broke down under the load of preaching and there were fever-ridden nights when people would sit with him until the morning. By August 1747 his first visit to Hanover was over and he was fit enough to ride the 100 miles back to Delaware, in time to witness the sudden death of his wife and the infant she was carrying on 15 September. Grief and depression were added to his own bodily weakness: 'After I returned from Virginia I spent near a year under melancholy and consumptive languishments, expecting death.' All this was undoubtedly part of God's preparation for his future usefulness. As Archibald Alexander wrote in another context, 'Too much applause is a dangerous thing to a young minister.' Davies was soon to see much success, but before it came he had been deeply chastened by a sense of his own infirmity and by the consciousness of the brevity of all earthly things.

In 1748 the people of Hanover renewed their endeavours of

---

[1] Alexander, *Log College*, p. 208. [2] Davies, vol. 4, p. 455.

the previous year to call Davies as their pastor, and he was finally constrained by the 'urgent necessity and importunity of the people': 'I put my life in my hand and determined to accept their call, hoping I might live to prepare the way for some more useful successor, and willing to expire under the fatigue of duty rather than in voluntary negligence.'[1] When he wrote in his Bible the brief sentence

Settled in Hanover Virginia May 1748

the words were more momentous than he could then realize. There is no indication that he had a presentiment such as Whitefield recorded in his journal when he was in Virginia on 16 December 1739: 'could not but think that God intended, in His own time, to work a good work in these southern parts of America. At present they seem more dead to God but far less prejudiced than in the northern parts.'[2]

*   *   *

One hundred and fifty heads of families signed Davies' call to Hanover. A meeting-house, 'a plain, unpretending wooden building, capable of containing about five hundred people',[3] was built in the neighbourhood of the Reading Room. In addition to this, there were three other preaching places established in Hanover and Henrico counties. These soon proved to be insufficient. In a letter dated 23 May 1749 Jonathan Edwards reported to a friend: 'I heard lately a credible account of a remarkable work of conviction and conversion, among whites and negroes, at Hanover, Virginia, under the ministry of Mr Davies, who is lately settled there and has the character of a very ingenious and pious young man.' Soon the total number of preaching places rose to seven, with an eighth added in 1750. Three years after his settlement there were 300 communicants, and in 1753 some 500 or 600

---

[1] W. H. Foote, *Sketches of Virginia*, first series (Philadelphia, 1850; Richmond, Va.: John Knox Press, 1966), p. 163.

[2] *George Whitefield's Journals* (London: Banner of Truth, 1960), p. 372.

[3] The description is that of Foote, who reported that it was still standing in 1850 (*Sketches*, p. 172).

adherents, in these various places.[1] But Davies' concern for the unreached did not permit him to be content even with these large parish boundaries. He was ready to travel to all parts of Virginia and sometimes beyond. There were occasions when he journeyed 500 miles in two months, during which time he might preach forty sermons. Individual converts, the fruit of such visits, became the nucleus for new churches, one of the most significant of these being at Briery in Prince Edward County (a name that will be noted later). Such was the geographical spread of his labours that when a Presbytery was first formed in Virginia in 1755 five ministers served an area that Davies had previously served alone.

That Davies was able to pursue work of this magnitude was due in no small measure to the help of his second wife, under whose care he regained his health. His marriage to Jane Holt of Williamsburg (in October 1748) was also important in other respects. In her father, a former mayor of that colonial capital, he had the support of a well-to-do family in a class-conscious society. Williamsburg, according to W. H. Foote, 'was the centre of taste and fashion and refinement. Wealth, dress and address were everything.' Davies' own bearing often won him influence in unexpected places, but there can be little doubt that his relation to the Holts also brought him favour in the town where Anglican authorities repeatedly sought to put restraints on his influence. Licenses had to be sought at Williamsburg, under the terms allowed to 'Dissenters' by the Toleration Act of 1688, for new preaching points which were opened. They were gained only after stiff opposition. 'Since Mr Davies has been allowed to officiate in so many places,' the Anglican Commissary of the colony wrote to the Bishop of London, 'there has been a great defection from our Religious Assemblies. The generality of his followers, I believe, were born

---

[1] 'Adherents', in Presbyterian terminology, are people in regular attendance at public worship who have not yet been admitted as communicant members. Prior to the Great Awakening it was customary 'that at a certain age nearly all who had been baptized should be received to the Lord's Supper without giving any evidence of a change of heart'. The revival restored the biblical standard for communicant membership. See Thomas Murphy, *The Presbytery of the Log College; or, The Cradle of the Presbyterian Church in America* (Philadelphia: Presbyterian Board of Publication, 1889), pp. 163, 180; Davies, vol. 2, pp. 266–95.

and bred in our Communion.'[1]

Davies' connection with the Holts brought a further important advantage. John Holt, his brother-in-law, worked with the public printer of the colony and the publisher of the *Virginia Gazette*. His support gave Davies a ready entrance into the publishing world, and his sermons and poems[2] regularly appeared in the *Gazette* or, under John Holt's direction, as separate publications. Davies was content to leave all literary arrangements in the hands of his brother-in-law, for, as he told him in a letter of 13 August 1751, the 'hurries' and 'copious entertainments' of Williamsburg held no charms for him. In his rural retreat he wrote: 'I am as happy as perhaps creation can make me: I enjoy all the necessaries and most of the conveniences of life; I have a peaceful study, as a refuge from the hurries and noise of the world around me; the venerable dead are waiting in my library to entertain me . . . I very much question if there be a more calm, placid and contented mortal in Virginia.'

As to the kind of people who made up the growing membership of Davies' church, there is reason to believe that many were in the category that had caused the commissary to complain. These were people, however, who had been brought not so much from one denomination to another as from nominal to real Christianity. They had heard and come to believe the Hanover preacher who said that lukewarm religion which did not make God the end for which men lived would take no one to heaven:

How common, how fashionable is this lukewarm religion! This is the prevailing epidemical sin of our age and country . . . We have thousands of Christians, such as they are; as many Christians as white men; but, alas! they are generally of the Laodicean stamp; they are neither hot nor cold. But it is our first concern to know how it is with ourselves; therefore, let this inquiry go round this congregation: Are you not such lukewarm Christians? Is there any fire and life in your devotions? Or are not all your active powers engrossed by other pursuits?

---

[1] Pilcher, *Davies*, p. 88.
[2] The only verse by Davies which is remembered in the present century is his hymn 'Great God of wonders! all Thy ways/Are matchless, godlike, and divine'.

On Davies' first visit to Hanover in 1747 two of the local gentry had been converted and it was from this class that conversions continued to be seen. When episcopal complaint was made that Davies, by preaching 'on working-days to poor people, his only followers', was depriving men of their necessary livelihood, the pastor was able to reply: 'A great number of my hearers are so well furnished with slaves that they are under no necessity of confining themselves to hard labour. They redeem time from the fashionable riots and excessive diversions of this age. The religion of labour is held sacred among us, as the flourishing circumstances of my people demonstrate.'[1]

It is striking that Davies' preaching appealed equally to the black slave population and to the plantation-owners.[2] 'His success', noted Richard Webster, 'mostly lay in the two extremes, gentlemen and slaves.' Numbers of the latter attended his services and among the 300 communicants three years after his settlement, forty were blacks who had come to faith in Christ. In a letter of 1755 to the Society for Promoting Religious Knowledge in London, Davies wrote of his black hearers:

The number of those who attend my ministry at particular times is uncertain, but generally about three hundred, who give a stated attendance; and never have I been so struck with the appearance of an assembly, as when I have glanced my eye to that part of the meeting-house where they usually sit, adorned, for so it has appeared to me, with so many black countenances eagerly attentive to every word they hear, and frequently bathed in tears. A considerable number, (about an hundred) have been baptized, after a proper time for instruction, and having given credible evidence, not only of their acquaintance with the important doctrines of the Christian religion, but also a deep sense of them upon their minds, attested by a life of strict piety and holiness.[3]

[1] Richard Webster, *A History of the Presbyterian Church in America From its Origin until the year 1760* (Philadelphia, 1857), p. 553.

[2] Ibid., p. 551. In 1755 Davies wrote, 'The inhabitants of Virginia are computed to be about 300,000 men, the one half of which are supposed to be negroes.'

[3] Foote, *Sketches*, p. 285. Charles Colcock Jones, writing in the South nearly a century later, had 'seen persons, born in Africa, who were baptized by Mr. Davies, and by his care had been taught to read: and have seen in their hands the books given to them by this eminent preacher'. *Biblical Repertory and Princeton Review* (Philadelphia, 1843), 26–7.

If the gospel preached was the occasion for the great change in Hanover, there is good reason to believe that the spread of the work owed as much to the impression made by transformed lives as it did to the pulpit. Davies was speaking from observation as well as from Scripture when he said, 'I know of nothing in the world that would have a more efficacious tendency to propagate Christianity through the nations of the earth than the good behaviour of the professors'. He saw families blessed, lives purified, education spread, and happiness multiplied. Serious Christian books came into demand among many who recently had shown no interest in such reading at all. He observed the 'passionate gratitude' with which 'poor slaves' would receive good books. And the truths they read they loved to sing in psalms and hymns: 'Sundry of them have lodged all night in my kitchen and, sometimes, when I waked about two or three o'clock in the morning, a torrent of sacred harmony poured into my chamber, and carried my mind away to heaven. In this seraphic exercise some of them spend almost the whole night.'[1]

A correspondent in nearby Richmond County wrote in 1755: 'When I go amongst Mr Davies' people, religion seems to flourish; it is like the suburbs of heaven: it is very agreeable to see the gentlemen at their morning and evening prayers, with their slaves devoutly joining with them.'[2]

*   *   *

After five years at Hanover, Davies' work was interrupted by an episode which occasioned his keeping a diary for nineteen months. This document is one of the most informative journals of the eighteenth century. From December 1753 to December 1754 Davies was in Britain on a deputation with the Rev. Gilbert Tennent on behalf of the infant College of New Jersey. This College will figure largely in later pages and we must pause here to mention its small beginnings.

At the time of The Great Awakening the log colleges of such men as William Tennent at Neshaminy and Samuel Blair at Fagg's Manor had done more to supply able men for the

---

[1] Pilcher, *Davies*, p. 110.   [2] Webster, *Presbyterian Church*, p. 557.

ministry than had such older institutions as Harvard and Yale which had identified themselves with criticism of the revival. But the evangelical or 'New Light' leaders of the Presbyterians in the Middle Colonies saw the need of more advanced learning than could be well supplied by ministers through their log colleges, especially as the congregations in which they ministered were 'vigorous, united and growing' and now provided 'a very considerable number of candidates'.[1] But while a charter for the College of New Jersey was obtained in 1746 and Jonathan Dickinson appointed as president, lack of financial support meant that little more could be done from Dickinson's parsonage than had been done at the log colleges. The College of New Jersey was opened in May 1747 but the death of Dickinson five months later necessitated a removal of the students to the home of his successor, Aaron Burr, at Newark, New Jersey. In 1752 the Presbyterian Synod of New York settled on Princeton as the permanent site for the College and, to raise the capital necessary to make it a reality, endorsed a request from the trustees of the College that Gilbert Tennent and Samuel Davies 'take a voyage to Europe on the important affairs of the said college'. The idea of a fund-raising mission had been urged by George Whitefield on his American brethren as early as 1748 and on hearing news of the Synod's decision he immediately wrote: 'I am glad Mr Tennent is coming with Mr Davies, if they come with their old fire I trust they will be able to do wonders.'[2]

Only twenty-nine years of age, Davies was apprehensive as he anticipated a visit on which much depended, the more so when he saw a letter from London stating that 'the principles inculcated in the College of New Jersey are generally looked upon as antiquated and unfashionable by the dissenters in England'.[3] A few weeks in the English capital – where Tennent and Davies arrived on 25 December 1753 – was to confirm this opinion as far as the majority of the English Presbyterians were concerned. 'The most numerous and rich', the Presbyterians

[1] Webster, *Presbyterian Church*, p. 251.
[2] *The Works of George Whitefield* (London, 1771), vol. 3, p. 16.
[3] Foote, p. 232. Davies' journal is printed in full in this volume. 'Dissenters' was the name commonly given to the Protestants who had remained apart from the Church of England on the Act of Uniformity of 1662.

were also the leaders 'of the general apostasy of the dissenters from the principles of the Reformation'. News was spread by some in England that the infant College adhered to the 'Calvinistic Scheme' and was 'in the hands of bigots', and this closed both pulpits and purses to the visitors. The Independents (Congregationalists) and Baptists, who, Davies noted, 'are more generally Calvinists than the Presbyterians', gave the two preachers a better welcome. But these groups had little numerical strength ('the congregations are so small that it is enough to damp one's zeal in preaching to them'), a fact not unrelated to the 'dry orthodoxy' and 'Antinomianism' which Davies also observed among them. Dr John Gill was supportive but 'he modestly pleaded that his name would be of little service and that the Baptists in general were, unhappily, ignorant of the importance of learning'.

Aid for the College was not, however, to be restricted to the English Dissenters. While in London, Davies noted in his journal for 1 February 1754 'that the revivals of religion which they had were chiefly in the Church of England by means of Mr Whitefield'. From that Church and its 'Methodists', Davies and Tennent received much of the help that came from England. Whitefield himself was their main patron but they also had help from other clergy, including John and Charles Wesley, despite differences in theology. 'The despised Methodists, with all their foibles, seem to me to have more of the spirit of religion than any set of people in this island', wrote Davies after ten months in Britain. The longer the visit went on the more the interest in their mission deepened among those who loved 'experimental religion', and Davies regarded the success that followed the initial difficulties and disappointments as evidence 'of the remarkable interposition of Providence in favour of the college'. In Britain as a whole something like £4,000 appears to have been raised.

The benefits of this deputation, which resulted in the establishment of the College building (Nassau Hall) at Princeton, were to be seen generations later. To Davies it was given to believe in a harvest of men for the ministry which he did not live to see. He wrote in his journal for 7 May 1754:

I have often walked the tedious crowded streets of London from morning to evening, till my nature has been quite exhausted, and I have been hardly able to move a limb. It was but seldom that I could relax myself in conversation with a friend, by reason of incessant hurries: and when I have had an opportunity, my spirits have been so spent, that I was but a dull companion. My hurries have also denied me the pleasure of a curious traveller, in taking a careful view of the numerous curiosities of nature and art in London. But all these disadvantages have been more than balanced by the success we have had . . . 'Tis but little that so useless a creature can do for God, during the short day of life; but to be instrumental in laying a foundation of extensive benefit to mankind, not only in the present but in future generations, is a most animating prospect: and if my usefulness should thus survive me, I shall live to future ages in the most valuable respects.

The demands of the College of New Jersey were not to end for Davies when he was at last joyfully home again in Hanover on 15 February 1755. Aaron Burr, president of the College, died in 1757, and Jonathan Edwards, his father-in-law and successor, the following year. The trustees then turned to the thirty-five-year-old pastor of Hanover whom they elected to the vacant position. Their decision brought Davies to one of the most difficult and anxious periods of his life. His people and his Presbytery pleaded against his removal. Davies himself wished to remain and he refused the call although, as he told his hearers, its acceptance would have been to his temporal advantage:

Had interest been my motive, I should undoubtedly have preferred two hundred a year before a scanty hundred. Had honour been my motive, I should have chose to have sat in the president's chair in Nassau Hall, rather than continued a despised and calumniated new-light parson in Virginia. Or had ease been my motive, I should have preferred a college life, before that of a hurried, fatigued itinerant.[1]

But applications to Davies from the trustees continued and he stood in doubt of the correctness of his initial decision. He was clear that considerations of usefulness should guide his choice: 'the service of God and mankind is not a *local* thing in my view; wherever it appears to me I may perform it to the greatest advantage, there I hope I should choose to fix my residence,

---

[1] Davies, vol. 4, p. 440.

whether in Hanover, Princeton, or even Lapland or Japan.'[1] At length the same motives that had led him to take the long journey to Britain prevailed. His vision for what Whitefield earlier called the 'grand plan' for the College in the Jerseys filled him with hope for the future. As he reminded his Hanover people in a Farewell sermon on 1 July 1759, 'The College of New Jersey, though an infant institution, is of the utmost importance to the interests of religion and learning in several extensive and populous colonies'. His removal, Davies told his mourning people, was as unexpected to him as his first settlement among them had been, and from a full heart he exhorted them to see that the work continued as it had begun:

It is the cause of liberty and the gospel, and not a carnal faction, or a schismatical body, that you, my dissenting brethren, have been promoting: and this is the true grace of God in which you stand. The longer I live, the more I am confirmed, that the simple method of worship I have practised, free from the ceremonies of human invention, and those doctrines of grace so mortifying to the pride of man, and so unfashionable in our age and country, which I have taught you, are agreeable to the pure gospel of Christ, pleasing to God, and conducive to your salvation. I am so far from advising you to give up this cause for the sake of peace, that, on the other hand, it is my solemn charge to you, in the name of God, zealously to maintain and promote it.

Farewell, ye saints of the living God, ye 'few names even in Hanover, that have not defiled your garments'. Ye shall fare well indeed. That God, whose the earth is, and the fulness thereof, is your God and has undertaken your welfare. That God will be your God for ever and he will be your guide even until death. He will guide you by his counsel through the intricacies of life, and then receive you into glory. Survey the sacred treasure of the divine promises laid up for you in the Bible, and stand lost in delightful wonder at your own riches. Behold the immense inheritance which the blood of Christ has purchased for you . . . It doth not yet appear what you shall be. I have known you broken-hearted penitents; honest, laborious, weeping seekers of Jesus, and conscientious, though imperfect observers of his will: I have known you poor mortal creatures, sometimes trembling, sometimes rejoicing, sometimes nobly indifferent at the prospect of death. But I hope yet to know you under a higher character; glorious Immortals, perfect in holiness, vigorous and bright, and full of

---

[1] Pilcher, *Davies*, p. 173.

devotion, 'as the rapt seraphs adore and burn', and qualified to bear a part in the more sublime and divine worship of the heavenly temple. There I hope to find some humble seat among you, and spend a blessed eternity in the divine intimacy of immortal friendship, without interruption or the fear of parting. Therefore adieu; but not for ever. Adieu for a few years, or months, or days, till death collects us to our common home, in our Father's house above. You have been the joy of my life, under all the discouragements and fatigues of my ministry; and to your prayers I owe the comfort and success I have had among you.[1]

Davies was to serve the college at Princeton for a brief eighteen months. His health had been poor in 1757 and it deteriorated again in 1760. During his illness in 1757 he had written to a friend in London:

Formerly I have wished to live longer, that I might be better prepared for heaven; but this consideration had very very little weight with me, and that for a very unusual reason, which was this: – after long trial I found this world a place so unfriendly to the growth of every thing divine and heavenly, that I was afraid if I should live any longer, I should be no better fitted for heaven than I am. Indeed I have hardly any hopes of ever making any great attainment in holiness while in this world, though I should be doomed to stay in it as long as Methuselah. I see other Christians indeed around me make some progress, though they go on with but a snail-like motion. But when I consider that I set out about twelve years old, and what sanguine hopes I then had of my future progress, and yet that I have been almost at a stand ever since, I am quite discouraged. O, my good Master, if I may dare call thee so, I am afraid I shall never serve thee much better on this side the regions of perfection. The thought grieves me; it breaks my heart, but I can hardly hope better. But if I have the least spark of true piety in my breast, I shall not always labour under this complaint. No, my Lord, I shall yet serve thee; serve thee through an immortal duration; with the activity, the fervour, the perfection of 'the rapt seraph that adores and burns'.[2]

Thus believing that 'to die is gain', Samuel Davies departed on 4 February 1761, at the age of thirty-seven. The only words to have been recorded of those present at his death were those of his mother: 'There is the son of my prayers and my hopes – my only son, my only earthly supporter; but there is the will of God and I am satisfied.'

*   *   *

[1] Davies, vol. 4, pp. 467–70.   [2] Ibid., vol. 1, p. 31.

Samuel Davies and 'Revival'

On several occasions in these pages we have already used the term 'revival' and at this point we must pause to clarify the sense in which it is to be understood. Although the word was only in occasional use before the 1740s as a descriptive term, the *idea* that it denoted was common enough from the time of the Reformation in Europe two centuries earlier. The Reformers recovered from Scripture the forgotten truth that the work of Christ in salvation did not end with his ascension, thereafter to be carried on by the church and human energies. Rather, Christ remains the source of all authority, life, and power. It is by him that his people are preserved and their numbers increased. But this on-going ministry he exercises through the Holy Spirit, whose work it is to apply to sinners the blessings purchased for them at Calvary. Davies was subscribing to the Pauline theology of the Reformation when he said that men

are estranged from God, and engaged in rebellion against him; and they love to continue so. They will not submit, nor return to their duty and allegiance. Hence there is need of a superior power to subdue their stubborn hearts, and sweetly constrain them to subjection; to inspire them with the love of God, and an implacable detestation of all sin. And for this purpose, the holy Spirit of God is sent into the world: for this purpose, he is at work, from age to age, upon the hearts of men.[1]

The ministry of the Spirit remains subject to Christ in whom alone he dwells without 'measure' (John 3.34). It is through Christ as mediator and head of his body that the Spirit continues to be communicated to the church and that his 'actual influence' is known.[2] Thus, although the Spirit was

[1] Ibid., vol. 2, p. 116.
[2] 'Actual influence' is the phrase of the Westminster divines in distinguishing between the once-for-all giving of the Spirit to a believer at regeneration and his continuing work. On the relationship between Christ's headship and the on-going communication of the Spirit see e.g. Eph. 4:7; Phil. 1:19; Rev. 3:1. On Ephesians 1:17 Bishop Moule wrote: 'We are not to think of the "giving" of the Spirit as of an isolated deposit of what, once given, is now locally in possession. The first "gift" is, as it were, the first point in a series of actions, of which each one may be expressed also as a gift.' Were it not for this truth, prayer for the Spirit (Luke 11:13) would be meaningless. For further references on the subject see my *David Martyn Lloyd-Jones: The Fight of Faith 1939–1981* (Edinburgh: Banner of Truth, 1990), pp. 381–2.

initially bestowed on the church by Christ at Pentecost, his influences are not uniform and unchanging; there are variations in the measure in which he continues to be given. In the book of Acts times of quickened spiritual prosperity and growth in the church are traced to new and larger measures of the influence of the Holy Spirit (Acts 4.31–3; 11.15–16; 13.52–14.1), and so, through Christian history, the church has been raised to new energy and success by 'remarkable communications of the Spirit of God . . . at special seasons of mercy'.[1] At such periods, to quote further from Jonathan Edwards:

The work of God is carried on with greater speed and swiftness, and there are often instances of sudden conversions at such a time. So it was in the apostles' days, when there was a time of the most extraordinary pouring out of the Spirit that ever was! How quick and sudden were conversions in those days . . . So it is in some degree whenever there is an extraordinary pouring out of the Spirit of God; more or less so, in proportion to the greatness of that effusion.[2]

These words convey the doctrinal understanding of revival that prevailed among the evangelical leaders of the eighteenth century. Edwards' phraseology was common to them all. Whitefield saw the great change that began in America in the winter of 1739–40 'as an earnest of future and more plentiful effusions of God's Spirit in these parts'.[3] Samuel Blair wrote of the same change: 'It was in the spring of 1740 when the God of salvation was pleased to visit us with the blessed effusions of his Holy Spirit in an eminent manner.'[4] Similarly, Jonathan Dickinson observed of the same period that 'they were again visited with the special and manifest effusions of the Spirit of God'.[5] For these men the words 'effusion', 'baptism', and 'outpouring of the Spirit' were synonymous in meaning with 'revival of religion'. The latter term, which was beginning to come into standard use only in the 1740s, was always understood in this sense and, as we shall see, nearly a hundred years were to pass before it began to be obscured.

---

[1] *The Works of Jonathan Edwards* (London, 1834; Edinburgh: Banner of Truth, 1974), vol. 1, p. 539.

[2] Ibid., p. 660.   [3] *Journals*, p. 378.

[4] Alexander, *Log College*, p. 157.   [5] Ibid. p. 239.

In so speaking of the Spirit's work in revival these evangelical leaders were not disparaging the reality of his normal and regular work in the church. They were far from believing that true Christianity can *only* spread in the manner that it did in 1740. They were simply affirming that there are times when the Spirit is given in exceptional measure and that such times may come suddenly, even when deadness is general in the church and indifference to biblical religion prevails in society at large. There are eras, said Davies, when only a large communication or outpouring of the Spirit can 'produce a public general reformation'. Thus, preaching on 'The Happy Effects of the Pouring Out of the Spirit' from Isaiah 32.13–19, he argued that 'the outpouring of the Holy Spirit is the great and only remedy for a ruined country – the only effectual preventative of national calamities and desolation, and the only sure cause of a lasting and well-established peace'.[1]

It is not in every era that the foundations of a new and great nation are laid, as they were being laid in North America in the eighteenth century. Had these men not been stirred up to believe that God has special help to give at critical points in history and had they not possessed the common heritage of biblical exposition on the work of the Spirit from the Puritans and Reformers, the subsequent history of America would have been very different.

In speaking of the meaning of revival it is also essential to note that what Davies and his brethren believed about revival was not something separate from, or additional to, their main beliefs; it was, rather, a necessary consequence. Such is man's state in sin that he cannot be saved without the immediate influence of the Holy Spirit. Regeneration, and the faith that results from it, are the gifts of God. Therefore, wherever conversions are multiplied, the cause is to be found not in men, nor in favourable conditions, but in the abundant influences of the Spirit of God that alone make the testimony of the church effective. No other explanation of revival is in harmony with the truths that are 'the essence of the Christian scheme – the utter depravity of man, the sovereignly-free grace of Jehovah, the

---

[1] Davies, vol. 4, p. 44.

divinity of Christ, the atonement in his blood, regeneration and sanctification by the Holy Spirit.'[1]

This school of preachers held that the Holy Spirit has appointed means to be used for the advancement of the gospel, pre-eminently the teaching of the Word of God accompanied by earnest prayer. Yet no human endeavours can ensure or guarantee results. There is a sovereignty in all God's actions. He has never promised to bless *in proportion to* the activity of his people. Revivals are not brought about by the fulfillment of 'conditions' any more than the conversion of a single individual is secured by any series of human actions. The 'special seasons of mercy' are determined in heaven. Thus, for a modern biographer of Davies to say that Blair 'began a revival of religion in 1740'[2] is to assert the opposite of what they believed. For the same reason it would have been obnoxious to these preachers to hear themselves described as 'revivalists'. Davies took up the very theme at length in a sermon on 'The Success of the Ministry Owing to a Divine Influence':

The different success of the same means of grace, in different periods of the church, sufficiently shews the necessity of gracious influences to render them efficacious . . . it is not by power, nor by might, but by the Spirit of the Lord of Hosts that the interests of religion are carried on, Zech. 4.6. Our own experience and observation furnish us with many instances in which this great truth has been exemplified. Sometimes the reading of a sermon has been the means of awakening careless sinners, when at other times the most solemn and argumentative preaching has been in vain. Sometimes we have seen a number of sinners thoroughly awakened, and brought to seek the Lord in earnest; while another number, under the very same sermon, and who seemed as open to conviction as the former, or perhaps more so, have remained secure and thoughtless, as usual. And whence could this difference arise, but from special grace? We have seen persons struck to the heart with those doctrines which they had heard a hundred times without any effect.[3]

Davies spoke these words to people who remembered well how the work of God had begun among them by truths *read* aloud from a book. When he preached this particular sermon in 1752,

[1] J. H. Rice describing Davies' preaching, quoted in Webster, *Presbyterian Church*, p. 563.
[2] Pilcher, *Davies*, p. 11.   [3] Davies, vol. 3, pp. 309–12.

the sermons which he had seen marked by such success at Hanover had apparently been heard to little effect at his preaching places in Henrico and Caroline. But in May 1754 – when he was away in England – it was in those two places that there were 'considerable appearances of success where he thought he had laboured in vain'. Whitefield's ministry exemplified the same lesson on a larger scale. Although his preaching was continually used of God to the end of his life in 1770, the evangelist never saw the same amazing harvest as had marked the years of the Great Awakening. Far from being discouraged, he regarded this variation as fully in accord with the workings of divine grace. 'I should be glad to hear of a revival at Cambuslang,' he wrote to his friend, the Rev. William M'Culloch in 1749, 'but, dear Sir, you have already seen such things as are seldom seen above once in a century'.[1]

From the above it can be further noted that what happens in revivals is not to be seen as something miraculously different from the regular experience of the church. The difference lies in degree, not in kind. In an 'outpouring of the Spirit' spiritual influence is more widespread, convictions are deeper, and feelings more intense, but all this is only a heightening of normal Christianity. True revivals are 'extraordinary', yet what is experienced at such times is not different in essence from the spiritual experience that belongs to Christians at other times. It is the larger 'earnest' of the same Spirit who abides with all those who believe.

Thus Davies and his brethren repudiated the idea that revivals restore miraculous gifts to the churches. They regarded revivals as more wonderful than that: they brought salvation to a larger number of the lost and gave Christians a greater conception of the glory of their Redeemer. The Spirit magnifies Christ, and the more abundantly his influence is possessed by believers the more they will live for his praise. When we meet with lives such as those of Davies, Whitefield ('he had such a sense of the incomparable excellence of the person of Christ'), Aaron Burr, Sr., ('a perpetual holocaust of adoration and praise'), and many others in the revival period, we are tempted to suppose that theirs was a different Christian-

---

[1] *Works of Whitefield*, vol. 2, p. 252.

ity. It was not so but rather, as Thomas Murphy wrote, it was 'the baptism of the Holy Ghost which caused the infant Church [in America] to become animated by the most fervent piety'.[1] The same writer said of these preachers: 'They believed in refreshings from on high, felt some of them in their own souls, and were ready for still more . . . These bright and cultured souls were stirred to their very depths, and blessings untold were involved therein. They awoke to a life not new in kind, but new in degree, and in all truth and soberness a new prospect opened before our Church and country.'[2]

If revival is a larger giving to the church of grace already possessed – a heightening of the normal – then it follows that the evidences by which revivals are to be judged are the same as those which form the permanent evidences of real Christianity. Foremost in the New Testament list is the evidence of love to God and men. At all times to all true believers Christ 'is precious'. Preaching on those words, Davies said:

Because he loves him he longs for the full enjoyment of him . . . Because Christ is precious to him, his interests are so too, and he longs to see his kingdom flourish, and all men fired with his love. Because he loves him, he loves his ordinances; loves to hear, because it is the word of Jesus; loves to pray, because it is maintaining intercourse with Jesus; loves to sit at his table, because it is a memorial of Jesus; and loves his people because they love Jesus.[3]

For revivals to be judged to be true we are to look for no greater proof than the increase of this same grace. Love is not uniform in its strength but it knows many degrees. Although it is an 'active principle' in all Christians, love can also blaze and burn. Men filled with the Spirit are filled with love (Eph. 3.16–19) and 'the sacred fire of love' (to use Davies' words) will affect all that they do. They cannot be other than 'fervent in Spirit' as well as dissatisfied with their own coldness:

Love is naturally productive of love; it scatters heavenly sparks around, and these kindle the gentle flame where they fall . . . Let a minister of Christ ascend the sacred desk, with a heart glowing with the love of souls, and what an amiable, engaging figure does he

[1] *Presbytery of Log College*, p. 295.
[2] Ibid., pp. 150–1.   [3] Davies, vol. 1, p. 355.

make . . . Love gives a smooth, though sharp edge to his address.
Love animates his persuasions and exhortations. Love breathes
through his invitations and renders them irresistible. Love brightens
the evidence of conviction, and sweetly forces it upon unwilling
minds . . .

My glorious and condescending Lord has appointed me the most
pleasing work – the work of love and benevolence. He only requires
me to shew myself a lover of souls – souls, whom He loves, and whom
he redeemed – souls, whom his Father loves, and for whom he gave up
his own Son unto death – souls, whom my fellow-servants of a
superior order, the blessed angels, love, and to whom they concur
with me in ministering – souls, precious in themselves, and of more
value than the whole material universe – souls, that must be happy, or
miserable, in the highest degree, through an immortal duration –
souls, united to me by the endearing ties of our common humanity –
souls, for whom I must give an account to the great Shepherd and
Bishop of souls. And, oh! can I help loving these souls? Why does not
my heart always glow with affection and zeal for them! Oh! why am I
such a languid friend, when the love of my Master and his Father is so
ardent! when the ministers of heaven are flaming fires of love, though
they do not share in the same nature! and when the object of my love is
so precious and valuable! The owners of those souls often do not love
them; and they are likely to be lost for ever by the neglect. Oh! shall
not I love them! shall not love invigorate my hand, to pluck them out
of the burning! Yes, I will, I must love them. But, ah! to love them
more! Glow, my zeal! kindle, my affections! speak, my tongue! flow,
my blood! be exerted, all my powers! be, my life! if necessary, a
sacrifice to save souls from death! Let labour be a pleasure: let
difficulties appear glorious and inviting in this service. O thou God of
Love! kindle a flame of love in this cold heart of mine, and then I shall
perform my work with alacrity and success.[1]

In cold print such words may appear a touch theatrical, but
those who saw and heard the man never entertained such
thoughts. They knew that Davies felt as well as believed what
he preached, and such words are characteristic of times of
revival. John H. Rice, the first biographer of Davies, drawing
on first-hand memories which survived into the nineteenth
century, remarked that his 'preaching combined a solemnity,
pathos and animation, with a most tender, fervent benevolence
to souls'.[2] How is such abounding sympathy and compassion to

---

[1] Davies, vol. 4, pp. 327–38.
[2] Quoted in Webster, *Presbyterian Church*, p. 562.

be explained if not in terms of a larger giving of the Spirit of Christ and a closer approximation to the testimony of Paul, 'the love of God is shed abroad in our hearts by the Holy Ghost which is given unto us' (Rom. 5.5)?

*　　　*　　　*

If love is the gift of the Spirit, it follows that an eminent degree of the Holy Spirit's working will be marked by eminent degrees of love between Christians. A narrow party spirit cannot coexist with a larger giving of the Spirit whose communion extends to the whole body of Christ. Exclusive attention to denominational interests may prevail among Christians in a period of spiritual decline; it never does so in days of enlarged blessing. Thus Davies, like Whitefield[1] and other evangelical leaders, was marked by catholicity of spirit to a conspicuous degree. Some of the most fervent words he ever wrote were called forth by the suggestion that he was primarily interested in building dissent from the Church of England in Virginia. He wrote to the Bishop of London on that subject:

For my farther vindications, my lord, I beg leave to declare that in all the sermons I have preached in Virginia, I have not wasted one minute in exclaiming or reasoning against the peculiarities of the established church; nor so much assigned the reasons of my own non-conformity. I have not exhausted my zeal in railing against the established clergy, in exposing their imperfections, or in depreciating their characters. No, my lord, I have matters of infinitely greater importance to exert my zeal and spend my time and strength upon; – To preach repentance towards God, and faith towards our Lord Jesus Christ – to alarm secure impenitents; to reform the profligate; to undeceive the hypocrite; to raise up the hands that hang down . . . These are the ends I pursue and if ever I divert from these to ceremonial trifles, let my tongue cleave to the roof of my mouth.[2]

[1] 'Happy they, who, with a disinterested view, take in the whole church militant, and, in spite of narrow-hearted bigots, breathe an undissembled catholic spirit towards all'; 'Do not tell me you are a Baptist, an Independent, a Presbyterian, a Dissenter, tell me you are a christian, that is all I want; this is the religion of heaven and must be ours upon earth'. *Works of Whitefield*, vol. 2, p. 226; *Sermons on Important Subjects* (London, 1825), p. 684.

[2] Quoted in Foote, *Sketches*, p. 194. The letter, dated 10 January 1752, at Hanover, 'was never submitted to the Bishop's inspection'. Further on the

Davies went on to declare that he made no effort to win over any true Christian from the Church of England and that he would rather that men were 'made members of the church triumphant in the regions of bliss' by the preaching of a minister of the Church of England than that they should remain unconverted in a Presbyterian church. But it was his distress that the clergy of Virginia did not prepare men for eternity:

I find to my sorrowful surprise, that the generality of them, as far as can be discovered by their common conduct and public ministrations, are stupidly serene and unconcerned, as though their hearers were crowding promiscuously to heaven, and there were little or no danger; – that they address themselves to perishing multitudes in *cold blood*, and do not represent their miserable condition in all its horrors; do not alarm them with solemn, pathetic and affectionate warnings, and expostulate with them with all the authority, tenderness and pungency of the ambassadors of Christ to a dying world, nor commend themselves to every man's conscience in the sight of God; that their common conversation has little or no savour of living religion . . . that instead of intense application to study, or teaching their parishioners from house to house, they waste their time in idle visits, trifling conversation, slothful ease, or at best, excessive activity about their temporal affairs . . . The plain truth is, a general reformation *must* be promoted in this colony by some means or other, or multitudes are eternally undone: and I see alas! but little ground to hope for it from the generality of the clergy here, till they be happily changed themselves; this is not owing to their being of the Church of England, as I observed before: for were they in the Presbyterian Church, or any other, I should have no more hopes of their success; but it is owing to their manner of preaching and behaviour. This thought, my lord, is so far from being agreeable to me that it at times racks me with agonies of compassion and zeal intermingled: and could I entertain that unlimited charity which lulls so many of my neighbours into a serene stupidity, it would secure me from many a melancholy hour, and make my life below a kind of anticipation of heaven. I can boast of no high attainments, my lord; I am as mean

---

above theme see Samuel Davies, *Charity and Truth United; or, The Way of the Multitude Exposed in Six Letters to the Rev. Mr. William Stith*, ed. T. C. Pears (Philadelphia: Department of History of the Office of the General Assembly of the Presbyterian Church in the U.S.A., 1941).

and insignificant a creature as your lordship can well conceive me to be: but I dare profess I cannot be an unconcerned spectator of the ruin of my dear fellow mortals: I *dare avow* my heart at times is set upon nothing more than to snatch the brands out of the burning, before they catch fire and burn unquenchably. And hence, my lord, it is, I consume my strength and life in such great fatigues in this jangling ungrateful colony.[1]

In these passages compassion for men and women are more prominent than catholicity, yet the two belong together, as Davies himself asserted elsewhere. He believed that a real concern to see people made Christians would keep believers from any primary desire to see their own denomination advanced. His own practice certainly exemplified that belief. His preaching in Virginia and North Carolina prepared the way for numbers of Christians who were to be of Baptist, Methodist, and other persuasions in their church connections. A few years later it was common for converts joining Baptist churches to say, 'At such a time and place I heard the Rev. Mr Davies preach and had my mind deeply impressed.'[2] Had Davies given more prominence to the distinctives of his own church it would have been to the numerical advantage of the Presbyterians, but his prime concern was to serve a much greater cause. And he sought to implant that same cause in his hearers. In a sermon on Acts 11.26, 'The Sacred Import of the Christian Name', he argued:

What an endless variety of denominations, taken from some men of character, or from some little peculiarities, has prevailed in the Christian world, and crumbled it to pieces, while the Christian name is hardly regarded? . . . what party-names have been adopted by the Protestant churches, whose religion is substantially the same common Christianity, and who agree in much more important articles than in those they differ. To be a Christian is not enough now-a-days, but a man must also be something more and better; that is, he must be a strenuous bigot to this or that particular church . . .

Every man will find that he agrees more fully in lesser as well as

---

[1] Ibid., pp. 204–5.

[2] Quoted in 'A Recovered Tract of President Davies', *Biblical Repertory* (1837), pp. 349–64. Baptist causes spread rapidly in Virginia in the 1760s and '70s, aided by preachers of similar spirit to Davies. Their liberty of worship was eloquently defended by Patrick Henry who sat under Davies' ministry in his youth. See Foote, *Sketches*, pp. 314–18.

more important articles with some particular church than others; and thereupon it is his duty to join in stated communion with that church; and he may, if he pleases, assume the name which that church wears, by way of distinction from others: this is not what I condemn. But for me to glory in the denomination of any particular church, as my highest character; to lay more stress upon the name of a presbyterian or a churchman than on the sacred name of Christian; to make a punctilious agreement with my sentiments in the little peculiarities of a party the test of all religion; to make it the object of my zeal to gain proselytes to some other than the Christian name; to connive at the faults of those of my own party and to be blind to the good qualities of others, or invidiously to represent or diminish them: these are the things which deserve universal condemnation from God and man; these proceed from a spirit of bigotry and faction, directly opposite to the generous catholic spirit of Christianity, and subversive of it. This spirit hinders the progress of serious practical religion, by turning the attention of men from the great concerns of eternity, and the essentials of Christianity, to vain jangling and contest about circumstantials and trifles. Thus the Christian is swallowed up in the partisan, and fundamentals lost in extra-essentials . . .

Endeavour to find out the truth, even in these circumstantials, at least so far as is necessary for the direction of your own conduct. But do not make these the whole or the principal part of your religion: do not be excessively zealous about them, nor break the peace of the church by magisterially imposing them upon others. 'Hast thou faith in these little disputables,' it is well; 'but have it to thyself before God,' and do not disturb others with it. You may, if you please, call yourselves presbyterians and dissenters, and you shall bear without shame or resentment all the names of reproach and contempt which the world may brand you with. But as you should not be mortified on the one side, so neither should you glory on the other. A Christian! a Christian! let that be your highest distinction, let that be the name which you labour to deserve. God forbid that my ministry should be the occasion of diverting your attention to anything else.[1]

If this emphasis is the New Testament's own emphasis, it may well be wondered why it has too often ceased to be as prominent in preaching as it was in the ministry of Davies and Whitefield. The answer is surely that catholicity thrives in the large measure of love that marks the churches in days when the Spirit of God is poured out. With few exceptions, the leaders of the

[1] Davies, vol. 1, pp. 298–300.

work of God in days of revival have always been men of this type.[1]

There is a final practical consequence which flows directly from the above understanding of revival. If revival consists in a larger giving of God's Spirit for the making known of Christ's glory, then it follows that a sense of God will always be evident at such times – evident not only in conviction of sin but equally in the bewildered amazement of Christians at the consciousness of the Lord who is in their midst. Then, indeed, to use the words of A. J. Gossip, people are 'awed and solemnized, they meet the Almighty face to face; and the hush of eternal things drowns the noises of earth and soaks into the soul'.[2] Such a sense of God invariably marks men with humility. They feel that they have scarcely begun to be Christians. Far from talking about their experiences and their achievements, they will say with Samuel Davies: 'I have but little, very little, true religion . . . Perhaps once in three or four months I preach in some measure as I could wish . . . It is really an afflictive thought that I serve so good a Master with so much inconstancy . . . I am at best smoking flax; a dying snuff in the candlestick of his church . . . The flame of divine love, sunk deep into the socket of a corrupt heart, quivers and breaks, and catches, and seems just expiring at times.'[3] These are not the words of a depressive and an introvert. They are the feelings of one who has seen something of the greatness of his Saviour. He would have been happy that posterity should best remember him, not by any biography, but by the words

> Great God of wonders! all Thy ways
> Are matchless, godlike, and divine;
> But the fair glories of Thy grace
> More God-like and unrivalled shine:
> Who is a pardoning God like Thee?
> Or who has grace so rich and free?

[1] For another example see 'Letter on Communion with Brethren of Other Denominations', *Robert Murray M'Cheyne: Memoir and Remains* (1844; London: Banner of Truth, 1966), pp. 605–12.

[2] *In the Secret Place of the Most High* (London: Independent Press Ltd, 1946), p. 117.

[3] From letters he wrote to Thomas Gibbons in London (Davies, vol. 1, pp. 28–9).

Samuel Davies and 'Revival'

Angels and men, resign your claim,
    To pity, mercy, love, and grace;
These glories crown Jehovah's name
    With an incomparable blaze:
Who is a pardoning God like thee?
Or who has grace so rich and free?

O may this strange, this matchless grace,
    This godlike miracle of love,
Fill the wide earth with grateful praise,
    And all the angelic choirs above:
Who is a pardoning God like thee?
Or who has grace so rich and free?

PRINCETON AND THE FIRST FRUITS
OF 'A GLORIOUS PLAN'

John Witherspoon (1722–1794)

2

At the time of Samuel Davies' death in 1761, when the total population of all the Thirteen Colonies was little more than 1 million, it was not difficult to note the main Christian figures who had moulded the development of the future nation. But the population was growing rapidly. By 1776 it was 2.5 million and the increase was reflected in the churches. Among Presbyterians, for example, in the seventeen years from 1741 to 1758 the number of ministers rose from fifty-one to ninety-two. Greater growth for all the evangelical denominations was to follow. Not surprisingly, therefore, the records of the churches of the later eighteenth century contain a near-bewildering mass of names of people unknown to our generation. At first sight the very number may appear to make it impossible to put them into any kind of order as far as their relative importance is concerned. Where there were only ten preachers or thereabouts in the 1740s, whose lives overlapped much of the history of the Great Awakening, there were now hundreds.

A closer inspection, however, of the mass of data to be found in such volumes as Sprague's invaluable *Annals of the American Pulpit* reveals that there are threads which tie many things together and by means of which the main lines of spiritual influence can be traced. Persons and events are often not so disconnected as they may first seem: there are significant links, and while attention to these links will still leave much in the shadows, it does give a clearer conception of the larger picture. This chapter aims to show how a number of key figures in the later eighteenth century were providentially related to one another.

[35]

As a starting-point we cannot do better than return to the New Brunswick Presbytery which prepared Samuel Davies for the work of the ministry. John Rodgers and Robert Smith were fellow students with Davies at Samuel Blair's school at Fagg's Manor, in that Presbytery. Rodgers, born in Ireland in 1727, was converted under Whitefield's preaching at the beginning of the Great Awakening. Given the duty of holding a lantern beside the preacher as he preached on the steps of the Court-House in Philadelphia one evening, Rodgers 'became so deeply impressed with the truth to which he was listening that, for a moment, he forgot himself and the lantern fell from his hand and was dashed in pieces.'[1] In 1743 Rodgers joined Blair's school to prepare for the ministry and soon became one of Davies' closest friends. They often preached together and when Davies declined to go to St George's, Delaware, and removed to Virginia, it was Rodgers who went to Delaware. On the death of Davies, Rodgers took Davies' mother into his home and when he was called to the Presbyterian church in New York in 1765 Martha Davies went with his family. In the opinion of some of his contemporaries, Rodgers was 'nearly equal to the late Mr Davies'. Preaching until 1809, and dying two years later after sixty-four years in the Christian ministry, he outlived all the ministers who had seen 'the Great Revival' of the 1740s.

Robert Smith, born in the same year as Davies, never occupied a major pulpit in the land. He spent his entire ministry (1751–93) at Pequea, Pennsylvania. But, in part through the influence of the pupils of the school he founded and in part through his three sons, Samuel, John and William – who were all to be eminent in the Presbyterian Church – he was to affect the lives of thousands. After his death one of Smith's contemporaries wrote of him:

[1] W. B. Sprague, *Annals of the American Pulpit*, vol. 3 (New York, 1858), p. 154. Many years after this incident, when Rodgers was in the ministry, Whitefield stayed at his home. Asked by his host whether he remembered the broken lantern, the evangelist replied, 'Oh yes, I remember it well; and have often thought I would give almost anything in my power to know who that little boy was, and what had become of him'. To his astonishment Rodgers then said with a smile, 'I am that little boy'. Whitefield confided in him that he was the fourteenth preacher he had met on this visit of whose hopeful conversion he had been the instrument.

Few men in the holy ministry have been more useful or more esteemed than Dr Smith. His whole soul was devoted to the faithful discharge of the duties of his sacred office. Though remarkably modest and even diffident in the deliberative assemblies of the Church, he has often been heard to say that in the pulpit he never knew the fear of man. He was so occupied with the solemnity and importance of his duties, that the opinions of men were forgotten: his mind was so filled with the Divine presence before which he stood, that wealth, station, talents, whatever is most respected by the world, was lost to him in the majesty of God. The character of his preaching, therefore, as was to be expected from a frame of mind so habitually devout, was remarkably solemn and fervent. He was uncommonly successful in convincing secure sinners, in comforting and establishing believers in the faith of the Gospel and in conciliating the affections and confidence of pious persons of all denominations. Preaching the Gospel and publishing the grace of the Redeemer was his most delightful employment.[1]

Another man who came to the ministry through the New Brunswick Presbytery in the 1740s was Samuel Finley. In all probability, he had been a pupil at William Tennent's original log college. Finley itinerated as an evangelist for two years before settling at Nottingham, Maryland, in 1744, and was an influential member of the circle of men mentioned above. He preached at the installation of Rodgers to the church of St George's and finished his life-work as Davies' successor at Princeton. At Nottingham he also ran an academy which, according to Archibald Alexander, 'acquired a higher reputation than any other in the Middle Colonies'.[2] Among the future leaders of state and church who came from Finley's Nottingham school I shall here mention only one. Alexander McWhorter, also of Scots-Irish descent, and a native of New Castle County, Delaware, found spiritual peace and direction for his life in his two years under Finley's ministry and instruction. From there he went to the College of New Jersey where he graduated a few days after the death of Aaron Burr in 1757. Two years later McWhorter began a near lifelong connection with Burr's former congregation at Newark, New Jersey. He was still at work there more than forty years later. Situated less than ten miles from his friend John Rodgers in New York, across the Hudson River, McWhorter was also to be

---

[1] Ibid., p. 174.   [2] Alexander, *Log College*, p. 186.

a key figure in events relating to the advancement of the kingdom of God. In the early 1800s Edward Griffin testified that the influence of Rodgers 'and that of McWhorter, in their old age, was most healthful and kept alive in our church a remembrance of the years of the right hand of the Most High, a sense of the importance of revivals and a longing for their return, such as was not to be found in New England'.[1]

*   *   *

The unifying influence of the New Brunswick Presbytery was to be far exceeded by the greatest institution to which it gave rise, Nassau Hall, the College of New Jersey, established at Princeton in 1756. All the evangelical leaders of the Great Awakening were ardent supporters, if not trustees, of the College – none more so than George Whitefield. He called it 'a glorious plan set on foot' and expressed the conviction that 'the spreading of the gospel in Maryland and Virginia in a great measure depends upon it'.[2] These hopes were to be abundantly fulfilled. By 1772 Princeton's president could say that the number of its undergraduates 'is near four times that of any college on the continent to the southward of New England and probably greater than all the rest put together'.[3] Men of Christian convictions from Nassau Hall soon filled important stations in society, and around 500 of the 2,500 graduates of the first eighty years fulfilled the primary intention of its founders by becoming preachers of the gospel.[4] To follow the course of some of the foremost of the 500 is to see a pattern in the unfolding events of this momentous era of history.

Princeton stamped these men with some common marks and to understand them aright we need first to look briefly at what made this New Jersey village the centre that it became.

---

[1] Quoted in Webster, *Presbyterian Church*, p. 581.

[2] *Works of Whitefield*, vol. 2, pp. 345, 349.

[3] 'Address to the Inhabitants of Jamaica and Other West-India Islands in Behalf of the College of New Jersey', *The Works of John Witherspoon*, (Edinburgh, 1804–5), vol. 8, p. 325.

[4] This figure is given in Robert Baird, *Religion in the United States of America* (Glasgow and Edinburgh, 1844), p. 544.

W. G. T. Shedd, one of the leading theological educators of the nineteenth century, believed that three conditions were required for the preparation of good students: first, a location free from other distractions; secondly, thorough teachers and the discipline of a curriculum; and thirdly, access to large libraries. On the last point he wrote: 'The consciousness of ignorance, which is generated by an exhibition upon the shelves of a library of what the human mind has accomplished in the past, is one of the sharpest spurs to personal investigation.'[1]

In its village location, the College of New Jersey perfectly fulfilled the first of these conditions. Although it was on 'the great post road', it was almost midway between New York and Philadelphia and beyond reach of such diversions as either city might provide. All students were boarded together at Nassau Hall for an annual fee (in the 1760s) of £26 6s. The cost was made up as follows: £4 for tuition; £15 for boarding ('steward salary and servants' wages inclusive'); £1 for room rent; £3 for washing; £2 for wood and candles; which left 6 shillings for 'contingent charges'. All meals were in the dining-hall and under the steward's direction. Samuel Finley, the first historian of the College, thought the cuisine mattered enough to warrant mention:

Tea and coffee are served up for breakfast. At dinner, they have, in turn, almost all the variety of fish and flesh the country here affords; and sometimes pies; every dish of the same sort, and alike dressed, on one day; but with as great difference, as to the kinds of provision and manner of cookery, on different days, as the market and other circumstances will admit. Indeed, no luxurious dainties, or costly delicacies, can be looked for among the viands of a college, where health and economy are alone consulted in the furniture of the tables. These, however, are plentifully supplied, without weight or measure allowance: and the meals are conducted with regularity and decorum; waiters being constantly in attendance. The general table drink is small beer or cider. For supper, milk only is the standing allowance, chocolate is sometimes served as a change.[2]

For teachers and libraries, what Princeton lacked in quantity

[1] W. G. T. Shedd, *Theological Essays* (New York, 1887), pp. 366–7.
[2] Quoted in Ashbel Green, *Discourses Delivered in the College of New Jersey, Including an Historical Sketch of the College* (Philadelphia, 1822), p. 368.

in its early years was fully made up for in quality. Dickinson, Burr, Edwards, Davies, and Finley were all outstanding men. A student at the College during the presidency of Finley recorded:

Doctor Finley, was a man of small stature, and of a round and ruddy countenance. In the pulpit, he was always solemn and sensible, and sometimes glowing with fervour. His learning was very extensive – Every branch of study taught in the college appeared to be familiar to him. Among other things, he taught Latin, Greek and Hebrew, in the Senior year. He was highly respected, and greatly beloved by the students . . .

As to revivals of religion, there were some partial ones in college before Dr Finley's time; but in his time there was something general. It began in 1762, in the Freshman class, to which I then belonged. It was a pretty large class, containing between 25 and 30 members. Almost as soon as the session commenced, this class met, once in the week, for prayer. One of the members became deeply impressed; and this affected the whole class. – The other classes, and the whole college, soon became much impressed. Every class became a praying society; and the whole college met once a week, for prayer – There was, likewise, a private select society. Societies were also held, by the students, in the town and in the country. I suppose there was not one that belonged to college but was affected more or less. There were two members of the Senior class who were considered as opposers of the good work at first. Yet both of these persons were afterwards preachers of the gospel. The work continued about one year. Fifteen, or about the half of my class, was supposed to be pious; and in the college about Fifty, or nearly one half of the whole number of students.[1]

Taken ill at the age of fifty, President Finley went to Philadelphia for medical help, only to find that nothing could be done for his condition. He died in July 1766 when the heat of the summer prevented the removal of his body for burial at Princeton. What was carried back to the College, and far beyond, was the record of his final triumphant testimony. 'The Lord Jesus will take care of his cause in this world!' He repeatedly affirmed in his last days: 'A Christian's death is the best part of his experience. The Lord has made provision for the whole way; provision for the soul and for the body . . . Blessed

[1] Ibid., p. 377.

be God, eternal rest is at hand. Eternity is but long enough to enjoy my God. This has animated me in my secret studies. I was ashamed to take rest here. O, that I could be filled with the fulness of God!'

With the death of Finley, Princeton had lost four presidents in under nine years, and obvious choices for a successor in the Thirteen Colonies had come to an end. The trustees turned instead to Scotland and called John Witherspoon, minister at Paisley, near Glasgow. The forty-five-year-old Scot did not find it an easy decision. In a rare passage of autobiography he was to tell Princeton students:

Nothing would give me a higher pleasure, than being instrumental in furnishing the minds, and improving the talents of those who may hereafter be the ministers of the everlasting gospel. The hope of it is indeed the chief comfort in my present station. Notwithstanding the many encouraging circumstances that have happened since my arrival here, and the evident smiles of Providence upon the College, yet I confess I have often regretted the want of a pastoral charge. After having been for twenty-three years constantly employed in preaching the gospel to a numerous, obedient, and affectionate people, to be employed in a way of life so considerably different, must have created some uneasiness. Just figure to yourselves, one that had been so long accustomed to preach to a crowded audience of from twelve to fifteen hundred souls every day, and all subject to my private oversight and discipline; now to have such a thin and negligent assembly, and mostly composed of those who think themselves under no obligation to attend but when they please.[1] In such a situation the sphere of usefulness seems to be greatly narrowed; but if I am made instrumental in sending out faithful labourers into the harvest, it will be an ample recompense. For as one of great zeal and discernment expressed himself to me in Britain: 'You will be greatly mortified to see the difference between a small country society in America, and a large city congregation in Scotland; but if you be instrumental in sending out ministers of the New Testament, it will be a still more important station, for every gownsman is a legion.'[2]

[1] A small church and congregation had been formed in Princeton during Finley's presidency, over which Witherspoon was the pastor throughout the period of his presidency.

[2] 'Lectures on Divinity' in Witherspoon, *Works*, vol. 8, pp. 10–11. The biographical notice of Witherspoon in Sprague's *Annals* notes that: 'He introduced the method of teaching by lecture, which seems previously to have been unknown in our American Colleges' (vol. 3, p. 292).

[41]

Witherspoon's unnamed counsellor was George Whitefield, with whom he conferred before leaving Britain. If the Scot was not as fully persuaded as Whitefield that Princeton was 'a glorious plan', he certainly believed that there was no 'surer mark that God intends effectual benefit to any part of the world or the church than when he raises up and commissions men eminently qualified to plead his cause'.[1] With that hope before him his mind was made up.

The calling of a Church of Scotland minister to New Jersey tells us much about the unity that existed among the greater part of the ministry on both sides of the Atlantic. The Princeton trustees had appointed a man whom they had not seen or heard. What they had read of his writing and learned by repute was enough, and their judgement proved correct. As we have seen, the revived Christianity of the log-college men was not idiosyncratic: it was in the same mould as the witness of the British evangelicals. Their views on Protestant Christianity and on preaching were identical. Thus, unknown to each other, Samuel Davies preached at Hanover on 'The Happy Effects of the Pouring Out of the Spirit', while Witherspoon, over 3,000 miles away, took up the same theme in addressing his Paisley hearers on 'Prayer for National Prosperity, and for the Revival of Religion, Inseparably Connected'.[2]

The Scotsman's first sermon at the church in Princeton, at the start of more than twenty-six years of service, could have been preached by any of his predecessors. From 1 Corinthians 3.5–7 he took as his subject 'The Success of the Gospel Entirely of God'. The application – the reality of dependence on God must lead to earnest prayer – was equally familiar to his hearers, although, as he pleaded his own personal need of their prayers, he included testimony not heard there before:

I make no merit at all of having left country, and kindred, and connexions of the dearest kind, in order to serve the interest of the church of Christ in this part of the globe; for I consider with pleasure the oneness of his body, and the extent of the catholic church, that there shall come from the east, and from the west, and from the north, and from the south, and sit down with Abraham, and Isaac, and

[1] Witherspoon, *Works*, vol. 5, p. 137.
[2] Davies' sermon was preached on 16 October 1757 and Witherspoon's on 16 February 1758 (Ibid., pp. 57–89).

Jacob, in the kingdom of their Father. Could we but think as we ought of the great removal which we are making from time to time into an eternal state, the removal of our bodies, and the change of our scene of service from Europe to America, would appear altogether unworthy of notice.[1]

The secret of Princeton's spiritual success did not lie in its curriculum, which differed very little from the other undergraduate colleges of the English-speaking world. It was not a divinity school, still less 'a clerical manufactory', as its critics sometimes claimed. The four-year course, taught by the president and three tutors, was designed 'to afford a solid basis equally for all the liberal professions'.[2] It aimed to make men think, study hard and acquire lifelong habits of reading. Any policy of hurrying men who possessed only religious experience and a gift of speech into the ministry, was entirely alien to Princeton. Whitefield, Davies, and others had seen the effect of that policy and were alarmed at the long-term consequences. 'You would do well to read more', Whitefield told an aspiring Christian worker in 1750. 'It has long since been my judgment that it would be best for many of the present preachers to have a tutor, and retire for a while, and be content with preaching now and then, till they were a little more improved. Otherwise I fear many who now make a temporary figure will grow weary of the work and leave it.'[3] With Princeton's emphasis on the liberal arts, and the fact that students for the ministry had to undertake additional studies after graduation (either under the president at Princeton or elsewhere), it may seem surprising that the College was, in Ashbel Green's words, 'eminently instrumental in preparing men to preach the gospel with ability and success'. In part this was due to the standpoint from which the curriculum was taught. 'Unsanctified learning' – that is scholarship detached from religion – was treated as a danger and not as an acquisition to be admired. If 'the fountains of science' were without 'the salt of revealed truth' they would become a curse. All that was taught thus gave men a heightened view of the importance of the Word of God.

---

[1] Ibid., pp. 164–5.   [2] Green, *Discourses*, p. 293.

[3] *Works*, vol. 2, pp. 363–4. For Davies on the same subject see Foote's *Sketches*, p. 275. 'It is a dreadful thing', Davies once commented to John Rodgers, 'to talk nonsense in the name of the Lord.'

The chief influence that confirmed undergraduates in a desire to serve in the Christian ministry undoubtedly came from the personal example and spirit of their instructors. While the presidents were men of scholarship and ability, this was not their first characteristic. As Green reminded a later generation of students in the College chapel, more was needed for teaching to be effectual: 'If a man of learning appears who is confessedly and eminently pious; who, it is acknowledged by all, considers religion as superior to learning itself – superior to every earthly object and consideration; whose holy life and ardent labours in the cause of Christ have put him above all suspicion; *this man* they will hear; to him they will listen.'[1]

The trustees of Princeton had never heard the term 'role model' but they understood the idea very well. It was pre-eminently because they appointed presidents who were proven as pastors and preachers that the College, in turn, affected the churches for years to come. Furthermore, while the presidents were all Presbyterians, their evangelical catholicity was far more prominent than their churchmanship. From the outset it could be said of Princeton that 'to inculcate or even recommend the discriminating opinions of any one protestant denomination, in preference to another, is carefully avoided'.[2] Something greater was in view, namely, the need to transmit to posterity the kind of preaching of the gospel that had returned with the Great Awakening. The trustees knew what they were doing when they put a younger generation in daily contact with men who were exponents of preaching which Richard Webster described in these words: 'If their sermons were bare of ornaments as skeletons, they were compacted together with the joints and bands of doctrines, precepts and promises. Though very dry to the cursory inspection of the caviller and the trifler, yet, like the dead bones of Elisha, they gave life even to the dead.'[3]

---

[1] *Discourses*, p. 13.

[2] Ibid., p. 370. Green says that in nearly forty years' acquaintance with the College, 'In regard to the making of proselytes . . . he has never known or heard of an attempt to make one; or that one has actually been made' (pp. 291–2).

[3] *Presbyterian Church*, p. 272. 'Why, Doctor,' a lady said to Witherspoon one day, 'I see no flowers in your garden'. 'No, Madam,' he replied, 'no flowers in my garden, nor in my discourses either.' (The practical Scot apparently excelled in 'kitchen gardening'.)

The Princeton leaders had consciously faced the key question: What was it that gave life to plain, scriptural preaching? And their united answer was, it was preachers knowing and feeling in their own experience the realities of which they spoke.

True Christianity cannot exist without real communion with God, and neither can true preaching. So while the technical aspects of public speaking were not ignored, this was not where the emphasis lay. 'It is an easy thing to make a noise in the world,' said Davies, 'to flourish and harangue, to dazzle the crowd and set them all agape; but deeply to imbibe the Spirit of Christianity, to maintain a secret walk with God, to be holy, as he is holy – this is the labour, this is the work.'[1] In his first sermon at Princeton Witherspoon affirmed as a certainty that 'true religion in the heart is of far greater importance to the success and efficacy of the ministry than eminence or gifts',[2] and the same note ran through his teaching at Nassau Hall. He enlarged on it, for example, in his 'Lectures on Eloquence'. He had no hesitation as to what ought to be at the head of the list of 'the qualities of most importance' for the preaching of the gospel:

1 Piety – To have a firm belief of that gospel he is called to preach, and a lively sense of religion upon his own heart . . .

2 It gives a man the knowledge that is of most service to a minister. Experimental knowledge is superior to all other, and necessary to the perfection of every other kind. It is indeed the very possession, or daily exercise of that which it is the business of his life, and the duty of his office, to explain and recommend. Experimental knowledge is the best sort in every branch, but it is necessary in divinity, because religion is what cannot be truly understood, unless it is felt.

3 True piety will direct a man in the choice of his studies. The object of human knowledge is so extensive, that nobody can go through the whole, but religion will direct the student to what may be most profitable to him, and will also serve to turn into its proper channel all the knowledge he may otherwise acquire.

4 It will be a powerful motive to diligence in his studies. Nothing so forcible as that in which eternity has a part. The duty to a good man

---

[1] Davies, vol. 1, p. 28. The words were written to Thomas Gibbons but we can be sure that he said similar things at Nassau Hall.

[2] *Works*, vol. 5, p. 160.

is so pressing, and the object so important, that he will spare no pains to obtain success.

5 True religion will give unspeakable force to what a minister says. There is a piercing and a penetrating heat in that which flows from the heart, which distinguishes it both from the coldness of indifference, and the false fire of enthusiasm and vain-glory. We see that a man truly pious has often esteem, influence, and success, though his parts may be much inferior to others, who are more capable, but less conscientious. If, then, piety makes even the weakest venerable, what must it do when added to the finest natural talents, and the best acquired endowments?

6 It adds to a minister's instruction, the weight of his example. It is a trite remark, that example teaches better than precept. It is often a more effectual reprimand to vice, and a more inciting argument to the practice of virtue, than the best of reasoning. Example is more intelligible than precept. Precepts are often involved in obscurity, or warped by controversy; but a holy life immediately reaches, and takes possession of the heart.

. . . observe, as the conclusion of the whole, that one devoted to the service of the gospel should be *really, visibly,* and *eminently* holy.[1]

Such words might have meant little coming from other men but Nassau Hall students could not doubt what they saw as well as heard from their presidents. The ethos of Princeton was one in which men sought to walk with God and, like their teachers, the men most eminently used in later days were those whose lives carried the evidence of the truths they preached.

*   *   *

Mention of revival was rare in America in the 1760s. Nassau Hall in 1762 was an exception. Another and more widespread occurrence of the same phenomenon was to be seen in the Presbyterian churches at Morristown, Newark, and New York in 1764–5. The first of these charges was served by Timothy Johnes who had been there since 1742. A native of Long Island and a graduate of Yale, Johnes had joined the Presbyterians of the Middle Colonies and, living little more than thirty miles north of Princeton, was an active trustee of the College. 'He was much with his people', wrote Webster. 'He read accounts of

---

[1] *Works*, vol. 7, pp. 274–7.

revivals to them; but no instance of more than ordinary success is recorded during the first twenty-one years of his labours'. Then, on Sunday, 1 July 1764, 'the wonderful effusion of God's admirable grace' began and Johnes wrote: 'The Lord Jehovah has rent the heavens and come down and the mountains are fleeing at his presence. There is something of this blessed work all around me.' The lives of men and women who were formerly unconcerned were now marked by 'deep feeling and much anxiety' as they awoke to a knowledge of the nature of sin and of the justice of God. Ninety-four were added to the Morristown church in that one year.[1]

Sixteen miles away at Newark, which was in the pastoral charge of Alexander McWhorter, a similar extensive work of grace occurred in the winter of 1764–5 while McWhorter himself was away in North Carolina. Later in 1765, when Rodgers moved from Maryland to New York, Johnes presided at his induction, and 'a considerable revival of religion almost immediately ensued: a large number were brought to the knowledge of the truth'.[2] This success necessitated the erection of a new building – the Brick Church – of which we shall hear again in the later history of New York.

John Witherspoon was settled at Princeton in August 1768. A 'remarkable revival' occurred in 'the third and fourth years' of his administration of which we have almost no details. We do, however, know much about the calibre of the men who came out of the College following these years. Foote referred to the event as 'a great awakening which resulted in the hopeful conversion of many' and recorded that of the twenty-nine graduates of the Class of 1773, twenty-three became ministers of the gospel and three Governors of states.[3]

There is one fragment of autobiography from a student who saw the Princeton awakening in the early 1770s. The writer was John McMillan, a name to be remembered if one of the most exciting records of the spread of the gospel in the late eighteenth century is to be understood. Born at Fagg's Manor in 1752, McMillan had studied under Robert Smith at Pequea. 'While

[1] Information on Johnes is from Webster, *Presbyterian Church*, pp. 481–3.
[2] Ibid., p. 579.
[3] *Sketches*, p. 409. On p. 440, however, he gives a different figure (fourteen) for the number of the Class of 1773 who became ministers.

there,' he wrote, 'the Lord poured out his Spirit upon the students and I believe there were but few who were not brought under serious concern about their immortal souls; some of whom became blessings in their day, and were eminently useful in the Church of Christ.' But McMillan was not among those converted at the time. His convictions and observation of religious duties were superficial:

I never saw that I was a lost, undone sinner, exposed to the wrath of a justly offended God, and could do nothing for my own relief.

In this situation I continued until I entered College at Princeton, in the spring of 1770. I had not been long there, until a revival of religion took place among the students, and I believe, at one time, there were not more than two or three but what were under serious impressions. On a day which had been set apart by a number of the students to be observed as a day of fasting and prayer, – while the others were at dinner, I retired into my study, and while trying to pray, I got some discoveries of Divine things, which I had never had before. I saw that the Divine law was not only holy, just and spiritual, but that it was good also, and that uniformity to it would make me happy. I felt no disposition to quarrel with the law, but with myself, because I was not conformed to it. I felt that it was now easy to submit to the Gospel plan of salvation, and felt a serenity of mind to which I had hitherto been a stranger. And it was followed by a delight in contemplating God's glorious perfections in all his works. I thought I could see God in every thing around me.

I continued at College until the fall of 1772, when I returned to Pequea, and began the study of Theology, under the direction of the Rev. Robert Smith.[1]

'Of a large frame' and 'almost a Knox in boldness, energy and decision', McMillan was being prepared by God to be a leader among churches to be formed over 300 miles inland from Princeton and in territory unknown to Whitefield, who in his extensive journeys had never crossed the Allegheny Mountains into what was to be Western Pennsylvania. The Alleghenies themselves had not been the principal barrier. For most of Whitefield's lifetime the land west of the mountain range had been claimed by the French in agreement with their allies the Indians. Then in 1755 the Old French and Indian War began

---

[1] Sprague, *Annals*, vol. 3, pp. 350–1.

with the disastrous defeat of the British General Braddock near
Fort Duquesne, the future site of Pittsburgh. Almost 700
Indian warriors, with about 150 French Canadian militia,
overwhelmed the scarlet-and-blue-coated British and Virginian soldiers. In 1756 the conflict with France was extended to
an international scale, involving Europe, India, and even the
Philippines. Protestants saw the struggle as having momentous
repercussions for the spread of evangelical Christianity, and
the outcome was to prove them right. The Peace of Paris in
1763 brought French Catholic power in North America to an
end and opened the way for immigration into the vast
backwoods territory where Braddock was routed. Twenty
years after 1763 there were to be some 20,000 English-speaking
inhabitants in territory that had previously been a wilderness,
many of them Scots-Irish Presbyterians. Among this number
was a group of people who settled south of what is now
Pittsburgh around 1773, including men and women who had
been present in the 1764 revivals in New Jersey.

From these and other groups of early settlers reports found
their way eastwards of a concern for the preaching of the gospel
and for the establishment of churches. One of the first to
respond to their calls for help was Thaddeus Dod. Born in 1740,
Dod had already turned thirty when he was at Princeton in
the significant years 1771–3. But that College period did
not provide him with his first experience of revival, for it
appears that he already knew the New Jersey congregations
of Alexander McWhorter (Newark) and Timothy Johnes
(Morristown). Johnes had been his first teacher in Latin. To
these churches Dod returned after graduating from Princeton,
and studied theology first with McWhorter, then with Johnes.
In 1777 he made an exploratory visit into the desolate region
west of the Monongahela River and at Ten-Mile he met friends
whom he had previously known in New Jersey. In 1779 he
returned with his wife and child. Dod's settlement west of the
Monongahela took place one year before that of John
McMillan – the first minister to reside beyond that boundary
and who became known as 'the apostle of the West'. Licensed
by the Presbytery of New Castle in 1774, McMillan had
travelled as an itinerant and first crossed the Alleghenies the
following year. It was this visit that led to his call to the united

[49]

congregations of Chartiers and Pigeon Creek, south-west of Fort Pitt. As an old man in 1832, McMillan wrote of his arrival with his family in the winter of 1778:

When I came to this country, the cabin in which I was to live was raised, but there was no roof on it, nor chimney nor floor in it: the people, however, were very kind, assisted me in preparing my house, and on the 16th of December, I moved into it: but we had neither bedstead, nor table, nor chairs, nor stool, nor bucket. All these things we had to leave behind us: there being no waggon road at that time over the mountains, we could bring nothing with us but what was carried on pack horses. We placed two boxes on each other, which served us for a table, and two kegs served for seats; and having committed ourselves to God in family worship, we spread a bed on the floor, and slept soundly till morning. The next day, a neighbour coming to my assistance, we made a table and a stool, and in a little time had every thing comfortable about us. Sometimes, indeed, we had no bread for weeks together; but we had plenty of pumpkins, and potatoes, and all the necessaries of life; and as for luxuries, we were not much concerned about them. We enjoyed health, the Gospel and its ordinances, and pious friends: we were in the place where we believed God would have us to be, and we did not doubt but that He would provide for us every thing necessary.[1]

Two other Princeton graduates, James Power and Joseph Smith, associated with Dod and McMillan, and together they formed the first presbytery west of the mountains. Named the Presbytery of Redstone (after the name of a fort) it initially covered all Western Pennsylvania and a section of Western Virginia. Power and Smith had been trained under Samuel Finley, first at Nottingham, then at the College of New Jersey. Power had been with his teacher at his death in Philadelphia, which, it was said, 'left a powerful and enduring impression on his mind'. In 1776 he settled in the Mount Pleasant area of Westmoreland County, to the east of the Monongahela and Youghiogheny Rivers, where he served a church until 1817. 'In his doctrines, he was of the same school with the Tennents, Davies, Robert Smith and Samuel Finley.'[2] Joseph Smith was also with Finley at both Nottingham and Princeton. In 1780 he joined Dod and McMillan beyond the Monongahela, serving

[1] Sprague, *Annals*, vol. 3, pp. 351–2.   [2] Ibid., p. 328.

the congregations of Buffalo and Cross Creek in what is now Washington County.

These men, and the people whom they served, lived plain and resolute lives amid astonishing hardships. There were no mills to grind flour for bread and no roads bringing goods across the mountains. Such scarce commodities as iron and salt had all to be carried by pack-horse. No stone, brick, or frame house existed in the region in 1781; log cabins – made without saws, planes, or nails – provided the only homes, their small window-opening covered by oil paper or linen. Not a single church building existed in the region before 1785, some sources say 1790. Worse than these deprivations was the peril of attacks from Indians which did not finally end until 1794. The direct passage across the mountains, through Chambersburg and Bedford, had often to be abandoned in the 1770s on account of the numbers killed by Indians at such places as 'the Burned Cabins' and 'Bloody Run'. Many immigrants, including McMillan, were forced to take a longer southern route on a horse path of 120 miles over 'rocks, precipices and marshes'. All the graveyards of early settlers in the West contained evidence of lives cut short by tomahawk or scalping-knife. In Westmoreland County (which was less hazardous than further west) the seat of County justice was overrun in 1782, several people were killed or kidnapped and the whole place burned. A year earlier the meeting-place appointed for the first gathering of the presbytery had to be changed 'by reason of the incursions of the savages', as its Minutes recorded. In several districts Sunday services were for years often held within forts, especially in the summer and autumn when Indian attacks were most common.

Remarkably, it was amid such primitive conditions and at a time when, further east, the attention of the nation was still absorbed in the Revolutionary War (1775–83), that the first records of revival in western Pennsylvania are found. In the letter quoted above, McMillan wrote:

The first remarkable season of the outpouring of the Spirit, which we enjoyed in this congregation, began about the middle of December, 1781. It made its first appearance among a few who met together for social worship, on the evening of a Thanksgiving day, which had been appointed by Congress. This encouraged us to appoint other meetings for the same purpose on Sabbath evenings; and the appearances still increasing, Sabbath night societies were continued with but little interruption for nearly two years. It was then usual to spend the whole night in religious exercises; nor did the time seem tedious, for the Lord was there, and his work went pleasantly on. Many were pricked to the heart with deep convictions, and a goodly number, we hope, became the subjects of renewing grace. At the first sacramental occasion after the work began, forty-five were added to the church, many of whom continued bringing forth the fruits of righteousness, and filling important offices in the church, until they were removed to the world of spirits. This time of refreshing continued, in a greater or less degree, until the year 1794. Upon every sacramental occasion, during this period, numbers were added to the church, who gave comfortable evidence of having obtained a saving change of heart; but, as I neglected to keep a register of their names, I cannot now ascertain their number.[1]

At about the same time there were parallel events in the congregations of Thaddeus Dod and Joseph Smith. Dod's people in the early years met chiefly in Fort Lindley. There they formed a church with twenty-five members in August 1781. Not long afterwards, the services in the fort 'were attended by a revival of religion, as the fruits of which upwards of forty were admitted to the church'. The confined circumstances of the fort did not, apparently, permit a solemn celebration of the Lord's Supper and to gather in the open air was too hazardous on account of the danger from Indian attacks. In May 1783 they were able to assemble for the first time in a barn to share in a communion service, a day remembered by 'unusual tokens of the Divine presence'. 'Besides a regular increase of his church,' records his brief biography, 'there were several seasons of special religious interest, which brought in larger numbers.'[2] Of the ministry of Joseph Smith it was recorded:

In the winter of 1781 and 1782 God began to pour out His Spirit on the congregations of Upper Buffalo and Cross Creek. In the Autumn of 1782 the sacrament of the Lord's Supper was administered for the first time in Cross Creek. About fifty persons from both congregations were received into full membership. This work continued, with but little abatement, for six or seven years. The most gracious visitation

[1] Sprague, *Annals*, vol. 3, p. 352.   [2] Ibid., p. 358.

was in June, 1787, when about fifty members were added to the
church of Cross Creek.[1]

Summarizing what others said of Joseph Smith, E. H. Gillett
wrote:

A more devoted pastor was not to be found in the whole band of those
that preceded or followed him. He was a man of prayer and faith. In
the pulpit, and out of it, his power was wonderful. His soul was
thrown into his utterance. His voice was 'now like the thunder, and
now like the music of heaven.' His manner 'had a strange kind of
power about it, totally indescribable.' He had the peculiarity of
Whitefield, a slight look askance of one eye; and the piercing
brilliancy of his glance was remarkably impressive. 'I never heard a
man,' said the Rev. Samuel Porter, 'who could so completely unbar
the gates of hell and make me look so far down into the dark,
bottomless abyss, or, like him, could so throw open the gates of
heaven and let me glance at the insufferable brightness of the great
white throne.' 'He would often rise to an almost supernatural and
unearthly grandeur, completely extinguishing in his hearers all
consciousness of time and place.' No one could appreciate the man
merely from his written discourses. His tones, his emphasis, his holy
unction and the holy vitality of his soul made them indescribably
impressive.[2]

It is remarkable that, given the extent of the demands upon
the first pastors in Western Pennsylvania, they did not neglect
the establishment of schools. They remained as committed as
their forebears to the need to train the next generation. 'When I
had determined to come to this country,' McMillan wrote in
1832, 'Dr Smith enjoined it upon me to look out for some pious
young men and educate them for the ministry; "for", said he,
"though some men of piety and talents may go to a new
country, at first, yet if they are not careful to raise up others, the
country will not be well supplied".' Joseph Smith, John
McMillan, and Thaddeus Dod all undertook this work and
each had his own school, although at times, it seems, pupils
may have moved between them. It was said of McMillan:

---

[1] 'Presbyterian Church of Cross Creek', in *Encyclopedia of the Presbyterian
Church in the United States*, ed. Alfred Nevin (Philadelphia, 1884), p. 1203.
[2] *History of the Presbyterian Church in the United States of America* (Philadelphia,
1864), vol. 1, p. 264.

'Whenever he found a young man of piety, who appeared to have gifts promising extensive usefulness in the Church, he took him into his family, taught him without charge, and trained him up for the ministry . . . He was in the habit of furnishing indigent young men with the means of prosecuting their studies for the Gospel ministry – always as a loan, telling them to return it when they were able so that he might assist others.'[1] After an academy for general education was founded near Cannonsburg, McMillan confined his home teaching to theology 'and this he continued until Theological Seminaries were established'.

Existing on the frontiers of civilization, these schools, which lacked even a name at this early date, had far-reaching influence. From the training given by Joseph Smith, Dod, and especially McMillan there issued 'a hundred young men, many of whom afterwards became distinguished preachers'. It was not so much their number that was important. As Gillett observed, despite the crying need of missionary labour, the preachers of the Redstone Presbytery were very cautious in their selection of men for training and service: 'They wanted, and made provision to secure, *strong* men; and all who joined them seemed to be made partakers of their own spirit.'[2] The history of many of their students shows that they were not disappointed – James Hughes was much used in the same region before becoming principal of what became Miami University; Elisha Macurdy and Thomas Marques were eminent pastors, preachers, and missionaries; Joseph Patterson and Samuel Porter were leaders in the Pittsburgh area through the first quarter of the nineteenth century; James M'Gready we shall meet in our next chapter. The records of these men show how fully they belonged to the living tradition into which they had been introduced in their early years. Dr J. Smith calls them 'thorough revival men'; men of 'spirit and fire'; 'more cheerful men never lived'; they 'lured to brighter worlds, and led the way'.[3] Their preaching combined 'affection

---

[1] Sprague, *Annals*, vol. 3, pp. 354–5.
[2] Gillett, *Presbyterian Church in U.S.*, vol. 1, p. 268.
[3] Joseph Smith, *Old Redstone; or, Historical Sketches of Western Presbyterianism, Its Early Ministers, Its Perilous Times, and Its First Records* (Philadelphia, 1854), pp. 138, 125n, 137, 85.

with authority, and a Christ-like pungency in its personal applications with a holy unction which it belongs to the Spirit alone to impart'. They were all possessed of the same convictions about revival and saw not a little in their later lives of the same power as had built the churches of their teachers. We read of such events as 123 being added to Marques' congregations in the first four years of his pastorate, of Porter preaching at the opening of the Synod of Pittsburgh in 1805 on 'A Revival of True Religion Delineated on Scriptural and Rational Principles', and of Macurdy, when he was turned eighty years of age in 1842, meeting in conference and prayer with members of the Synods of Pittsburgh, Ohio, and Wheeling, 'to supplicate larger measures of the Divine influence'.

But we must return to note the passing of the three pioneers from whose labours so much came down to later generations. Joseph Smith was the first to die. He was fifty-six years of age when he ascended the pulpit at Cross Creek on the first Sunday of April 1792. Although his health was never strong, it seemed to others that day to be much as usual; yet Smith preached as though he knew it to be his last sermon. His text was Galatians 1.8: 'though we, or an angel from heaven, preach any other gospel unto you than that which we have preached unto you, let him be accursed.' As he drew to a conclusion, he gave such a summary view of his twelve years' preaching that his people sensed it was the winding up of his ministry. The whole congregation wept, the more so when they saw that the preacher they had heard for the last time could not move from the pulpit to his horse without help. When Smith died on 19 April, 'such were the feelings of his people that it was a common remark among them that the sun did not seem to shine with its natural brightness for many days afterwards'.[1]

For Thaddeus Dod the sorrow over the loss of his close friend – whose epitaph he wrote – was lessened by the joy of seeing another period of revival in his own congregations. It began in the summer of 1792 and continued through the autumn into the winter. Under the burden of that happy and abundant work Dod's own health failed. He was to preach in Smith's former pulpit at Cross Creek exactly one year after the end of his

[1] Sprague, *Annals*, vol. 3, p.279.

friend's ministry. That Sunday, the first in April 1793, was the occasion of his last service. The following month he was gone and John McMillan preached at his grave on 'Blessed are the dead which die in the Lord from henceforth: Yea saith the Spirit, that they may rest from their labours; and their works do follow them'.

Forty years later, in the summer and autumn of 1833, the old 'apostle of the West' was still preaching, it was said, 'with almost the energy of middle life'. McMillan died on 16 November 1833. James Carnahan, who remembered him well, observed of his preaching:

He had but little gesture, seldom moving his hands in the pulpit. The body of his discourse was generally doctrinal, divided into two or three heads, – the whole an hour long, – not five minutes more or less, – embracing, at different times, the whole system of doctrine taught in our Confession of Faith. In the application of his sermons, which he never omitted, he made appeals to the hearts and consciences of his hearers. In describing the wretchedness of the lost, especially of those who had enjoyed the privileges of the Gospel, he was tremendous. And God blessed his preaching in a remarkable manner. He would not be called a man of genius, or of splendid talents. He wrote and spoke plain English, which the most illiterate could understand. I have often seen him, when preaching to fifteen hundred or two thousand people, in the open air, under the shade of the native trees, take off his coat and neckcloth or stock, in the midst of his discourse, and proceed without exciting a smile in one of the audience.[1]

*　　　*　　　*

There are a few final observations to be made on the spread of the gospel in Western Pennsylvania before we follow our theme elsewhere. The overruling of God in history could be seen in the way this part of the country was opened for settlement. The opening came at a time when true religious experience had prepared men and women for the hardship and heroism that the advance westwards would require. Western Pennsylvania was to be the key to the occupation of the great valley of the Mississippi and to the movement towards the Pacific. Here

[1] Ibid., p. 354.

[56]

churches were needed that would have deep and sure foundations and whose example would give guidance and inspiration
to the many yet to be formed in the regions beyond. Just such
congregations came into being in the manner we have seen.

Furthermore, for such expansion to occur without
fragmentation and confusion required a united leadership. At
Princeton Witherspoon's students used to hear him say that
when the church was to prosper it was noticeable that her
leaders 'flourish in clusters',[1] each helping one another. What
Witherspoon had observed in Scotland was equally true in
America. The unity of the log-college men of the 1740s, of
Johnes, McWhorter and Rodgers around New York, and of
Smith, McMillan, Power and Dod in their shared work
between the Monongahela and the Ohio, was a vital part of
their success.[2] It was patently more than the same education
which gave the Redstone presbytery men the oneness they
enjoyed. They were possessed by the same conception of
Christianity. They knew fellowship with God. They believed in
a gospel which had to be felt in its power and in the Holy Spirit,
on whose energy all success depends. For these men, therefore,
as Gillett wrote: 'Revivals were not only favoured but expected
and longed for; . . . In spirit they were the successors to the
Blairs, Finleys and Smiths of the Revival period who during the
division adhered to the New Side and the cause of vital piety.
Many of them were rarely gifted, and would have done honor to
the most exalted station; and the influence which they exerted
upon the great Western field then opening with inviting
promise to Eastern emigration, cannot be estimated.'[3]

Another fact is too important to go unmentioned. It is that
the wives of these men were no less in stature as Christians than
their husbands. These were women not raised in the
backwoods but educated and accustomed to the established
communities in the East. We can well believe that it was only

---

[1] Quoted by Martha L. L. Stohlman, *John Witherspoon, Parson, Politician,
Patriot* (Philadelphia: Westminster Press, 1976), p. 106.
[2] On this same point Jonathan Edwards wrote in 1741, 'Ministers should
act as fellow-helpers in their great work. It should be seen that they exert
themselves with one heart and soul, and with united strength . . . and to that
end should often meet together and act in concert'. *Works*, vol. 1, p. 424.
[3] *Presbyterian Church in U.S.*, vol. 1, pp. 261, 267.

'uncommon piety' that enabled them to survive the hardship and loneliness, the early death of children, the fear of the frontier, and all else that became a part of their daily lives. Indeed, all the indications are that they did more than survive. They prayed and fasted; they improvised coats from skins or blankets for winter and made summer clothes from linen which they coloured from the dye from new-mown hay; they relearned some of their cooking in kitchens which had to be shared, at times, with their husbands' school pupils. All in all, they presided over homes that were happy both in life and death. When the wife of Joseph Patterson was dying, such were her 'views of the glory she was advancing to, and hopes of being soon in it', that the edge of sorrow was so dulled that he 'scarcely felt its sharp cutting'.[1] John McMillan wrote: 'My wife and I lived comfortably together more than forty-three years; and on the 24th of November, 1819, she departed triumphantly to take possession of her house not made with hands, eternal in the heavens.'[2]

On this same subject, Thomas Murphy directs attention to Catharine Kennedy, the wife of William Tennent (founder of the log-college), and asks whether that school would ever have been built without 'her counsel, cheer and self-sacrifice'. He goes on to express the opinion that 'on account of her position, usefulness and excellence, we consider that she deserves to stand highest of all . . . Unseen, unheralded, almost unknown, her influence was deeper, stronger, wider and more lasting than that of any other of the group.'[3] Probably the same could be said of many of the early pioneer Christian women across the Alleghenies; without them the story would certainly have been very different.

The tide of population movement which gathered momentum in the later eighteenth century had one effect that

[1] Sprague, *Annals*, vol. 3, p. 523. See also Smith's general remarks on these women upon whom 'too much praise cannot be bestowed': 'They trained their children to fear God, to tell the truth, to reverence the Sabbath and house of God, to work hard, and to be honest in all their dealings' (*Old Redstone*, pp. 109–10). For the view of this generation on Christian mother-hood see Archibald Alexander, *Thoughts on Religious Experience* (1844; London: Banner of Truth, 1967), pp. 318–28.

[2] Sprague, *Annals*, vol. 3, p. 352. More fully in *Old Redstone*, pp. 201–2.

[3] *Presbytery of Log College*, p. 118.

was mourned by some among a later generation of Christians. As people sought new lives on cheaper ground, the congregations of country churches in the East often dwindled until their old stone walls were at last deserted as other buildings were constructed to meet the needs of smaller numbers. Lines written by W. M. Nevin, when he went back to the church of his childhood at Middle Spring in the Cumberland Valley in 1847, record something of this change. As he revisited the scene of the Sundays of his youth and saw again in his mind's eye the crowds that had once filled the churchyard in the lunch-break between the services, he wrote the following lines, which help us to understand more of the era to which the pioneers belonged:

> They come not now, who gave that spot its zest.
>   Parent and brothers, sisters, all are gone
> To newer homes, far settled in the West, –
>   No more to walk, on holy days, this lawn.
>   Yet one here rests. O, most reveréd one!
> Dear parent mine! Say, is thy spirit near,
>   To whose green mound here have I first been drawn?
> Mark'st thou my sorrowing step and briny tear,
> To think I loved thee not the more when thou wast here?
>
> In this high burial-ground, in that below,
>   No massive structure stands of sculptured stone;
> No column's shaft, off broke, that it might show
>   Youth's vigour downwards all untimely thrown.
>   But humble slabs and headstones many strown,
> Simply the names and years and worth avow
>   Of those here laid. 'Tis well. They covet none.
> In life they were plain men of honest brow,
> They sought no honours then, nor do they seek them now.
>
> Here were they gathered every good Lord's day,
>   From town, from hamlet, and from country wide,
> In pleasant groups, but meek and staid alway,
>   They showed not often levity nor pride;
>   Yet sooth in some gay maids some pranks were spied,
> Misled by dress and spirits over light,
>   Out by yon firs, with beaux convened aside,
>   They laughed and joked; yes, some did shrill outright!
> And that it was God's day they had forgotten quite.

But these were few: and for that breach, I wote,
    At home their mothers did them well aread.
Others all o'er this place in solemn thought,
      Stood lone, or spoke with sanctimonious heed.
      Yet this to take full many had no need,
For they were grave in grain. Who would might scan,
      Still were they upright found in word and deed.
They knew, but most they felt, the gospel plan,
And loved their God supreme, and next their fellow-man.

Blest sight it was to mark that godly flock,
    At intermission, grouped throughout this wood.
Each log, each bench, each family upping-block,
      Some granddame held amidst her gathered brood.
      Here cakes were shared, and fruits, and counsel good;
Devoutly spoken 'twas of crops and rain;
      Hard by the church the broad-brimmed elders stood,
While o'er that slope did flow a constant train
Of bevies, springward bound, or coming back again.[1]

---

[1] W. M. Nevin, quoted in Alfred Nevin, *Churches of the Valley: or, An Historical Sketch of the Old Presbyterian Congregations of Cumberland and Franklin Counties, in Pennsylvania* (Philadelphia, 1852), pp. 40, 44–5.

3

GLORY IN VIRGINIA

Francis Asbury (1745–1816)

3

When Samuel Davies left Virginia in 1759, almost the only choice for church-goers in the colony was between the Church of England, with her cold, unevangelical clergy, and the few scattered Presbyterian churches in which the preaching recovered at the time of the Great Awakening had been continued. Devereux Jarratt, a Virginian born in 1733, wrote of this period: 'I knew of no other people that had any real appearance of religion . . . I scarcely thought there was any religion but among the Presbyterians.'[1]

The identification of evangelical Christianity with the Presbyterians was common enough in Virginia in 1760. But within a few years the whole church scene was to change and in that change Devereux Jarratt himself played a major part. Jarratt's account of his life (from which we have already quoted) tells us how he came to see that the Church of England was not to be judged solely by its representatives in the Old Dominion. After all, Whitefield and Wesley were numbered among her clergy and the doctrinal articles professed by Anglicans and Presbyterians were the same in substance. The real differences between the two denominations, he believed, had to do with non-essentials, and so considerations of spiritual expedience finally persuaded him to enter the Anglican rather than the Presbyterian ministry: 'The general prejudice of the people, at

---

[1] *The Life of the Reverend Devereux Jarratt, Rector of Bath Parish, Dinwiddie County, Virginia, Written by Himself to the Rev. John Coleman* (Baltimore, Md., 1806; Arno Press, New York, 1969), p. 56. References to Jarratt's ministry in the following pages are from this source unless stated otherwise.

that time, against dissenters and in favour of the church, gave me a full persuasion that I could do more good in the church than anywhere else.'

Jarratt went to England for episcopal ordination in 1762 and on his return the following year became the rector of Bath parish in Dinwiddie County. In that position he stood alone, 'not knowing of one clergyman in Virginia like minded with myself . . . I was called an enthusiast, fanatic, visionary, dissenter, Presbyterian, madman, and what not.' To his own hearers his evangelical preaching was 'strange and wonderful'. He summarizes their conversation about his preaching as follows: 'We have had many ministers and have heard many before this man, but we never heard any thing, till now, of conversion, the new birth, &c. – we never heard that men are so totally lost and helpless, that they could not save themselves, by their own power and good deeds; – if our good works will not save us, what will?' In his uncompromising preaching of the law and the gospel Jarratt proved to be the successor to Samuel Davies, and by 1765 there was the same evidence of concern among his people as had marked the work at Hanover County sixteen years earlier. His hearers multiplied and strangers began to attend from 'far and near'.

Jarratt's scattered parish was served by several buildings at different locations. One of these – the Butterwood church – had to be twice enlarged. Then, in 1770–71, he records, 'we had a more considerable outpouring of the Spirit at a place in my parish called White Oak'. This proved to be the beginning of a revival period:

In the year 1772, the revival was more considerable, and extended itself in some places, for fifty or sixty miles around. It increased still more in the following year, and several sinners were truly converted to God. In Spring, 1774, it was more remarkable than ever. The word preached was attended with such energy, that many were pierced to the heart. Tears fell plentifully from the eyes of the hearers, and some were constrained to cry out. A goodly number were gathered in this year, both in my parish and in many of the neighbouring counties. I formed several societies out of those which were convinced or converted; and I found it a happy means of building to those that had believed, and preventing the rest from losing their convictions.[1]

[1] Jarratt, *Brief Narrative of the Revival of Religion in Virginia, in a Letter to a*

Meanwhile, another evangelical influence, which was not connected with Anglicans or Presbyterians, was gaining momentum. In 1760 churches of Baptist persuasion, which were very few in number and of negligible influence in Virginia, saw the first in a succession of events which, within thirty years, was to make them one of the largest Christian groups in the state. The change came largely through Baptists of 'Separate' persuasion whose first congregation was established in Pittsylvania County in the south-west of the colony in 1760. A second congregation, north of the James River, followed in 1767. The witness of these and similar congregations spread both through the calibre of the preachers and by the lives of those converted under their ministry. Among the most notable of the preachers at the outset were Daniel Marshall and Samuel Harris. It was reported of Harris that he 'left a train of seriousness after him wherever he went'. He spoke to men's hearts in a manner which, it was said, 'perhaps even Whitefield did not surpass'. A younger generation of men, converted under this preaching, caught the same spirit and also became eminent ministers of the gospel. Among these was Lewis Lunsford (1753–93) who became an exhorter at the age of seventeen. Robert B. Semple, Lunsford's contemporary, called him 'an ambassador of the skies, sent down to command all men everywhere to repent . . . In his best strains he was more like an angel than a man. His countenance, lighted up by an inward flame, seemed to shed beams of light wherever he turned.'[1] The Presbyterian W. H. Foote similarly described Lunsford as 'a young preacher of extraordinary powers'.[2]

The second event precipitating the growth of the Baptists after 1760 was the settlement of David Thomas in northern Virginia. From his base in Fauquier County he began to itinerate and became, in Semple's words, 'the first Baptist preacher that ever proclaimed the Gospel of Peace in the

---

Friend [John Wesley] (London, 1778). See also *The Journals and Letters of Francis Asbury* (London and Nashville, Tenn., Epworth Press and Abingdon Press, 1958), vol. 1, pp. 207–24.

[1] Robert B. Semple, *History of the Baptists in Virginia* (1810, rev. edn 1894; Church History Research and Archives, Lafayette, Tenn., 1974), p. 473.

[2] *Sketches*, p. 314.

counties of Orange and Culpeper . . . His preaching was in power and demonstration of the Spirit.' Although he belonged to the Regular Baptists,[1] Thomas was working with Samuel Harris and other Separates by 1765.

These Baptist preachers were unconnected with Jarratt or the Presbyterians, but the movement to which they belonged also owed its resurgence to the influence of the Great Awakening. Their evangelistic preaching was the same in content to that of Whitefield and the other leaders of the 1740s. The Separate Baptists were immigrants from New England where Whitefield's ministry had influenced them deeply. Only on church polity and baptism did they differ from him, which is said to have occasioned the Englishman's humorous comment, 'My chickens have turned to ducks'. The influence of Whitefield had also moulded the thinking of David Thomas as he grew up in Pennsylvania. That the gospel preaching of the Baptists was readily identifiable with the teaching that many in Virginia had already heard from Presbyterian preachers was one reason for the support they received. The substance of their evangelical and Calvinistic message offered no novelties. When Anglican clergy attacked Baptists as 'false prophets', they replied that *they* believed their opponents' 'own Articles – at least the leading ones – and charged *them* with denying them, a charge which they could easily substantiate.'[2]

The new movement, however, reached further than the people in whom a hunger for biblical preaching had already been awakened; it soon extended to multitudes who had never heard the gospel before. At first regarded with suspicion and ridicule, then, for a season, exposed to persecution from the authorities, Baptist preachers pressed on with their work. No one could doubt that they believed men must be converted to God if they were to be saved. The old charge that Christians

---

[1] Whereas the Separate Baptists had originated in New England after the Great Awakening, the Regular Baptists were established in the Middle Colonies earlier in the century and their Philadelphia Association (holding to the 1689 revision of the Westminster Confession) was the oldest and largest Baptist association in America. The term 'Regular' seems to have originated in the 1760s as a distinction between them and the 'Separates'. It is estimated that total Baptist membership in 1775 was around 20,000 members, in 400 to 500 small churches.

[2] Semple, *Baptists in Virginia*, p. 382.

'turned the world upside down' (Acts 17.6) was heard again. A lawyer prosecuting them in court complained, 'These men are great disturbers of the peace; they cannot meet a man upon the road but they must ram a text of Scripture down his throat'. Another complainant alleged that in Loudoun County these men were 'quite destroying pleasure'. Yet their message continued to spread, in Semple's words, 'like the spread of a fire . . . it does not in all cases advance regularly; but a spark being struck, flies off and begins a new flame at a distance'. One writer estimates that in 1772 'as many as forty thousand Virginians may have heard the gospel from the Baptists'.[1] The growth in the Separate Baptist churches bears out the effects of this evangelism. In 1770, according to Semple, the Separates possessed only two congregations north of the James River and about four on the south side; two years later their number appears to have grown to twenty, with twenty-one branches. In 1774 they had thirty churches south of the James and twenty-four to the north.

Various factors have to be considered in interpreting the extraordinary speed of this growth. The prejudice in the common attitude towards the Baptists in the 1760s had gradually given way to admiration. The opposition of the unpopular Church of England, backed by the state – which had some of the Baptist leaders temporarily imprisoned – gave the new preachers the status of reformers. Poor and unlearned as they generally were, and entirely unsupported by patronage, the very contrast between them and the clergy told in their favour. People could scarcely doubt which of the two opposing religious professions was the more convincing, judged on the basis of consistency between life and message. While the established clergy, observed Foote, were contesting the question of their salaries and 'alienating the public mind from the established church herself, the zealous Baptist preachers were calling the attention of men to the great interests of religion, and preaching, according to their ability, the Gospel, without money and without price'.[2] Such was the change in popular sympathy towards them that it was to contribute significantly

---

[1] W. L. Lumpkin, *Baptist Foundations in the South* (1961), repr. in *Colonial Baptists and Southern Revivals* (Arno Press, New York, 1980), p. 100.
[2] *Sketches*, p. 315.

to the partial disestablishment of the Church of England in 1776 and its total disestablishment in 1784.

But the principal reason for the remarkable success of the gospel preaching of the Baptists lies elsewhere. The movement of the Spirit of God, which we have already noted among Devereux Jarratt's congregations in the early 1770s, was clearly equally in evidence in the Baptist churches. The dates of the revival of which Jarratt wrote, when compared with the period of the surprising Baptist advance, can be seen to be the same. Semple's statement is undoubtedly correct: 'The great success and rapid increase of the Baptists in Virginia must be ascribed primarily to the power of God working with them.'

Such is the partial-sightedness of even the best Christians that Jarratt himself did not share the interpretation Semple would later give. On the contrary, he complained vigorously of the hindrance he encountered through the proselytizing of the Baptists: 'I prevented this notion of going into the water, and its evil train of consequences, from breaking into the body of my parish. But I could not prevent its spreading in other counties where I used sometimes to preach. In these counties many were disunited, and the peace of neighbourhoods destroyed.'[1]

Jarratt went on to say that it was in part his need of help in counteracting Baptist influence which led him into a new alliance – an alliance that was to be of far greater consequence than he could have realized. Another new evangelical and Protestant group was also at the starting point of an ascendancy no less swift than that of the Baptists and no Anglican clergyman in the Thirteen Colonies contributed so largely in its beginnings as the rector of Bath parish.

In March 1773 ' a plain, simple-hearted, pious man' by the name of Robert Williams came to Jarratt's home in Dinwiddie County. 'He staid with me near a week,' wrote his host, 'and preached several sermons in the parish, most, or all, of which I heard. I liked his preaching in the main very well, and especially the affectionate and animated manner in which his discourses were delivered.'

Williams, who had come from England in 1769, was one of the first of John Wesley's preachers in America. He had arrived

_____
[1] *Life*, p. 107.

only a few months before Richard Boardman and Joseph Pilmoor, the two men officially sent out by Wesley's Conference. Wesley himself had been in Georgia as early as 1736, and it is therefore surprising that 'Methodism' did not reach America until more than thirty years later. The explanation is largely doctrinal. The Great Awakening of the 1740s had been led by men whose reformed and Puritan convictions made them unsympathetic to Wesley's evangelical Arminianism. The distinctive theology that came to be identified with Wesleyan Methodism scarcely existed in Protestant America for nearly 150 years after the landing of the Pilgrim Fathers. There was point, therefore, to Whitefield's remark to Boardman and Pilmoor on their arrival in America in October 1769, 'Ah, if ye were Calvinists, ye would take the country before ye'.[1] The English evangelist, who was to die in New England the following September, knew that there were no preachers of the Calvinistic persuasion belonging to Wesley's Conference.

Jarratt also knew this as he welcomed Williams to his home and pulpit, but it did not affect his decision to form an alliance with the Methodists. In the midst of a revival, there were opportunities enough for a score of men who were prepared to preach Christ crucified, and he believed that there was ample common ground to justify co-operation. After all, a large part of Methodist belief was common to the confession of all the Protestant churches. One of their first historians in America, Nathan Bangs, summarized the Methodists' teaching as follows:

While they held, in common with other orthodox Christians, to the hereditary depravity of the human heart, the deity and atonement of Jesus Christ, the necessity of repentance and faith; that which they pressed upon their hearers with the greatest earnestness was, the

[1] Reported by Francis Asbury in Nathan Bangs, *A History of the Methodist Episcopal Church*, third edn (New York, 1839), vol. 1, p. 325. 'I dread your coming over to America,' Whitefield wrote to Wesley on 24 May 1740, 'because the work of God is carried on here (and that in a most glorious manner) by doctrines quite opposite to those you hold' (*Works*, vol. 1, p. 182). It should be remembered that the word 'Methodist' was originally applied to Whitefield and other evangelicals in England. Only gradually did it become identified with the Wesleyan branch of the Evangelical Revival in England and that was the sense in which the word was later understood in America.

necessity of the new birth, and the privilege of their having a knowledge, by the internal witness of the Holy Spirit, of the *forgiveness of sins*, through faith in the blood of Christ; and as a necessary consequence of this, and as naturally flowing from it, provided they persevered, *holiness of heart and life*.[1]

In addition to these shared beliefs, the Wesleyan view of preaching was also the same as that recovered by the Great Awakening. Their preachers, observed Bangs, 'disturbed the false peace of the lukewarm, awakened the conscience of the sleeping sinner, and gave him 'no rest until he surrendered to Christ . . . and they accompanied all their efforts by earnest prayer, both public and private, that God would sanction their labors by sending upon them the energies of the Holy Spirit.'[2]

Another important factor that weighed with Jarratt in his decision to open his pulpits and merge his societies with the Methodists was their vigorous affirmation that Methodism existed only as an arm of the Church of England. It would establish societies only within that Church. It ordained no clergy and administered no sacraments. No separation from the Church of England was therefore threatened. On the contrary, Williams assured Jarratt in much the same way as Wesley himself might have done, that 'He that left the Church, left the Methodists'. Almost alone among Virginia's clergy, and pressed as Jarratt was by losses to the Baptists, this unexpected arrival of evangelical preachers who supported the Church of England was especially welcome. Thus, as Asbury recalled years later, 'Jarratt was the first who received our despised preachers – when strangers and unfriended, he took them to his house, and had societies formed in his parish'.[3]

From 1773, Jarratt reported, the work of the gospel in the adjacent counties of Sussex and Brunswick 'was chiefly carried on by the labours of the people called Methodists'. In 1774 other preachers joined Williams in the area, 'who gathered many societies both in this neighbourhood, and in other places, as far as North Carolina. They now began to ride the circuit, and to take care of the societies already formed, which was

---

[1] Bangs, *History*, vol. 1, p. 364.
[2] Ibid., p. 363.   [3] *Journals and Letters*, vol. 2, p. 292.

rendered a happy means, both of deepening and spreading the work of God.'

Jarratt's societies, he wrote, continued to pray 'for a larger outpouring of the Spirit of God', and towards the end of 1775 they began to experience 'a revival of religion as great as perhaps ever was known in country places':

It began in the latter end of the year 1775: but was more considerable in January, 1776, the beginning of the present year. It broke out nearly at the same time, at three places, not far from each other. Two of these places are in my parish; the other in Amelia county – which had for many years been notorious for carelessness, profaneness, and immoralities of all kinds. Gaming, swearing, drunkenness, and the like, were their delight, while things sacred were their scorn and contempt.

Last December one of the Methodist preachers, Mr. Shadford,[1] preached several times at the three places abovementioned. He confirmed the doctrine I had long preached; and to many of them not in vain. And while their ears were opened by novelty, God set his word home upon their hearts. Many sinners were powerfully convinced, and mercy! mercy! was their cry. In January, the news of convictions and conversions was common; and the people of God were inspired with new life and vigour by the happiness of others.

During this whole winter, the Spirit of the Lord was poured out in a manner we had not seen before. In almost every assembly might be seen signal instances of divine power, more especially in the meetings of the classes. Here many old stout-hearted sinners felt the force of truth, and their eyes were open to discover their guilt and danger. The shaking among the dry bones was increased from week to week: nay, sometimes ten or twelve have been deeply convinced of sin in one day . . . Numbers of old and gray-headed, of middle-aged persons, of youth, yea, of little children, were the subjects of this work. Several of the latter we have seen painfully concerned for the wickedness of their lives, and the corruption of their nature . . .

Many in these parts who had long neglected the means of grace now flocked to hear, not only me and the travelling preachers, but also the exhorters and leaders. And the Lord showed he is not confined to man; for whether there was preaching or not, his power was still sensible among the people. And at their meetings for prayer, some have been in such distress that they have continued therein for five or

---

[1] George Shadford was one of the most successful of Wesley's early preachers in America. He remained in Virginia for eighteen months.

six hours. And it has been found that these prayer meetings were singularly useful in promoting the work of God.

The outpouring of the Spirit which began here, soon extended itself, more or less, through most of the circuit, which is regularly attended by the travelling preachers, and which takes in a circumference of between four and five hundred miles. And the work went on, with a pleasing progress, till the beginning of May, when they held a quarterly meeting at Boisseau's chapel, in my parish. This stands at the lower line of the parish, thirty miles from White's chapel,[1] at the upper line of it, where the work began. At this meeting, one might truly say, the windows of heaven were opened, and the rain of Divine influence poured down for more than forty days. The work now became more deep than ever, extended wider, and was swifter in its operations. Many were savingly converted to God, and in a very short time, not only in my parish, but through several parts of Brunswick, Sussex, Prince George, Lunenburg, Mecklenburg, and Amelia counties.

The multitudes that attended on this occasion, returning home all alive to God, spread the flame through their respective neighbourhoods, which ran from family to family: so that within four weeks, several hundreds found the peace of God. And scarce any conversation was to be heard throughout the circuit, but concerning the things of God: either the complaining of the prisoners, groaning under the spirit of bondage unto fear; or the rejoicing of those whom the Spirit of adoption taught to cry, 'Abba, Father.' The unhappy disputes between England and her colonies, which just before had engrossed all our conversation, seemed now in most companies to be forgot, while things of far greater importance lay so near the heart.[2]

Had it not been for the alliance with the Methodists we would probably not have this account of what happened in 1775–6 for the above report is taken from a long letter which Jarratt wrote to John Wesley dated 10 September 1776. This was forwarded to England along with statements by other witnesses confirming the same facts. Thomas Saunders, who lived twenty-two miles away from Jarratt, wrote on 29 July

---

[1] The chapel at White Oak Creek. Mr Boisseau, a supporter of Jarratt's, had erected the other chapel which was known by his name. These chapels were distinct from Jarratt's three main churches, Butterwood, Hatcher's Run and Saponey. The last-named still exists and Jarratt and his wife are buried beneath the pulpit.

[2] Asbury, *Journals and Letters*, vol. 1, p. 207ff.

1776: 'Above seven years have I been exhorting my neighbours; but very few would hear. Now, blessed be God, there are few that will not hear.' Another man, describing how Christians were filled with love and praise, recorded: 'Surely this was one of the days of heaven! Such a day I never expected to see in time.' In a supplement to Jarratt's account of the revival. Thomas Rankin, another Methodist preacher, described a service at Boisseau's chapel on Sunday, 30 June 1776:

At four in the afternoon I preached again, from 'I set before thee an open door, and none can shut it.' I had gone through about two-thirds of my discourse, and was bringing the words home to the present – Now, when such power descended, that hundreds fell to the ground, and the house seemed to shake with the presence of God. The chapel was full of white and black, and many were without that could not get in. Look wherever we would, we saw nothing but streaming eyes, and faces bathed in tears; and heard nothing but groans and strong cries after God and the Lord Jesus Christ. My voice was drowned amidst the groans and prayers of the congregation. I then sat down in the pulpit; and both Mr Shadford and I were so filled with the divine presence, that we could only say, This is none other than the house of God! This is the gate of heaven!

In concluding his letter to Wesley, Jarratt warned the English leader against an overestimate of what was happening. He knew there was some 'wildfire' mixed with the true, and 'a great part of Virginia is still in a very dark and deplorable condition. This province contains sixty-two counties; and the late work has reached only seven or eight of them. Nor has it been universal even in these, but chiefly in the circuit which is regularly visited by the preachers. In this alone very many hundreds have in a few months been added to the Lord. And some are adding still.'

An idea of the numbers affected at this time can be judged from records kept by the Methodists. When ten Methodist preachers met for their first Conference in July 1773, the total number of men and women belonging to their societies had been 1,160. Virginia had 100, the lowest membership of the five colonies where societies existed. In May 1774 society membership had risen to 218 in Virginia, and a year later it stood at 800, and 811 more were added before the May Conference of 1776. It continued to rise to 2,456 in 1776 and to 3,449 in 1777. In

[73]

1780, when total Methodist membership in America stood at 8,540, 7,808 were to be found in the South – 'in spite of the fact,' notes William Warren Sweet, 'that Wesley's missionaries gave most of their attention to the societies in New York, Pennsylvania, New Jersey and Delaware'.[1] In 1784, its membership at 14,988, Methodism 'had increased approximately 1,400 percent in the short span of ten years, or at a rate of about six times the increase of the American population'.[2]

No real sense can be made of these figures without taking into account the awakening in Virginia. To call what happened in 1775–6 'the first great Methodist revival in America' is partially misleading, for much of the preparation and an important part of the leadership of the work belonged to Jarratt. Nor can the society-membership figures simply be equated with converts under Methodist preaching, for Jarratt had merged his own society members into the new organization transplanted from England. And while we lack Baptist documentation for these years, we do know that their congregations were caught up in a similar work of grace. True revivals rarely remain within denominational boundaries.

*   *   *

With the possible exception of Western Pennsylvania, there seem to have been no areas where there was general revival during the years of the War of Independence, from 1775 to 1783. In most of the country there was evident spiritual decline as political and military events dominated public attention. Prior to the Revolution there had been no deep-seated desire for the independence of the Thirteen Colonies. In a letter on 'The Contest between Great Britain and America' John Witherspoon wrote in 1778: 'I am a witness that the people of this country had an esteem of, and attachment to the people of Great Britain, exceedingly strong . . . When an American

[1] *Methodism in American History* (1953; Nashville, Tenn.: Abingdon Press, 1961), p. 60.
[2] R. Coleman, *Factors in the Expansion of the Methodist Episcopal Church from 1784 to 1812* (Ann Arbor, Mich.: University Microfilms, 1974), pp. 120–1.

spoke of going to England, he always called it going home.'[1] But in their ignorance of transatlantic affairs, and by no small bungling, the English Parliament at last drove their fellow countrymen past the point of return. They forgot, in Witherspoon's words, that 'the liberty which pervades the British constitution came with the colonists to this part of the earth'. When 12,000 German mercenaries were dispatched to America in 1776 it needed nothing more for Congress to resolve 'That these United Colonies are, and of right ought to be, Independent States'. The Union Jack, retained in one corner of the Patriots' flag, disappeared altogether the next year to be replaced by the Stars and Stripes.

Most Christians in America stood behind the Revolution. Witherspoon – the only minister to sign the Declaration of Independence – put into words what others must have felt. He judged that the outcome of the struggle would be 'a matter of truly inexpressible moment. The state of the human race through a great part of the globe, for ages to come, depends upon it.'[2] With shrewd foresight he judged (in 1778) that 'the separation of America from Britain will be to the benefit of this country, without injury to the other – perhaps to the advantage of both'.

In the short term, however, the sufferings brought by the War were considerable and in these sufferings the Presbyterians – united in support of independence – had a larger share than most. Among Princeton graduates who were killed were the Rev. John Rossburgh and twenty-five-year-old James Witherspoon, the son of the president. The former was shot by German mercenaries, as was the wife of the Rev. James Caldwell. Caldwell himself was murdered after the armistice of 1781, leaving nine children orphans.

Many parts of the country were ravaged by the War. Princeton was twice engulfed in battle and Nassau Hall left a wreck. When peace was at last restored, the Presbyterians could refer with justice to 'our burnt and wasted churches and our plundered dwellings'.

The Baptists of Virginia initially profited from the War in that it brought all persecution against them to an end. But the

---

[1] *Works*, vol. 9, pp. 168–9.   [2] Ibid., p. 87.

event also marked the end of their spiritual advance. Robert Semple, who was fourteen years of age when the Peace Treaty was signed in 1783, observed:

The war, though very propitious to the liberty of the Baptists, had an opposite effect upon the life of religion among them. As if persecution was more favorable to vital piety than unrestrained liberty, they seem to have abated in their zeal, upon being un-shackled from their manacles. This may be ascribed to several causes . . . Perhaps many did not rightly estimate the true source of liberty, nor ascribe its attainment to the proper arm. In consequence of which God sent them liberty, and with it leanness of soul. This chill to their religious affections might have subsided with the war, or perhaps sooner, if there had not been subsequent occurrences which tended to keep them down. The opening a free trade by peace served as a powerful bait to entrap professors who were in any great degree inclined to the pursuit of wealth. Nothing is more common than for the increase of riches to produce a decrease of piety. Speculators seldom make warm Christians. With some few excep-tions the declension was general throughout the State. The love of many waxed cold. Some of the watchmen fell, others stumbled, and many slumbered at their posts.[1]

The inhabitants of the American colonies were, of course, not all on the side of independence. One modern historian surmises that 40 per cent of the white population was actively Patriot, about 10 per cent actively Loyalist and 'about 50 per cent indifferent or neutral'.[2] Clergy of the Church of England were predictably Loyalist. Their public identification with the losing side contributed to bringing the Church to near extinction in several areas when the War was over. From ninety-one Anglican clergymen in Virginia in 1776 the number fell to twenty-eight in 1783, of whom only fifteen still served parishes.

[1] *Baptists in Virginia*, pp. 55–6.
[2] S. E. Morison, *The Oxford History of the American People* (New York, O.U.P., 1965), p. 236. On the percentage of Christians among the Patriots, Ashbel Green (Presbyterian chaplain to Washington's Congress) wrote: 'Many of those who took the lead in the arduous struggle which issued in the Independence of our country were . . . men of decided piety; and those of opposite character yielded to their influence, from a regard to popular opinion, which at that time was strongly in favor of religion' (quoted in Stohlman, *John Witherspoon*, p. 116).

From around 40,000 communicants in 1775 the number in the reconstituted Protestant Episcopal Church stood between 12,000 and 16,000 at the end of the century. Less predictably, Methodists, taking their cue from John Wesley, were often out of sympathy with the Revolution. By 1778, with one exception, every Methodist preacher who had been sent across the Atlantic had returned to England. The exception was Francis Asbury who had arrived in 1771. For nearly half a century Asbury's calm leadership in the work of evangelistic itinerary and church organization did more than any other figure to establish Methodism in North America. The opinion of Abel Stevens on Asbury is perhaps overstated but it bears repetition: 'Neither Wesley nor Whitefield labored as energetically as this obscure man. He exceeded them in the extent of his annual travels, the frequency of his sermons, and the hardships of his daily life.'[1]

If it had not been for American-born preachers raised up before the Revolution, Methodism might have suffered a decline similar to that of the Church of England. The Conference of 1778 recorded a loss of 873 members and seven preachers. During the War, Methodists were commonly treated as anti-Patriot. Asbury had to lie low for two years. Other leaders were arrested or, on occasion, mobbed. Methodist membership in New York fell from 200 at the outset of the War to 60 by the end.[2] But, unlike the Church of England, Methodism was inherently a spiritual movement and the temporary taint of political disloyalty was already fading by the time its societies became the Methodist Episcopal Church in 1784.

*   *   *

As we shall later see, an opinion originated in the nineteenth century to the effect that where revival has once occurred it is

[1] *A Compendious History of American Methodism* (New York, 1867), p. 118. On one important point Asbury was more consistent than the two Englishmen: he remained a bachelor while they too often pursued their itinerant work as though they were single.

[2] But there was growth in other areas during the war years, most notably in places least affected by the conflict.

most liable to be found recurring at regular, probably shorter, intervals. No such view existed in Virginia in the 1780s. An understanding of revival as a work of God kept Christians of all denominations from any such assumption. The general decline after 1776, according to Semple, 'induced many to fear that the times of refreshing would never come'.

It was among Baptist Churches on the James River that the first signs of a coming change were seen in 1785. From that date, reported Semple,[1] revival spread 'as fire among stubble, continuing for several years in different parts. Very few churches were without the blessing. How great the change!' It appears that this work began among Baptists while there was no sign of it as yet among Presbyterians or Methodists. At this date the centre of Presbyterian evangelical witness east of the Blue Ridge Mountains was no longer Hanover but Hampden-Sydney in Prince Edward County, where Princeton men had formed a college in 1776 – yet another seedling from William Tennent's first log college. In 1787 the President of Hampden-Sydney was John Blair Smith (son of Robert Smith of Pequea) who also served the congregations of Cumberland, Briery and Cub Creek in adjacent Charlotte County. Smith had been at Princeton at the time of the revival there in the early 1770s, and it would seem that the evidence he saw of revival among Baptist churches in Charlotte County in 1786 or 1787 encouraged him to establish a prayer meeting with his elders 'to pray for a special outpouring of the Spirit of God' upon their congregations and college.

All was quiet among the Presbyterians when Asbury visited them in April 1787. His journal record reads: '*Monday*, 23. We called at Hampden and Sydney college, in Prince Edward: the outside has an unwieldy, uncommon appearance, for a seminary of learning; what the inside is, I know not. The president, Mr J. Smith, is a discreet man, who conducts himself well. About half past eleven o'clock we reached John Finney's, in Amelia, having ridden about sixty miles. I want to live more constantly in the spirit of prayer.' Nor did Asbury notice anything unusual among Methodists in Virginia in the spring of 1787. By his next visit in October, however, the whole scene

[1] *Baptists in Virginia*, pp. 57–60.

had changed, as he wrote on 19 October 1787, 'a revival has taken place all round the circuit'. For more detail we must look to Jesse Lee, converted under Robert Williams and by this date a preacher himself. He described the year 1787:

There was a remarkable revival of religion in the town of Petersburgh, and many of the inhabitants were savingly converted; and the old Christians greatly revived. That town never witnessed before or since such wonderful displays of the presence and love of God in the salvation of immortal souls. Prayer meetings were frequently held both in the town and in the country, and souls were frequently converted at those meetings, even when there was no preacher present; for the prayers and exhortations of the members were greatly owned of the Lord.

The most remarkable work of all was in Sussex and Brunswick circuits, where the meetings would frequently continue five or six hours together, and sometimes all night.

At one quarterly meeting held at Mabry's Chapel[1] in Brunswick circuit, on the 25th and 26th of July, the power of God was among the people in an extraordinary manner: some hundreds were awakened; and it was supposed that above one hundred souls were converted at that meeting, which continued for two days, i.e., on Thursday and Friday. Some thousands of people attended meeting at that place on that occasion.

The next quarterly meeting was held at Jones's Chapel, in Sussex county, on Saturday and Sunday, the 27th and 28th of July. This meeting was favored with more of the divine presence than any other that had been known before . . .

The great revival of religion in 1776, which spread extensively through the south part of Virginia, exceeded any thing of the kind that had ever been known before in that part of the country. But the revival this year far exceeded it.

It was thought that in the course of that summer there were so many as sixteen hundred souls converted in Sussex circuit; in Brunswick circuit about eighteen hundred; and in Amelia circuit about eight hundred. In these three circuits we had the greatest revival of religion; but in many other circuits there was a gracious work, and hundreds were brought to God in the course of that year.

. . . the work was not confined to meetings for preaching; at prayer meetings the work prospered and many souls were born again . . . It

---

[1] A chapel built for preaching by the Mabry family in the mid-1770s. In his journal for 4 April 1804, Asbury noted it was 'made anew; now sixty by twenty-five feet'.

was common to hear of souls being brought to God while at work in their houses or in their fields. It was often the case that the people in their corn-fields, white people, or black, and sometimes both together, would begin to sing, and being affected would begin to pray, and others would join with them, and they would continue their cries till some of them would find peace to their souls.[1]

Various other witnesses confirm this account. John Lee in Prince George County wrote to his brother Jesse on 4 October 1787:

All the white persons in my father's family have joined in class with the Methodists, and profess to be happy. Our class has increased to forty members; and our circuit has been enlarged to six weeks; and I suppose near a thousand souls have been converted in this circuit within a few months past. Such a work of God we have never seen before. The great work began in July, and I was the third person that found peace with God. . . . Within four weeks from the time that I was converted, I believe one hundred of our neighbors were brought to God.[2]

On 8 January 1788, when Asbury was again in Virginia, he noted in his journal:

We came to James River: the ice was in the way, yet we pushed through safely to the opposite shore and arrived at Moorings just as the quarterly meeting ended; nevertheless, we too had a meeting, and the cry of glory! was heard in great life: God is among these people. Brother Cox thinks that not less than fourteen hundred, white and black, have been converted in Sussex circuit the past year; and brother Easter thinks there are still more in Brunswick circuit.[3]

In the spring of the same year (1788) Philip Bruce wrote from Portsmouth, Virginia to Asbury's fellow bishop, Thomas Coke:

vast numbers flocking into the fold of Christ from every quarter. In many places in this circuit, as soon as the preacher begins to speak, the power of God appears to be present; which is attended by trembling among the people, and falling down; some lie void of

---

[1] Quoted in Bangs, *History*, vol. 1, pp. 263–7.
[2] Jesse Lee, *Life of John Lee* (1805), p. 28, quoted in W. M. Gewehr, *The Great Awakening in Virginia, 1740–1790* (Gloucester, Mass.: Peter Smith, 1965), p.171.
[3] *Journal and Letters*, vol. 1, pp. 559–60.

motion or breath, others are in strong convulsions: and thus they continue, till the Lord raises them up which is attended with emotions of joy and rapture.[1]

According to W. W. Bennett, the historian of Methodism in Virginia, the whole area south of the James River, from the Blue Ridge to the sea, was affected by this awakening, which reached all classes of people. But whereas the revival was past its peak among the Methodists in 1788, it continued among the Baptists north of the James 'until about 1791 or 1792'. Semple, giving these dates, says briefly, 'Thousands were converted and baptized, besides many who joined the Methodists and Presbyterians'. More records are available for the Baptists in this period than ten years earlier. For example, from letters read at the Association meeting of May 1789, we learn that of the churches that made up the Dover Association (from the James north to the Potomac in eastern Virginia) twenty-one reported a great revival. The Tuckahoe church had seen 300 new members in the previous year; the Nomini church, constituted with seventeen members in April 1786, had grown to 222 in 1788 and to 300 in 1789. The Upper King and Queen congregation (two miles from Newtown) had gradually increased until 1788 when, Semple reported, 'God descended in mighty power. A greater work of grace has probably never been known in Virginia within the limits of one church.' For many months there were 'seldom, if ever, less than twenty baptised, but more frequently forty, fifty and sixty'.

Among the Baptist preachers singularly used at this period mention has already been made of Lewis Lunsford (pastor of the Morattico church from 1778 up to his death while still in his prime in 1793). Lunsford combined this pastorate with such far-flung preaching tours that one observer believed he had travelled far enough to have circled the globe twice. He served within a spiritual brotherhood made up of many similar men. The number included John Williams whose fervent preaching moved Charlotte County in 1787; Henry Toler, pastor of Nomini; and John Leland who had come to Virginia from Massachusetts in 1777. Leland's preaching, together with that

---

[1] *The Arminian Magazine (American)*, *11*, *p. 563, quoted in Gewehr, Great Awakening*, p. 172.

of Samuel Harris, in August 1786 is said to have awakened many. In Leland's view, the revival was at its greatest intensity from the fall of 1787 to the spring of 1789. Labouring mainly within some twenty square miles, covering Orange, Culpeper, Spotsylvania and Louisa Counties, Leland baptized around 400 people between October 1787 and March 1789.[1] He later returned to New England where he was still preaching when he was almost eighty-seven. 'For more than half a century,' he wrote in 1831, 'I have been trying to do a little for Him who has done so much for me; but now the time is gone and nothing has been done as I hoped. I die a debtor; let me then die a beggar.'

The work of grace among the Baptist Churches of Virginia in the late 1780s completed the transformation of a group which had been a despised and persecuted cause only fifteen years earlier. They had become possibly the largest denomination in Virginia. Baptist membership for the whole of America in 1792 consisted of 65,000 communicants, almost double the figure of six years earlier. It has been estimated that 22,793, or 35 per cent of them, came from Virginia.[2] As with the Methodists, the growth was invariably in the areas 'blessed with large effusions of the Spirit'. Not surprisingly, a Christian in Boston, who heard the news from Virginia, wrote on 4 November, 1789, 'By accounts from those parts it has seemed something like the day of Pentecost.'[3]

*　　*　　*

Before we turn to the Presbyterian participation in 'the Great Revival', a comment is needed by way of qualification of the above quotations. In times when it seems as though almost whole communities are entering into the kingdom of God, time must elapse before a more balanced assessment can be made. In all revivals there are admixtures. It cannot be supposed that, in the high excitement attending a work of the Spirit of God, God's saving work can be instantly distinguished from what

[1] *The Writings of Elder John Leland* (1845; Gallatin, Tenn.: Church History Research and Archives, 1986), p. 27.

[2] Coleman, *Expansion of M. E. Church*, pp. 78–9.

[3] Semple, *Baptists in Virginia*, p. 5.

moves men only temporarily or from what can be accounted for in psychological terms. The depth of feeling shown by professed converts, and physical phenomena such as falling and swooning, provide no safe means for distinguishing the permanent from the transitory.

For the most part, preachers of this period recognized the danger. They knew no procedures by which men could be led to a 'decision' which would classify them as Christians, and they avoided hasty admissions into the church. Nonetheless, Semple observed, 'Many ministers who labored earnestly to get Christians into their churches were afterwards much perplexed to get out hypocrites'.[1] A winnowing season generally follows revival: 'Many that seemed to be somewhat proved to be nothing.'[2]

Apart from misinterpreting the number of converts, another mistake common to revivals was also to be found in Virginia. In the midst of powerful evidence of the blessing of God it was all too easy for leaders – especially for young men – to suppose that everything they did or taught was prompted by the Spirit of God and had his approval. But human fallibility and pride never cease to be realities in Christian experience. Good and harm can be done by the same men, at the same time, even in a revival. Nathan Bangs, who was himself too ready to argue that the evidence of God's blessing proved that Methodist teaching and practice 'must therefore be pleasing to him', acknowledged that 'errors of judgment may very well exist among the best of men'.[3] That caution should have been heeded more than it was in Virginia in the 1770s and 1780s. In a time of high excitement, Semple noted, things entered many congregations which caused 'no little confusion and disorder after the revival had subsided.'

On this point the testimony of Devereux Jarratt is salutary, although one-sided. As we have seen, he was the next leader in the revival in Virginia after Davies and played a prominent part in the 1770s, but there is no indication that he was involved in the movement of 1787–90. From his letters to his fellow Anglican the Rev. John Coleman, written in 1794–97, we learn

---

[1] Ibid., p. 58.
[2] Ibid., p. 151.   [3] *History*, vol. 1, pp. 68, 87.

that his ministry in Bath parish was then being carried on in very changed circumstances:

I have found the minds of the people, in my own parish, and in other places, so alienated from me that my usefulness at present seems to be at an end. When I now go to places, where formerly some hundreds used to attend my sermons, I can scarcely get forty hearers . . . Instead of crowded churches, as formerly, my hearers seldom exceed, on Sundays, one hundred and fifty and, for the most part, hardly half that number. The communicants have decreased ten-fold.

Jarratt blamed this state of affairs on the men whom he had warmly welcomed among his people in 1773, whose aid, he had believed, would prevent defections from the Church of England. Little did he realize at the time, as he confessed to Coleman, that 'I only jumpt out of the frying pan into the fire', for, in 1784, 'the whole body of Methodists broke off from the church at a single stroke! What mighty magic was able to effect so great a change in one day!' Jarratt's congregation left him, encouraged, he alleged, by Methodist rumours that he was a money-lover. On that hurtful charge, he wrote to Coleman that in all his travel and preaching before the Revolution he had never accepted a single farthing and that, since his salary had been stopped, along with that of all the clergy in 1776, 'for these thirteen years, I may say with the apostle, "these hands" of mine "have administered to my necessities and to those that are with me".' But this was not all. Jarratt's faith also came under censure: 'you must know I am accused of preaching bad doctrine – at least such a thing is insinuated by some, and others are more pointed in contradicting the truths I advance, and have advanced for more than thirty years. But it is truly laughable to hear doctrines established and taught by the greatest divines, for so many centuries, now condemned as execrable, by those, who never studied divinity in their lives, nor never read any system of theology whatever.'[1]

The doctrine that was being controverted by Methodists was the same as that to which Whitefield had drawn the attention of Wesley's first representatives on their arrival in 1769. They had

---

[1] *Life*, p. 123. There is some obscurity over Jarratt's doctrinal position. See James W. Alexander, *The Life of Archibald Alexander* (New York, 1854), p. 150.

come to a country, he reminded them, unused to the distinctives of evangelical Arminianism. In 1783, on the eve of approving the Methodist Episcopal Church in America, Wesley had warned his transatlantic brethren of the great danger of men 'bringing in among you new doctrines, particularly Calvinian'.[1] It was in connection with these doctrines, and particularly that of imputed righteousness, that Jarratt now found himself opposed. He also differed from Wesley on the subject of Christian experience. While he admired the Methodist emphasis on holiness and may have had an element of sympathy with Wesley's ideas on 'Christian perfection' in the 1770s, it is clear that the strongly felt convictions on continuing sin in the believer which he expressed to Coleman in the mid-1790s were incompatible with that teaching. In words reminiscent of the testimony of Samuel Davies, he wrote on 17 January 1795: 'I find this world to be a climate very unfavourable to the growth and improvement of everything holy, spiritual and divine – so that I am sometimes tempted to think I shall never be much better prepared for heaven than I am now, though I should live to the age of six-score years and ten.'[2] Jarratt also told Coleman that, amid the discouragements of his situation, it was his theology that sustained him: 'when I consider that salvation belongeth unto God – that the conversion of sinners is a work of his power alone – that when he shall deign to take the work into his hand, the stoutest hearts must bend – that he does this work by the instrumentality of a preached gospel, and, that in the mean time that I am not accountable for the success of my own labours, I am still induced to hold on in calling sinners to repentance.'

Jarratt's experience among the Methodists reveals a different side of that movement. Given the way in which the American Methodists had been aided by the ministry that existed in America long before their arrival, it is ironic that Wesley should have warned against 'new doctrines' being brought among *them*. The Methodists in Virginia and elsewhere were preceded by generations of preachers of the Calvinistic doctrines of the Reformers and Puritans. The Methodists' success was not due to what was distinctive in their teaching,

---

[1] Bangs, *History*, vol. 1, p. 148.   [2] *Life*, p. 144.

but rather to what they held in common with others. Bangs' claim that God's blessing proved the truth of their distinctive teaching – much repeated by later Arminian evangelicals – ignored the facts of the situation.

By the time of the revival of 1787 the Methodists no longer needed Jarratt's support or leadership but there might have been fewer excesses among them if they had remained together. Their itinerants were younger men who needed the discernment of his maturity. Only once in his letters to Coleman did Jarratt refer to the awakening in the time of Davies. In doing so he records an anecdote which is relevant here. Jarratt confessed how he came to learn that a zeal to do good was not the only thing that could move men to be active in the propagation of the gospel. In his own case, he was energetic in his early years as a Christian, in holding meetings for prayer and for other spiritual purposes:

In doing this, I thought I was actuated by the purest and most laudable principles. But being, one evening, in company with an older and more experienced christian, I simply related to him my practice of meeting and the effects my efforts seemed to have on my hearers. The gentleman looked grave on the occasion, and, instead of his approbation, which, no doubt, I expected, he gave me a little history of his own proceedings. 'When religion, *said he*, first broke out in these parts (*Henrico and Hanover*) I used to hold meetings in our meeting-house, for prayer, reading, &c. and large congregations attended – the people were frequently much affected, and I thought my zeal for their souls was so great and ardent, that I could freely have laid my head under their feet, to promote their happiness, by turning them to the Lord: but, *added he*, after a while I found a devil of pride lay at the bottom of all my exertions.' – He made no application, nor was it necessary, for I felt the words applied with great power to my heart – I saw my own picture drawn to the life – I was ashamed and confounded, in the presence of the venerable man – when I discovered the same *devil* to lurk and predominate in my own heart, which I had not before discovered, nor even suspected. It was a good lesson to me, and I endeavored to profit by it. It is not therefore without a cause, that I am led to judge that pride is a principal agent in the mission of many in our day. Human nature is the same now, as when I was a young man.[1]

[1] *Life*, p. 128.

Jarratt went on to deplore the practice of making preachers of 'young volunteers', which tendency was 'rather to foster pride than to discover and destroy it'. Given his experiences, his view of the Methodists cannot have been altogether objective. By the mid-1790s he was largely out of touch with them and the Baptists. His health broken, he described himself to Coleman as 'a great recluse'.[1] But his opinions are a valuable reminder that revivals never usher in a state of perfection and that Christians can, unwittingly, become the means of spreading error as well as truth.

While these revivals were not an unmixed good, let it be emphasized that they represented a great spiritual advance. The Great Awakening had largely missed Virginia in the 1740s and left her one of the most materialistic of all the colonies, but in the Virginia of the 1780s an impetus for biblical religion affected large numbers of people and prepared the way for a major spiritual change in the South. For the first time, religion became identified in the public mind with evangelical Christianity. 'The Established Church was all but completely swept away,' wrote Wesley M. Gewehr, chiefly because of the distaste for its nominal Christianity created by the revivals 'rather than because of its political connections'.

This transformation was also attended by a new unity among the evangelical denominations. Some divisions and heartaches there indeed were, but, on the whole, Christians of different persuasions on church matters recognized that they were receivers in common of the abundant grace of God. Unity had now a higher priority. Regular and Separate Baptists settled their differences and became one.[2] '"United we stand, divided

---

[1] Jarratt had not, however, become an embittered old man. William Hill recorded the uplifting effect of meeting and hearing him in 1791 (W. W. Sweet, *Religion on the American Frontier*, vol. 2, *The Presbyterians, 1783–1840* (New York and London, 1936), pp. 771–2); and Asbury wrote of him in his Journal for 31 March 1801: 'The old prophet, I hear is dead. He was a man of genius, possessed a great deal of natural oratory, was an excellent reader, and a good writer . . . I have reason to presume that he was instrumentally successful in awakening hundreds of souls to some sense of religion in that day and time [before the Revolution]' (*Journals and Letters*, vol. 2, p. 289).

[2] The Philadelphia Confession became their common Confession of Faith: 'We do not mean that every person is bound to the strict observance of

we fall," overcome, at that time, all objections,' wrote John Leland.[1] New relationships were forged across denominational boundaries. Being a Christian was seen to be more important than being a Baptist or a Methodist or a Presbyterian. So buildings were frequently shared and a common witness engaged in where such co-operation had been scarcely known. John Williams, observing the 'harmony and union of the Spirit' which follows a time of refreshing, noted: 'It is no strange thing to see a Presbyterian and Baptist preacher in the same pulpit, each in turn addressing the congregation.'[2] There were Baptist commendations of Methodists ('Their ministers are very constant preachers, and they exceed all societies in the state in spreading their books and tenets among the people'[3]), while Methodists noted with thankfulness the blessing attending the gospel preaching of Baptists. As Francis Asbury observed in his Journal, 'The Baptists go ahead of the Methodists in this settlement: if it be well done, it matters little who does it.'[4]

As was seen in the time of Edwards, Whitefield and Davies, one mark of an outpouring of the Spirit of God is the presence of a stronger catholicity of spirit among believers. Only when churches put adherence to Christ first can the world begin to recognize the real identity of those who bear his name.[5]

---

everything therein contained, yet that it holds forth the essential truths of the Gospel, and that the doctrine of Salvation by Christ and free, unmerited grace alone ought to be believed by every Christian and maintained by every minister of the Gospel.' From this time (1787) the terms 'Regular' and 'Separate' fell into disuse in Virginia (Semple, *Baptists in Virginia*, p. 99).

[1] *Writings of Leland*, p. 114n.
[2] Semple, *Baptists in Virginia*, pp. 330–1.
[3] *Writings of Leland*, p. 101.
[4] *Journal and Letters*, vol. ii, p. 426.
[5] Witherspoon wrote: 'There are few surer marks of the reality of religion than when a man feels himself more joined in spirit to a truly holy person of a different denomination than to an irregular liver of his own.'

4

WHEN THEOLOGY TOOK FIRE

A Presbyterian Communion Gathering

4

'No church in America, at the close of the War of Independence, was in a better position for expansion than was the Presbyterian.' So wrote William W. Sweet, one of the best of twentieth-century church historians, but that was certainly not the feeling of William Hill, a young Presbyterian missionary, as he stood on a street in Williamsburg on the evening of 12 December 1790. He and a friend had just arrived in the town as strangers but with a letter of introduction to John Holt who, they had been informed, 'was a very pious Presbyterian and brother-in-law to President Davies'. When they reached Holt's home a servant kept them at the door while he fetched his master. Hill later recorded in his journal:

After a considerable delay, he made his appearance at the door. I told him who I was, and that I was a Presbyterian minister, and held a letter of introduction in my hand to him. He asked me from whom the letter was; I told him from Col James Gordon of Lancaster County – he replied that he knew no such man. I told him Col G— had said that he served with him in the Virginia Assembly. Without saying any more or taking the letter which I reached toward him, he turned about and shut the door, and left us standing in the street.

Only after Hill and his friend had spent the night with an 'hospitable pious Methodist, who received us very cordially and treated us with every possible kindness', did they hear the explanation for Holt's strange behaviour. His conversation with them the next day began with the words, 'My God has it come to this, that the only Presbyterian minister who had been at his door for about forty years, should have been rudely turned away in a cold winter's night.'[1] He had distrusted their account of their identity, he went on to say, for his second wife, whom he had married following the death of Davies' sister, had reduced him by her extravagance 'from affluence to bankruptcy', and he was afraid that they might have been the sheriff's officers sent to arrest him.

The young preacher's introduction to Williamsburg was characteristic of the conditions he was to discover in that part of Virginia as they affected his denomination. Permission to use either the church or the court-house for a service was denied him. His experience was similar in Petersburg: 'There was not a member of the presbyterian church that I could hear of in the place, and I could find no one who was willing to receive me and lend a helping hand.' There is no record of his visiting Davies' former charge in Hanover County. Perhaps he had heard the discouraging news that the revivals that had recently returned to Virginia had passed them by.

We must retrace our steps to gain a general impression of the Presbyterian churches in this part of the country. According to records for the year 1774, there were ten ministers in the Hanover Presbytery and nineteen congregations in Virginia that lacked pastors. By no means all these men or congregations, however, represented the evangelicalism which was seen in Samuel Davies. The Great Awakening of the 1740s, it is to be remembered, had divided the Presbyterians as it had other denominations, with what was called the 'Old Side' party remaining unmoved and critical of the preaching of Whitefield and the log college men. This viewpoint was to be found in Virginia, where across the Blue Ridge Mountains in the Shenandoah Valley the Scots-Irish congregations were untouched by the revival in the time of Davies, and across the state all the Presbyterian churches were unaffected by the movement of the 1770s. One Virginian Christian of this period (who with many others had moved from the Church of England

---

[1] The journal of William Hill is in the library of Union Theological Seminary, Richmond, Virginia. Extracts – from which these quotations are taken – have been published in Sweet, *Religion on the American Frontier*, vol. 2, pp. 755ff.

to the Baptists) was no doubt correct in believing that too many Presbyterians 'were sound in doctrine but deficient in experience'. Francis Asbury noted of one of their preachers whom he heard in 1775 that 'his discourse was systematical but if he had studied to pass by the consciences of his hearers, he could not have done it more effectively'. William Hill, whose visit to Williamsburg we have noted above, wrote of his experience in another place a few months later: 'We found Mr Sawyer a stiff bigoted Old Side Scotch Irish presbyterian, a bitter enemy to new lights and enthusiasm and I am afraid to all revivals and vital religion.'

For further evidence on the same point we turn to the biography of a man whose name is to feature in the following pages and has to be listed among the foremost of dependable commentators on the subject of revivals in the United States. Archibald Alexander was born in the Blue Ridge Mountains of Virginia, on an upper tributary of the James River, in April 1772. His grandfather, who had been converted in the Great Awakening in Pennsylvania thirty years earlier, had been one of the first settlers in that region. His grandmother had died in an Indian massacre. But experimental religion had not been preserved in the family line. Although Alexander's father was an elder, 'the few pious people in the land who kept up the power of religion' had no representative in his home: 'My only notion of religion was that it consisted in becoming better. I had never heard of any conversion among Presbyterians.'[1] This statement is the more surprising when we note that the minister whom he heard through his infancy and youth was the Rev. William Graham, one of those in Princeton's graduating class of 1773 who became ministers of the gospel. Perhaps Graham became distracted or discouraged from his main work during the turbulent years of the War of Independence. Certainly, he made no impression on Alexander whom he taught both in school and at church. His pupil was a great deal more interested in the skills of horsemanship, swimming and shooting, and later confessed: 'It is remarkable that I never paid any attention to what our own preacher said in the pulpit. His voice was very low, and much interrupted by continual

---

[1] *Life of Alexander*, p. 32.

hemming, or clearing the throat. I thought him the worst preacher of all I ever heard.'

When Alexander reached the age of seventeen, his father considered his education to be sufficient and arranged for him to become tutor to four children in the home of General Posey, 140 miles away across the Blue Ridge in the county of Spotsylvania. The destination was significant, for Spotsylvania was adjacent to Hanover County and was part of the area where Baptist witness had made such headway after the time of Davies. Living in Posey's home was an elderly lady, Mrs Tyler, whose life had been transformed by that witness, and the young tutor, whom she befriended, soon heard both her testimony and the preaching of Separate and Regular Baptists. A Baptist millwright who worked for General Posey also gave Alexander further cause for thought; one day, after business matters had been discussed, he unexpectedly asked the young tutor whether he believed that before a man could enter the kingdom of heaven he must be born again. Of that conversation Alexander wrote:

I knew not what to say, for I had for some time been puzzled about the new birth. However, I answered in the affirmative. He then asked whether I had experienced the new birth. I hesitated, and said, 'Not that I knew of.' 'Ah,' said he, 'if you had ever experienced this change you would know something about it!' Here the conversation ended; but it led me to think more seriously whether there were any such change. It seemed to be in the Bible; but I thought there must be some method of explaining it away; for among the Presbyterians I had never heard of any one who had experienced the new birth, nor could I recollect ever to have heard it mentioned. This became about the same time a subject of discussion at the table, after old Mrs Tyler had withdrawn, especially on Sunday. In these conversations Mrs Posey, who professed to be a 'seeker,' defended the Baptist opinions, and so did old Mrs William Jones, who I believe was a truly pious woman. General Posey declared that he did not believe in any such miraculous change, but added that he would credit it, if Mrs Posey should ever profess that she had experienced it.[1]

Alexander's attention was now thoroughly aroused and the final means of his conviction was at hand in the *Works of John*

---

[1] *Life of Alexander*, pp. 40–1.

Flavel, a large volume which belonged to Mrs Tyler. As her eyesight was failing, she sought his aid with a request that he should read the volume aloud to her. Alexander, supposing Flavel to be a genuine Presbyterian and eager to know what he might think on the subject of the rebirth, was not averse to this duty. The practice of secret prayer – hitherto an unknown thing with him – was soon joined to reading, and to further this exercise he found a quiet place of retirement amid trees on the edge of the plantation. One Sunday night an event occurred which he described as follows:

My services as a reader were frequently in requisition, not only to save the eyes of old Mrs Tyler, but on Sundays for the benefit of the whole family. On one of these Sabbath evenings, I was requested to read out of Flavel. The part on which I had been regularly engaged was the 'Method of Grace'; but now, by some means, I was led to select one of the sermons on Revelation 3.20, 'Behold I stand at the door and knock', etc. The discourse was upon the patience, forbearance and kindness of the Lord Jesus Christ to impenitent and obstinate sinners. As I proceeded to read aloud, the truth took effect on my feelings, and every word I read seemed applicable to my own case. Before I finished the discourse, these emotions became too strong for restraint, and my voice began to falter. I laid down the book, rose hastily, and went out with a full heart, and hastened to my place of retirement. No sooner had I reached the spot than I dropped upon my knees, and attempted to pour out my feelings in prayer; but I had not continued many minutes in this exercise before I was overwhelmed with a flood of joy.[1]

These were some of Alexander's first spiritual experiences. The 'utter aversion to what was spiritual', which had marked his days until now, was at an end. The true way of acceptance with God and other truths, 'now appeared as if written with a sunbeam'.

Alexander was in Spotsylvania in the years 1788–89. Unknown to him, a great transformation was occurring among other Presbyterians in a different part of Virginia at this time. We noted John Blair Smith, who served churches in and around Prince Edward County and Hampden-Sydney College, had called his elders to prayer after being stirred by the fresh anointing of the Spirit of God which he saw in other denomina-

---

[1] Ibid., pp. 44–5.

tions. There were no apparent signs of the prayer being answered when Asbury passed through this mainly Presbyterian county in April 1787, but it was at hand. The elders' prayer meeting, wrote Foote, 'had become a delightful place' and what had been a private meeting now developed into praying circles 'in different parts of the congregations where a few could assemble'. Slowly, convictions among the people deepened and 'the spirit of prayer and inquiry increased together'. One of Smith's students at this date recalled:

I was born in the year 1772; I was myself deeply exercised on the subject of religion from a child, through the instrumentality of my parents who were pious. But I saw nothing, heard nothing like an awakening among the people, till I was a student at Hampden Sidney a while. I went there at the age of fourteen years, the only serious boy amongst sixty or eighty students, and was often laughed at on account of my religious principles: but by the grace of God, I was never ashamed on that account; but reproved them for their want of reverence for the authority of God. At that time I did not think I had religion, but was much engaged in the use of all appointed means to obtain it. After I was there one or two sessions, I saw and heard of, for the first time, a seriousness and deep concern in Briery congregation; and about the same time, in Cumberland congregation. Christians became greatly quickened, and awakenings amongst the dead in sins multiplied in quick succession.[1]

In September 1787, when the College resumed after the summer vacation, one student had become a Christian and two more were earnestly seeking. One of the seekers was William Hill whom we have already seen as a missionary-preacher in Williamsburg a few years after this. Hill provides more details of what happened at the College in the fall of 1787. Three or four of them began to meet for prayer on Saturday afternoons in woods some distance from the College. One Saturday, anticipating rain, they changed the meeting-place to a room in the College. Fears that they would be interrupted were realized:

We locked our door and commenced. Although we sung and prayed with suppressed voices, not wishing it should be known what we were about, we were overheard by some of the students, when it was noised about through every room in College, and a noisy mob was raised,

[1] Foote, *Sketches*, pp. 413–14.

which collected in the passage before our door, and began to thump at the door, and whoop, and swear, and threaten vengeance, if we did not forbear and cease all such exercises in College for the future. We had to cease, and bear the ridicule and abuse of this noisy riot, which could not be quieted until two of the Professors interfered and ordered them all to their rooms. Information of this riot was given to Mr Smith. In the evening the College was rung to prayers. When the prayers were ended, Mr Smith demanded the cause of the riot, and who were the leaders in it. Some of the most prominent leaders stepped forward and said, there were some of the students, who had shut themselves up in one of the rooms in College, and began singing and praying and carrying on like the Methodists, and they were determined to break it up. We had nothing to say; we were not absolutely certain that we were justifiable in introducing such exercises in College without first obtaining permission to do so.[1]

Smith was far from requiring any explanation from the holders of the prayer meeting. He was overjoyed at this first evidence he had seen of a spiritual concern among his students. After soundly rebuking the complainers – 'who will neither serve God themselves, nor suffer others to do so' – he told the originators of the prayer meeting: 'I rejoice, my young friends, that you have taken the stand you have; you shall not be interrupted in your meetings for the future. Your appointment next Saturday afternoon shall be held in my parlour; and I will be with you, conduct your meeting for you, and render you all the assistance you may need.'

Surprise was general when, at the appointed hour the next Saturday, the rector's parlour was full. Smith called on the nervous members of the original group to pray in turn and then 'from a heart full to overflowing', he fervently addressed the whole gathering. 'The next Saturday afternoon,' writes Hill, 'nearly the whole of the students came out, and many from the neighbourhood around, so that the parlour and other rooms were crowded. As the neighbourhood generally got word of what was going on in the College, they all wished to attend; so we had to appoint the next meeting in the large College Hall, which was filled upon subsequent occasions. Within two weeks or thereabouts, fully half of the students in the College appeared deeply impressed, and under conviction for their sins.

[1] Ibid., p. 417.

Deep impressions and concern were generally made throughout the neighbourhood.'

Prayer meetings now multiplied, and John Blair Smith
seems to have given himself entirely to preaching both in the
College and in his congregations. 'Every other business,' says
Foote, 'appeared for a time forgotten in the all-absorbing
interests of religion. The awakening in the congregations
received a great impulse in every direction . . . by the commencement of the year 1788, there was a general awakening in
Prince Edward, Cumberland and Charlotte counties. The
professors of religion awaked as from sleep and put on the
armour of godliness; some declared themselves convinced that
their former profession had been a lifeless one and professed
conversion anew.'

Among the visitors who now came to Prince Edward County
was the rector's father, Robert Smith of Pequea in
Pennsylvania. In a letter written on 26 October 1788, a few
days after he had returned to Pequea, the old preacher, who
had been converted under the ministry of George Whitefield at
the time of the Great Awakening of 1740–41, reported to a
friend:

A few days ago I returned from Virginia, where I preached five
Sabbaths, one at Alexandria, and four for my son, besides several
week days.

The half was not told me of the display of God's power and grace
among them; no, not the tenth part. I have seen nothing equal to it for
extensive spread, power, and spiritual glory, since the years '40 and
'41. The work has spread for an hundred miles, but by far the most
powerful and general in John Smith's congregations, which take in
part of three counties.

Not a word scarcely about politics; but all religion in public and
private. They run far and near to sermons, sacraments and societies.
They have six or seven praying societies, which meet every
Wednesday and Saturday evenings, and at College on Sabbath
evenings also. Numbers of the students have been convinced, and
several of them hopefully converted.

. . . The blessed work has spread among people of every description, high and low, rich and poor, learned and unlearned, orthodox
and heterodox, sober and rude, white and black, young and old;
especially the youth, whom it seems to have seized generally. Two
hundred and twenty-five hopeful communicants have been added to

the Lord's table among John Smith's people, in the space of eighteen months, chiefly of the young people.

When they go to sermons or societies, they commonly go in companies, either conversing on spiritual subjects or singing hymns. When they arrive at the place of worship, they enter the house and sing hymns till the minister enters.

Such sweet singing I never heard in all my life. Dear young Christians, how engaged, how heavenly, how spiritually and innocently they look and speak. I have seen an hundred wet cheeks, some deeply penetrated with convictions, some fainting with love-sickness as it were, in the Saviour's arms, and others rejoicing for the day of God's power and grace, all under the same sermon. The rejoicings were much among some old disciples.

When I went and heard, and saw, I felt richer in my mind than if I had seen my son mounted upon a throne; yet I confess I felt several pangs for my beloved child, lest he should wear his life to an end too soon. He had certainly the work of three men to do. All the time of College vacation he will be riding to sacraments and preaching everywhere. For the importunities of the people are pressing and his desires are strong.[1]

In later years Hill recalled the influence of the revival:

Persons of all ranks in society, of all ages, both old and young, became the subjects of this work so that there was scarcely a magistrate upon the bench, or a lawyer at the bar in Prince Edward and Charlotte, but became members of the church. Young men and women were generally heartily engaged in the work, so that it was now as rare a thing to find one who was not religious, as it had been formerly to find one that was. The frivolities and amusements once so prevalent, were all abandoned, and gave place to singing, serious conversation, and prayer-meetings – very few comparatively, who appeared to become serious, afterwards lost their impressions, or apostatized; and the cases which did occur were chiefly those who never became members of the church.[2]

Archibald Alexander concluded his work at General Posey's and recrossed the Blue Ridge to his home near Lexington some time in the first half of 1789. His route did not take him near Prince Edward and it was only after his return that he heard the rumour that 'had come to that quiet settlement of an extraordinary religious awakening on the other side of the Mountain, as the great dividing Blue Ridge is familiarly called'.

[1] Ibid., pp. 422–4.   [2] Ibid., pp. 427–8.

Speaking of Presbyterian congregations at this point in time, Foote observed that while 'the whole region south of the James River, east of the Blue Ridge, was greatly excited by the preaching of the gospel, the congregations of the [Shenandoah] Valley and those north of the James River were entirely unmoved'. There does not seem to have been much interest in and around Lexington in the news from Hampden-Sydney. Alexander noted:

There had never been any revival in the Valley, and few of the Scottish Presbyterians there resident had much faith in these sudden awakenings. They had heard of a work of this kind in Western Pennsylvania, under the labours of the Rev. Joseph Smith, the Rev. John M'Millan, and others; but the general impression was that these religious commotions would pass away like the morning cloud.[1]

Another reason seems to have prevented William Graham from making closer enquiries. Although he and John Blair Smith had been fellow students in the Princeton graduating class of 1773, the two men had drifted apart. There was possibly an element of rivalry between the two preachers who had both established academies – Graham wished 'to rear a seminary after the model of Princeton College', while Smith was no less ambitious for Hampden-Sydney. They were also known to have had some difference on political questions at the end of the War of Independence. According to Alexander, 'Mr Graham had enjoyed very little friendly intercourse with Mr Smith for a number of years; indeed a certain coolness existed between them in consequence of some difference in Presbytery, which was not however of a personal nature.'[2]

Smith took the initiative to end the coolness by a personal invitation to Graham, as Alexander put it, 'to come over and see the great works of the Lord'. But it was only in August 1789, nearly two years after the commencement of the revival at Hampden-Sydney, that the minister of the Lexington district accepted and set off on horseback for Briery, taking Alexander and another young man with him. The weeks that followed were to be the most unforgettable in the whole of Alexander's life. As they drew near to their destination, situated on the border of Charlotte and Prince Edward counties, they began to

---

[1] *Life of Alexander*, p. 52.   [2] Ibid., p. 52.

hear news of remarkable conversions. Men who had until recently been conspicuous for their profanity and infidelity were now reported to be fervent witnesses to the truth. On the Saturday night of their arrival they witnessed the novel and surprising sight of young people on horseback who were singing hymns as they rode along. Many of them were young converts who had travelled fifty miles from North Carolina. That same night there was a service at which Alexander first saw and heard John Blair Smith: 'His appearance was more solemn than that of any one I had ever seen and caused a feeling of awe to come over me.'

'On the morning of the Sabbath,' Alexander continued, 'the roads were covered with multitudes flocking to the place of worship at Briery. The house was not sufficient to hold half the people.' The Lord's Supper was to be administered during the morning service and so another service was appointed for non-communicants in the open air which Alexander attended as he had not yet professed faith. Both services had been in progress for some time when a violent rainstorm made continuation outdoors impossible, and as many as could press into the house did so, Alexander among them. The first thing that arrested him was the attitude of the congregation: 'There was on the face of the assembly an appearance of tender and earnest solemnity.' But his attention was soon fixed on the speaker. Smith had preached prior to the administration of the sacrament and the second preacher was Alexander's own pastor who was half-way through his sermon when the newcomers found admittance. William Graham was as a man suddenly transformed as he addressed the people from the words of Isaiah 40.1, 'Comfort ye, comfort ye my people, saith your God'. Alexander recalled:

The good people of Briery were entranced. They had expected a very cold and dry discourse. Dr Smith afterwards said to me of this sermon, that it was the best he had ever heard, except one; and the one excepted was preached during the revival by the Rev. James Mitchell, who was never reckoned a great preacher. Every mouth was filled with expressions of admiration, and from this time, Mr Graham was considered one of the ablest preachers in the land.[1]

---

[1] Ibid., p. 58.

Foote confirmed the observable change in the minister of Lexington. On the previous evening, 'the apparent tone of Mr Graham's feelings did not exactly suit the ardour of some of the young converts and they requested Mr Smith not to let him preach'.[1] Happily, Smith ignored that advice. 'This sermon of Mr Graham made an unusual impression. There are still living a few who heard it; and these, after a lapse of about sixty years, speak of the immediate influence and the abiding impression of that discourse.'[2]

*   *   *

A new era had begun in Graham's life. While he had not forgotten the awakening of Princeton in his student days, the intervening years among an unresponsive people may have dimmed his expectations. But if he had come to entertain any doubts they were all swept away in the experiences of that weekend in August 1789. Remembering his own state of mind as they later journeyed back across the Blue Ridge Mountains, Alexander recalled, 'I now fully calculated on a revival in Lexington'. He was not alone in his anticipation. 'News of the spirit in which we had returned spread rapidly' and in consequence there was a great congregation collected at the Monmouth church for the service on the following Sunday morning. After the sermon from a visiting preacher, Graham gave an account of all they had seen, 'which he followed', according to an eye-witness, 'with one of the most affecting exhortations I ever heard, during which he poured out a torrent of tears; and very few eyes in the house were dry. The impression on the minds of the assembly was very general.'[3] Alexander confirmed this with his own testimony:

Another meeting was appointed for the evening, in the town, in a large room which had been used for dancing. Here the solemnity was greater, if possible, than at the church. Many remained to converse with the ministers, and a person of the most sedate habits and moral life cried out in an agony, 'What must I do to be saved!' Every thing went on prosperously, and I was in expectation that all, or nearly all, the people would be awakened.[4]

<hr />

[1] *Sketches*, p. 420.   [2] Ibid., p. 466.
[3] *Life of Alexander*, p. 67.   [4] Ibid., p. 67.

In the opinion of F. N. Watkins, probably 'one hundred persons were now brought under serious impressions of religion' at Monmouth and Lexington, although all 'did not become true converts'.

It was not long before opposition was encountered from formalists who had previously been left in peace, 'but the work went on, and we were gratified to find that cases of awakening occurred at almost every meeting, and the religious concern continued to diffuse itself through the country. These were halcyon days for the church.' As had happened in Prince Edward, the series of services that marked communion seasons were now attended by large numbers coming to Lexington from many places. One of these occasions, when the preacher was Drury Lacy from Hampden-Sydney College, was recalled by Moses Hoge when he preached at Lacy's funeral in 1815:

> The Lord's Supper was administered on the Sabbath; and on Monday Mr Lacy was called upon to address an audience, of not less, I suppose, than 2000 people. His discourse was a *word in season* and in power. I could not observe an individual in that numerous assembly, who appeared inattentive or unimpressed. It was a discourse that will, I doubt not, be remembered by a large number of his hearers, as long as they live. Never shall I forget with what a moving emphasis he exclaimed toward the end of his discourse, *Where is the Lord God of Elijah!* He was, most undoubtedly, there to assist his servant to declare with extraordinary energy, his holy word.[1]

Although Graham had been living near Lexington for a few years, it was only now, in 1789, that a church was formed. As a later pastor of the congregation remarked, 'It had its birth in a revival.'[2] The session records in the first year of the congregation's history note with thankfulness 'a drawing off on the part of young people from public halls', and the new interests they now showed included 'a taste for reading, and especially an increased attention to the Shorter Catechism'.[3] These same session records set down five seasons of revival from this date to

[1] *Sermons of Moses Hoge* (Richmond, Va., 1821), p. 417.
[2] H. M. White (ed.), *Rev. William S. White and his Times: An Autobiography* (1891; Harrisonburg, Va., Sprinkle Publications, 1983), p. 136.
[3] Howard McKnight Wilson, *The Lexington Presbytery Heritage* (Verona, Va.: McClure Press, 1971), p. 79.

the year 1831, with 253 members added during that period.

To the Presbyterians, the movement of the Holy Spirit in the years 1787–89 was also to be known as 'the Great Revival' on account of the extent to which its influence spread and the permanence of its effects. North Carolina was almost immediately affected, in part through a visit of the Rev. Henry Pattillo to Hampden-Sydney. Pattillo had been a student under Davies at Hanover in the 1750s. He then moved to North Carolina where he later became minister of the congregations of Natbush and Grassy Creek – 'composed originally of emigrants from Virginia who had been trained under the ministry of the Rev. Samuel Davies and his coadjutors'.[1] Pattillo's diary of his student days recorded that one of his principal petitions in his private prayers was 'that religion may revive where it is professed, and spread where it is not known'. He was to see his youthful hopes fulfilled in his own ministry in a way he had not seen before. He took a number of his young people with him on a visit to Hampden-Sydney and 'they carried the sacred fire home with them, from whom it communicated to others, and a glorious revival broke out in Granville and Caswell counties, North Carolina'.[2] Foote was no doubt referring to the same awakening which he elsewhere dated at 1791 and, more generally, 1789–91.[3]

Pattillo had not been alone in supplying that region with faithful preaching. David Caldwell, a Princeton graduate of the class of 1761, had been in Caswell county since 1766, as a missionary and a schoolmaster. His congregations were among those that now shared in the revival: 'Many professors of religion renounced their hopes and became, as they thought, truly converted to God; others were greatly enlivened and strengthened in their faith, and rejoiced in renewed graces: and many hopeful converts were added to the church.'[4] Foote also tells us that this was the second revival of religion in North Carolina 'of any extent, of which any account or tradition has been preserved'. The first was in the Iredell district in 1784 in the congregations of James Hall, who had been another contemporary of John Blair Smith and William Graham at Princeton.

[1] Sprague, *Annals*, vol. 3, p. 197.   [2] Foote, *Sketches*, p. 419.
[3] *Sketches of North Carolina* (New York, 1846), p. 226.   [4] Ibid., p. 375.

The effects of the revival in Virginia were further seen in a whole generation of younger men who were now called to the work of the gospel ministry. From the time of the formation of the Lexington Presbytery in 1786 there had been no candidates for the ministry until the beginning of the revival. Then seven or eight able men came forward, including Archibald Alexander, to be taught theology by William Graham.[1] The numbers entering the ministry from Hampden-Sydney were still larger. As Foote observed: 'But for the influence of the revival of 1788, east of the Ridge, and of 1789, west of the Ridge, in sending into the ministry that eminent company of young men . . . there is reason to fear the churches would in great measure have been swept away.'[2] The same was in evidence following the revivals in North Carolina. It was supposed that of David Caldwell's pupils 'about fifty became ministers of the gospel', although it was often said that, in terms of human instrumentality, the main credit for it belonged elsewhere – 'Dr Caldwell makes the scholars', the saying went, 'and Mrs Caldwell makes the ministers'.[3] James Hall, who lived his eighty-two years as a bachelor, had no such assistant in the Iredell district, but in Foote's opinion the school he ran was 'the birth-place of the most laborious ministers of the last generations'. Hall, preacher, teacher, and evangelist, devoted 'all his time to build the church of the living God'. Such was his spirit that in the latter part of his long life he took immense missionary journeys as far afield as Natchez in Mississippi. On one occasion he covered 1,485 miles in four months and fifteen days and preached fifty-eight times in the process.[4]

The most important consequence of the Great Revival for the Presbyterians was the new ethos which came to prevail in the churches. Old Side prejudices lost their hold and a 'unanimity of sentiment' came to distinguish the denomination in the South. The main cause for this was undoubtedly the priority now given to experimental religion. Prayer was restored to its rightful place and 'fervent charity' came to be expected among

---

[1] Others followed: 'From 1792 through 1822 the Presbytery of Lexington enrolled thirty-seven ministerial candidates' (Wilson, *Lexington Presbytery*, p. 80).
[2] *Sketches*, p. 475.   [3] Foote, *Sketches of N.C.*, p. 235.
[4] For Hall, a student of Witherspoon's, see *Sketches of N.C.*, pp. 315–35.

all Christians. The same influence inevitably brought a return to biblical standards of church membership. It was no longer assumed that those who attended church from birth were Christians, nor was 'profession of faith' henceforth taken as sufficient evidence of conversion. Ministers and elders considered how people lived, and what they did, as well as what they said. It was understood afresh that the true usefulness of the church is bound up with her spirituality and her unity. The premature admission of men and women and young people to the Lord's table (communicant membership), which had formerly been too common, now gave way to a more faithful examination of candidates. The wisdom of the counsel of John Blair Smith was universally recognized: 'He advised those who were awakened not to be too hasty in professing conversion, and urged them to examine the foundations of their hopes well before they entertained a hope they had made their peace with God . . . Generally months, and in some instances a year or more was suffered to pass before they were received into the church.'[1]

William Hill believed that the revival 'gave a character to the Presbyterian Church of the South for vital, exemplary piety, which has pervaded several States and given a tone to religious exercises far and wide'. How this affected the churches in a practical way is well illustrated by a statement of principles drawn up by one of the many new churches of the 1790s:

1 A church is a society of Christians, voluntarily associated together, for the worship of God, and spiritual improvement & usefulness.
2 A visible church consists of visible or apparent christians.
3 The children of visible christians are members of the visible church, though in a state of minority.
4 A visible christian is one, who understands the doctrines of the Christian religion, is acquainted with a work of God's Spirit in effectual calling, professes repentance from dead works, and faith in our Lord Jesus Christ, and subjection to him as a king; and whose life and conversation corresponds with his profession.
5 Sealing ordinances ought not to be administered to such as are not visible christians.
6 A charitable allowance ought to be made for such, whose natural

[1] Foote, *Sketches*, p. 427.

[106]

abilities are weak, or who have not enjoyed good opportunities of religious instruction, when they appear to be humble and sincere.

7 Children and youth, descended from church members, though not admitted to all the privileges of the church, are entitled to the instructions of the church, and subjected to its discipline.[1]

As we have seen, all the evangelical denominations in Virginia benefited largely from the revival of 1787–90, but in certain respects the Presbyterians had particular advantages. Before the revival they already had in the South a degree of organization, a policy of planting schools and colleges to gain the youth, and an inheritance of spiritual literature, which were all major assets. These things alone, however, could not bring spiritual advance, but wedded to new life and to renewed evangelistic passion they became powerful advantages. Thus, while the Baptists of Virginia faced a lack of procedures to bring candidates forward for the gospel ministry,[2] the Presbyterians had structures ready to hand. And whereas the Baptists were still cautious of 'book-learning', the old Puritan literature became an invaluable school of instruction for a whole new generation of Presbyterian ministers. Authors long dead – Alleine, Flavel, Owen, Baxter, Bates, and others – became again a living force as there developed a 'new taste' for their writings.

Revival was earlier defined as a larger giving of the Holy Spirit, or a new accession of his influence. Something should be said here of how this manifested itself in individuals. Archibald Alexander drew attention to the striking change in William Graham as a preacher. In addition to being a Christian, before 1789 Graham was both able and orthodox, but it is evident that from that date there was a degree of authority, warmth and joy that had not been there before. John Blair Smith also experienced a similar change. More lively in his temperament than

---

[1] These are the principles of the united congregations of Cincinnati and Columbia. Sweet, *American Frontier*, vol. 2, p. 394.

[2] The reasons adduced for a lack of young preachers among the Separate Baptists after the Great Revival include: (1) old preachers standing in the way; (2) too little prayer for laborers; and (3) prejudice against a paid ministry (see W. L. Lumpkin, *Colonial Baptists and Southern Revivals*, 1961), p. 137.

These words could equally have been written of Graham or Smith. The Great Revival taught the Presbyterian churches that orthodoxy and correct preaching, indispensable though they are, are not enough. Authority, tenderness, compassion, pity – these must be given in larger measure from heaven, and when they are it can truly be said that theology has taken fire.

5

THE AGE OF THE SECOND GREAT AWAKENING

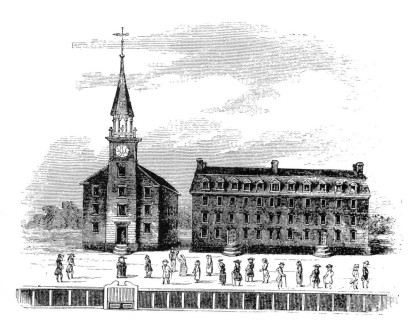

Yale College, New Haven

5

The extent to which the Christian faith remained dominant in America in the later eighteenth century has been a subject of some disagreement. The years 1775–81, when the War of Independence saw the end of colonial status and the emergence of the nation, have often been regarded as marking an ebb tide of Christian influence. Similarities between the revolution in North America and the French Revolution (which was soon to follow) seem to bear out that idea. Both revolutions asserted 'liberty, equality and fraternity', both represented a rejection of established authority, and both gave the individual the right to think for himself. French support for the emancipation of Britain's Thirteen Colonies opened the way for a wider hearing of her philosophers of the so-called Enlightenment, who treated Christianity as a fable imposed on oppressed peoples. Before long, America had her own anti-Christian literature, headed up by the writings of the son of an English Quaker who emigrated to America at the beginning of the war. Thomas Paine gave the rest of his life to opposing Christianity. His *Rights of Man*, published in London in 1791–2 was said to have sold a million and a half copies and his *Age of Reason*, which argued for deism, was possibly still more popular. 'I have gone through the Bible', the new American claimed, 'as a man would go through a wood with an ax and felled trees. Here they lie and the priest may replant them, but they will never grow.'[1]

[1] Quoted in Arthur B. Strickland, *The Great American Revival* (Cincinnati: Standard Press, 1934), p. 36.

There were others who, while unimpressed by Paine's boasts, nevertheless saw cause for concern. After William Wilberforce, a rising British parliamentarian, met John Jay, the American ambassador in London in the summer of 1794, he wrote in his journal, 'I feel there is little spirit of religion in America.'[1] Many Christians in America were expressing the same fear. Bishop Mead wrote: 'Every educated young man in Virginia whom I met I expected to find a sceptic, if not an avowed unbeliever.' Speaking of sober Connecticut in the same years, another contemporary later recalled: 'Infidel opinions came in like a flood. Mr Paine's *Age of Reason*, the works of Voltaire, and other deistical books, were broadcast, and young men suddenly became, as they thought, wiser than their fathers.'[2] Robert Smith had similar memories of Kentucky: 'Youth became scoffers at religion and blasphemers against God. Such a thing as a young man of talents turning his attention to the ministry was so rare that it would have excited astonishment.'

But this is not the whole picture. While an ebb tide had set in, a strong religious element – in large part the fruit of the Great Awakening – remained in the later eighteenth century. The parallel with the French Revolution was superficial. The argument for independence owed much to Protestant and Puritan sources, and no small part of America's strength in the War of Independence came from Christians. Men such as John Witherspoon were leaders in the new nation. Charles Thomson, secretary to the Continental Congress under successive presidents, was a man of real piety who accomplished a translation of the whole Bible. George Washington himself had no conceptions of a democracy which could be sustained without a religious base. 'Religion and Morality', said the father of the nation on his retirement in 1797, 'are the essential pillars of civil society.'[3] While Thomas Jefferson had no such

[1] R. I. and S. Wilberforce, *The Life of William Wilberforce* (London, 1838), vol. 2, p. 57.

[2] E. E. Beardsley, *The History of the Episcopal Church in Connecticut*, vol. 1, p. 432, quoted in C. R. Keller, *The Second Great Awakening in Connecticut* (New Haven: Yale University Press, 1942), p. 190.

[3] Quoted in J. H. Jones, *The Life of Ashbel Green* (New York, 1849), p. 615. Washington also said, 'It is substantially true, that religion or morality is a necessary spring of popular government' (Marshall, *Life of Washington*, vol. 5, pp. 699–700, quoted in *Biblical Repertory* 1834), p. 120.

belief, it tells us much that he took care that his infidelity was 'not openly avowed till after his death'.[1] Public opinion as a whole was clearly not with the young men whose views alarmed their elders.

Philadelphia, America's first city in the 1790s, where Congress sat, had only one newspaper that showed sympathy towards disbelief in the Bible. Such was the abiding public recognition of the Ten Commandments in that city that legislation required chains to be extended across streets in front of churches during the hours of Sunday worship so as to ensure quietness. No one knew his fellow countrymen better than Benjamin Franklin, the politician and publisher, and he was not out of touch with them when he declined to accept publications from Paine. In his response to the offer of one of Paine's books, Franklin wrote to him: 'Though your reasons are subtle and may prevail with some readers, yet you will not succeed so as to change the general sentiments of mankind on that subject and the consequences of printing this piece will be a great deal of odium drawn on yourself . . . He that spits in the wind, spits in his own face.'[2]

It may therefore be concluded that the opinion which Wilberforce formed in London was exaggerated. There was no general prevalence of irreligion towards the end of the eighteenth century. Yet the balance of evidence justified the apprehension that many felt. While a number of churches continued to grow slowly, Christians commonly spoke of 'dark times', of 'low conditions', and of a 'falling off'.[3] It was universally believed that there had been no general awakening since the 1740s. Edward Dorr Griffin, who commenced his ministry in 1792, observed that 'Long before the death of Whitefield in 1770, extensive revivals in America had ceased'. And Heman Humphrey, who was a youth in Connecticut in the 1790s, wrote: 'While the form of godliness remained there was little of the power . . . from 1745, to near the close of the century, the Holy Spirit withheld in great measure those

---

[1] J. H. Jones, *Life of Green*, pp. 262–3.
[2] Quoted in Strickland, *Great American Revival*, p. 31.
[3] For a good summary of testimonies see John Boles, *The Great Revival 1787–1805* (Lexington: University Press of Kentucky, 1972).

copious refreshings which turned so many parched fields into gardens of the Lord.'[1]

A further indication of the low spiritual condition lies in the extent to which controversies occupied the attention of churches. Methodists debated church government and the Methodist Episcopal Church saw a 25 per cent loss of membership as James O'Kelly and his supporters complained of ecclesiastical despotism, and seceded. At a time when the population of the United States rose by 32 per cent in the period 1790–1800, Methodist membership rose by only 12.6 per cent. The infant Presbyterian Church in Kentucky was similarly torn by controversy as one of its ministers led a campaign against the use of any hymns other than the Psalms of David. 'Infidelity was just beginning to come in like a flood,' wrote Robert Davidson, 'and the sacramental host, instead of rallying round the standard, were wasting their energies in intestine feuds.'[2]

The decline of Christian influence before a revival has sometimes been exaggerated in order to emphasize the scale of the subsequent transformation. The Second Great Awakening in America requires no such distortion of history in order to justify its title. By any assessment, an extraordinary period of Christian history began around the beginning of the new century. Voltaire is said to have claimed that by the early nineteenth century the Bible would have passed 'into the limbo of forgotten literature'. Instead, by 1816 many Americans considered themselves to be living in 'the age of Bibles and missionaries'. The annual report for 1816 of the Fairfield County Bible Society in Connecticut, went on to say: 'The atheism of Voltaire and his associates is gone down, almost with their dust to the grave. The blasphemies of Paine are remembered only to be abhorred.'[3]

Mrs Mary Winslow, visiting New York from England in 1833, wrote: 'There is not a country in the world where religion and religious intelligence are so constantly and prominently brought before the attention as this. In fact it is, at least at the present time, one continued, interesting topic of conversation.'[4]

[1] Heman Humphrey, *Revival Sketches and Manual* (New York, 1859), p. 94.
[2] Robert Davidson, *History of the Presbyterian Church in the State of Kentucky* (New York, 1847), pp. 97–8.
[3] Quoted in Keller, *Second Great Awakening*, p. 223.
[4] *Life in Jesus: A Memoir of Mrs Mary Winslow* (London, 1855), pp. 112–13.

The Second Great Awakening

Drs Andrew Reed and James Matheson, as deputies to the United States from the Congregational Union of England and Wales, travelled widely in America in 1834, and their conclusion was similar to Mrs Winslow's:

Allowing, as I did, for the difficulties of a newly settled country, and for the disadvantages of emigration, the state of education, morals and religion, was decidedly better than I expected to find it. Indeed, I have never visited a country in which I have seen them equalled. England herself painfully suffers in comparison . . . appearances in favour of religion are to their advantage. They have no law for the regulation or observation of the Sabbath, but public sentiment secures its sanctification better with them than with us. I have never seen that day observed in Bristol or Bath as it is in Boston and Philadelphia. In the large town, the people attend in larger numbers at their respective places of worship; there are more places for their accommodation; and the average size is greater with them than with us. The communicants are far more numerous than in this; and you will regard this as important evidence on the subject, especially when it is known that the principle of strict communion prevails . . . I regard the entire exigencies of this great country with the assurance of hope.[1]

Such comments were by no means confined to those who professed to be Christians. Alexis de Tocqueville, from France, noted with surprise in 1831, 'There is no country in the world where the Christian religion retains a greater influence over the souls of men than in America.'[2]

The speed and extent with which Christian churches were revitalized and multiplied at the beginning of the nineteenth century constitutes the era before us as the most important in the whole period under consideration in these pages. More than that, the Second Great Awakening has to be one of the most significant turning-points in church history. 'One of the most remarkable and extensive revivals ever known has passed over this people', Reed and Matheson wrote in 1835.[3] Similarly,

[1] Andrew Reed and James Matheson, *A Narrative of the Visit to the American Churches by the Deputies of the Congregational Union of England and Wales* (London, 1835), vol. 2, pp. 273–7.
[2] *Democracy in America*, vol. 2, p. 388, quoted in Keller, *Second Great Awakening*, p. 223.
[3] *Visit to the American Churches*, vol. 2, p. 2.

The Biblical Repertory and Theological Review, a journal not known for exaggeration, believed that it had pleased God to make America 'the theatre of the most glorious revivals that the world has ever witnessed'.[1]

While its name rightly puts the Second Great Awakening in succession to the first of the 1740s, it fails to alert us to the measure in which they differed. For one thing, there was a remarkable difference in time scale. The duration of the first Great Awakening extended through three to five years at most; the duration of the second was not less than a quarter of a century and, in the opinion of most, several years longer. Writing of the situation in the Northeast, Gardiner Spring recalled:

From the time I entered College, in 1800, down to the year 1825, there was an uninterrupted series of these celestial visitations, spreading over different parts of the land. During the whole of these twenty-five years, there was not a month in which we could not point to some village, some city, some seminary of learning, and say: 'Behold what hath God wrought'.[2]

Spring's contemporaries generally regarded this age of revival as continuing further than 1825. Edward Griffin, who dated the beginning of the general awakening in Connecticut in 1798, could write in January 1832, 'Since that time revivals have never ceased.'[3] William B. Sprague, also in 1832, described 'the wonderful change' in God's providence towards America which had begun 'near the beginning of the present century', as something that was still continuing. Unlike earlier times when the church was 'enlarged by very gradual additions . . . a different state of things seemed to commence, in the more copious and sudden effusions of the Holy Spirit; and now it has come to pass in these days in which we live, that far the greater number of those who are turned from darkness to light, so far as we can judge, experience this change during revivals of religion'.[4] Similarly, Heman Humphrey observed that

---

[1] *Biblical Repertory* (1832), p. 456.

[2] *Personal Reminiscences of the Life and Times of Gardiner Spring* (New York, 1866), vol. 1, p. 160. In an address in 1856, Spring gave the year 1842 as the termination of the period remarkable for 'copious effusions of the Holy Spirit'.

[3] W. B. Sprague, *Lectures on Revivals of Religion*, (1832; London: Banner of Truth, 1959), appendix, p. 151.

[4] Ibid., p. 3.

The spiritual harvests were more productive in some years than in others – in some thirty-fold, in some sixty, and in some a hundred – a period which will ever be referred to as one of the most extraordinary hitherto in the religious history of our country. We began to hope that these showers would continue to pour down righteousness, without any intermission as had so often occurred. Oh, it would be delightful to take a full survey of the great field while Christ was so gloriously triumphing everywhere.[1]

Humphrey's last sentence brings us to a second major difference between the two periods of awakening. The first reached only to the eastern seaboard and to part of the comparatively small population of the 1740s. The second was of far greater geographical extent and reached far more people. Abel Stevens, the Methodist historian, believed that at the beginning of the nineteenth century 'religious interest' was 'universal, if not simultaneous, from Maine to Tennessee, from Georgia to Canada'.[2]

It is partly the sheer scale of the Second Great Awakening that makes it impossible to point to where it began. For many in the South it was customary to regard Kentucky and Tennessee in 1800 as the starting-point. Referring to it as 'the great Revival', the Presbyterian writer W. H. Foote said that 'it spread over the Southern and Western, and portions of the Middle States, with a power almost terrific'.[3] But Francis Asbury in Pennsylvania had a different perspective when he wrote in his journal for 8 June 1800:

I spoke only once at the conference; my subject was Psalm 39.9: 'And in his temple doth everyone speak of his glory'; truly fulfilled at that time and place. Surely we may say our Pentecost has fully come this year, when we recollect what God hath wrought in Edisto in South, and Guildford in North Carolina; in Franklin, Amelia and Gloucester in Virginia; in Baltimore and Cecil in Maryland; in Dover, Duck Creek and Milford in Delaware![4]

Kentucky and Tennessee are not even mentioned in his statement and probably he was also unaware of what had

---

[1] *Revival Sketches*, pp. 212–3.   [2] *American Methodism*, p. 348.
[3] *Sketches*, p. 164.   [4] *Journal and Letters*, vol. 2, p. 235.

begun in New England. 'In 1799', wrote Edward Griffin of Connecticut, 'I could stand at my door in New Hartford, Litchfield county, and number fifty or sixty contiguous congregations laid down in one field of divine wonders, and as many more in different parts of New England.'[1]

Abel Stevens recorded an opinion that the new age of revivals began neither in the South nor in New England but under the ministry of Hezekiah C. Wooster in Canada. It was a view he did not favour, for he understood revival better than to suppose it to be a phenomenon that can only spread from place to place from a given starting-point. The awakening was, he said, 'one of those mysterious "times of refreshing" which appear at intervals in Christian communities, pass through their salutary cycle, and subside, to reappear in due time'. After reflecting on the record increase in numbers in his own denomination, Stevens expressed the opinion that 'the great revival of the times, which prevailed over most of the nation, seemed to centralize' in Baltimore:

In Baltimore it prevailed mightily. It extended all through Maryland and Delaware; the chapels and meetings in private houses were crowded in the evenings, and by day the harvest fields, work shops, the forests where the woodmen were cutting timber, were vocal with Methodist hymns. It seemed, remarks a witness of the scene, that all the population were turning to the Lord.[2]

This report, together with others from Methodist sources, is a reminder of another way in which the Second Great Awakening far exceeded the first in its scope. In the 1740s few congregations outside the Presbyterian and Congregational bodies were stirred into new life even though Whitefield, the foremost preacher, was an Anglican. But in the early 1800s, in addition to these two denominations, Baptists, Methodists and others, including the Episcopal Church, were all affected. This being so, it might be supposed that a series of writers would have arisen to give permanent records of this remarkable period. Certainly, there was information for books in abundance. The Congregational pastors who in July 1800 launched a forty-page

[1] Sprague, *Lectures*, appendix, pp. 151–2.
[2] *American Methodism*, p. 348.

The Second Great Awakening

monthly entitled *The Connecticut Evangelical Magazine* believed that they could sustain it chiefly with news of revivals. In an editorial to their first annual volume, published in 1801, they wrote:

The late wonderful out-pouring of the Holy Spirit and revival of experimental religion, in large districts of the American Church, will furnish much matter for publication to delight the hearts and satisfy the benevolence of the children of God. There has not been so great and extensive a work of divine grace in this land since the years 1742 and 1744 . . .
Such displays of divine power and grace ought to be faithfully narrated to the world for the purpose of awaking the secure. Great revivals of religion have been so rare for the last half century that multitudes began to believe the accounts received from the lips of their parents to have been fabulous. Indeed, it was time for God to work marvellously to set evidence before a sleeping generation of his mighty power in awakening and sanctifying sinners, and convincing them of the truth of Christ's words, 'Except a man be born again, he cannot see the kingdom of God'.[1]

In 1802 the first general volume on the awakening appeared under the title *Surprising Accounts of the Revival of Religion in the United States*,[2] with reports from Vermont, Connecticut, Western Pennsylvania, Kentucky, Tennessee, Georgia, North Carolina and other places. But instead of this hurriedly compiled book becoming the first of a long series, no other general account covering the Second Great Awakening seems to have been published until 1859. The author of the latter volume was Heman Humphrey who was well qualified for the task both as a preacher and as a participant in the awakening. He had long believed that 'the revival period at the close of the last century and the beginning of the present, furnishes ample materials for a long and glorious chapter in the History of Redemption'. But, sadly, he gave up his first attempt at a volume 'as a task beyond my powers, and for which I could not then command the time'. Thirty years later, at the age of eighty, and still conscious of the unmet need, the old preacher returned to the subject and issued

[1] *Connecticut Evangelical Magazine* (Hartford, 1801), vol. 1 (July 1800–June 1801), p. 6.
[2] 'Collected by the publisher', William Woodward of Philadelphia.

his *Revival Sketches and Manual*. Valuable though it is, the book provides, as he himself acknowledged, only 'a few selections from the mass'. A fuller work executed long before 1859 would have provided a volume of a different order. After Humphrey's volume little of significance on the subject appeared until Charles Roy Keller's *The Second Great Awakening in Connecticut* came out in 1942. Keller's book, far removed in time from the events it seeks to describe, was proof at least that, in his words, 'the Second Great Awakening deserves a place not hitherto accorded to it'.

The paucity of literature from participants in the Second Great Awakening constitutes a major loss to the church. Too often it meant that a later generation were left without information. W. H. Foote, in his *Sketches of North Carolina* (1846), regretted that 'We have no written account of the progress of the revival in the lower part of the State'. Other authors faced the same problem.

Various reasons for the literary failure have been offered, some of them coming from the period itself. Humphrey was far from alone in feeling that the subject was beyond him and that he could not command the time to do it justice. In May 1802 the Rev. James Hall wrote a lengthy letter from North Carolina describing a work of grace spreading 'two hundred miles, in a greater or lesser degree, from east to west, and near one hundred miles from north to south'. At the end of his narrative he concluded: 'What I have written are mere introductory sketches to what might be said on what I have seen during the last three months. Volumes might be written on the subject. Many of the scenes to which I have been a witness baffle description'.[1]

Joseph Bradley, a Baptist pastor in Albany, New York, writing in 1818, believed that a record covering one area of New England alone 'would fill many volumes'. But seeking to do *something*, Bradley confined himself to a four-year period and brought out a comparatively small book entitled *Accounts of Religious Revivals in Many Parts of the United States, from 1815 to 1818*. In these pages Bradley offered another reason why so few people were setting down the extraordinary events of their

---

[1] Foote, *Sketches of N.C.*, p. 390.

times: 'Within a few years, the churches have been so constantly favoured with refreshing streams of salvation, and large additions of members, that they seem to view these manifestations so common, that they have neglected to give information to the world that the Lord is among them of a truth.'[1] A writer in the *Biblical Repertory* of 1832, also commenting on this lack of writers, set down his understanding of the main reason in these words: 'It is, no doubt, an impression of holy awe and conscious unfitness for the important work, that has deprived the world of a connected history of Revivals in our age and especially in our own country. This is deeply to be regretted.'[2]

Notwithstanding what has been said on information unrecorded or lost, there are enough reliable statistics from the period to confirm the greatness of the work. These statistics are of new communicants and church members and to understand their significance it has to be remembered they are not hastily announced figures of 'converts'. The latter practice was generally unknown at this period; rather, the churches looked for the evidence of changed lives before permitting additions to their membership and the belief prevailed that true revival always proved itself by a change in conduct in communities. James H. Hotchkin, for example, in his *History of Western New York*, observed that the period of the Second Great Awakening raised the moral standard of the region, 'giving a character to this part of the State which laid a foundation for its large prosperity and improvement in all things useful'. A good deal more weight can therefore be given to admission figures from the early decades of the nineteenth century than can be done at a later date.

In the ten years from 1800 to 1810, the membership of the Presbyterian Church grew from 70,000 to 100,000. A statement authorized by the General Assembly of the denomination in 1803 remarked:

There is scarcely a Presbytery under the care of the Assembly from

---

[1] *Accounts of Religious Revivals in Many Parts of the United States, from 1815 to 1818*, (Albany, NY, 1819; Wheaton, Ill.: Richard Owen Roberts, 1980), p. 77.
[2] *Biblical Repertory* (1832), pp. 455–6.

which some pleasing intelligence has not been announced; and from some of them communications have been made which so illustriously display the triumphs of evangelical truth, and the power of sovereign grace, as cannot but fill with joy the hearts of all who love to hear of the prosperity of the Redeemer's kingdom.

In most northern and eastern Presbyteries, revivals of religion of a more or less general nature have taken place. In these revivals, the work of divine grace has proceeded, with few exceptions, in the usual way. Sinners have been convinced and converted by the still small voice of the Holy Spirit, – have been brought out of darkness into marvellous light, and from the bondage of corruption into the glorious liberty of the sons of God, without any remarkable bodily agitations, or extraordinary bodily agitations or extraordinary affections. In this calm and ordinary manner, many hundreds have been added to the church in the course of the last year; and multitudes of those, who had before joined themselves to the Lord, have experienced times of refreshing, from his presence.

In many of the southern and western Presbyteries revivals more extensive and of a more extraordinary nature have taken place . . . But, forbearing to enter into details on this subject, they would only in general declare that in the course of the last year there is reason to believe that several thousands within the bounds of the Presbyterian Church have been brought to embrace the gospel of Christ, and large accessions of zeal and strength as well as of members given to the people.[1]

Baptist membership rose still more dramatically in the same ten-year period, from 95,000 in 1800 to 160,000 in 1810. David Benedict (1779–1874), who published his two-volume *General History of the Baptist Denomination in America* in 1813, concurred with the opinion of the writers of other denominations given above. Writing well before this era had come to an end, he said: 'From 1799 to 1803, there were, in most parts of the United States, remarkable out-pourings of the Divine Spirit among different denominations; multitudes became the subjects of religious concern and were made to rejoice in the salvation of God.'[2]

In Connecticut powerful awakenings occurred among a

---

[1] Quoted in *Connecticut Evangelical Magazine*, vol. 4 (July 1803–June 1804), pp. 68–9.

[2] *A General History of the Baptist Denomination in America and Other Parts of the World* (Boston, 1813), vol. 2, p. 251.

number of Baptist churches in 1798. In 1800 Isaac Backus, the best-known Baptist leader of New England, noted, 'The revivals of religion in different parts of our land have been wonderful.'[1] In 1803 it was among Baptist churches in Boston, under cautious, Calvinistic preaching, that revival began: 'It continued,' noted Benedict, 'for more than two years', during which time 'about two hundred' were added to the Second Church 'and about the same number to the First'.[2] In Connecticut there were fifty-nine Baptist churches in 1800, with 4,600 members; by 1820 there were seventy-three churches with 7,500 members; and by 1830 eighty-three churches with 9,200 members.

Figures relating to the increase in the Methodist Episcopal Church are probably the most specific. In the nine consecutive years from 1801 to 1809 the totals of its annual increase in membership were: 7,980; 13,860; 17,336; 9,064; 6,811; 10,625; 14,020; 7,405; and 11,043. As Robert Coleman has pointed out, these figures mean that in the first decade of the nineteenth century the Methodist Episcopal Church saw an increase of 167.8 per cent while, in the same period, the population of the United States increased by only 36.4 per cent. Some of the stories that lie behind these bare figures can be found for example in Asbury's Journals;

[10 June 1801] The Lord appears glorious upon our Continent, and my soul exults in Zion's prosperity.

[30 May 1802] My soul hath been suppressed with deep and sore temptations: it may be thus, that I should not be lifted up at the prosperity of the Church, and increase of ministers and members. I have a variety of letters, conveying the pleasing intelligence of the work of God in every State, district, and in most circuits in the Union . . . Ride on blessed Redeemer, until all the states and nations of the earth are subdued unto thy sacred sway! . . . I read letters concerning the great revival of religion westwards and southwards.

[14 January 1804] I have been unwell; but I am cheered by the glorious prospects of Zion's welfare: I mark this year, 1804, as the greatest that has ever yet been in this land for religion.

The same spirit of thanksgiving, as it ran through the whole

---

[1] Alvah Hovey, *A Memoir of the Life and Times of Isaac Backus* (1858; Harrisonburg, Va., Gano Books, 1991), p. 304.

[2] *Baptist Denomination in America*, vol. 1, p. 410.

denomination, is well reflected in 'The Address of the General Conference of 1812 to the Members of the Methodist Episcopal Church in the United States of America':

Dearly Beloved Brethren: When we retrospect the divine goodness towards us as a people, our hearts are animated with sentiments of praise. The Redeemer has planted his standard in the midst of us, and given astonishing success to our labors, and annually made accessions of thousands to our number. From the cold provinces of Canada to sultry regions of Georgia – from the shores of the Atlantic to the waters of the Mississippi – in populous cities, improved countries, and dreary deserts, God has extended the triumphs of his grace . . . In the revolution of a few years our number has almost amounted to two hundred thousand . . .

The blessings you have received from God should humble you to the dust . . . All the divine benedictions conferred upon you have been unmerited and free . . . You are therefore under peculiar obligations to grace.

*　　　*　　　*

From the general introduction to the period of the Second Great Awakening we turn to some particular observations.

In the first place, if it be asked, What special means were used to promote these revivals? the answer is that there were none. The significance of this fact will be the more apparent in later pages. This is not to say that the spiritual leaders of this new era held the view that the gospel could be advanced without means being employed. They were united in regarding such an attitude as a serious abuse of the doctrine of divine sovereignty. As Ebenezer Porter affirmed:

The God of this universe is not dependent on instruments . . . He could fill the world with Bibles by a word, – or give every inhabitant of the globe a knowledge of the gospel by inspiration. But he chooses that human agency should be employed in printing and reading and explaining the Scriptures. God is able to sanctify the four hundred millions of Asia, in one instant, without the agency of missionaries; but we do not expect him to do this without means, any more than we expect him to rain down food from the clouds, or turn stones into bread.[1]

[1] E. Porter, *Letters on the Religious Revivals which Prevailed about the Beginning of the Present Century* (Boston, 1858), pp. 15–16.

These men were united in the belief that God has appointed the means of prayer and preaching for the spread of the gospel and that these are *the great means* in the use of which he requires the churches to be faithful. There are no greater means which may be employed at special times to secure supposedly greater results. It is therefore the Spirit of God who makes the same means more effective at some seasons than at others.

This has perhaps not always been as evident as it was in 1800. Sometimes revivals have coincided with the emergence of hitherto unknown preachers whose abilities have been credited with securing change. But in the case of the Second Great Awakening, nearly all the preachers prominent at the outset had already been labouring for many years. Asbury had been twenty-nine years in America before 1800. Timothy Dwight, grandson of Jonathan Edwards, was ordained in 1783 and had worked for twenty years before he saw revival under his ministry. What Asa Rand wrote of Dr Seth Payson could have been written of many others. Dr Payson was for thirty-seven years (1782–1819) minister at Rindge, in New Hampshire. In a tribute to his memory written in 1849 Rand said of that long ministry:

During the first half of that period the ministers and churches in that region were generally unblest by copious showers of Divine grace. They were unacquainted with revivals of religion . . . Dr Payson held on his way, faithfully declaring the gospel on the Sabbath, and was blessed in building up a comparatively enlightened and spiritual church, enlarged by occasional additions from the world. Early in the present century, his people were favoured with times of refreshing . . . The latter part of his ministry was far more successful and happy than the former. He lived to produce *permanent* effects and the results are witnessed to this day.[1]

The facts are indisputable. A considerable body of men, for a long period before the Second Great Awakening, preached the same message as they did during the revival but with vastly different consequences – the same men, the same actions, performed with the same abilities, yet the results were so amazingly different! The conclusion has to be drawn that the change in the churches after 1798 and 1800 cannot be explained

---

[1] Sprague, *Annals*, vol. 2, p. 213.

in terms of the means used. Nothing was clearer to those who saw the events than that God was sovereignly pleased to bless human instrumentality in such a way that the success could be attributed to him alone. Many pastors included this observation in their narratives of revival published in *The Connecticut Evangelical Magazine*. Samuel Shepard of Lenox, Massachusetts, described what had happened in his congregation in 1799, concluding: 'The immediate hand of omnipotence was strikingly exhibited in this work . . . Religious instruction was no other now than it had been . . . The apostle knew what he said when he spoke these memorable words, "We have this treasure in earthen vessels, that the excellency of the power might be of God, and not of us".'[1] Jeremiah Hallock, a leader in Connecticut, wrote: 'As means did not begin this work of themselves, so neither did they carry it on. But as this was the work of the Omnipotent Spirit, so the effects produced proclaimed its sovereign, divine author.'[2] Asahel Hooker, another eminent Connecticut pastor, drew the same conclusion after seeing the same change among his own people: 'It is the evident design of Providence to confound all attempts which should be made by philosophy and human reason to account for the effects wrought without ascribing them to God, as the marvellous work of his Spirit and grace.'[3]

Such are a few of the testimonies of Congregationalists, but men of other denominations spoke in similar terms. A Baptist author, for instance, describing the revival at Hartford in 1798–1800, wrote: 'The Lord seems to have stepped out of the usual path of ordinances, to effect this work more immediately in the displays of his Almighty power, and outpouring of his

---

[1] *Connecticut Evangelical Magazine*, vol. 2 (July 1801–June 1802), p. 140. This 40-page monthly is the source for much of the revival material of the period from New England. Some of its narratives are reprinted in abridged form in Bennet Tyler, *New England Revivals, as They Existed at the Close of the Eighteenth, and the Beginning of the Nineteenth Centuries*, (Boston, 1846; Wheaton, Ill., Richard Owen Roberts, 1980); Humphrey, *Revival Sketches*; and elsewhere.

[2] Quoted in Porter, *Letters on Revivals*, p. 101.

[3] Ibid., pp. 101–2. Porter also quoted these words of personal testimony from Asahel Hooker: 'I never fully understood the apostle's comparison of ministers to "earthen vessels", till I saw, in a revival, the utter inefficacy of my own preaching to save a single soul, without divine influence'.

Spirit; probably to show that the work is his own.'[1]

Thus what characterizes a revival is not the employment of unusual or special means but rather the extraordinary degree of blessing attending the normal means of grace. There were no unusual evangelistic meetings, no special arrangements, no announcements of pending revivals. Pastors were simply continuing in the services they had conducted for many years when the great change began. That is why so many of them could say, 'The first appearance of the work was sudden and unexpected.' Their theology taught them that there is no inherent power in the truth to convert sinners and they rejoiced in the knowledge that the size of the blessing which God is pleased to give through the use of means is entirely in his own hands. As William Rogers of Philadelphia wrote to Isaac Backus in 1799, 'The revivals of religion which you speak of are peculiarly illustrative of the glorious doctrines of grace, – "the wind bloweth where it listeth".'[2]

On the subject of means, something needs to be said more particularly on prayer. As with the truth that is preached, prayer has no inherent power in itself. On the contrary, true prayer is bound up with a persuasion of our inability and our complete dependence on God. Prayer, considered as a human activity, whether offered by few or many, can guarantee no results. But prayer that throws believers in heartfelt need on God, with true concern for the salvation of sinners, will not go unanswered. Prayer of this kind precedes blessing, not because of any necessary cause and effect, but because such prayer secures an acknowledgement of the true Author of the blessing. And where such a spirit of prayer exists it is a sign that God is already intervening to advance his cause. One thing that can be said with certainty about the 1790s, before any general indications of a new era were to be seen, is that there was a growing concern among Christians to pray. Later on, when the evidence of records from those years was compared, it was recognized that across the Union, from Connecticut to Kentucky, the 1790s were marked by a new spirit of intercession.

[1] Robert Turnbull, *Memorials of the First Baptist Church, Hartford*, pp. 15–16, quoted in Keller, *Second Great Awakening*, p. 195.
[2] Hovey, *Memoir of Backus*, p. 295.

In New England Congregationalists and Baptists united – in the words of a letter of the Stonington Baptist Association in 1798 – in 'supplications that God would avert his judgments; prevent the spread of error and iniquity – and pour out his Spirit in plentiful effusions on our guilty land'. The General Assembly of the Presbyterian Church called for 'Solemn humiliation, fasting and prayer' and urged the same petition. Both public statements and private journals (such as Asbury's) show how Methodists emphasized the same duty at this period. Their Church appointed the first Tuesday in March 1796 to be set aside for fasting and prayer, and Nathan Bangs recorded that, until the end of the century, the first Tuesday in each quarter was observed for this purpose. Among the local churches of whose practice we have more detailed information are those of Logan County, Kentucky, which were under the care of the Rev. James M'Gready. At the time M'Gready wrote: 'We feel encouraged to unite our supplications to a prayer hearing God for the outpouring of his Spirit, that his people may be quickened and comforted, and that our children and sinners generally may be converted.' Of the year 1799, he observed: 'A remarkable spirit of prayer and supplication was given to Christians, and a sensible, heart-felt burden of the dreadful state of sinners out of Christ: so that it might be said with propriety, that Zion travailed in birth to bring forth her spiritual children.'

This is well summarized in the report of the General Assembly of the Presbyterian Church for 1803. The writers considered it worthy of special attention

that most of the accounts of revivals communicated to them stated that the institution of prayer societies, or seasons of *special prayer to God*, generally preceded the remarkable displays of Divine grace with which our land has been recently favored. In most cases, preparatory to signal effusions of the Holy Spirit, the pious have been stirred up to cry fervently and importunately that God would appear to vindicate his own cause.

'Does God always hear prayer and answer it?' Asbury asked himself in his journal on one occasion. The other leaders in the Second Great Awakening would have agreed with the answer he recorded: 'If it is in the Spirit's groaning, and in purity of intention, and in faith, doubtless he does.'

*   *   *

A second general observation to be noted is the unprecedented upsurge of evangelical and interdenominational activity which resulted from the Second Great Awakening. Narratives of revivals tend to concentrate on the people converted, but every true revival begins in the church and a proof of the genuineness of the work is that it does not leave believers where they were before. They are filled with new wonder, joy and praise, with a new sense of the privilege of serving God, and with renewed energy that comes from being constrained by the love of Christ. What Christians had thought impossible in former years was now attempted with a faith and sacrificial abandon that was to astonish the world. Humphrey, who saw it happen, remarked:

> Whatever view we take of the work of God at the beginning of this century, it was a glorious period in the religious history of the country . . . those revivals stand connected, in the history of Redemption, with those aggressive agencies by which He is now turning our own moral wildernesses into fruitful fields, and sending the gospel to all heathen lands.
>
> When that era dawned, there were no Missionary societies, foreign or domestic, no Bible societies, no Tract societies, no Education societies, no onward movements in the churches of any sort, for the conversion of the world. At home it was deep spiritual apathy; abroad, over all the heathen lands, the calm of the Dead sea – death, death, nothing but death.[1]

These conditions quickly changed in the opening years of the nineteenth century as scores of new evangelical agencies sprang into existence. Local missionary societies, such as those formed in Connecticut (1798) and Massachusetts (1799) were soon overtaken by larger institutions such as the American Board of Foreign Missions (1810), whose first missionaries went to Calcutta two years later. By 1821 the Board had sent out eighty-one missionaries. Baptist (1814), Methodist Episcopal (1819) churches, and others, soon followed with their own foreign missionary societies. The same pattern of local agencies

[1] *Revival Sketches*, pp. 200–1.

[131]

multiplying spontaneously occurred with Bible and tract societies, and these also became nation-wide in the American Bible Society (1816) and the American Tract Society (1825). New spiritual endeavours of many kinds originated in the same period, including Sunday School unions, work among black people, monthly magazines, and societies for educational or humane objectives. All these and other agencies owed their beginnings to the impulse that came from the awakening. Such phenomenal development could never have taken place if thousands of Christians had not seen the wonderful works of God and been energized to labour so that the same blessings could be imparted to others.

*   *   *

A third general observation relates to the colleges, both old and new. The revivals, far from being merely emotional events which influenced the uneducated, made a profound impression on almost all the main centres of learning. It is a striking fact that many of the best-known preachers of the era – men who were convinced believers in the outpouring of the Spirit – were themselves often heads of colleges during at least part of their ministries. A list of college presidents in this period is almost a list of revival preachers; it includes such names as Moses Waddel, inspirer of the University of Georgia; Philip Milledoler of Rutgers; Timothy Dwight of Yale; Edward Griffin of Andover and Williams; Ebenezer Porter of Andover and Heman Humphrey of Amherst.

What happened at Yale may be taken as an example of what occurred more widely. When Dwight became president of the college in 1795, it was suffering from the disbelief then in fashion among the young. One entering student of 1793 reported that the college church 'was almost extinct. Most of the students were skeptical, and rowdies were plenty.'[1] Another student, a few years later, recalled, 'There was but one professor of religion in the Freshman class, not one in Sophomore, only one in the Junior, and not more than ten in

---

[1] Charles Beecher (ed.), *Autobiography of Lyman Beecher*, (New York, 1864; Cambridge, Mass., Harvard University Press, 1961), vol. 1, p. 27.

the Senior.'[1] Bishop Hurst wrote in praise of Dwight, 'From the day that the young president faced his students in the chapel of Yale College, infidelity has been a vanishing force in the history of the American people'. The statement is plainly wrong: in the seven years from 1795 to 1802 Dwight's influence placed a restraint on wayward students and may have reclaimed some but, Humphrey (a Freshman at the time) observed, the change at Yale came suddenly in the spring of 1802 'with such power as had never been witnessed within those walls before . . . It was like a mighty rushing wind. The whole college was shaken. It seemed for a time as if the whole mass of students would press into the kingdom of God.'[2] Only then, in the words of another observer, did the Christian influence become 'positive and pervading'. About seventy-five out of Yale's 230 students were converted and united to churches.

The Yale revival of 1802 was marked by a feature that became characteristic of the new era: the number of men coming forward for the gospel ministry was suddenly greatly multiplied. Prior to this date candidates for the ministry had been dwindling, as is generally the case when the world's influence gains ascendency in the church. As William Speer remarked:

No motives but those with which the Holy Spirit moves the souls of men can draw gifted and energetic young men from the overwhelming attractions which the world has to offer, and lead them heartily to consecrate themselves to the comparatively toil-some, ill paid and anxious office of the ministry . . . Thus it is that the cause of Ministerial Education is one of the first to feel the influences of a genuine outpouring of the Holy Spirit; and these influences it soon sends streaming, in an energized generation of ministers, through every branch and fibre of the Church's outward life.[3]

Heman Humphrey noted that in the four classes preceding his at Yale only thirteen men became ministers of the gospel. In the next four years there were to be sixty-nine, 'nearly if not quite all of them brought in by the great revival'. Writing at a later

[1] Bennet Tyler, *Lectures on Theology*, with a Memoir by Nahum Gale (Boston, 1859), p. 16.
[2] *Revival Sketches*, p. 198.
[3] *The Great Revival of 1800* (Philadelphia, 1872), p. 86.

date, when the pattern had again changed, Humphrey had no doubt of the reason why so many men were prepared to come forward at the beginning of the nineteenth century:

As he loveth much to whom much is forgiven, so he who has most deeply felt the plague of his own heart, and the justice of his condemnation under discriminating preaching – he who has most deeply felt his own perishing need of a Saviour – will feel more constrained by the love of Christ to enter the ministry, that if possible he may save some who are under the same condemnation, than if the terrors of death had not taken hold upon him when he was passing through the deep waters. Such were the preachers who came out of the revivals now under review, and who were to carry forward the work when the fathers had fallen asleep. They knew what truths had taken the deepest hold of their own minds, and made them the basis of their ministry.[1]

Seminaries specifically designed for men preparing to preach were almost unknown prior to the beginning of the nineteenth century. As we have seen, men such as William Graham in Virginia and John McMillan in Western Pennsylvania made a beginning in this field but it was the appearance of a new generation of younger men with a call to preach that now drew attention to the need for more theological training. Among the earliest of these new schools were Andover in Massachusetts (1808) and Yale Divinity School in Connecticut (1822). But Princeton Theological Seminary, established in 1812, has special significance for its long-term influence in the interest of orthodox Christianity, and fuller mention needs to be made of its origins.

While Princeton Theological Seminary resulted from the combined action of the Presbyterian Church, there were two men in particular whose work and vision shaped its course: Ashbel Green (1762–1848) and Archibald Alexander (1772–1851). Green, the son of one of Whitefield's ministerial friends, was converted during the Revolutionary War, and entered the College of New Jersey at Princeton in 1787. Such was his early brilliance that he was invited to dine with Washington and the Congress when he was only twenty-one. He became first a tutor and then a professor at Princeton, under

---

[1] *Revival Sketches*, p. 200.

Witherspoon, before being called to the Second Church at Philadelphia in 1787. This was a church initially composed largely of converts from the Great Awakening and Green was entirely at home in its ethos. He had witnessed 'two or three' times of revival in his father's congregation and one of his life-long petitions was that God would 'Visit us with a day of Almighty power'.[1] Green believed in preaching ('there is no employment in this world that I love half as well'[2]), and Samuel Miller wrote of his ministry in what was then America's foremost city: 'Crowds flocked to hear him, more than the place of worship could contain. His evening services especially were attended by all denominations.'[3] By 1800 the status of the minister of Philadelphia's Second Church as an evangelical leader was such that he was one of the first men to whom personal reports were sent of awakenings in different places.[4]

Archibald Alexander was converted, as we have already seen, in the period of the revival in Virginia (1787–9), and was a student for the ministry under the training of William Graham. Thereafter he became an itinerant preacher before settling as pastor of John Blair Smith's former congregations of Briery and Cub Creek (1794), in close proximity to the College at Hampden-Sydney. In 1802 he married Janetta Waddel, the daughter of the Rev. Dr James Waddel, an eminent blind preacher who had trained under Samuel Davies. Preaching and college work filled Alexander's time until 1807, when, as minister of the Third Church, he joined Ashbel Green in Philadelphia. The two men were soon working together and with others for the establishment of a theological seminary. Both held the conviction that the existing schools of learning – including Princeton College – were failing to 'furnish preachers' and that this failure was not due simply to the breadth of the general education they offered. They believed that preparation for the ministry was much more than the acquisition of intellectual attainments, and this conviction is well stated in a report towards the founding of a Seminary which became an Act of the Presbyterian General Assembly:

[1] Jones, *Life of Green*, pp. 246, 343, 431.
[2] Ibid., p. 573.   [3] Ibid., p. 526.
[4] See e.g. William Woodward, *Surprising Accounts of the Revival* (Philadelphia, 1802), pp. 25, 53.

That, as filling the Church with a learned and able ministry without a corresponding portion of real piety, would be a curse to the world and an offence to God and his people, so the General Assembly think it their duty to state, that in establishing a seminary for training up ministers, it is their earnest desire to guard as far as possible against so great an evil. And they do hereby solemnly pledge themselves to the churches under their care, that in forming and carrying into execution the plan of the proposed seminary, it will be their endeavour to make it, under the blessing of God, a nursery of vital piety as well as of sound theological learning, and to train up persons for the ministry who shall be lovers as well as defenders of the truth as it is in Jesus, friends of revivals of religion, and a blessing to the Church of God.[1]

When the new Seminary was at length established at Princeton in 1812, Alexander was appointed its first professor and Green the first president of its board. It was Green who wrote its constitution and personally donated half the land on which the Seminary was to be built. An unforeseen development further strengthened the Seminary's beginnings. At the same time as Alexander moved to start the new Seminary, Green was elected president of Princeton College, so that through the vital first years of the Seminary's life he was to be at hand to help and encourage. In 1813 the village church at Princeton was destroyed by fire and as a consequence the students of the Seminary and the College began to meet together for services on the Lord's Day in the dining-hall of Nassau Hall, with Alexander and Green undertaking the preaching in turn. Spiritual interest among the College – as distinct from the Seminary students – was small. When the winter session began in November 1814 there were only twelve 'professors of religion' out of 105 students in the College. Within three months of that date the situation had changed and Green could write: 'there were very few individuals in the College edifice who were not deeply impressed with a sense of the importance of spiritual and eternal things. There was scarcely a room – perhaps not one – which was not a place of earnest secret devotion.'[2]

This was the first (in Green's words) 'great revival' at Princeton since 1772 and the results were no less far-reaching.

---

[1] *Life of Alexander*, pp. 325–6. [2] Jones, *Life of Green*, p. 619.

Some of the men whose lives took a new spiritual direction were to become leaders in civil and political office: they included William Pennington and James McDowell, later Governors of New Jersey and Virginia respectively. Others were to become eminent ministers of the gospel – their number included two future bishops of the Episcopal Church, and Charles Hodge whose life-work was to be in the Seminary. It was Hodge who founded *The Biblical Repertory* in 1825.

There is considerable documentation on the 1815 revival at Princeton which it is unnecessary to quote here.[1] What needs to be remembered, in the light of later controversy, is that the founders of the Seminary were men who belonged whole-heartedly to the same tradition as Whitefield and Samuel Davies. In the phrase of the above assembly report, they were emphatically 'friends of revivals of religion'.

*   *   *

A final general observation arising out of this period has to do with the manner in which the unusual sense of the presence of God was recognized in the churches which experienced these revivals. It was not because men saw weeping multitudes, unrestrained noise and high excitement that they believed a revival had begun. On the contrary, such things – which are sometimes supposed to be of the essence of revival – were almost entirely absent in the Northeast during the greater part of the Second Great Awakening. Ebenezer Porter noted 'as a remarkable characteristic of these revivals, that there was no instance of outcries, or of any public disorders, in religious assemblies'.[2] The presence of God and the measure of his working was not judged by such things but rather by the deep impression made on people by 'the power of divine truth'. Far from aiming at stirring excitement, the preachers sought to avoid it. 'It was their object, indeed, to make deep impressions on the hearts of sinners', observed Porter, 'but to do this only by means of the truth. Accordingly, the whole tendency of things

[1] Ibid., pp. 619–22; W. M. Baker, *Life and Labours of Daniel Baker* (Philadelphia, 1858, 3rd. ed.), pp. 64–71.
[2] *Letters on Revivals*, p. 58.

was to produce exercises of the calm, solemn, pungent kind, rather than passionate and clamorous excitement.'[1] Heman Humphrey wrote of the preachers in similar terms: 'They laid more stress upon "fervency of spirit", than upon strength of lungs, or muscular contortions.'[2] Edward Griffin, reviewing the whole period in 1832, wrote: 'The means employed in these revivals have been but two, – the clear presentation of divine truth and prayer: nothing to work upon the passions but sober, solemn truth, presented, as far as possible, in its most interesting attitudes, and closely applied to the conscience. The meetings have been still and orderly, with no other sign of emotion in the hearers than the solemn look and the silent tear.'[3]

As we have seen, it was when these pastors were continuing in their normal preaching ministries that revivals began and the first appearance of change was commonly the mysterious influence, 'like the silent dew of heaven', which took from men's minds all save the truth they were hearing. Congregations were then awed and subdued and it was often the degree of silence and stillness, more than anything else, which showed that a new day had come. There are unanimous testimonies to this from the many eyewitnesses who have left records. The Rev. Jeremiah Hallock reported what happened in his congregation of West Simsbury, Connecticut in 1798–9:

The solemnity of this season cannot be communicated. It can only be known by experience . . . The work was by no means noisy, but rational, deep, and still. Poor sinners began to see that every thing in the Bible was true, that they were wholly sinful and in the hand of a sovereign God. The first you would know of persons under awakening was, that they would be at all the religious meetings, and manifest a silent and eager attention.[4]

The Rev. John B. Preston of Rupert, Vermont, wrote:

Our Prayer-meetings were crowded, and solemn to an amazing degree. No emotions more violent than shedding of tears, and no appearance of wildness and disorder occurred. Nothing appeared but a silent, fixed attention, and profound solemnity, the most resembling

[1] *Letters on Revivals*, p. 75. [2] Sprague, *Lectures*, appendix, p. 119.
[3] Ibid., p. 158. [4] Humphrey, *Revival Sketches*, p. 127.

my idea of the day of judgment of any scene I ever witnessed. Infidelity retired, or was overcome by the bright manifestations of divine power and grace.[1]

Sometimes this same spirit possessed whole places. Dr Noah Porter, describing the revival at Farmington, Connecticut, wrote: 'The state of feeling which, at this time, pervaded the town, was interesting beyond description. There was no commotion; but a stillness, in our very streets; a serenity in the aspect of the pious; and a solemnity apparent in almost all, which forcibly impressed us with the conviction, that, in very deed, *God was in this place*.'[2]

This same feature was particularly noted in what was called 'the Great Revival' in the southern part of Saratoga County, New York, in 1820. Of one village it was said: 'Every house exhibited the solemnity of a continued Sabbath. So profound was the stillness, that a recent death could have added nothing to it, in many families. Common conversation was rarely engaged in, and every ear was open to hear the gospel.'[3] At another location, 'A deep solemnity spread over the whole community, and everywhere meetings were crowded.'[4]

That the young were affected in this manner in the same way as the old is clear from the record of many instances of revival in colleges. A student who was converted at Amherst, during the presidency of Heman Humphrey, described how the change in his life began in these words:

The first circumstance which attracted my attention, was a sermon from the President on the Sabbath. I do not know what the text and subject were, for, according to a wicked habit, I had been asleep till near its close. I seemed to be awakened by a *silence*, which pervaded the room; a deep solemn attention which seems to spread over an assembly when all are completely engrossed in some absorbing theme. I looked around, astonished, and the feeling of profound attention seemed to settle on myself. I looked towards the President,

---

[1] Ibid., p. 172.

[2] Sprague, *Lectures*, appendix, p. 72.

[3] Reuben S. Smith, *Recollections of Nettleton and the Great Revival of 1820* (Albany, N.Y.), 1848, pp. 55–6.

[4] Ibid., p. 60. Quoted in Reed and Matheson, *Visit to the American Churches*, vol. 1, pp. 394–5.

and saw him calm and collected, but evidently most deeply interested in what he was saying, – his whole soul engaged, and his
countenance beaming with an expression of eager earnestness,
which lighted up all his features, and gave to his language unusual
energy and power.

What could this mean? I had never seen a speaker and his audience
so engaged. He was making a most earnest appeal to prevent those
who were destitute of religion *themselves*, from doing any thing to
obstruct the progress of the revival which he hoped was approaching;
or of doing any thing to prevent the salvation of others, even if they did
not desire salvation for themselves. He besought them, by all the
interests of immortality, and for the sake of themselves, and of their
companions, to desist from hostilities against the work of God.

The discourse closed, and we dispersed. But many of us carried
away the arrow in our hearts. The gayest and the hardiest trembled at
the manifest approach of a sublime and unwonted influence . . . in the
aspect of the pious; and a solemnity apparent in almost all, which
forcibly impressed us with the conviction, that, in very deed, *God was
in this place.*[1]

Bennet Tyler's account of his spiritual experiences includes
the following account of the changed appearance of the campus
at Yale in the awakening of 1802 to which we have already
referred:

In the spring of 1802, while I was Sophomore, that great revival
commenced in Yale College, to which reference has often been made,
and which issued in the hopeful conversion of about seventy of the
students. This revival commenced a few weeks before the spring
vacation. I knew very little of it, however, at the time, as I was
confined with the measles, and as soon as I was able, had gone home,
on account of the weakness of my eyes. I continued at home during the
remainder of the term, and, owing to the sickness and death of my
father, I did not return to college till one or two weeks after the
commencement of the summer term. A great change had taken place
during my absence. Many who were thoughtless when I last saw
them, were now rejoicing in hope, and others were deeply anxious for
their souls. Meanwhile I had been called to pass through a most
affecting scene. My father had died in the triumphs of faith. His
death, the funeral sermon which was preached on the following
Sabbath, and the intelligence which I had received from college, had
made a deep impression on my mind. I returned to college. When I

---

[1] Sprague, *Lectures*, appendix, p. 72.

entered the college yard, an awful solemnity seemed to rest upon every object on which I cast my eyes. The buildings were solemn. The trees were solemn. The countenance of every individual whom I saw was solemn. 'How dreadful is this place,' was the exclamation which seemed naturally to force itself from me. I went into my room. On the table was a letter addressed to me from a classmate with whom I had been intimate, and whom I had left in a state of thoughtless security. His attention had been called up to the concerns of his soul; and having heard of my affliction in the death of my father, he had written me a very affectionate letter, urging upon me an immediate attention to the concerns of my soul. My room-mate soon after came from his closet, with a solemn, joyful countenance, and told me what God had done for his soul since we had parted. My feelings at this time can be better imagined than described. Suffice it to say, an impression was now made upon my mind which was never effaced. I no longer halted between two opinions.[1]

Princeton students were characterized by the same spirit in the revival of 1815. Charles Pettit McIlvaine, one of the students in that year, was Bishop of Ohio when he recalled what that time meant to him:

It is more than forty years since I first witnessed a revival of religion. It was in the college of which I was a student. It was powerful and pervading, and fruitful in the conversion of young men to God; and it was quiet, unexcited, and entirely free from all devices or means beyond the few and simple which God has appointed, namely, 'prayer and the ministry of the word.' In that precious season of the power of God, my religious life began. I had *heard* before; I began then to *know*. I must doubt the deepest convictions of my soul, when I doubt whether that revival was the work of the Spirit of God.[2]

The last observation on the manner in which God's presence was known, is crucial to any assessment of this period of history. Too often, modern writers have regarded the Second Great Awakening as though it were simply a movement of religious excitement. The first-hand accounts cannot be reconciled with that idea. It was not mere emotion that restored faith in the Bible and put an end to the advance of unbelief, that changed the moral character of oncoming generations and

---

[1] *Lectures*, pp. 17–18.
[2] Humphrey, *Revival Sketches*, pp. 220–1. See also W. Carus, *Memorials of Charles Pettit McIlvaine* (London, 1882), p. 11.

made them servants of God. In subsequent pages we shall not ignore the fact that there were places where excitement was sometimes allowed to take control and times when tares even choked the wheat, but in this chapter we have been concerned to look at the work as a whole. Such a survey ought to lead to one great conclusion: 'in the mercy of God, a glorious harvest was gathered to eternal life.'[1]

---

[1] Foote, *Sketches*, p. 545.

6

John McMillan (1752–1833),
tutor of James M'Gready of Kentucky

6

At the first census of the population of the United States in 1790 it was found that out of some 4 million people only 5 per cent were living west of the Appalachian Mountains. Among that minority on the frontier the fastest-growing population was that of Kentucky. From the first few settlers in 1774, numbers grew to 176 in 1779, 75,000 in 1790, and had reached 220,955 by 1800. Initially considered a part of a county of Virginia, Kentucky became the fifteenth state in the Union in 1792 and thirty years later it had the sixth largest population among all the states. It was predicted that whatever happened in this 'Mother of the West' would affect a much wider region, and so it proved.

If, as it is claimed, the first emigrants to Kentucky were men of religious convictions, it was rather as Indian fighters that they were remembered by posterity. The belief that the land was unsettled by any major Indian tribe was disputable given the struggle that took place before *Can-tuck-kee* (commonly interpreted to mean 'the dark and bloody ground') was secured. As late as 1790, a Kentucky judge reported that in the previous seven years 'fifteen hundred souls had been killed or taken prisoner' by the Indians. When Asbury paid his first visit to Kentucky in that year, he passed the graves of twenty-four settlers slain in a surprise attack. Such hardship, and the homesickness that many found harder to endure, did not hinder the movement westwards chiefly from Virginia, which increased after the Revolutionary War.

Among the newcomers were Baptists and Presbyterians.

Two Baptist congregations were established in Kentucky in 1781. One of them had formerly been the Upper Spotsylvania Church, the first Separate church north of the James River. With 200 church members and another 300 to 400 children and adherents, this congregation seems to have removed almost in its entirety from Virginia, with its pastor, Lewis Craig. It became the South Elkhorn Baptist Church, about five miles from Lexington. Craig was one of the well-known preachers in the revival period of the 1770s. Other leading Baptist pastors who removed to Kentucky were John Taylor (whom Semple called 'a preacher of weight, wisdom and usefulness'), John Tanner, and John Gano. David Thomas also from Virginia was to follow in the 1790s. It is said that between 1791 and 1810 a quarter of all the Baptists in Virginia removed to Kentucky.

At first, the numbers of Presbyterians may have kept pace with the Baptists. From 1783 they had the leadership of the mature David Rice. Rice was born in 1733 and converted under the preaching of Samuel Davies. When Davies went to Princeton in 1759 Rice went with him as a student. A description of the kind of people who formed the nuclei of the first Kentucky churches served by Rice is provided by Jane Trimble who crossed the Appalachians a year after him. She rode with an infant on her lap and a three-year-old boy behind her. All the other adults in the party, she wrote,

rode upon horses, and upon other horses were placed the farming and cooking utensils, beds and bedding, wearing apparel, provisions, and last, but not least, the libraries, consisting of two Bibles, half a dozen Testaments, the Catechism, the Confession of Faith of the Presbyterian Church, and the Psalms of David. Each man and boy carried his rifle and ammunition, and each woman her pistol.[1]

By 1785 there appear to have been twelve Presbyterian and eighteen Baptist churches established in Kentucky. That year John Taylor saw the first local revival to be recorded in the region. Two years later Baptist numbers were above 3,000, with their churches divided into three Associations, two of them Regular and one Separatist.

[1] Quoted in Henry Alexander White, *Southern Presbyterian Leaders* (New York, 1911), p. 207.

An element of mutual support clearly existed between Baptists and Presbyterians, for Robert Davidson, the Presbyterian historian of Kentucky, recorded the debt of Rice to John Gano in the early years when there was much cause for discouragement. Rice had been called to Kentucky by 300 Presbyterians, but while they supported him by their attendance at church, he was dismayed at the extent to which their Christianity was merely traditional, despite their certificates of communicant membership from former churches. Rice 'found scarcely one man, and but few women, who supported a credible profession of religion. Some were grossly ignorant of the first principles of religion . . . perhaps most of them totally ignorant of the forms of religion in their own houses.' It was the friendship of John Gano, the 'devout old Baptist preacher', according to Davidson, that 'reanimated' Rice at a time of depression and encouraged him to redouble his zeal and his labours. This led to 'a refreshing revival', both in Rice's and in other congregations around 1790.[1]

The local encouragement that was seen by Taylor, Rice, and others did not affect the general trend of decline in both religion and morals which marked the 1790s on the frontier. The population had multiplied far faster than the provision of churches. The conditions that led to the weakening of Christian influence in other parts of the Union were also in evidence in Kentucky. Peter Cartwright, who grew up in Logan County during this period, remarked that the county was nicknamed 'Rogues' Harbour' on account of those who had moved there to escape the consequences of their law-breaking in the East. As for the population in general, 'Sundays were days set apart for hunting, fishing, horse-racing, card-playing, balls, dances, and all kinds of jollity and mirth.'[2] In his history Davidson named two factors that hindered Christian testimony. First, controversy was prevalent within the churches: 'The Presbyterian churches were convulsed by a sharp dispute about Psalmody . . . while the Baptists were similarly occupied with wranglings between Regulars and Separates. Instead of husbanding their resources, the churches were impairing their

[1] Robert Davidson, *Presbyterian Church in Kentucky*, p. 68.
[2] W. P. Strickland (ed.), *The Backwoods Preacher: An Autobiography of Peter Cartwright* (London, 1859), pp. 5–6.

strength by intestine feuds and exposing their weakest points to the contempt of their enemies.'[1] This failure was probably connected with the second factor, the poor leadership given by some of the ministers. Many of them, because they were inadequately supported, gave too much time to their own maintenance. In Rice's words, 'the people starved the ministers and the ministers starved the people'. Although the number of ministers steadily increased, they were 'mediocre'. One preacher, according to Davidson, 'chilled and petrified every one that listened to him'; another 'was a good but weak man; punctual and steady, but an indifferent preacher'. Of the Presbyterian ministry in general in Kentucky in the early 1790s he concludes:

Had they all been men of marked ability, devoted piety, and unblemished reputation, the salutary influence they might have exerted in moulding the character and institutions of the growing West would have been incalculable. Unhappily, with two or three shining exceptions, the majority were men of barely respectable talents, and a few hardly above mediocrity; and so far from being patterns of flaming zeal and apostolic devotion, a dull formality seems to have been their general characteristic.

A more fatal mistake can scarcely be committed, than to suppose that a mere handful of half-educated, feeble-minded missionaries will do for the West.[2]

This assessment contrasts with the quality of the men who pioneered in Western Pennsylvania and, as we shall see in the outcome, it throws some light on the different courses which revival took in these two areas.

The Baptists and Presbyterians were soon followed into Kentucky by the Methodists who by 1792 had 2,235 members, if we include their Cumberland circuit which overlapped with Tennessee. Despite early reports of success, it appears that the Methodist itinerants made no more headway than anyone else; indeed Asbury, on his first visit in 1790 thought it was less, 'The Methodists do but little here – others lead the way.'[3] As for the people, 'not one in a hundred came here to get religion, but rather plenty of good land'.

---

[1] *Presbyterian Church in Kentucky*, p. 100.
[2] Ibid., pp. 129–30.   [3] *Journal and Letters*, vol. 1, p. 638.

It is commonly believed that the Great Revival in Kentucky began among the Presbyterians. William Sweet, a leading church historian of the frontier period from a Methodist background, remarked: 'It is an interesting fact that most of the great American revival movements have come largely through Presbyterianism, and the great Revival in the West is no exception.'[1] For the most part, the men who became the leaders were not the early associates of David Rice, but a younger generation who arrived during the 1790s, eight of whom were trained in Virginia under John Blair Smith or William Graham. These were men

whose hearts God had touched in the blessed revival of 1787–88, which commenced in Hampden-Sydney College and extended to Liberty Hall. Their education, and the training they had received in revivals and itinerant service, pre-eminently fitted them for the responsible positions they were called to occupy; and as we trace their connection with the subsequent history of the Church, we shall find the integrity and purity of the Presbyterian communion preserved, under God, mainly through the vigilance and fidelity of these men. One of the number indeed, strayed lamentably, but it was only a temporary delusion; his own naturally strong mind, and a radical principle of piety, assisted by the affectionate expostulations of his brethren, brought him back again to the truth. The rest never wavered for an instant. They all stood firm in the perilous hour, and intrepidly offered battle to the adversaries of the evangelical system; and their efforts were finally crowned with success.[2]

Another Presbyterian newcomer was James M'Gready who arrived from North Carolina in 1796 at the age of thirty-three. M'Gready had become a communicant in North Carolina at the age of seventeen. He later trained for the ministry under John McMillan in Western Pennsylvania, during which time he became convinced that he lacked personal experience of the gospel in which he thought he believed. His belief was orthodox, his outward practice correct, but 'when he came to examine *his feelings*, to try them by such passages as, being "filled with the Spirit; filled with joy; filled with the Holy Ghost; joy of the Holy Ghost; the fruit of the Spirit is love, joy, peace",

---

[1] *Religion on the American Frontier*, vol. 2, p. 84.
[2] *Presbyterian Church in Kentucky*, p. 104–5.

it seemed to him that he did not understand these things experimentally'.[1] His conversion from nominal Christianity which began in this way was to colour his future preaching. 'Formal professors had generally a very great dislike to him', according to Foote, because they could not remain comfortable under his searching words. From Western Pennsylvania he had travelled back to North Carolina through Hampden-Sydney at the time of the revival in the College, and soon afterwards he was prominent in the awakening already mentioned in North Carolina. One of his hearers testified: 'Such earnestness, such zeal, such powerful persuasion, enforced by the joys of heaven and miseries of hell, I had never witnessed before . . . His concluding remarks were addressed to the sinner to flee the wrath to come without delay. Never before had I comparatively felt the force of the truth. Such was my excitement that, had I been standing, I should have probably sunk to the floor under the impression.'[2]

M'Gready was called to Logan County in south Kentucky, where there were a number of his former hearers from North Carolina. As was customary, the three congregations he came to serve were named after the local geography, Red River, Muddy River, and Gasper River. The 'universal deadness and stupidity' which he found in the district led to the call to prayer which we noted in the last chapter. The first signs of a different spirit among the people were seen in the Gasper River congregation in 1797 when people began to ask, 'Is Christianity a felt thing? If I were converted would I feel and know it?' In the summer of 1798 there was some movement among all three congregations and M'Gready reported 'a very general awakening'. The spirit of prayer deepened and twelve months later it was apparent that a powerful work of conversion was in progress. At the Red River communion services at the end of July 1799 'many of the most bold and daring sinners of the country were brought to cover their faces and weep bitterly'. A month later the same 'heart-piercing conviction' was in evidence at services at Gasper River, some individuals being so overcome with emotion that they fell to the floor. Much more

[1] Foote, *Sketches of N.C.*, p. 369.
[2] Quoted in Boles, *The Great Revival*, pp. 39–40.

was to follow: M'Gready wrote:

The year 1800 exceeds all that our eyes ever beheld on earth. All the blessed displays of Almighty power and grace, all the sweet gales of the divine Spirit, and soul-reviving showers of the blessings of Heaven which we enjoyed before, and which we considered wonderful beyond conception, were but like a few scattering drops before a mighty rain, when compared with the overflowing floods of salvation, which the eternal, gracious Jehovah has poured out like a mighty river, upon this our guilty, unworthy country. The Lord has indeed shewed himself a prayer-hearing God: he has given his people a praying spirit and a lively faith, and then he has answered their prayers far beyond their highest expectations.[1]

*　　　*　　　*

By 1801 the revival had become general – northwards in Kentucky and southwards in Tennessee – and other denominations were quickly affected. On 20 October 1800 Asbury attended a Presbyterian service in Tennessee led by ministerial friends of M'Gready's, at which he estimated the number present to be 1,000. When the preaching continued the following day, the Methodist leader recorded, 'Methodists and Presbyterians united their labours . . . mercy flowed in abundant streams of salvation to perishing sinners . . . I rejoice that God is visiting the sons of the Puritans.'[2]

The years 1800–1801 witnessed the advent of a new phenomenon, 'the camp-meeting'. This originated among the Presbyterians and was initially a development brought about only by a practical necessity. Following the Scottish tradition, the Lord's Supper was administered infrequently in Presbyterian churches, but the occasion was marked by special services

---

[1] M'Gready's *Short Narrative of the Revival of Religion in Logan County, in the State of Kentucky, and the adjacent Settlements in the State of Tennessee, from May 1797, until September 1800* was published in four instalments in the *New York Missionary Magazine*, 1802. A briefer account is given in a 'Letter to a Friend', dated 23 October 1801, *The Posthumous Works of James M'Gready*, ed. James Smith, (Louisville, Kentucky, 1831), vol. 1, pp. ix-xvi. It is unclear what document Asbury possessed when, at the earlier date of 20 October 1801, he notes in his Journal: 'I read James M'Gready's narrative of the work of God in Logan County, Kentucky'.

[2] *Journal and Letters*, vol. 2, pp. 257–8.

which were often attended by visitors from other congregations who would be offered hospitality for the four or five days of the communion season. When numbers increased these services had to be held in the open air, and once the revival began the provision of hospitality became entirely inadequate. Wagons and tents were therefore brought into use for overnight shelter. At the communion services held at Gasper River in July 1800, M'Gready made it known beforehand that visitors should come prepared to camp on the ground. Attendance at these services was unprecedented, some travelling distances of forty or even 100 miles, and the communion season became 'the camp meeting'. These occasions quickly multiplied and, becoming interdenominational in character, were later called 'general camp meetings'. That term does not appear to have been applied to perhaps the best-remembered of the meetings, a Presbyterian communion season at Cane Ridge, Bourbon County, in August 1801. In addition to eighteen Presbyterian ministers, Baptist and Methodist preachers also took part in the services which lasted for a week. A temporary village of tents, 'laid off in regular streets', was estimated to shelter between 10,000 and 21,000 people. A man in Lexington, Kentucky, described the Cane Ridge gatherings in a letter to his sister in Philadelphia, dated 7 August 1801:

I arrived there on Saturday about 10 o'clock: I then began to note some of the extraordinary particulars: I first proceeded to count the wagons containing families, with their provisions, camp equipage, etc to the number of 147: at 11 o'clock the quantity of ground occupied by horses, waggons, etc was about the same size as the square between Market, Chestnut, Second and Third-streets, of Philadelphia – There was at this place a stage erected in the woods, about 100 yards from the place of the meeting-house, where there were a number of Presbyterian and Methodist ministers; one of the former preaching to as many as could get near enough to hear – in the house also, was another of the same denomination, preaching to a crowded audience – at the same time another large concourse of people collected about 100 yards in an east direction from the meeting-house, hearing a Methodist speaker – and about 150 yards in a fourth course from the house was an assembly of black people, hearing the exhortations of the blacks, some of whom appeared deeply convicted, and others converted. The number of communicants who received tokens were 750, nor was there a sufficiency of them – these tokens are small pieces of lead, the size of a five-penny bit, with the letter A or B impressed thereon, and are distributed by ministers to the members of the several churches, not excluding any baptists who apply for them.[1]

Many other eyewitness accounts of these open-air communion services confirm the enormous numbers who assembled. It is clear from the number of recorded communicants that a large majority of the people were not members of churches. At another communion season (camp meeting), although 8,000 people were estimated to be present, only 350 of them were communicants, and at another gathering, said to number 5,000, only 300. When it is remembered that the population of Lexington, Kentucky's largest town, was only 1,797 (including 439 slaves) in 1800, the percentage of the community being arrested by the awakening can be better judged. Of course, the crowd figures given by those present were only conjectures, but the writer quoted above was not alone in counting wagons and estimating the size of the ground in use. When every allowance has been made for exaggeration, there remain indications enough that the meetings were extraordinary in their size. For a time, a concern to hear preaching gripped a major part of the population. In the words of Robert Davidson: 'Business of all kinds was suspended; dwelling houses were deserted; whole neighbourhoods emptied; bold hunters and sober matrons, young men, maidens, and little children, flocked to the common centre of attraction; every difficulty was surmounted, every risk ventured, to be present at the camp-meeting.'[2]

Another first-hand account can be found in the diary of the Rev. John Lyle, a fellow student with Archibald Alexander under William Graham, who had moved to Kentucky. His description of events in and around Lexington in June 1801 shows that services were being carried on simultaneously at many places among different denominations, with people sometimes remaining far into the night. Lyle also provides a full account of the Cane Ridge communion services of August 1801, quoted above, where services were held concurrently in different parts of the camp as well as in the meeting-house. From the meeting-house, where he found a minister exhorting,

---

[1] John Lyle, quoted in Woodward, *Surprising Accounts*, p. 57.
[2] *Presbyterian Church in Kentucky*, p. 136.

he noted how he went to hear one of the Presbyterians in the open air, and then returned to the full meeting-house where another sermon was in progress with a different speaker. Of the large congregation in the meeting-house, 'Many appeared to be Methodists, they shouted before he was done, but afterwards they shook hands and got into a singing extasy.'[1]

The number of those who professed to have become Christians at this time further confirms the extent of the revival. M'Gready reported that 330 persons known to him in various locations had professed conversion in 1800, and 144 in the first ten months of 1801. Scarcely any of these, he wrote in October 1801, have 'given us any ground to doubt their religion'.[2] Other areas, he believed, saw 'the conversion of hundreds of precious souls'.

David Benedict believed that the Kentucky revival had its origins among Baptist churches in Boone County on the Ohio River in 1799.[3] Possibly, he was unaware of details of the movement among the Presbyterians at the southern end of the state or, more probably, the Great Revival began almost simultaneously in the two areas. The Methodist William McKendree, writing in Kentucky on 10 October 1802, referred to 'a great ingathering among the Baptists' which had occurred 'about two years ago'. George Baxter, in the Fall of 1801, learned that 'last winter appearances were favorable among Baptists and great numbers were added to their churches'.[4]

Baptist records confirm these words. The Great Crossing church recorded a 'cold condition' between 1795 and 1800 when only six new members were added 'through experience and baptism' (that is they were not new settlers from the East). But 175 members were brought in during 1800 and 186 the following year. The South Elkhorn church had apparently made no numerical progress since its removal from Virginia in

---

[1] The manuscript of the diary of John Lyle (June 1801 to July 1803) is in the possession of the Kentucky Historical Society, Frankfort, Kentucky. Quotations are from excerpts published in Catherine Cleveland, *The Great Revival in the West 1797–1805* (Gloucester, Mass., 1959), appendices 4 and 5.

[2] *Posthumous Works*, vol. 1, pp. xv–xvi.

[3] *Baptist Denomination in America*, vol. 2, p. 251. There is variation in the figures quoted by different writers.

[4] Woodward, *Surprising Accounts*, p. 106.

1781, as its membership stood at 127 at the end of the century, but during the revival period its congregation saw 318 baptized. Among the other churches, Bryant's reported 367 additions, Clear Creek 326, and there were smaller but significant numbers in many more. The Elkhorn Association, which included the churches of Boone County, consisted of twenty-seven churches, made up of 1,642 members, in 1800. Its printed minutes of 8 August 1801 showed a gain of 3,011 members in one year. By 1802 its number of churches had risen to forty-eight. Commenting on the association, J. N. Bradley wrote: 'During the Great Revival many were added to the church who afterwards were influential members and occupied positions, not only in the church, but also in our denomination at large in the community.'[1] Elsewhere in Kentucky there was similar growth among the Baptists. Towards the end of 1800 it was said that revival began suddenly in the Sandy Creek Association. The membership figures for all six Baptist associations in Kentucky show an increase from 4,766 to 13,569 between 1800 and 1802.[2]

Methodist weakness in Kentucky has already been noted, and it remained so at the beginning of the nineteenth century. 'It is plain there are not many mighty among the Methodists in Kentucky', Asbury wrote when he was there in October 1800 and left William McKendree as the new presiding elder of the Kentucky district. It must have been soon after this that the same great change began in Methodist congregations. We hear of it affecting Methodists in the eastern part of the state by the early summer of 1801.[3] At the Western Conference of September 1801, convened for the churches of Tennessee, Kentucky and Ohio, Asbury noted the non-attendance of 'our brethren in Kentucky' on the grounds of 'the greatness of the work of God'. Abel Stevens remarked on the 'unprecedented

---

[1] *Elkhorn Association: Minutes of 1875*, quoted Strickland, *Great American Revival*, p. 95.

[2] John B. Boles, *Religion in Antebellum Kentucky* (Lexington: University Press of Kentucky, 1976), p. 29.

[3] Col. Robert Patterson wrote of 'the extraordinary work' beginning in that area in May 1801 which 'is not altogether confined to the Presbyterian Society, it appears among the Methodists and Baptists' (quoted in Cleveland, *Great Revival in West*, pp. 196–201).

vigor' that appeared in the Kentucky churches at this time and wrote of conditions by the time the Western Conference met in 1802: 'The mere handful of members, scattered here and there in the settlements, now numbered at least eight thousand, having increased more than five thousand in the last two years'.[1] Stevens' figure is on the high side, though not by a great deal. Peter Cartwright gives the membership of the churches comprising the Western Conference as 7,201 for the Fall of 1802. But the growth was clearly phenomenal. 'We have added three thousand this year', Asbury noted at the Western Conference just mentioned. At the Conferences of 1803 and 1804 the increases were 1,500 and 2,400 respectively. A letter by William McKendree confirms the extent of the change in his district. He attended meetings extending from two to four days for over thirteen weekends in succession and reported: 'Our congregations were generally large, (in places where fifty formerly made a respectable congregation, a thousand is now a tolerable gathering) and blessed by God we were generally favoured with distinguishing marks of the divine presence.'[2] It is not surprising to find Asbury saying in a letter of 16 August 1804, 'Kentucky, which was a few years [ago] a dangerous frontier, is the centre of the western front of our empire where we behold a second part of the new world.'

*   *   *

A religious change of this extent could not take place without being seen by the whole community, and the transformation was a matter of general comment. One man visiting Lexington in October 1802 heard 'of but little else than the great revival of religion'. Another wrote on 25 December 1802: 'It is a very comfortable thing to be in a country where religion has obtained the pre-eminent influence.'[3] One of the most widely circulated contemporary accounts was written by the Rev. George Baxter, successor to William Graham in the teaching work in Lexington, Virginia. Baxter described his extended

[1] *American Methodism*, pp. 404–5.
[2] Letter of 10 October 1802, quoted in Cleveland, *Great Revival in West*, pp. 202–5.
[3] Boles, *The Great Revival*, p. 68.

visit to Kentucky in the autumn of 1801, in a letter to Archibald Alexander, dated 1 January 1802:

The power with which this revival has spread, and its influence in moralizing the people, are difficult for you to conceive of, and more difficult for me to describe . . . On my way to Kentucky, I was told by settlers on the road, that the character of Kentucky travellers was entirely changed, and that they were now as distinguished for sobriety as they had formerly been for dissoluteness; and indeed, I found Kentucky the most moral place I had ever been in; a profane expression was hardly heard; a religious awe seemed to pervade the country; and some deistical characters had confessed that from whatever cause the revival might originate, it certainly made the people better . . .

Upon the whole, sir, I think the revival in Kentucky among the most extraordinary that have ever visited the Church of Christ, and, all things considered, peculiarly adapted to the circumstances of that country. Infidelity was triumphant, and religion at the point of expiring. Something of an extraordinary nature seemed necessary to arrest the attention of a giddy people, who were ready to conclude that Christianity was a fable, and futurity a dream.[1]

Perhaps the most important assessment of the revival from the Presbyterian side comes from a sermon preached by the patriarchal and long-experienced David Rice at the Synod of Kentucky in 1803. We restrict our quotation to his main points. They provide a good conclusion to this chapter:

1 This revival has made its appearance in various places, without any extraordinary means to produce it. The preaching, the singing, the praying, have been the same to which people had been long accustomed, and under which they had hardened to a great degree; and the first symptoms of the revival have been a praying spirit in the few pious people found among us.

2 As far as I can see, there appears to be in the subjects of this work a deep heart-humbling sense of the great unreasonableness, abominable nature, pernicious effects and deadly consequences of sin; and the absolute unworthiness in the sinful creature of the smallest crumb of mercy from the hand of a holy God. There appears to be in them a deep mourning on account of their own sins, the sins of their fellow professors, and the sins of the careless and profane, and

---

[1] The whole letter is in Woodward, *Surprising Accounts*, pp. 105–13 and, in part, in Ernest Trice Thompson, *Presbyterians in the South* (Richmond, John Knox Press, 1963), vol. 1, pp. 138–9.

particularly for the base sin of ingratitude to God for his many mercies; and conviction of the justice of God in condemning and punishing his offending creatures.

3 They appear to have a lively and very affecting view of the infinite condescension and love of God the Father, in giving his eternal and only-begotten Son for the redemption of mankind; and of the infinite love of the Redeemer, manifested in the great and gracious work of redemption; manifested in the labors and sorrows of his life and of his death: an affecting view of the astonishing goodness of the adorable Trinity.

4 They seem to me to have a very deep and affecting sense of the worth of precious immortal souls, ardent love to them, and an agonizing concern for their conviction, conversion and complete salvation . . . This love, this compassion, this ardent desire, this agonizing, this fervent pleading for the salvation of sinful men and for Zion's prosperity, far exceed any thing I have ever seen. This love, these fervent supplications, are not confined to a particular spot or a particular party. They extend to and include men of every description: Catholics and Protestants, Jews, Moham-medans and Pagans. The most savage nations, who are sunk almost beneath the notice of others, are embraced in the arms of their benevolence . . . O thou Fountain of mercy, give me, give to all, this spirit of love, of grace and of supplication!

5 A considerable number of individuals appear to me to be greatly reformed in their morals. This is undoubtedly the case within the sphere of my particular acquaintance. Yea, some neighborhoods, noted for their vicious and profligate manners, are now as much noted for their piety and good order. Drunkards, profane swearers, liars, quarrelsome persons, etc., are remarkably re-formed. The songs of the drunkard are exchanged for the songs of Zion; fervent prayer succeeds in the room of profane oaths and curses; the lying tongue has learned to speak truth in the fear of God, and the contentious firebrand is converted into a lover of peace. . .

6 A number of families, who had lived apparently without the fear of God, in folly and in vice, without any religious instruction or any proper government, are now reduced to order, and are daily joining in the worship of God, reading his word, singing his praises, and offering up their supplications to a throne of grace . . .

7 The subjects of this work appear to be very sensible of the necessity of *Sanctification* as well as Justification, and that 'without holiness no man can see the Lord;' to be greatly desirous that they themselves and 'all that name the name of Christ should depart

from iniquity,' should recommend the religion of Jesus to the consciences and esteem of their fellow men, that the light of their holy conversation should so shine before men that they, seeing their good works, might give glory to God. A heaven of perfect purity and the full enjoyment of God appears to be the chief and ultimate object of their desire and pursuit.

Now I have given you my reasons for concluding the *morning is come*, and that we are blessed with a real revival of the benign, the heaven-born religion of Jesus Christ, which demands our grateful acknowledgments to God the Father, Son and Holy Ghost.[1]

[1] *A Sermon on the Present Revival of Religion, Preached at the Opening of the Kentucky Synod* (Lexington, Ken., 1803).

7

THE EMERGENCE OF REVIVALISM

A Common Scene in Kentucky after 1800

7

There was another side of the revival in Kentucky, a side to which so much attention has often been given that the whole work has tended to be discredited in terms of excess and emotionalism. But if the excesses in Kentucky have been exaggerated by some writers, their existence cannot be questioned, and they had major consequences for subsequent evangelical history.

All awakenings begin with the return of a profound conviction of sin.[1] From attitudes of indifference, or of cold religious formality, many are suddenly brought by the hearing of the truth to a concern and distress so strong that it may even be accompanied by temporary physical collapse. The phenomenon of hearers falling prostrate during a service or crying out in anguish is not uncommon at the outset of revivals. It happened during the Great Awakening and, to some extent, in Virginia in the 1770s and 1780s. A revival is, by its very nature, bound to be attended by emotional excitement. But the course of a revival, together with its purity and abiding fruit, is directly related to the manner in which such excitement is handled by its leaders. Once the idea gains acceptance that the degree of the Spirit's work is to be measured by the strength of emotion, or that physical effects of any kind are proofs of God's action,

---

[1] 'All great religious awakenings begin in the dawning of the august and terrible aspects of the Deity upon the popular mind, and they reach their height and happy consummation, in that love and faith for which the antecedent fear has been the preparation'. William G. T. Shedd, *Sermons to the Natural Man* (New York, 1876; Edinburgh: Banner of Truth, 1977), p. 331.

then what is rightly called fanaticism is bound to follow. For those who embrace such beliefs will suppose that any check on emotion or on physical phenomena is tantamount to opposing the Holy Spirit.

The Presbyterian ministers among whom the work began were the first to be put to the test on this score. One of the first indications of impending trouble occurred among some 400 or 500 of M'Gready's people assembled at the Red River church in June 1800 for four days of services in connection with the administration of the Lord's Supper. Three Presbyterian ministers were present besides M'Gready and a Methodist named John McGee from Tennessee, who was a brother of one of the Presbyterians. At the final service on the Monday there was an outcry from a woman present during the sermon. After the service had concluded, while some prepared to go home, the majority remained seated in silence. McGee then rose in the pulpit and indicated that it was his turn to preach. But, he assured the people, One much greater than he was already preaching in their midst. Similar words brought general shouts of praise from some in the congregation, led, it seems, by the woman who had cried out earlier. While the other ministers sat uncertain as to what to do in the mounting excitement and confusion, McGee began to descend from the pulpit to exhort among the people. As he did so, one of his Presbyterian brethren warned him of the danger of encouraging emotionalism, and the visitor from Tennessee hesitated: in his own words, 'I turned to go back, and was near falling; the power of God was strong upon me, I turned again, and losing sight of all the fear of man, I went through the house shouting and exhorting with all possible ecstasy and energy, and the floor was soon covered with the slain', that is by people who had collapsed.[1]

Of the physical phenomena attending the revival that of 'falling' became the most common. People dropped 'as if shot dead' and they might lie, unable to rise, conscious, or unconscious, for an hour or for much longer. Some fell who had previously been sceptical of everything. Many – 150, 250, even 800 – were recorded as falling during camp meetings. Others

---

[1] John McGee, *Methodist Magazine*, 4, p. 190; quoted in Boles, *The Great Revival*, p. 54.

fell while hastening from services. One case Lyle records was that of an elder who had scorned the phenomenon and yet became subject to it himself: 'When we got to him he was not speechless. I asked what was the matter, if he found himself a sinner, yes he said what he never before believed to be a reality. He found himself to be a great sinner. He groaned deeply but talked sensibly.'

The potential for disorder increased when the numbers assembling necessitated open-air gatherings and camp meetings. While some degree of control could be exercised in a meeting-house, when thousands were assembled in makeshift villages of tents and wagons the difficulty of maintaining any kind of order was virtually insuperable. The reasons that brought the crowds together were not necessarily spiritual ones. As W. B. Posey wrote: 'The camp meeting's appeal was not just to the spirit of man hungering after righteousness but to his gregarious nature seeking surcease from the loneliness and hardship of the frontier.'[1] Others present at camp meetings, such as sellers of liquor, were there from less innocent motives.

Presbyterian ministers were divided in their response to the physical phenomena that were attending many services by the summer of 1801. The Rev. James Finley (nephew of an earlier president of Princeton College), writing in the Fall of that year, was hopeful that excesses could be controlled: 'The work of the Lord appears to be progressing, though attended with some enthusiasm. But this is generally confined to the grossly ignorant; for whom we must make every apology, as they are just emerging, as it were, out of heathenish darkness.' Some of the excitement, Finley could see, was to be understood in purely natural terms. It reminded him of the excess shown by some at the beginning of the War of Independence in 1776, 'so is human nature everywhere; sitting up whole nights is extravagant, but you cannot bid them quit, or you need not'. On the whole, he was rather uncertain of the right response to the unusual at this date: 'The falling down of multitudes, and their crying out (which happened under the singing of Watts' hymns, more frequently than under the preaching of the word)

---

[1] *Frontier Mission: A History of Religion West of the Appalachians* (Lexington: University of Kentucky Press, 1966), p. 25.

was to us so new a scene, that we thought it prudent not to be over hasty in forming any opinion of it.'[1]

Moses Hoge on 10 September 1801 reported the words of another minister in Kentucky:

In time of preaching, if care is taken, there is but little confusion: when that is over, and the singing, and praying and exhorting begins, the audience is thrown into what I call real disorder. The careless fall down, cry out, tremble and not infrequently are affected with convulsive twitchings. Among these the pious are very busy, singing, praying, conversing, falling down in extacies, fainting with joy . . . A number, too, are wrought upon in the usual way, and hopefully get religion without any of these extraordinary appearances.[2]

Other ministers, however, were entirely uncritical. Richard M'Nemar was one of the foremost among them. It did not trouble him at all that 'meetings exhibited nothing to the spectator but a scene of confusion that could scarce be put into human language'. He describes scenes of great excitement which 'would continue for several days and nights together', and had no doubt that it was all of God. He gives us details of two camp meetings in May and early June 1801. At the second he supposed 4,000 people to be present, with seven Presbyterian ministers:

The meeting continued five days, and four nights; and after the people generally scattered from the ground, numbers convened in different places, and continued the exercise much longer. And even where they were not collected together, these wonderful operations continued among every class of people, and in every situation; in their houses and fields, and in their daily employments, falling down and crying out, under conviction, or singing and shouting with unspeakable joy, were so common, that the whole country round about, seemed to be leavened with the spirit of the work.[3]

A number of Presbyterians tried to check the emotionalism that was becoming confused with the work of God. John Lyle recorded of a service in Lexington in June 1801:

I prayed against enthusiasm and in my sermon gave marks of true

---

[1] Quoted in Woodward, *Surprising Accounts*, pp. 53–4.
[2] Ibid., p. 55. The overuse of singing clearly encouraged the high emotion.
[3] Richard M'Nemar, *The Kentucky Revival; or, A Short History of the Late Extraordinary Outpouring of the Spirit of God* (New York, 1846), pp. 24–5.

illumination and true faith, mentioned the parable of the Tares, exhorted them to guard against enthusiasm &c. that it like a worm destroyed the beauty of a revival and would ere long discredit the work of God. I said people and ministers might go wrong, referred to the history of Whitefield's day &c, &c. Davenport's retractions respecting himself and those who followed him.[1]

Two months later, hearing M'Nemar and others at the Cane Ridge camp meeting, Lyle was certain that the danger had increased: 'I expect the conduct of these hot-headed men and the effect of their doctrine will separate the church of Christ and quench the revival.' With one exception (Robert Marshall), all the young Virginian ministers trained at Hampden-Sydney and Liberty Hall stood against any encouragement of excitement and against the identification of 'bodily exercises' with spiritual experiences. They noted that some who 'fell' had within months gone back to the world, and supported 'Father' Rice when he took the lead in trying to prevent excess. In the Fall of 1801 Rice proposed rules for the ordering of camp meetings and, according to Lyle, 'exhorted powerfully against noise and false exercise'.[2] Robert Davidson records a memory of Rice passed on to him by a woman who, as a child, was present in one of the services at the time of the revival. She recalled that from her seat in the gallery

she looked down upon the body of the building, where a great crowd were collected, some praying, some singing, and some going through the bodily agitations. While she gazed in wonder, Father Rice rose in the pulpit, with his commanding form and his silver locks, and in the most solemn manner began to repeat those words of Scripture, 'HOLY! HOLY! HOLY! IS THE LORD GOD ALMIGHTY!' Never was anything more impressive. There was an instantaneous hush through the whole house. The venerable old patriarch having thus secured their attention, proceeded to express his sentiments on the Bodily Exercises, and to dissuade from encouraging them.[3]

The incident confirms Posey's belief that 'The attitude and behaviour of the preacher affected the incidence of these

---

[1] On this subject see my *Jonathan Edwards: A New Biography* (Edinburgh: Banner of Truth, 1987), pp. 216–56.
[2] Davidson, *Presbyterian Church in Kentucky*, p. 161.
[3] Ibid., p.161

displays of nervous agitation'.[1] Similarly, Cleveland observed: 'Those opposed to the excitement soon realized that the attitude of the preacher has a great influence upon the character of the meeting. A peremptory command from him upon the first appearance of undue excitement sufficed in most cases to quiet those affected, and prevented contagion.'[2] But too few were willing to believe that not everything was of the Holy Spirit and so the tide could not be stemmed. Rice, Lyle, and others were dubbed 'anti-revival' men, whereas had Rice's advice been followed 'shocking disorders might have been prevented and the revival have gone on with greater purity, power and splendor'.[3] Many of the popular leaders either did nothing to prevent excess or acted as though the physical phenomena – 'the falling exercise' and other things – were miraculous. This is not to say that all the vast gatherings had degenerated into confusion by the Fall of 1801. George Baxter speaks of attending three sacramental seasons in October: 'At each there were supposed to be four or five thousand people, and everything was conducted with strict propriety. When persons fell, those who were near took care of them, and everything continued quiet until the worship was concluded.'

John B. Boles believes that the physical 'exercises,' including 'twitchings' or 'jerks', and dancing, 'which have been cited widely to discredit the revival, were probably restricted to a comparative few'.[4] While that may be true, it is evident that there was much unrestrained emotionalism in a number of places from 1801 and that it attained such popular support that it could not be checked. In the general camp meetings attempts at control were often abandoned. Since in a concourse of people no one preacher could possibly be heard, many simultaneous meetings became the pattern, with spectators wandering in between, 'confused and careless, talking and laughing'.[5] Voices, hymns, and shouts were blended in a sound 'like the roar of Niagara'. Lyle even heard preachers call on people to

---

[1] *Frontier Mission*, p. 27.
[2] *Great Revival in West*, p. 125.
[3] Davidson, *Presbyterian Church in Kentucky*, p. 160.
[4] *Great Revival*, p. 68.
[5] Davidson, *Presbyterian Church in Kentucky*, p. 160. For other quotations from Lyle see Cleveland, *Great Revival in West*, appendices 4 and 5.

cry aloud because God 'can hear us, should we all speak at once'. Further, those who believed that a new age of the miraculous had dawned came to regard men regularly set aside to preach as no longer necessary. The people themselves, now endowed with visions, dreams, and prophecies, could all minister to one another. M'Nemar described this wonderful new 'freedom':

All distinction of names was laid aside, and it was no matter what any one had been called before, if now he stood in the present light and felt his heart glow with love to the souls of men; he was welcome to sing, pray, or call sinners to repentance. Neither was there any distinction, as to age, sex, color, or anything of a temporary nature; old and young, male and female, black and white, had equal privilege to minister the light which they received, in whatever way the Spirit directed.[1]

In 1803 the Presbyterian Synod was about to examine the teaching of M'Nemar and other men when the suspects and three other ministers left to form a presbytery of their own. According to M'Nemar, a spirit of persecution had forced them to take this step; yet their 'sufferings', he went on to say

were not a little alleviated by the many extraordinary signs and gifts of the Spirit, through which they were encouraged to look for brighter days. Among these innumerable signs and gifts, may be ranked, The spirit of prophesy – Being caught up or carried away in this spirit, and remaining for hours insensible of anything in nature – Dreaming of dreams – Seeing visions – Hearing unspeakable words – The fragrant smell and delightful singing in the breast. This spirit of prophesy is particularly worthy of notice; which had its foundation in a peculiar kind of faith, and grew up under the special influence of visions, dreams, &c. The first thing was to believe what God had promised, with an appropriating faith – cast anchor upon the thing promised though unseen; and hold the soul to the pursuit of it, in defiance of all the tossing billows of unbelief. This faith so contrary to the carnal heart, they concluded must be of God. It must be the Spirit of Christ, or God working in the creature, both to will and to do. What is the promise, but the purpose of God? Upon this principle, all were encouraged to believe the promise, and immediately set out, in co-operation with the promiser; and in proportion to the strength of their

[1] *Kentucky Revival*, p. 31.

faith, to predict the certain accomplishment of that purpose of God which they felt within them.[1]

With such ideas in circulation and urged on by impetuous and immature preachers, it is no wonder that Kentucky came close to being a maelstrom of confusion. Too many, in the opinion of Rice, 'were like a parcel of boys suddenly tumbled out of a boat, who had been unaccustomed to swim, and knew not the way to the shore. Some fixed upon one error, and some upon another'. From these conditions, it has been said, the Kentucky Baptists largely escaped. Certainly, none of their leaders is known to have treated 'bodily exercises' as evidence of the Spirit's power and this was salutary. But it is clear from David Benedict, who was in Kentucky in 1809–10, that the Baptist Associations soon had difficulties and controversies enough:[2] Of the Elkhorn Association in particular, he says that 'perilous times have succeeded' the 'joyful scenes' of the early years of the revival.

While the unity of the Methodists seems to have been largely unaffected, for reasons yet to be noted, the Presbyterians were virtually shattered by divisions. A number existed among the latter who were prepared to receive any new teaching provided it was preached warmly enough, and they criticized those who did not share their enthusiasm as cold or dead: 'The more sober and discreet were now stigmatized as *Anti-Revival* men. They were denounced as "hindrances to the work", as "standing in the way" . . . "Father" Rice was singled out as the chief offender. The *Revival* men, meanwhile, as the other party styled themselves, affected a kind of holy superiority.'[3]

A number of years were to pass before the full effects of this were worked out. One Presbyterian minister became a Quaker; another finally took his people into union with Alexander Campbell's Disciples of Christ; M'Nemar and two others went the full distance into delusion to become Shakers and

[1] *Kentucky Revival*, pp. 67–8.
[2] *Baptist Denomination in America*, vol. 2, pp. 230–57. Speaking of one of the most common of the phenomena, he wrote: 'These jerking exercises were rather a curse than a blessing. None were benefited by them. They left sinners without reformation and Christians without advantage. Some had periodical fits of them seven or eight years after they were first taken.'
[3] Gillett, *Presbyterian Church in U.S.*, vol. 2, pp. 172–3.

supporters of Ann Lee's prophecies; three formed the nucleus for what became the Cumberland Presbyterian Church (the first Presbyterian denomination to reject a Calvinistic confession of faith); while others, including M'Gready and Marshall, who had been temporarily carried away, finally remained with their brethren. In the course of all these changes the membership of the Presbyterian church fell dramatically.

It can thus be seen that no balanced assessment of the revival in Kentucky was possible until some time after the event.

Benedict concluded his account of the revival with the words: 'On the whole, it appears there was in Kentucky in 1799, and for two or three succeeding years, a precious work of grace. Towards the close of it, a set of men arose, who attempted to carry the work farther than the Lord had done; and among them were exhibited those astonishing scenes of fanaticism we have described.'[1] In 1846 Archibald Alexander gave his final verdict on the subject on which his friend George Baxter had first written to him in 1802:

Many facts which occurred at the close of the revival, were of such a nature, that judicious men were fully persuaded that there was much that was wrong in the manner of conducting the work, and that an erratic and enthusiastic spirit prevailed to a lamentable extent. It is not doubted, however, that the Spirit of God was really poured out, and that many sincere converts were made, especially in the commencement of the revival; but too much indulgence was given to a heated imagination, and too much stress was laid on the bodily affections, which *accompanied the work*, as though these were supernatural phenomena, intended to arouse the attention of a careless world . . .

Thus, what was really a bodily infirmity, was considered to be a supernatural means of awakening and convincing infidels, and other irreligious persons. And the more these bodily affections were encouraged, the more they increased, until at length they assumed the appearance of a formidable nervous disease, which was manifestly contagious, as might be proved by many well-attested facts.

Some of the disastrous results of this religious excitement were, – 1st. A spirit of error, which led many, among whom were some Presbyterian ministers, who had before maintained a good character, far astray.

[1] *Baptist Denomination in America*, vol. 2, pp. 256–7.

2dly. A spirit of schism; a considerable number of the subjects and friends of the revival, separated from the Presbyterian Church, and formed a new body, which preached and published a very loose and erroneous system of theology; and though a part of these schismatics, when the excitement had subsided, returned again to the bosom of the Church, others continued to depart farther from the orthodox system, in which they had been educated, and which they had long professed and preached . . .

3dly. A spirit of wild enthusiasm was enkindled, under the influence of which, at least three pastors of Presbyterian churches in Kentucky, and some in Ohio, went off and joined the Shakers. Husbands and wives who had lived happily together were separated, and their children given up to be educated in this most enthusiastic society. I forbear to mention names, for the sake of the friends of these deluded men and women. And the truth is – and it should not be concealed – that the general result of this great excitement, was an almost total desolation of the Presbyterian churches in Kentucky and part of Tennessee.[1]

Alexander's emphasis was occasioned by his belief that the terrible mistakes of 1800 were being repeated as he wrote.

Other Presbyterian writers have emphasized the permanent good which was done. Dr Thomas Cleland, a Kentuckian, wrote in 1834: 'The work at first was no doubt a glorious work of God. Many within my knowledge became hopefully pious, the most of whom continue unto this present day, and many are fallen asleep in Jesus. The number of apostates was much fewer than I supposed.'[2] William Martin, another contemporary witness, concluded in 1843 that 'the great revival of religion which took place in this country in 1800 (and continued several years)' was 'the most extraordinary in many respects that has been witnessed in modern times' and that notwithstanding the fanaticism which he saw 'much good appears to have been done'.[3] Boles, a modern historian, gives this verdict:

---

[1] Alexander's letter was first published in the *Watchman and Observer* and reprinted in the *Presbyterian Magazine*, ed. C. Van Rensselaer (Philadelphia, 1855), pp. 225–6. In 1830, when the population of Kentucky was 700,000, regular members of the Presbyterian Church in the state were reckoned at around 10,000 (W. W. Sweet, *Religion on the American Frontier*, vol. 2, p. 33).

[2] Quoted in Humphrey, *Revival Sketches*, p. 190.

[3] Quoted in Cleveland, *Great Revival in the West*, p. 129.

The Great Revival altered the course of Kentucky and southern history . . . evangelical Protestantism, especially in its Baptist and Methodist varieties, was placed on such a foundation that never again was Protestant dominance threatened in the South . . . Much that is associated with the southern character may be linked to conservative religion, and the Great Revival, beginning in Kentucky, and spreading into the remainder of the South, was largely responsible.[1]

*   *   *

Hysteria was the chaff attending the awakening in Kentucky and such has been the attention drawn to it that it has tended to dominate all subsequent discussions. Even those who have read little on the subject have gained an abiding impression from artists' portrayals of disorderly camp meetings. But hysteria was not the only chaff; there were more permanent evils which belong to this same period and at them we must now look.

The first of these evils was the sudden growth of new denominations, all claiming to represent true religion. Instead of the few church bodies of 1800, there was, within a short period, what has been called 'a sea of sectarian rivalries'. Some of the new groupings, such as the Marshallites, the Cumberland Presbyterians, and the Disciples of Christ, were close enough to the older denominations to be able to draw away members without the departure of their beliefs from historic Christianity being too apparent. Others, such as the Mormons and the Shakers, made no claims for continuity but simply saw themselves as custodians of truth miraculously received from heaven.[2] The stage was being set in the West for a growing confusion in which, as Philip Schaff later deplored, 'Every

---

[1] *Religion in Antebellum Kentucky*, pp. 29–30.

[2] The Shakers were a sect founded in Britain in 1747. Ann Lee, their most notable convert, emigrated to America. Her disciples grew considerably in Kentucky after 1800. For a contemporary account of the Shakers see Timothy Dwight, *Travels in New England and New York*, vol. 3, (1822), pp. 152–69. Lee 'professed that she was able to work miracles and that she was endued with the power to speak in tongues . . . They hold all books to be useless, except that which they have published themselves'.

theological vagabond and peddler may drive here his bungling trade.'[1]

On a superficial view this fragmentation may seem enough to discredit any belief in the revival as God-given. Such belief has always appealed to the evidence that the genuine work of the Holy Spirit always unifies churches by a common faith in the Bible and by the deepening of a catholicity of spirit. How, then, can such a belief be harmonized with the disruption which came to Kentucky after 1800?

The answer is that, powerful though such a revival was, it did not obliterate other influences which were working concurrently in American history. The 'heathenish darkness' of many before the awakening did not mean that people's minds were a blank as far as *all* ideas were concerned. The War of Independence had not only established a new form of government it had given rise to a whole ferment of thought which could not readily be contained in the existing moulds and channels. The War had been a successful appeal against the old order. If men are naturally equal, then it seemed to follow that the judgment of the common man would hold sway in the future. Democracy had begun to change the whole orientation of society. Together with the assertion of the right of private judgment, there came a new faith that majorities were right. Confidence was now to be put in the view and decision of the majority – 'populism' – rather than in the judgment of history or of the educated few.

The Second Great Awakening broke into this historical process. To a major extent, it gave men the Bible as their guide instead of the goddess Reason whose reign had begun in France. But the experience of Kentucky also demonstrated what could happen where men and women who were untaught in the Bible decided its meaning for themselves. Such people, while claiming the Bible as their only authority, could all too easily be carried away by things to which Scripture gives no sanction. And while they supposed they were following their own judgment, the fact might be that they were the victims of demagogues who knew how to manipulate populist opinion. Commenting on the dangers of camp meetings, Richard Furman, the Baptist leader

---

[1] B. Thompson and G. H. Bricker (eds.), *The Principle of Protestantism* (1845); quoted in Nathan O. Hatch, *The Democratization of American Christianity* (New Haven: Yale University Press, 1989), p. 164.

of Charleston, wrote in 1802, 'Men of an enthusiastic disposition have a favourable opportunity at them for diffusing their
spirit and they do not fail to use it.'[1] With further experience,
Furman would state that more forcefully.

The new denominations and sects were generally formed by
men and women who claimed to be so much on the side of the
supernatural that they would allow only 'Bible words', not
words 'invented' by theologians. Some went further and
promised the miraculous – revelations and healings – in
exchange for the outmoded and the traditional. The old
denominations, these self-appointed leaders also claimed, had
made the Bible needlessly complex. Instead, their message was
'simple' and was always accompanied by the promise that it
would secure true unity. Nathan Hatch puts this well in
describing the motivation of Alexander Campbell, founder of
the Disciples of Christ:

> Like many of his generation, Campbell believed that stripping away
> the accretions of theology and tradition would restore peace,
> harmony, and vitality to the Christian church. Only slightly temp-
> ered by a sense of their own limitations, these reformers espoused
> private judgment as the sure route to coherence and harmony.
> Unfortunately, the more confidently they attacked the traditional
> order and espoused individual autonomy, the more confusing their
> limitless world became.[2]

Another factor in the situation was largely contributory to the
populist mood. If sympathy lay with the new and the changing,
over against any conservation of the past, then the institution of
the Christian ministry could readily be made suspect; the more
so as the writings of Thomas Paine and others spread abroad
the spectre of 'priestcraft'. Men such as M'Nemar, whom we
have noted celebrating the end of all 'distinctions', were
moving with the current of the times in claiming the same
absolute freedom in the church as the Revolution had supposedly secured for the nation. Where previously men were well
prepared for the ministry of the Word, it was now claimed that
every American had the right to be a preacher. A day had come
when 'all human creeds and confessions had been disannulled,

---

[1] *Baptist Denomination in America*, vol. 2, p. 171.
[2] *Democratization*, p. 163.

or rolled out of the way: the power and authority of the modern clergy . . . was renounced'.[1]

The point is that the ideas that led to fragmentation in Kentucky were in men's heads before 1800, for the errors that spread so suddenly had been clearly warned against in other parts of the country before the end of the eighteenth century. For example, Nathan Perkins, a Connecticut leader in the Second Great Awakening, had preached a series of sermons in Hartford in the 1790s on the very themes that were to receive such acceptance in the West – including the rejection of the ministerial office and a readiness to believe in the restoration of miraculous gifts: 'No man can tell what fanaticism, or a heated imagination, or an erroneous conscience will do.'[2] Given the absence of biblical teaching, and the weakness of instruction, which were common in Kentucky before the revival, some confusion was inevitable. As a contributor to *The Connecticut Evangelical Magazine* wrote on 16 September 1800: 'Where persons who have been but poorly indoctrinated are made the subjects of conviction and conversion, they frequently run into many wild and erroneous opinons, which not only tend to cramp their minds, and to destroy their peace, but prove prejudicial to the interest of religion.'[3] These words were written well before any news of excesses reached New England. And if this could happen to true converts, what might be said of those who became religious but remained unregenerate?

The situation in Kentucky was further fuelled by the shortage of able teachers and leaders in all the denominations. John Miller, a visitor to Kentucky in 1817, reviewed in his journal the evils that had arisen and drew particular attention to this fact: 'At the time the want of clergymen was great and, in order to supply this want, many clergymen were desirous of having young men licensed who were not duly qualified.'[4] On the same subject, Samuel Miller wrote: 'A number of hot-headed young

[1] *Kentucky Revival*, p. 46.

[2] Nathan Perkins, *Twenty-four Discourses* (Hartford, Conn., 1795), p. 392. He considered the 'Discourses as being *peculiarly* adapted to the day in which we live, and the state of Religion in our nation' (Dedication).

[3] *Connecticut Evangelical Magazine*, vol. 1, p. 158.

[4] 'John Miller's Missionary Journal – 1816–1817', *Journal of the Presbyterian Historical Society* (Sept. 1969), p. 250.

men, intoxicated with the prevailing element of excitement, and feeling confident of their own powers and call to the work – though entirely destitute of any suitable education – assumed the office of public exhorters and instructors . . . When once this door was opened it was found difficult to close it.'[1]

The situation we have considered was no proof that there had been no genuine revival. In 1817 John Miller concluded that in Kentucky and Tennessee 'there is far more attention to religion and literature than in the Southern States'. But it certainly showed that revival as such provides no safeguard against ignorance and error and that these dangers are increased rather than lessened when connected with fervent professions of faith in the Bible. Where there existed leadership and well-taught congregations in the Second Great Awakening, unity and catholicity were generally maintained. Where these were absent the opposite could well result.

*   *   *

We have considered the general detrimental effects which accompanied the awakening in the churches of Kentucky, and noted how these effects gained strength on account of the low level of biblical instruction that was prevalent. Ideas popularized by the spirit of the age were too strong to be counteracted by preachers who were too few in number, or inadequately prepared, for a situation of such an extraordinary character. But in addition to the fragmentation of church structures – and contributing largely to it – a specific area of theology was now for the first time generally challenged in America. All the new sects and denominations had one thing in common – they rejected the Calvinistic understanding of the gospel that had hitherto prevailed among all evangelical Christians. Up to this period, the only sizeable exception to the common understanding of orthodoxy was the Methodists, who began to arrive in 1769.[2] We have quoted above the words of the Methodist

---

[1] Sprague, *Lectures*, appendix, p. 33.

[2] See above, pp. 68–9. There were Arminian Baptists in America at an earlier date, but their numbers were few and most of their congregations appear to have either died out or become Calvinistic during the eighteenth century. A group of Freewill Baptists was formed in New England in 1780 but their influence was minimal at this date.

historian, William Warren Sweet, that 'most of the great American revival movements have come through the Presbyterians'. By the term 'Presbyterian' Sweet was thinking not only of church polity but of the Calvinistic confession which identified the denomination as well as the Baptists and Congregationalists. In the 1780s Witherspoon could affirm, 'The Baptists are Presbyterians, only differing in the point of infant baptism.'[1] Sweet observed that as late as 1820 'the Colleges of the country were largely under Calvinistic control'.[2] M'Nemar acknowledged in 1807 that 'The people among whom the revival began were generally Calvinists'.[3] He was thinking of Presbyterians but, again, the Baptist churches could be included.

We need to be clear how the Methodist understanding of the gospel differed from the common consensus of belief. Their evangelical Arminianism was formulated largely by John Wesley and diverged from the creeds and confessions of the Reformation and Puritan eras. Both Calvinistic and Arminian schools of belief held to the message of salvation as the gift of God through Christ crucified, and both taught the necessity of rebirth, faith, and holiness of life. Disagreement entered over the interpretation of these biblical truths. Evangelical Arminians claimed that grace extends equally to all men and its acceptance or rejection must therefore depend ultimately on human decision. Calvinists believed that such is the ruined state of human nature that no man would respond to the gospel if repentance and faith are conditions to be fulfilled before grace renews him. They saw repentance and faith, rather, as *parts* of the salvation which God bestows: 'by grace are ye saved through faith; and that not of yourselves; it is the gift of God' (Eph. 2:8). Both sides – as exemplified in the ministries of Wesley and Whitefield – believed that God commands all men to repent and believe the gospel; both showed that Christ is to be preached with compassion to all men; both taught human responsibility and insisted that sin alone is the cause of man's ruin; both knew that God is longsuffering towards all, 'not willing that any should perish'. But Calvinists believed the

[1] *Works*, vol. 9, p. 203.
[2] *Methodism in American History*, p. 177.   [3] *Kentucky Revival*, p. 27.

Scriptures to teach that, in a sovereignty unaccountable to us, those who actually receive Christ are those for whom God intended salvation from all eternity.[1] And further, they believed, that the work of Christ is so definite and particular that he *will save* all those for whom he died. Arminians held that such an understanding of the gospel must obstruct evangelism because it would prevent a preacher telling his hearers that they were able to exercise faith at any time. Calvinists responded that their hope of success in preaching salvation to sinners did not depend in any degree on what they thought man was able to do.

Orthodoxy and evangelism in America had for so long been identified with the creeds of the Reformation and Puritan eras that it was no small task for Christians of Arminian persuasion to set about to change the landscape. By the 1790s Methodists were making a major effort to effect just such a transformation. They boldly let it be known that it was Arminianism that was to be regarded as scriptural. Francis Asbury and Thomas Coke, launching the first American Methodist paper in 1789, did not hesitate to call it *The Arminian Magazine*. The opening lines of their Preface to the first issue read:

Brethren and Friends:
    We are not ignorant that the Gospel has been preached in the eastern and northern parts of these United States, from the earliest settlement of the country; but this has been done chiefly, though not entirely, through the Calvinistic medium . . . However, in this magazine very different opinions will be defended.[2]

This magazine was, of course, following Wesley's British magazine of the same name, but just how strongly Asbury believed in the need for doctrinal change in America can be judged from his words to Wesley in a personal letter of 20 September 1783:

I see clearly that the Calvinists on one hand, and the Universalists on the other, very much retard the work of God, especially in Pennsylvania and the Jerseys . . . Maryland does not abound with Calvinism; but in Virginia, North and South Carolina, and Georgia, the Baptists labour to stand by what they think is the good old cause. I

[1] e.g. Matt. 11:25; John 6:37; Acts 13:48.
[2] *The Journal and Letters*, vol. 3, p. 67.

think you ought always to keep the front of the Arminian Magazine filled with the best pieces you can get, both ancient and modern, against Calvinism: they may be read by future generations.[1]

Presbyterians, who often loaned their buildings to Methodists before the latter became well established, were sometimes taken by surprise by their dogmatism. William Hill, for example, itinerating in Virginia in 1790, discovered that when it came to a Presbyterian preaching in a Methodist meeting-house the invitation was hedged about by conditions. He met a Methodist preacher on the road who asked him to preach for him that day:

I agreed to do so. But says he, as I suppose you are a calvinist you must promise not to preach these doctrines, or we cannot suffer you to preach. I told him, if I preached at all, I should preach what I believed to be the truths of Gods words, & I would suffer no man to control me in matters of that kind, but would act as duty & prudence might seem to prompt me. He told then plainly that I should not be suffered to preach; otherwise they should be obliged to oppose my doctrine.[2]

The distinctive aspects of Methodist belief were pushed in Virginia in the 1790s and not without results. Some Baptist pastors were won over and became protagonists for the new convictions. One of these men was answered by Moses Hoge in 1793 in his *Strictures on a Pamphlet by the Rev. Jeremiah Walker, entitled The Fourfold Foundation of Calvinism Examined and Shaken.* Hoge did not

think it very proper that our religious opinions should receive their denomination from any man. The doctrines commonly denominated Calvinism might with greater propriety be called the doctrines of the Reformed churches; for they were generally received by the Churches of that description until Arminius arose to propagate a different system of religious sentiments.[3]

David Benedict, who in the early years of the nineteenth century, travelled widely to collect materials for his *General History of the Baptist Denomination in America*, commented on this subject: 'I was often not a little surprised at the bitterness of

---

[1] Ibid., pp. 30–1.   [2] Sweet, *American Frontier*, vol. 2, p. 770.
[3] John Blair Hoge, *The Life of Moses Hoge*, (Union Theological Seminary in Virginia, Historical Transcripts No. 2, 1964), pp. 70–71.

feeling which, in many cases, was displayed by the anti-Calvinists against the doctrine of election,' and he referred particularly to the Methodists who 'were extremely severe in their feelings and comments on the orthodox faith, so far as Election, etc., were concerned. Some of their circuit riders of that age conducted as if they considered themselves predestinated to preach against Predestination.'[1] Perhaps the worst example of this animosity is to be found in the ministry of Lorenzo Dow who itinerated mainly among the Methodists, though he is said to have had a Masonic burial on his death in 1834. Dow was a New-Englander and according to him, 'Satan with the help of Calvinism and Universalism had succeeded in keeping out the Methodists.'[2] After, as he believed, he had received a call to preach from John Wesley in a dream, 'he began in earnest his life-long polemical war on Calvinism in general.'[3]

The Methodists were not alone in their opposition to the older evangelicalism. As a recent writer has noted: 'No theme united the interests of insurgent groups between 1780 and 1830 more than an exaggerated opposition to official Christianity . . . The organization and rhetoric of this revolt against Calvinism remains elusive and neglected.'[4] Contemporary Calvinists believed that the main reason Arminianism gained ground was that it was more congenial to men's natural understanding, or, in the words of Robert Semple 'more palatable to the self-righteous heart of man'.[5] Man unhumbled before God believes that God has no right to give to any what he will not equally give to all. The aged Isaac Backus wrote to a fellow Baptist in 1797:

The enmity which men have discovered against the sovereignty of the grace of God, as revealed in Holy Scriptures, hath now prevailed so far that every art is made use of to put other senses upon the words of revelation than God intended therein. He said to Moses: 'I will have mercy on whom I will have mercy, and I will have compassion on

---

[1] *Fifty Years Among the Baptists* (New York, 1860; Little Rock, Ark.: Seminary Publications, 1977), p. 139.

[2] C. C. Sellers, *Lorenzo Dow, The Bearer of the Word* (New York, 1928), pp. 34–5.

[3] Ibid., p. 47.   [4] Hatch, *Democratization*, p. 170.

[5] Semple, *Baptists in Virginia*, p. 385.

whom I will have compassion. So then it is not of him that willeth, nor of him that runneth, but of God that showeth mercy, Rom. 9:15–16. This was the doctrine that God made use of in all the reformation that was wrought in Germany, England and Scotland after the year 1517; and by the same doctrine he wrought all the reformation that has been in our day, both in Europe and America.[1]

This argument, which satisfied many Christians before the Kentucky revival, was to command less influence afterwards. There was to be a major shift in the whole argument for which the Methodists again were principally responsible. If evangelicalism came out of the revival numerically stronger, it was at the expense of the older unity of belief, for Arminianism received a new and powerful impetus. How this happened must now be considered.

The Presbyterians, among whom the awakening commenced, did not regard such an extraordinary opportunity for evangelism as a suitable time for theological debate, and M'Gready's churches had an early Methodist helper in the person of the Rev. John McGee, as we have seen. We also noted McGee's authoritative and emotional intervention and its effect on the congregation at the Red River church in June 1800. By 1801 there seems to have been general Methodist participation at the great Presbyterian communion seasons. On the subject of the opening freely given to Methodist preachers, Davidson commented: 'Mr Lyle, indeed, mentions an instance when they were discouraged, and stood aloof; but such cases were rare exceptions. It appears evident that they soon obtained predominance, and from assistants became leaders.'[2]

One reason for the Methodist ascendency in the later stages of the revival was that they were not distracted by internal divisions as the Presbyterians and Baptists were. There does not seem to have been any sign of dissent among them over the issue of emotionalism and physical phenomena, which put such a strain on other churches. Methodist writers deny that their men encouraged excesses. It would be foolish to blame them exclusively, but we know no reason to doubt David Benedict's statement that 'when the work arose to an enthusiastick

[1] Hovey, *Memoir of Backus,* p. 356.
[2] *Presbyterian Church in Kentucky,* p. 141.

height. . . The Methodists had no scruples of its being genuine.'[1] Instead of recognizing and restraining natural excitement and wildfire, and probably losing the headstrong as a consequence, the Methodists willingly accommodated themselves to it. Overbalanced on an experience-centred Christianity, and too ready to exalt zeal above knowledge, the Methodist tendency was to treat such things as loud emotion, shouting, sobbing, leaping, falling, and swooning as though they were 'the true criteria of heartfelt religion.'[2] This is a generalization, but support for it is not hard to find. Thomas Cleland, a schoolboy in Kentucky at the time of the revival, and later a preacher in revivals himself, described how his Methodist schoolmaster worked children up into religious hysteria.[3]

It may be argued that Methodist failure at this point was simply a failure in balance rather than the result of any difference in belief. Perhaps so, but the institution which Methodism took out of the camp meetings and made permanent clearly *was* a matter of belief. Prior to 1800 there were times when large crowds attending Methodist preaching made open-air gatherings a necessity. But after 1800, when Presbyterians and Baptists generally gave up planning such mass meetings, Methodists made them a key part of future evangelism. The term 'camp meeting' first appears in Asbury's journals in 1802. Thereafter, it gained increasing prominence. 'We must attend to camp-meetings,' the Methodist leader wrote in 1809, 'they make our harvest time . . . I hear and see the great effects produced by them.'[4] In Kentucky, on 21 October 1810, he noted, 'The Methodists are all for camp-meetings.' By 1812, it was estimated that at least four hundred Methodist camp meetings, large and small, were held annually in the United States.[5]

The crux of the difference over this new institution was not whether one was for or against large numbers. Crowds as such

---

[1] *Baptist Denomination in America*, vol. 2, p. 252.
[2] *Presbyterian Church in Kentucky*, p. 141.
[3] *Life of Cleland*, p. 34, quoted in Gillett, *Presbyterian Church in U.S.*, vol. 2, p. 171.
[4] *Journals and Letters*, vol. 3, p. 141.
[5] Sweet, *Methodism in America*, p. 160.

were not the issue. Throughout the period vast congregations were to be found in all denominations. But the Methodists, harnessing, as they thought, a lesson from Kentucky, came to believe that the organization of mass meetings was a very effective part of evangelism. Emotion engendered by numbers and mass singing, repeated over several days, was conducive to securing a response. Results could thus be multiplied, even guaranteed. Calvinists, using their Bibles rather than any knowledge of psychology, saw from the New Testament that no technique could produce conversions. On the contrary the use of techniques was calculated to confuse the real meaning of conversion. Thus the opposition to the camp-meeting psychology was theological, and Richard M'Nemar was correct to identify Calvinism as the main hindrance to the type of meeting in which excitement was given full sway. If the viewpoint M'Nemar represented was to succeed then 'all creeds, confessions, invented by men, ought to be laid aside, especially the distinguishing doctrines of Calvin'.[1] The seceding Cumberland Presbyterians similarly regarded Calvinistic beliefs as a hindrance to success in evangelism. They both dropped their Calvinistic confession and endorsed the camp meeting.

Unlike M'Nemar and the Cumberland Presbyterians, the Methodists already had a theology which was more amenable to the new institution. There was also an element in their practice which had further prepared the way for the new development. Prior to 1800, Methodism in America – despite its concern not to admit any into church membership prematurely – had begun to record the number of supposed converts at particular services. This was a practice studiously avoided by the older evangelicalism,[2] and it was not used by John Wesley. How converts were counted is not always clear.

[1] *Kentucky Revival*, p. 30.
[2] 'It was not the custom of Whitefield or of the various pastors who published detailed reports of the course of the revival in their congregations to state the number of conversions' C. H. Maxson, *The Great Awakening in the Middle Colonies* (1920; Gloucester, Mass., 1958), p. 33. Referring to some who professed to 'know when persons are justified', Whitefield declared: 'It is a lesson I have not yet learned. There are so many stony-ground hearers which receive the word with joy, that I have determined to suspend my judgement till I know the tree by its fruits.' His rule was, 'A holy life is the best evidence of a gracious state'.

Jesse Lee, one of the best-known of the Methodist itinerants, spoke of men stationed in the congregation to keep an accounting. Christians, he believed, who saw people when they were careless, and then under conviction, 'can tell pretty well whether they are deceived or not when they professed to be converted'.

To this attempt to secure a speedy knowledge of conversions among the American Methodists before 1800, a new practice now came to be commonly added. The excitement of the camp meetings had brought much attention to the visible. It became common to count the number of those who 'fell' during services and, as we have seen, some took the figure as an indication of permanent results. Certainly, if the response to gospel preaching could be made instantly visible, there would be a far readier way of assessing success. But incautious as they tended to be, Methodists knew too much of true religion to make 'the falling exercise' the test of the number of converts. Something else was needed and it was found in what became known as 'the invitation to the altar'. The origin of this procedure is obscure. It was unknown in England, but the term reveals the Church of England background of its first promoters, who referred loosely to the end of a church building, in front of the communion table, as the altar. Before the end of the eighteenth century, in some congregations of the Methodist Episcopal Church the innovation had been introduced of inviting 'mourners' to come to the front, metaphorically, 'to the altar'.

As early examples of this new procedure the following can be noted. Jesse Lee recorded in his journal for 31 October 1798: 'At Paup's meeting-house Mr. Asbury preached on Eph 5:25, 26, 27 . . . I exhorted, and the power of the Lord was among us . . . John Easter proclaimed aloud, "I have not a doubt but God will convert a soul today". The preachers then requested all that were under conviction to come together. Several men and women came and fell upon their knees, and the preachers for some time kept singing and exhorting the mourners . . . two or three found peace.' In 1801 another Methodist in Delaware reported: 'After prayer I called upon the persons in distress to come forward and look to the Lord to convert their souls. Numbers came forward.'[1]

---

[1] John Atkinson, *Centennial History of American Methodism* (New York, 1884), p. 468.

There were no 'altar calls' in the early great communion services and camp meetings in the Kentucky revival but, with the impetus that high emotion imparted to the immediate and the visible, it was a short step to its introduction by the Methodists. When they began to organize their own camp meetings an area was railed off to serve as the altar and to this mourners were summoned. The initial justification for the new practice was that by bringing individuals to identify themselves publicly it was possible for them to be prayed with and to be given instruction. Nobody, at first, claimed to regard it as a means of conversion. But very soon, and inevitably, answering the call to the altar came to be confused with being converted. People heard preachers plead for them to come forward with the same urgency with which they pleaded for them to repent and believe.

Speaking of a camp meeting in 1806 Peter Cartwright, a Methodist itinerant, said: 'The altar was crowded to overflowing with mourners . . . young ladies asked permission to set down inside it. I told them that if they would promise to pray to God for religion they might take a seat there.'[1] He shared services with a fellow preacher, after they had settled procedure in advance: 'Said he to me: "If I strike fire, I will immediately call for mourners, and you must go into the assembly and exhort in every direction, and I will manage the altar. But," said he, "if I fail to strike fire, you must preach; and if you strike fire, call the mourners and manage the altar. I will go through the congregation and exhort with all the power God gives me."'[2]

It is significant that when people fell in sufficiently large numbers in the meetings Cartwright considered the altar call unnecessary, as though the work of conversion had already been done. On the other hand, when parents belonging to other churches hindered their children from 'going to the altar', Cartwright regarded their action as hindering salvation: 'I fear they were hindered for life, if not finally lost.'[3] As the idea gained ground that coming forward was the alternative to being lost,

[1] *The Backwoods Preacher: An Autobiography of Peter Cartwright* (London, 1859), p. 37.
[2] Ibid., p. 63.   [3] Ibid., p. 184.

[186]

results and successes on an unprecedented scale were witnessed. Statements like the following became commonplace:

The invitation was no sooner extended than the mourners came pouring forward.[1]
The enclosure was so much crowded that its inmates had not the liberty of lateral motion, but were literally hobbling *en masse*.[2]

Five hundred persons pressed forward.[3]

Exhortation and singing were renewed; and it was proposed that [visiting preachers also on the platform] should go down and pass among the people for the purpose of conversing with them and inducing them to come forward.[4]

The record of camp meetings in Asbury's journal give confident figures of conversions. On 12 December 1805 he noted from letters received, 500 souls at one meeting and 400 at another who all 'profess to have received converting grace'. From then on these assessments of numbers commonly became related to the altar call and in 1810 Asbury, not surprisingly, required that in the building of new meeting-houses there should be 'as much as one seat left before the pulpit for mourners'.[5]

There are many reasons why Methodist thinking and practice came to have much wider influence after 1800. Its ethos coincided more readily with the new mood in the country than did that of the older denominations. Methodist criticism of the past, with its theological inheritance and creeds, found a ready hearing in a generation prone to erase what was old. The Methodist appeal to the 'simple Bible', shorn of difficulties, made traditional doctrinal preaching look unnecessary. In particular, their idea that men cannot repent and believe *unless* they have the *ability* to do so seemed logical and reasonable to the common man. 'He could prove

---

[1] Related by circuit-rider Stephen R. Beggs, and quoted in Charles A. Johnson, *The Frontier Camp Meeting* (Dallas: Southern Methodist Univ. Press, 1955), p. 135. Johnson comments: 'Many refused to apologize for the weapon of emotional excitement that they used. It was the very element of power by which most people were "thoroughly and speedily affected"' (p. 237).
[2] Ibid., p. 136.   [3] Ibid., p. 138.
[4] Ibid., p. 142.   [5] *Journals and Letters*, vol. 3, p. 436.

his doctrine from Scripture and reason' was often said of the Methodist preachers.[1]

But it was the evangelism of camp meetings and of altar calls that did most to popularize the distinctive beliefs of Methodism. What the intellectual arguments of *The Arminian Magazine* failed to achieve was accomplished by another kind of 'proof'. Before 1800, as Isaac Backus knew, any argument that Arminianism was more effective in evangelism than Calvinism would have been regarded as absurd. After the Kentucky revivals that claim was presented with a good deal more credibility. If the immediate and the visible were to be the tests then the Methodist novelties had the advantage, and any theology that took an opposing view, it was said, was hostile to evangelism and revival. Apparent success added weight to the case. The numbers who made a public response were held up as unanswerable proof, and many preachers whose beliefs had not previously been Arminian were carried away.[2]

The change did not, of course, come overnight. There was, at first, a mixture of old and new. David Rice, one-time student of Samuel Davies, complained in 1803 of sermons which contained 'Calvinism, perhaps in the beginning, Antinomianism in the middle, and Arminianism at the end'. Davidson speaks further of the entrance of this new style of preaching and calls it, 'a mongrel mixture of Antinomianism and Arminianism . . . It blended high pretensions to sanctification with equally high exaltations of human agency in believing and a studious silence

[1] This and similar quotations are given in Hatch, *Democratization*, p. 174. 'No theme drew more humorous barbs from Methodists, Christians, and Mormons alike than the conundrums of Calvinistic orthodoxy'. The idea that if man is 'unapt to any good and prone to all evil' he cannot be held responsible was treated at the Reformation as a charge against Scripture. Question 9 of the Heidelberg Catechism asked: 'Does not God then wrong man, by requiring of him in his law that which he cannot perform?' Answer: 'No; for God so made man that he could perform it; but man through the instigation of the Devil, by wilful disobedience deprived himself and all his posterity of this power. 2 Cor. 11:3; Rom. 5:10.'

[2] Prominent among these was Barton W. Stone, initially a Presbyterian, who took up the use of 'a mourner's bench and teaching immediate conversion in contrast to his Presbyterian heritage' (Posey, *Frontier Mission*, p. 89). One opponent of the advocates of the new evangelism complained, 'They measure the progress of religion by the numbers who flock to their standard' (quoted by Hatch, *Democratization*, p. 135).

upon the subject of the Holy Spirit and his operations.'[1] The same author quotes a Methodist writer who affirmed, 'It was now obvious that the subjects of this work, very generally, had embraced the doctrine of grace as held by the Methodists.'

From the same date there came into existence a caricature of the earlier beliefs and the men who held them. William M'Gready wrote clearly on this point. Although temporarily thrown off balance by the excitement of the early 1800s, as Foote says, M'Gready was 'always a warm experimental calvinistic preacher' and he awoke to the danger of the beliefs which were gaining ground. In M'Gready's view, as he expressed it in 1809, a weakening of real religion was bound to follow from the erroneous teaching which he was grieved to see men accepting:

Those who are led off by the schismatic preachers (who are very numerous) are entirely unhinged from every system of doctrine. They have rejected the doctrines of the Confession of Faith. They appear to be ignorant of the doctrines of their own teachers, whilst their minds are filled with enmity against Calvinism and absolute election; there are but few of them that know what Calvinism or absolute election is. As I lodged with some of them I found that their preachers had told them that the calvinistic doctrines just taught that men were like passive machines bound in unalterable fate by the absolute decrees of God.[2]

Feeling, not thinking, M'Gready believed had become the rule for too many professing Christians: 'The greatest divine and greatest Christian upon earth if he have a calm, dispassionate address, cannot move them more than he could move the leviathan.'[3]

Early nineteenth-century Methodism contained within it much that was scriptural; and Stevens' claim for its leaders is largely true: they 'were mighty in the scriptures; they preached and loved and lived holy'. As models of prayerfulness, self-denial, and compassion for souls, many Methodist itinerants

---

[1] *Presbyterian Church in Kentucky*, p. 166.
[2] Report by M'Gready in *The Religious Intelligence* quoted by Thompson, *Presbyterians in the South*, vol. 1, p. 164.
[3] *Presbyterians in the South*, vol. 1, p. 165.

were an example to any age. But while their establishment of camp meetings and of altar calls arose from the best of motives, it was the result of an erroneous theology and it led to a system with consequences that they failed to see. If camp meetings and altar calls could produce the same number of 'converts' as revivals, what was the difference between them? Could a revival ritual replace real revival? Arminianism shielded the Methodists from appreciating the force of such questions. They believed that God had set his own seal on their work, and to question such success appeared to them akin to blasphemy. So, in due course, 'The seemingly miraculous new revival technique was disseminated throughout the length and breadth of the southern states.'[1] Revivalism had been born. We shall meet it again, but before we do so, we must go to another part of the country where the spirit of the old evangelicalism prevailed in the Second Great Awakening.

[1] Boles, *The Great Revival*, p. 89.

8

FIVE LEADERS IN THE NORTHEAST

The East Hampton Church, Long Island, built 1717, scene of
Lyman Beecher's pastorate during the opening years of the
Second Great Awakening

8

The period of the Second Great Awakening, and most especially with regard to the Northeast, is forceful evidence that the extent to which posterity remembers men is no true indication of the stature and influence they had in their own day. Heman Humphrey's list of the spiritual leaders in 1800 – men whose 'preaching was not in man's wisdom, but in demonstration of the Spirit and with power' – is of men whose names are unknown today. They were preachers who 'would quote chapter and verse from all parts of both Testaments, without turning over a single leaf', whose congregations saw the awakenings recorded in *The Connecticut Evangelical Magazine*, and under whom 'not far from four-fifths of the younger pastors of evangelical churches, who were especially blessed during the succeeding twenty years, were themselves converted'.[1] Humphrey knew them 'and often heard them preach, before and during the revivals. Now, after more than fifty years, I have a distinct recollection of their countenances, their tones of voice, their earnest and solemn appeals, their going out and coming in among the people.'[2] But when his generation died there seems to have been little on paper to keep such memories alive.

Happily, it is different with the generation of preachers who immediately followed the leaders of 1800. These were men whose names were to become well known before the age of revivals was over and they all had biographers or wrote

[1] Humphrey, *Revival Sketches*, p. 208.   [2] Ibid., p. 102.

autobiographies. Humphrey, who was their contemporary, drew attention to two of them, Edward Dorr Griffin and Asahel Nettleton. If we add to those names Lyman Beecher, Edward Payson, and Gardiner Spring, and consider some of the main features of their ministries, we may have an insight into what made the first three decades of the nineteenth century such a remarkable era.

Lyman Beecher was the son of a New Haven blacksmith who was 'one of the best-read men in New England, well versed in Astronomy, Geography and History, and in the interests of the Protestant Reformation'.[1] Lyman was born in 1775 and, living until 1863, he possessed the strength and vigour of his father at an age when other men have usually expended all their energies. Edward Griffin and Asahel Nettleton were both sons of Connecticut farmers, the former born in 1770 and the latter in 1783.

Edward Payson also started life in 1783 in the parsonage of Rindge in New Hampshire where his father, Seth Payson, had become the Congregational minister twelve months earlier. Spring, the last of the five, was born in 1785 at Newburyport, where his Princeton-trained father ministered from 1777 until his death in 1819.

Edward Payson alone of the five was a Harvard man. From Harvard he entered the teaching profession at Portland, Maine, but soon answered a call to the ministry and, for the twenty years from 1807 to 1827, served the Second Church of Portland. On his death in 1827 at the age of forty-four a writer likened his earthly path to that of 'an angel standing in the sun' (Rev. 19:17), and even those who knew him only from his biography came to understand why he was spoken of as the 'seraphic Payson'. It is a pity that the biography does not also show the more human side of the man who had eight children and invented games for their amusement.[2] But despite its inadequacies, Asa Cummings' memoir of Payson was probably the most influential ministerial biography to appear in the

---

[1] *Autobiography of Beecher*, vol. 1, p. 9.
[2] We have a glimpse of this in the biography of his daughter, G. L. Prentiss, *The Life and Letters of Elizabeth Prentiss* (New York, 1882), p. 11. Two of the Payson children died in infancy. Elizabeth, the fifth in the family, wrote the hymn 'More Love to Thee, O Christ.'

United States in the first half of the nineteenth century.[1]

The other four men all went through college at Yale in New Haven, during which time Griffin and Beecher nearly lost their lives. Griffin was thrown by a wild horse which then fell on him, and Beecher fell through thin ice while skating alone. Griffin left Yale intent on being a lawyer and 'a man of the world': 'I had been habituated to pour contempt on the ministry.' When he was converted in 1791, it was to that work, however, that he was called. His first charges were at New Hartford (1795–1801) and Newark, New Jersey (1801–09). Thereafter, he attempted to serve the new seminary at Andover concurrently with Park Street Church, Boston. The teacher's desk at Andover gave way wholly to Park Street from 1811. The latter part of his life was spent in a second period at Newark (1815–21), then in the presidency of Williams College at Williamstown, before a brief retirement among the people whom he had so long loved in Newark. On his death in Newark in 1837 a friend remarked, 'It was fitting that he who came in his youth to teach us how to live should come, when his head was grey, to show us how to die.'[2]

Lyman Beecher graduated from Yale in 1797 and studied for the ministry before taking up his first pastorate at East Hampton, Long Island, in 1799. From there he moved to Litchfield, Connecticut, where through the years 1810 to 1826 he came to be regarded as one of the first preachers of New England. Seemingly boundless in his energy and vitality, men spoke of him as 'thoroughly alive'. At Boston (where he served the church at Hanover Street from 1826 to 1832) ministerial visitors would be astonished to see the use he made of parallel bars and other gymnastic apparatus in his backyard. At the age of fifty-eight Beecher took on a new challenge by moving west to the thriving river town of Cincinnati where he was both president of Lane Seminary (1832–50) and minister of the Second Presbyterian Church (1833–43). One of his daughters, Harriet, married C. E. Stowe, a professor at Lane Seminary,

---

[1] First published in 1829, it went through a number of editions and printings before being reissued, in *The Complete Works of Edward Payson* (Philadelphia and London, 1859), vol. 1.

[2] *The Life and Sermons of Edward D. Griffin* (1839; Edinburgh: Banner of Truth, 1987), vol. 1, p. 237. The valuable biography of Griffin by W. B. Sprague takes up nearly half of volume 1.

and subsequently wrote one of America's most famous novels, *Uncle Tom's Cabin*. Stowe, who later became a professor at Andover, provides one of the last descriptions of Beecher, at length retired at Boston: 'The day he was eighty-one he was with me in Andover, and wished to attend my lecture in the Seminary. He was not quite ready when the bell rang, and I walked on in the usual path without him. Presently he came skipping along across lots, laid his hand on top of the five-barred fence, which he cleared at a bound, and was in the lecture-room before me.'[1]

Gardiner Spring, as did Payson, spent the whole of his ministry in one congregation. Having also turned from law to the ministry, he was pastor of the Brick Church, New York City, from 1810 until his death in 1873. When he wrote his *Personal Reminiscences* in 1865, there were only four people remaining in the congregation who had called him to their pulpit in his youth. He lived to see New York grow from a population of under 100,000 to 1 million, and the number of Protestant churches increase to over 300. When he became the pastor of the Brick Church in Beekman Street, it was eight years before the commencement of regular shipping communication with Liverpool, and twenty-eight before the first steamer reached New York Bay. By the time of his death his adopted city had become one of the great ports and business centres of the world.

Asahel Nettleton, the only bachelor among the five, differed most from the others in the outward course of his life. From the time he was licensed to preach at New Haven in 1811, his ministry was owned with such success that his brethren urged him to delay leaving the country for the missionary work abroad on which he had set his hopes. At a time when itinerant evangelists were virtually unknown among the Congregational churches of New England, the calls for Nettleton's help were so widespread and the revivals that he witnessed so numerous that he was detained for far more years than he had ever anticipated. It was only after his health failed in 1822 that Nettleton reluctantly gave up his hope of ever being a foreign missionary. The men who were inspired by his ministry to serve

---

[1] *Autobiography of Beecher*, vol. 2, p. 412.

overseas were probably able, together, to accomplish far more than he could have done if he had gone himself in 1811. From 1822 to 1824, when it was thought that he was close to death, Nettleton preached little, but then his work resumed and, although he never fully recovered, he lived until 1843.

The five men were all personally known to one another and shared a common, in some cases close, friendship. Griffin was an early encourager of Spring, and when he had a free Sunday in New York he would sit under the ministry of the younger man. The two men, according to Sprague, knew one another 'long and intimately'. Spring wrote of Griffin with great affection in his *Reminiscences*:

I have ever felt a deep interest in revivals of pure and undefiled religion. The Church of God from the beginning has been enlarged, beautified, and perpetuated by them. My venerated instructor, the Rev. Dr. Griffin, who, from his settlement in New Hartford, through his happy pastorate in Newark, during his official services at Andover and Park Street, and his presidency at Williamstown College, lived almost incessantly under their blessed influence, and who, with the exception of Dr. Nettleton, was better acquainted with them than any other man, once said to me, 'There never has been the time since 1792, in which the Spirit of God has not been poured out on some of the American churches'.[1]

It was Spring who preached at Griffin's funeral in 1837. He acknowledged it was Griffin, Nettleton and Payson who served as his 'models for the services of the pulpit'.[2]

Lyman Beecher became one of the leading figures in New England during his ministries at Litchfield and Boston. He was a welcome visitor to Spring's home and pulpit in New York, as can be judged from remarks in Spring's *Reminiscences*, for example: 'I had refreshing interviews this week with Brother Beecher of Litchfield. We conferred on the subject of revivals, and prayed together for one among my own people. I feel the need of such ministerial friends.'[3] Many years later Spring remembered their meeting: 'Well do I recollect his influence on my own mind during a few days when he was my guest at

---

[1] *Personal Reminiscences*, vol. 1, p. 170.
[2] Ibid., pp. 113–14.   [3] Ibid., vol. 2, p. 63 (7 May 1814).

Beekman Street.'¹ Beecher also visited Griffin at Newark in 1807, during 'a time of revivals through the bounds of Synod': 'We called on the doctor, and he marched into the parlor big as Polyphemus. "How is it with you, Brother Griffin?" said Woolworth; "I hear there are good things among you here." He swelled with emotion, and his strong frame shook, and the tears rolled down his cheeks. "Thank God!" said he, "I can pray once more." '²

After Beecher had been widowed in 1816, with eight young children, his thoughts turned to a woman in Edward Payson's congregation whom he had met in Boston, and he and Harriet Porter were married by Payson at Portland in the autumn of 1817. Beecher later wrote of his wife's spiritual experience: 'It was about 1812, as nearly as I remember, when her pastor, Dr. Payson was in his meridian of usefulness, that she with many others of her intimate associates, was awakened to religious enquiry by the preaching of that remarkable man.'³ Beecher was to preach on the installation of Payson's successor, Bennet Tyler.

While Beecher knew Griffin, Spring, and Payson, his friendship with Nettleton was closest. The two men first met in 1813, on the eve of Nettleton's visit to the parish of Milton, which was adjacent to Beecher's in Litchfield, and at that time without a pastor. Nettleton stayed at Milton three or four months and there, and at nearby South Farms in 1814, saw some of the first powerful revivals of his ministry.⁴ From that time the itinerant preacher was often in Beecher's home and pulpit. When the latter's health temporarily broke down in 1821 it was Nettleton who supplied his pulpit from the beginning of September to the middle of January 1822. 'During this period,' according to Beecher's son, Edward, 'Mr. Nettleton was the instrument in the hand of God of a powerful revival, in which there were seventy or more hopeful converts.'⁵ When Beecher, convalescing in Boston, heard of this

¹ Ibid., vol. 1, p. 114. See also *Autobiography of Beecher*, vol. 1, pp. 248–50, 315, 325.
² *Autobiography of Beecher*, vol. 1, p. 113.   ³ Ibid., p. 262.
⁴ Bennet Tyler and Andrew Bonar, *Nettleton and his Labours* (1854; Edinburgh: Banner of Truth, 1975), pp. 68–78.
⁵ Quoted in Sprague, *Annals*, vol. 2, p. 552.

awakening at Litchfield, he wrote to his wife on 20 October 1821: 'Some have suggested to me, perhaps God has granted this success in my absence to humble me . . . That the event will humble me I earnestly hope, but it will be by such a sense of his undeserved goodness in sending me away when I could not endure the labor of bringing forward a revival, and in sending to be an instrument one whom of all others I should have chosen to leave my people with at such a time.'[1] Beecher, both in his own congregation and elsewhere, had first-hand opportunity to see the changed lives of those converted under Nettleton's preaching, and it was his stated opinion in later years that the revivals with which Nettleton had been connected 'showed less of defect and more of moral power than I have ever known or ever expect to see again'. In recollections of his one-time fellow labourer, he wrote:

Nettleton's personal attention to the critical state of individuals in the progress of a revival was wonderful. This is a field in which the greatness of his vigilance, and wisdom, and promptness, and efficacy lay, the wonders of which, though much may be told, can never be recorded. His eye was open on every side so far as to see if any danger betided, and his solicitude was intense and his adaptations wonderful and efficacious . . .

The power of his preaching included many things. It was highly intellectual as opposed to declamation, or oratorical, pathetic appeals to imagination or the emotions. It was discriminatingly doctrinal, giving a clear and strong exhibition of doctrines denominated Calvinistic, explained, defined, proved, and applied, and objections stated and answered. It was deeply experimental in the graphic development of the experience of saint and sinner. It was powerful beyond measure in stating and demolishing objections, and at times terrible and overwhelming in close, pungent, and direct application to the particular circumstances of sinners . . .

But there was another thing which gave accumulating power to his sermons. They were adapted to every state and stage of a revival, and condition of individual experience. His revivals usually commenced with the Church in confessions of sin and reformation. He introduced the doctrine of depravity, and made direct assaults on the conscience of sinners, explained regeneration, and cut off self-righteousness, and enforced immediate repentance and faith, and pressed to immediate submission in the earlier stages.[2]

[1] *Autobiography of Beecher*, vol. 1, p. 345.   [2] Ibid., vol. 2, pp. 363–5.

All five of these men, as New Englanders, belonged to the Congregational churches which constituted the great majority of congregations. But three of the five – Griffin, Spring, and Beecher – served Presbyterian churches beyond New England. This represented no significant change on their part for they shared a common Calvinistic doctrinal heritage with the largely Scots-Irish Presbyterians of the Middle and Southern States. There were thus many and increasing contacts between the work in New England and the Presbyterians. Since the Plan of Union of 1801, the annual General Assembly of the Presbyterian Church was open to Congregationalists, and we read of Payson being as far from home as Philadelphia for such an occasion. The revivals in New England also quickly drew the sympathy and interest of the Presbyterians. Archibald Alexander paid a lengthy visit there in 1801 and saw the beginnings of the great change in various places. All his days, writes his son, 'his acquaintance with New England, its clergy, its manners and its revivals, he always returned to with pleasure'.[1] In New York, Spring had time to form an enduring friendship with his Presbyterian colleague in the city Samuel Miller, before the latter left to become the second professor of the new Princeton Seminary in 1813. Relations between the pastor of the Brick Church and Princeton were so close that when he visited Europe in 1835 he left the care of his pulpit in the hands of the Seminary's professors.

A similarly close bond came to exist between Nettleton and his Presbyterian brethren. From the Fall of 1827 Nettleton spent two years in the South among the Presbyterian churches of Virginia. At this time the College at Hampden-Sydney again saw such days as had been witnessed in 1788 with more than a hundred enquiring 'What must we do to be saved?' Thankful reports of Nettleton's preaching reached Alexander at Princeton and the New Englander was thereafter in much closer touch with the Seminary.

*   *   *

[1] *Life of Alexander*, p. 268. At Hartford, Connecticut, Alexander observed in his journal that 'there had been a glorious revival more considerable than any which had occurred since the great awakening in the time of President Edwards . . . A similar awakening was experienced in most of the congregations in the State' (ibid., p. 238).

We must now turn to some general principles arising from this period.

In the first place, the lives of these men show the clear difference between knowing revival and being a 'revivalist'. It was in this era that the term 'revivalist' was first used but, significantly, it was employed not by these men but by Unitarians and other opponents of revival. The term implied that there were certain men capable of producing the emotion and excitement which, in the judgment of critics, was the essence of revival. Not believing in the work of the Spirit of God, such observers saw no distinction between revivalism and revival.[1] They could see no meaning in Gardiner Spring's affirmation, 'Revivals are always spurious when they are got up by man's device and not *brought down* by the Spirit of God.'[2]

Revivalism *aims* to produce excitement. No such intention marked the ministries of those who saw revival in the Northeast. It was something of a different order which was changing lives and churches. These preachers, unlike some of a later date, had more biblical sense than to accept their opponents' description of them as revivalists. Revival is not something that men can plan or command as they will; the revivals in the Northeast, which occurred over a period of thirty years, followed no pattern or sequence. For example, the most notable years in Connecticut after 1802 were 1807–8, 1812, 1815–16, 1820–21, and 1825–26, but why these were years of great harvest rather than others no one can explain. It was certainly not because of 'protracted meetings' (special evangelistic services), for they were unknown in Connecticut before 1831. This mysterious periodicity is evident in the ministries of all five preachers. The only explanation which they knew for the times of special blessing was that the Spirit of God, like the wind, 'bloweth where it listeth' (John 3:8). What an observer wrote in 1801 remained true of the whole period: 'The history of the late awakenings is calculated to impress the mind with a view and sense of the *sovereignty* of God in the bestowment of the

[1] I cannot prove that it was New England Unitarians who first used the term 'revivalist' but it seems probable. The same term was unwisely adopted by those of Arminian persuasion.

[2] *Personal Reminiscences*, vol. 1, pp. 217–8.

influences of his Spirit . . . In the late effusions of the divine Spirit, although many places have been visited, yet it has been far from universal or general. It has rained upon one place and not upon another.'[1] God sovereignly determined places and times.

In Griffin's case he was almost immediately involved in revival both in his first pastorate at New Hartford, Connecticut, and then at Newark, New Jersey, where he became a colleague of Alexander McWhorter in 1801. McWhorter, a man who kept the example of Spirit-anointed preaching before his generation, was then near the close of his ministry. He had seen the Spirit of God poured out at Newark in 1772, 1784, and, more briefly, in 1796. In 1802–3 Griffin and McWhorter together saw the last awakening of the veteran preacher's ministry. There were over 100 converts and some twenty other congregations in the area also experienced 'the mighty power of God'.[2] A still greater revival occurred soon after McWhorter's death. It began at Elizabethtown and Orange, to the south and west of Newark, in August 1807. Speaking of a meeting on the first Monday night in September 1807, Griffin wrote:

the first feelings which denoted the extraordinary presence of God, and the actual commencement of a revival of religion, were awakened, perhaps in every person that was present. It was no longer doubtful whether a work of divine grace was begun. During that and the following week, increasing symptoms of a most powerful influence were discovered. The appearance was as if a collection of waters, long suspended over the town, had fallen at once, and deluged the whole place. For several weeks, the people would stay at the close of every evening service, to hear some new exhortation; and it seemed impossible to persuade them to depart, until those on whose lips they hung had retired.[3]

In a terse record Griffin noted: 'Sept. 1807. Began a great revival of Religion in the town. Ninety-seven joined the church in one day, and about two hundred in all.'[4] Griffin knew that it

[1] *Connecticut Evangelical Magazine*, vol. 1, p. 286.
[2] Sprague, *Lectures*, appendix, p. 153.
[3] Letter from Griffin to Ashbel Green, *Life and Sermons of Griffin*, vol. 1, p. 92.
[4] Ibid., p. 90.

was due to the sovereign appointment of God that his early ministry was marked with such success. When he moved on to Boston he wrote to one of his successors at Newark, warning of the danger of supposing that what had happened in 1807–8 was normal for the congregation: 'You went to Newark at the close of a great revival. The thing was done, and could not be continued. I had the privilege of being there in harvest time; and you came in the fall of the year; a winter followed of course; but a spring you will see, and then a harvest.'[1]

Beecher began his first pastorate in 1799 and saw his first harvest in December 1807. Payson, who was ordained at Portland in 1807, was noting 'considerable attention to religion' among his people in 1809. Forty-two were added to his church in 1810, and much more was to follow in 1814. Preaching in another town in December 1813, he spoke of never having 'seen so much of God's power displayed in the same space of time'. He had to end six days of preaching there in order to return for a church fast and communion at Portland. He wrote to his mother on 7 January 1814, describing what happened on his return:

I came home thoroughly drenched by the shower of divine influences, which began to fall at——, and soon found that the cloud had followed me, and was beginning to pour itself down upon my people. Instead of a fast, we appointed a season of thanksgiving. A blessing seemed to follow it. I then invited the young men of the parish to come to my house, on Sabbath evening, for religious purposes. The church thought none would come. I expected twenty at most. The first evening forty came; the second, sixty; and the third, seventy. This was the last Sabbath. Six stopped, after the rest were dismissed, to converse more particularly respecting divine things. About thirty persons are known to be seriously inquiring, and there is every appearance that the work is spreading. Meanwhile, I am so ashamed, so rejoiced, and so astonished, to see what God is doing, that I can scarcely get an hour's sleep.[2]

Although in that year and the next there were repeated evidences of God's presence in Payson's congregation at Portland, it was the year 1816 that 'was the most remarkably

---

[1] Ibid., p. 124.   [2] *Works of Payson*, vol. 1, p. 294.

distinguished for the effusions of the Holy Spirit on his people of any year of his ministry, with the exception of that in which his happy spirit took its flight'. The following are extracts from letters he wrote to his mother in that year:

March 1, 1816 . . . We have about eighty inquirers, and several I hope are converted; but this is nothing to what we expected. However, we would be thankful for a drop if we cannot have a shower. It has been a trying season to me this winter. While pursuing the revival, it seemed as if I must die in the pursuit and never overtake it.

April 1, 1816 . . . Our revival still lingers : it, however, increases slowly. I have conversed with about forty who entertain hopes, and with about sixty more who are inquiring. Twenty-three have joined the church since the year commenced. The work is evidently not over; but whether it will prove general, is still doubtful. There is quite a revival at Bath, below us. Nearly two hundred have been awakened. In Philadelphia, seventy one were added to a single church at one time, a few weeks since. In New York and Baltimore, also, there are revivals.

September 19, 1816. . . On the whole, the past summer has been the happiest which I have enjoyed since I was settled. Were it not for the dreadfully depressing effects of ill health, I should be almost too happy. It seems to me, that no domestic troubles, not even the loss of wife and children, could disturb me much, might I enjoy such consolations as I have been favored with most of the time since the date of my last letter. Soon after that, the revival, which I feared was at an end, began again, and things now look as promising as ever. My meeting-house overflows, and some of the church are obliged to stay at home, on account of the impossibility of obtaining seats. I have, in the main, been favored with great liberty for me, both in the pulpit and out; and it has very often seemed as if – could I only drop the body, I could continue, without a moment's pause, to praise and adore to all eternity. This goodness is perfectly astonishing and incomprehensible. I am in a maze, whenever I think of it . . . Never did God appear so inexpressibly glorious and lovely as he has for some weeks past. He is, indeed, all in all. I have nothing to fear, nothing to hope from creatures. They are all mere shadows and puppets. There is only one Being in the universe, and that Being is God; may I add, He is my God. I long to go and see him in heaven. I long still more to stay and serve him on earth. Rather, I rejoice to be just where he pleases, and to be what he pleases. Never did selfishness and pride appear so horrid. Never did I see myself to be such a monster; so totally dead to all wisdom and goodness. But I can point up, and say –

There is my righteousness, my wisdom, my all. In the hands of Christ I lie passive and helpless, and am astonished to see how he can work in me. He does all; holds me up, carries me forward, works in me and by me; while I do nothing, and yet never worked faster in my life. To say all in a word – 'My soul followeth hard after thee; thy right hand upholdeth me.'

Our inquirers are about seventy. We are building a conference-house, to hold 500 people. Some of the church, who can ill afford it, give fifty dollars each towards it.

December 9, 1816. . . In a religious view, things remain very much as they have been. We have about fifty inquirers; but they do not seem, except in a few instances, to be very deeply impressed, and their progress is slow. We have admitted seventy-two persons into the church during the present year. Our new conference-house has been finished some weeks; cost about twelve hundred dollars. At its dedication, and at a quarterly fast held in it the same week, we enjoyed the divine presence in a greater degree, I think, than we ever did before as a church. I would not have given a straw for the additional proof, which a visible appearance of Christ would have afforded of his presence.[1]

Payson had completed twenty years in his Portland pulpit when he died in October 1827. Throughout his ministry he witnessed a regular increase of members interspersed with periods of larger, sudden blessing when the numbers multiplied. After 1816 there were further revivals in 1822 and in 1827, the year of his death. Over the period of his ministry the average increase in membership was more than thirty-five a year; in 1827 the figure was seventy-nine.

This periodicity is also to be seen in the work of Gardiner Spring. In 1864 he wrote: 'There have been five seasons of special outpouring of the Holy Spirit during my ministry. They occurred between 1812 and 1834, more or less copious, but all seasons of refreshing.' He describes only the first of these in any detail:

Sparse clouds of mercy had been hovering over the congregation during the first four years of my ministry . . . and not a few, especially of those in middle life, had been brought into the kingdom of God.

The year 1814 was a year of great labor and deep solicitude. Many a time after preaching did I remain long in the pulpit, that I might not

[1] Ibid., vol. 1, pp. 365–8.

encounter the reproaches of the people of God for my heartless preaching, and many a time, as I left it, has my mind been so depressed that I have felt I could never preach another sermon. But I did not know to what extent the Spirit of God was carrying forward his own noiseless work . . .

God was already beginning a precious work of grace among the people. He had taken it into his own hands, and was conducting it in his own quiet way, convincing the church and the world that it is 'not by might, nor by power, but by his own Spirit,' as the Author and Finisher of the whole. The spirit of grace and supplication was poured out upon the people, and they 'looked on Him whom they had pierced.' The weekly prayer-meeting and the weekly lecture were full of interest. Days of fasting and prayer were occasionally observed, and a Saturday evening prayer-meeting was established by the young men of the church, for the special purpose of imploring the divine presence and blessing upon the services of the approaching Lord's day . . . Our Sabbaths became deeply solemn and affecting. We watched for them as those who 'watch for the morning.' I verily believe we anticipated them with greater pleasure and more buoyant expectation, than that with which the sons and daughters of earth ever anticipated their brightest jubilee.

This was the first strongly-marked work of grace among my people. I take this notice of it for two reasons. God is wont to give every generation some inviting day of grace; to 'set before them an open door.' There were members in the congregation past the mid-day of life, who knew little of such seasons of awakening, and who had not become hardened by that resistance to the Holy Spirit which so often seals the damnation of scoffers. And this was chiefly the class that were the subjects of this blessed work.

Again: this season of mercy was an emphatic expression of God's goodness to the youthful minister. He had been but six short years in the ministry, but God foresaw that he was to occupy a place in his earthly sanctuary for more than half a century. It was a weary wilderness he was appointed to traverse, and the God of Israel refreshed him with some of the grapes of Eshcol. Poor a thing as I have been, and still continue to be, with devout gratitude I record it here, that it was this work of grace that made me what I am; which enlarged my heart, gave vigor to my thoughts, ready utterance to my tongue, new views of the great object of the ministry, made my work my joy, and stimulated me to reach forward to greater measures of usefulness. I loved preaching the Gospel before, but never as I have loved it since. But for this early season of mercy during the summer of 1814, I should have changed from place to place, and turned out what the Scotch call a 'sticket minister.' It was the Lord's doing, and marvellous in our eyes. The ingathering was not great, but it was the 'finest of the wheat' . . .

The commencement of the year 1815 was the dawning of a still brighter day. The last Sabbath of the 'Old Year,' and the evening services of that Sabbath, will be long remembered . . . Eight or ten persons, during the following week, were found to be anxiously inquiring for the way to Zion, with their faces thitherward; weeping Marys and bold young men, startled from the grave of trespasses and sins. The whole winter proved to be a 'day of the right hand of the Most High' . . .

The third Thursday of January, by a private arrangement, was set apart by about thirty members of the church as a day of fasting, humiliation, and prayer. It was at a private house in Church-street, just in the rear of St. Paul's; and such a day I never saw before, and have never seen since. Such self-abasement, such confession of sin, such earnestness and importunity in prayer, and such hope in God's almightiness, I have rarely witnessed. And what deserves to be recorded is, that as the devotions of the day were drawing to a close, there was a *strong and confident expectation* that the Holy Spirit was about largely to descend upon the people. And so it was. He was even then descending. That cry: 'Where is thy hand, even thy right hand? Pluck it out of thy bosom,' was heard in heaven, and echoed by our great High Priest. A delightful impulse was given to the work by this day of prayer. The promise was made good, 'Before they call I will answer, and while they are yet speaking I will hear.'

Our weekly lecture occurred on the evening of the same day; and I may say, it was the most solemn service of my ministry. The subject of the lecture was, 'Marvel not that I said unto you, ye must be born again.' God was with the hearers and the preacher; his Spirit moved them as 'the trees of the wood are moved with the wind.' There is good reason to believe that *more than one hundred persons* were deeply impressed with their lost condition as sinners, and their need of an interest in Christ, on that evening. It was not then with us as it is now. *Now* few attend our weekly lectures except the professed people of God; *then* the impenitent rushed to the house of prayer. Enemies were silenced; members of other churches came among us, some to spy out our liberty, and some to mark the character of the work for themselves, and all classes were constrained to confess, 'This is the finger of God.' Between one and two hundred attended the private meetings for religious instruction, and great solemnity pervaded the whole people.[1]

---

[1] *Personal Reminiscences*, vol. 1, pp. 161–7.

The experience of all five men points to the same conclusion: revivals did not occur in conjunction with any special efforts. They were not worked up, but were witnessed in the course of the ordinary services of the churches. Far from their being planned or announced in advance, those who experienced them were all united in the conviction that God alone had determined the time. So while they used the analogy of springtime and harvest, they were careful to assert that in the work of grace there is no corresponding set period of time between sowing and reaping. The duration of the cycles of time are known only to him before whom 'a thousand years are but as yesterday when it is past and as a watch in the night'.

*   *   *

A second general lesson may be drawn from the history of this period as exemplified in the lives of the five men. It has to do with the wisdom required of those who would be physicians of souls. The mishandling of would-be converts is a disaster at any time but pre-eminently in times of revival when numbers are multiplied. If scriptural truth is not preached in its right proportions, if due emphasis is not given both to human responsibility and to dependence on divine grace, and if people affected by the superficial and the emotional are brought to a premature profession of 'faith', then serious consequences are bound to follow. The fruit of true revival will be marred, as happened in Kentucky, and the reputation of evangelical Christianity discredited. Ebenezer Porter, writing in 1832, believed that the difference in this regard between the work in Kentucky and the revivals in the Northeast was due to the fact that in the latter area the leaders were more mature pastors.[1] This observation was well founded. New England had suffered in the 1740s (as Kentucky did after 1800) on account of some revival preachers whose zeal was far in excess of their understanding.[2] In the Northeast that lesson had not been forgotten and the necessity of scriptural wisdom, of caution,

---

[1] *Letters on Revivals*, p. 59.
[2] This subject is treated in some detail in my *Jonathan Edwards: A New Biography*, pp. 216–48.

and of patience was well understood by the leaders of the Second Great Awakening.

There is much in the pages of *The Connecticut Evangelical Magazine* on the ways in which souls are to be guided to Christ and confirmed in the faith. The writers (commonly men who were themselves prominent in the revivals) knew that God's ways in dealing with sinners follow no stereotyped procedure. No two conversions are identical; nonetheless, they believed that there were definite biblical guide-lines to be taught and followed.

In the first place, they put the truth that real conversion entails a change of nature – a change from 'supreme selfishness to universal love, from enmity against God to supreme attachment to Him'[1] – and that no one will be conscious of their need of *such a change* until 'brought to see their true character and condition'. The work of the Holy Spirit therefore always begins with conviction of sin, and where the influences of the Spirit are abundantly evident, as in a revival, there will always be numbers of people who can be described by such terms as 'the awakened', 'the concerned', and 'enquirers'. When many people are suddenly brought under conviction the scene of distress may be similar to what was seen on the day of Pentecost.

But outward signs of conviction are not to be identified with regeneration. The light of truth by which the Spirit first deals with men is not always the same as the power by which he immediately changes their nature. The conscience of the unconverted may be so strongly accused by the truth that they are brought into a state of physical shock. They may be alarmed to the point of trembling, as Felix under the preaching of Paul, yet with no saving result. These wise pastors, therefore, counted it essential to understand that to be awakened is not the same as to be saved. And in their view, to lay importance on outward signs of conviction, such as tears, was a sure way to confuse the natural with the spiritual. They also knew that if displays of emotion were allowed to go unchecked in large congregations then, by a principle of natural sympathy, others would soon be affected. The consequent heightened emotion, far from advancing a true revival, could well bring it to an end.

[1] Edward Griffin, *A Series of Lectures Delivered in Park Street Church Boston* (Boston, 1813), p. 113.

For this reason, when people gave way to audible distress in a service, it was the common practice to have them removed from the meeting.

These preachers regarded the emotional danger as usually greatest at the beginning of a revival when the natural element of surprise was likely to be at its strongest. Griffin wrote to Ashbel Green of what happened at Newark in 1807: 'a multitude weeping and trembling . . . I presume not less than a hundred were in tears at once.' But far from regarding this as of special significance, he went on to say: 'But this excitement of animal feelings, incident to the commencement of revivals of religion, soon subsided, and the work has ever since proceeded in profound silence . . . This work, in the point of power and stillness, exceeds all that I have ever seen. While it bears down everything with irresistible force, and seems almost to dispense with human instrumentality, it moves with so much silence that, unless we attentively observe its effects, we are tempted, at times, to doubt whether any thing uncommon is taking place.'[1]

Nettleton remarked of a revival beginning in Salisbury, Connecticut, 'A number were anxious and a few in awful distress of soul.' During his temporary absence from Salisbury some would-be helpers, whom he describes as 'ignorant' and 'officious', encouraged the display of emotion so that the troubled 'were set to groaning and screaming':

Having heard the tidings, I hastened to the spot, and, with kind but decided severity, called them to order. My attempts, by those who had given the work that turn, were considered as very obtrusive and daring. It was reported all over town, that a revival had begun in Salisbury, and that I had put a stop to it. They seemed to be very much grieved and shocked at my conduct. It took a number of days to restore order; but when it was done, the work of God advanced, silently and powerfully, until all classes, old and young, were moved all over town. The language was: 'The fountains of the great deep are broken up.' Not far from three hundred were numbered as the hopeful subjects of divine grace in that revival.[2]

Another example of this procedure was described by Nettleton's biographer with reference to revival in the parish of

[1] *Life and Sermons of Griffin*, vol. 1, p. 93.
[2] *Nettleton and his Labours*, p. 83.

Milton, Litchfield:

It was soon manifest that God was in the place of a truth. The work increased rapidly, and became very powerful. It was characterized by remarkably clear and distressing convictions of sin. The subjects of it had a vivid sense of the opposition of their hearts to God; and, in some instances, their distress was overwhelming.

On one evening, two or three individuals were in such horror of mind, that it became necessary to remove them from the meeting to a neighbouring house. This, for a moment, created some confusion, but order was soon restored, when Mr. N. addressed the people in the following manner: 'It may, perhaps, be new to some of you, that there should be such distress for sin. But there was great distress on the day of Pentecost, when thousands were pricked in the heart, and cried out: "Men and brethren, what shall we do?" Some of you may, perhaps, be ready to say: If this is religion, we wish to have nothing to do with it. My friends, this is not religion. Religion does not cause its subjects to feel and act thus. These individuals are thus distressed, not because they have religion, but because they have no religion, and have found this out. It was so on the day of Pentecost. The thousands who were pricked in their heart, had found that they had no religion, and were unprepared to meet their God. They had made the discovery, that they were lost sinners, and that their souls were in jeopardy every hour.'[1]

Such a state of concern may lead to salvation but it may not, and therefore must not be treated as evidence of the regenerating work of the Spirit. Thus Payson wrote on one occasion: 'A great many seem to be somewhat alarmed but I see none of those convictions of sin which I used to see; it is only the mere workings of natural fear.'

This point corresponds with what was considered in a previous chapter, namely, that it is reverence, humility, and stillness rather than noise and excitement which mark the nearness of God to a people. When people are conscious of God, like Moses, they bow their heads and worship (Exod. 34:8). A recent writer describes Nettleton as 'encouraging in his meetings a hushed, mysterious stillness'.[2] For Nettleton and his brethren, however, such an effect had to come from heaven.

[1] Ibid., pp. 69–70.
[2] Keith J. Hardman, *Charles Grandison Finney 1792–1875* (Syracuse, N.Y.: Syracuse University Press, 1987), p. 120.

[211]

Excitement might be worked up but not this. The subject cannot be better stated than it is by Payson in a sermon entitled, 'God Heard in the Still Small Voice', based on the experience of Elijah in 1 Kings 19:12–13:

Ministers may give voice and utterance to the Bible which is the word of God. Like James and John they may be sons of thunder to impenitent sinners. They may pour forth a tempest of impassioned, eloquent declamation. They may proclaim all the terrors of the Lord; represent the earth as quaking and trembling under the footsteps of Jehovah; flash around them the lightnings of Sinai; borrow, as it were, the trump of the archangel, and summon the living and the dead to the bar of God . . . and still God may not be there; his voice may not be heard either in the tempest, the earthquake, or the fire; and if so, the preacher will have labored but in vain; his hearers, though they may for the moment be affected, will receive no permanent salutary impressions. Nothing effectual can be done unless God be there, unless he speaks with his still small voice. By this still, small voice we mean the voice of God's Spirit; the voice which speaks not only to man, but in man; the voice, which, in stillness and silence, whispers to the ear of the soul, and presses upon the conscience those great eternal truths, a knowledge and belief of which is connected with salvation . . . Large congregations often sit and hear a message from God, while perhaps not a single individual among them feels that the message is addressed to himself, or that he has any personal concern in it. But it is not so when God speaks with his still small voice. Every one, to whom God thus speaks, whether he be alone, or in the midst of a large assembly, feels that he is spoken to, that he is called, as it were, by name. The message comes home to him, and says, as Nathan said to David, Thou art the man. Hence, while multitudes are around him, he sits as if he were alone. At him alone the preacher seems to aim. On him alone his eye seems to be fixed. To him alone every word seems to come . . . And when God thus speaks to the whole or the greatest part of an assembly at once, as he sometimes does, when he comes to revive his work extensively, these effects are experienced, and these appearances exhibited by all. No scene, on this side the bar of God, can be more awfully, overpoweringly solemn, than the scene which such an assembly exhibits. Then the Father of spirits is present to the spirits he has made; present to each of them, and speaking to each. Each one feels that the eye of God is upon him, that the voice of God is speaking to him. Each one therefore, though surrounded by numbers, mourns solitary and apart. The powers of the world to

[212]

come are felt. Eternity, with all its crushing realities, opens to view, and descends upon the mind. The final sentence, though uttered by human lips, comes with scarcely less weight, than if pronounced by the Judge himself. All countenances gather blackness, and a stillness, solemn, profound, and awful, pervades the place, interrupted only by a stifled sob, or a half repressed sigh. My hearers, such scenes have been witnessed. Within a very few years they have been witnessed in hundreds of places.[1]

These pastors knew nothing more demanding and exacting than preaching for conviction and then dealing wisely with those in that condition. Certainly, they taught the immediate responsibility of every soul to repent and believe the gospel. They pleaded with their hearers to do so without delay. But they also considered it a part of faithful preaching not to hide from men their sinful inability. True conversion is not made easier if conviction of sin can somehow be bypassed, and they regarded a recognition of the fact that sinners cannot convert from enmity to holiness at their own decision as integral to conviction. Porter observed: 'I have seen sinners in those assemblies agitated with awful anxiety, and crushed down with conviction of their guilt, under the pressure of two truths; one, that heaven is now offered to their acceptance as a free gift, and that they have no excuse for remaining impenitent a single moment; the other, that their hearts are so deeply wicked that their only hope is in the sovereign mercy of God.'[2]

In the West, as we saw earlier, some evangelists believed that they had found a way to aid the release of the convicted from any continuing anxiety. Let enquirers 'stand up' or 'come to the altar,' and their peace with God was virtually assured. Such counsel was almost unheard of in New England, as Porter observed:

During a powerful work of grace, which prevailed in my childhood, a zealous preacher, at the close of a public lecture, called on all impenitent sinners, 'who would then make up their minds to be on the Lord's side,' to rise and declare that purpose by speaking aloud. Scores of hearts in the assembly were ready to burst with deep anxiety, but the incongruity of such a proposal, in the regular worship

[1] *Works of Payson*, vol. 2, pp. 500–2.
[2] *Letters on Revivals*, p. 29.

of God, was instinctively and generally felt. After a dead silence of a few moments, five or six men rose, and made the declaration which was desired. I was old enough to observe them all as they spoke; but among the blessed fruits of that work not one of these was numbered, and some of them soon became open infidels. But one other instance like this occurred within my knowledge till I became a preacher myself, and not one in all the revivals during my pastoral life.[1]

These pastors believed that to persuade the convicted to engage in an external act as an aid to conversion, if not as an act of conversion itself, was to ignore the magnitude of the spiritual change that brings men from death to life. Those whom God brings to salvation will repent, believe, and confess Christ but to issue instructions that lead men to regard the change as a physical, observable action, to be performed at a moment determined by the preacher, can only mislead and multiply spurious religious experience.

In guiding souls to Christ, these men did not know *when* God would grant regeneration.[2] It was in his hands. Joel Hawes' description of a revival at Hartford in 1820, in which he was helped by Beecher, was fairly characteristic: 'Conviction of sin was often deep and pungent, and lasted from two to three and four weeks, or longer, and was then succeeded by submission and peaceful hope.'[3] Hawes was deliberately inexact. Nettleton distinguished between conviction and what he called '*extreme distress*'. The latter, he observed, 'does not generally continue long, especially in seasons of revival; sometimes but a few moments; *commonly* a few hours; and rarely over three days. And when this extreme distress exceeds this time I begin to fear that it may subside (as it has sometimes done) without a change of heart.'[4]

There is no doubt that the full preaching of the gospel in this

[1] *Letters on Revivals*, pp. 89–90.

[2] From biblical descriptions of rebirth as 'creation' and 'resurrection' Griffin proved that regeneration is instantaneous and supernatural. The time of its occurrence is not always known to the individual, although its result – a new principle of sanctification – will always be evident. 'Show me a man in whom holiness and sin are struggling for dominion, and I will show you one who is already born again' (*Lectures in Park Street*, p. 124).

[3] Edward A. Lawrence, *The Life of Joel Hawes* (Hartford, Conn., 1871), p. 100.

[4] *Nettleton and his Labours*, p. 122.

era made assurance, *humanly speaking*, more difficult. Bennet Tyler, summarizing the preaching, says it was not a message which spoke only of 'escaping future punishment and obtaining eternal happiness'; rather, conversion was shown to be 'a deep, radical change of all the moral feelings' and thus, when men came under conviction, 'it became difficult for them to persuade themselves that they had become Christians till a real change had been wrought in them'.[1]

For this reason these leaders were against treating anyone as a convert simply on profession of faith. Beecher's warning against 'the hasty recognition of persons as converted upon their own judgement, without interrogation or evidence',[2] was echoed by all his brethren. Tyler remarked of Nettleton: 'He never told persons that they had reason to hope. He would set before them, with great plainness, the distinguishing evidences of regeneration, and enjoin it upon them to be faithful and honest in the application of these evidences to themselves.'[3] In Nettleton's opinion, 'Many an awakened sinner had his convictions all talked away, and he talked into a false hope.'[4] These preachers did not regard an individual's own feelings as any sure spiritual sign. 'The young convert, in judging of the reality of his conversion, lays much stress upon having a great deal of joy; and regards that as a very decisive proof that he is a disciple of Christ. But this is one of the most fallacious proofs, and no dependence ought to be placed on it.'[5] Much more is needed to distinguish the true from the false:

The manner in which people obtain a false hope is generally this: they first believe that God is reconciled to them, and then are reconciled to him on that account; but if they thought that God was still displeased with, and determined to punish them, they would find their enmity to him revive. On the contrary, the Christian is reconciled because he sees the holiness of the law which he has broken, and God's justice in punishing him; he takes part with God against himself, cordially submits to him, and this when he expects condemnation. He is

[1] *New England Revivals*, p. ix.
[2] Letter to N. S. S. Beman, Jan. 1827, *Letters of the Rev. Dr. Beecher and Rev. Mr. Nettleton, on the 'New Measures' in Conducting Revivals of Religion* (New York, 1828), p. 83.
[3] *Nettleton and his Labours*, p. 135.
[4] Ibid., p. 256. [5] Payson, *Works*, vol. 1, p. 268.

reconciled, because he is pleased with the character of God; the false convert, because he hopes God is pleased with him.'[1]

These preachers all believed in the occasional use of 'inquiry meetings' but at such meetings they sought only to advise individuals from Scripture and never supposed that they could deliver any from spiritual distress. It is in God's hands as to when those under conviction enter into peace and joy. Often the consolation would come as surprisingly as the initial conviction. Nettleton described an inquiry meeting where distress was so great, with very few finding relief, that Christians dreaded attending the next such meeting:

> They could hardly endure the thought of passing through such a scene of distress a second time. And I can truly say that, for the first time, I felt the same reluctance. But, to the astonishment of all, instead of an anxious, we had a joyful meeting. Most of those in such distress at our last meeting for inquirers, had found relief, and were exceeding joyful. What an astonishing change in one week! I felt that it could hardly be possible. We had lost our anxiety, and had little else to do but to render united thanks to God for what He had done.[2]

The extent to which these accounts will be seen as wise dealing with the spiritual needs of men and women must depend on our own convictions regarding the biblical teaching. They certainly demonstrate that doctrinal convictions on the nature of conversion have very practical consequences in pastoral ministry. To sum up the subject we have been considering: true conversion involves a radical break with the principle of sin and self-interest which controls the natural man. To be born of the Spirit is to become 'spiritual', to possess a new nature which loves holiness and conformity to God. So whether it be one professed conversion or hundreds in revival, the test is the evidence of *moral* transformation. Where any other test is elevated, and regarded as of primary importance, the inevitable result will ultimately be that the whole idea of revival becomes discredited. To claim as the work of the Holy Spirit anything that does not show itself first by purity of life is to undermine the real meaning of Christianity. What made the

---

[1] Ibid., p. 269.   [2] *Nettleton and his Labours*, p. 128.

revivals of the early nineteenth century so powerful in the conviction and silencing of unbelief was their indisputable effects in changing men's habits, subduing their selfishness and pride, and rendering visible the apostolic assertion, 'if any man be in Christ, he is a new creature: old things are passed away; behold, all things are become new' (2 Cor. 5:17). Joshua Bradley, writing in 1819, gives testimony to this:

God has delivered his cause from reproach, and laid waste the systems of infidels. These are confounded, and stand with silent astonishment, to see such a striking alteration, as evidently appears in many old hardened sinners, who they thought, were inaccessible to the influences of religion. But they are not more astonished than many of the converts are themselves, to find such a change in their own feelings, views, motives and desires. Who can behold the blessed effects of the religion of Jesus, and not be convinced of its divine original?[1]

*   *   *

In concluding this chapter some comment is needed on the personal character of these five men. With one possible exception (the reason for which will be clearer in a later chapter), the impression that they leave on those who read their writings, as of those who heard them, is that the things about which they spoke were great realities in their own lives. Their lives and preaching illustrated the words of the apostle John, 'That which we have seen and heard declare we unto you.' They appeared to men not so much as eloquent preachers but as Christians for whom fellowship with God was a living experience. The evidence of their personal papers abundantly confirms the truth of that impression. Their work was not their first business. They aimed to live near to Christ. To know him in private was more important than to speak for him before men. They depended on Christ as 'the foundation of every good thought, desire and affection' in order to live and not simply for their public work. 'At times,' wrote Payson, 'God is pleased to

---

[1] *Accounts of Religious Revivals in Many Parts of the United States, from 1815 to 1818*, p. 129.

admit his children to nearer approaches and more intimate degrees of fellowship with himself and his Son, Jesus Christ.' From diary entries which were never intended to be published we occasionally see something of the experiences that lay behind such words. For example, Payson wrote on 22 April 1807:

Spent this day in fasting and prayer. At first was stupid; but soon God was pleased to lift up the light of his countenance upon me, and visit me with his free Spirit. O how infinitely glorious and lovely did God in Christ appear! I saw, I felt, that God was mine, and I his, and was unspeakably happy. Now, if ever, I enjoyed communion with God. He shone sweetly upon me, and I reflected back his beams in fervent, admiring, adoring love. Had a most ravishing view of the glories of heaven, of the ineffable delight with which the Lord Jesus beholds the happiness which he has purchased with his own blood.[1]

The secret of the influence of these men was that in their being much with Christ they were indeed the reflectors of 'his beams'.

But if it be asked how they attained to being such close disciples the answer may be surprising. It was not that they had reached some higher ground in the way of holiness. On the contrary, what marked them most was their low views of themselves. 'The leading element of Doctor Griffin's Christian character', remarked Sprague, 'was a deep sense of his own corruptions and of his entire dependence on the sovereign grace of God.'[2] 'I fear that I am little better than a cumberer of the ground,' Spring recorded in his diary,[3] and Payson, similarly, often noted the pain of his unworthiness and his failure as a Christian. On 18 December 1817 he recorded in his diary: 'Began to think, last night, that I have been sleeping all my days; and this morning felt sure of it . . . How astonishingly blind have I been, and how imperceptible my religious progress.'[4] Again, in 1821 he told a ministerial friend, 'My parish, as well as my heart, very much resembles the garden of the sluggard; and, what is worse, I find that most of my desires

---

[1] *Works*, vol. 1, pp. 92–3.
[2] *Life and Sermons of Griffin*, vol. 1, p. 250. See also p. 138.
[3] *Personal Reminiscences*, vol. 2, p. 60.
[4] *Works*, vol. 1, p. 369.

for the melioration of both proceed either from pride, or vanity or indolence.'[1]

Statements such as these show us the nature of the relationship with God that these men had. Their felt need lay behind their frequent prayer and their dependence on Christ. Earnestness in prayer, says Payson, requires a true view of oneself: 'You cannot make a rich man beg like a poor man; you cannot make a man that is full cry for food like one that is hungry: no more will a man who has a good opinion of himself cry for mercy like one who feels that he is poor and needy.' This was the heart of Christian experience:

As our views of our own sinfulness, and of the abominable malignity of sin, are always in direct proportion to our views of the divine purity and glory, the Christian never appears to himself so unspeakably vile, so totally unworthy of his Saviour's love, or so unfit to enjoy his presence, as at the very time when he is favored with these blessings, in the highest degree. The consequence is that he is astonished, confounded, crushed and overwhelmed by a display of goodness so undeserved, so unexpected. When he has perhaps been ready to conclude that he was a vile hypocrite, and to give up all for lost; or, if not to fear that God would bring upon him some terrible judgment for his sins, and make him an example to others – then to see his much-insulted Saviour, his neglected Benefactor, his injured Friend, suddenly appear to deliver him from the consequences of his own folly and ingratitude; to see him come with smiles and blessings, when he expected nothing but upbraidings, threatenings, and scourges – it is too much; he knows not how to bear it; he scarcely dares take the consolation offered him; he sinks down ashamed and broken-hearted at his feet; feels unworthy and unable to look up; and the more condescendingly Christ stoops to embrace him, so much lower and lower does he sink in the dust. At length his emotions find utterance, and he cries, O Lord, treat me not thus kindly. Such favors belong to those, only, who do not requite thy love as I have done. How can it be just, how can it be right to give them to one so undeserving? Thy kindness is lavished upon me in vain; thy mercies are thrown away upon one so incorrigibly vile. If thou pardon me now, I shall offend thee again; if thou heal my backslidings, I shall again wander from thee; if thou cleanse me, I shall again become polluted: thou must, O Lord, give me up – thou must leave me to perish, and bestow thy favors on those who are less unworthy, less incurably prone to offend thee. Such are often the feelings of the broken-hearted penitent.[2]

---

[1] Ibid., p. 252.   [2] Ibid., pp. 513–4.

Broken-hearted penitents were what these men knew themselves to be all their days. They sought to live in the experience of the grace of God to the wholly undeserving and never ceased to pray for the Spirit who shed the love of God abroad in their hearts. This was the desire that kept them coming back to him. So as an old man Griffin was still pursuing the hope of his youth: 'I long and pray for high communion with God, and for affections toward him more ardent and delightful than I ever felt before.'[1] The same motivation entered into their keenest anticipations of heaven. Thus Nettleton wrote to young converts in 1820: 'No friendship, no attachment in this world, is equal to that created in a revival of religion . . . But, my dear friends, after all, *the milk and the honey lie beyond this wilderness world.*'[2]

It will always be true that the further preachers enter into true evangelical experience, and the more they know of the Spirit of Christ, the more will the elements of tenderness and love, doxology and praise enter into their ministries. Looking back on his long ministry, and on those of others, Spring made an important observation on this point. He noted that while the experience of an 'alarmed conscience' can enable a man to preach on 'fearful themes', it requires 'a loving heart' to preach Christ as he should be preached. So deficient did Spring feel himself to be in this regard that he wrote: 'The difficulty of *preaching well* on the more attractive and winning themes has sometimes alarmed me, and made me fear lest after having preached to others, I myself should be a cast-away.'[3]

Payson entered deeply into this love, and reflected it to an eminent degree, although that was not how he regarded himself and his preaching, as he wrote to his mother:

I have sometimes heard of spells and charms to excite love, and have wished for them, when a boy, that I might cause others to love me. But how much do I now wish for some charm which should lead men to love the Saviour! . . . Could I paint a true likeness of Him, methinks I should rejoice to hold it up to the view and admiration of all creation, and be hid behind it forever. It would be heaven enough to hear Him

[1] *Life and Sermons*, vol. 1, p. 209.
[2] *Nettleton and his Labours*, pp. 131–2.
[3] *Personal Reminiscences*, vol. 1, p. 110.

praised and adored. But I can not paint Him; I can not describe Him; I can not make others love Him; nay, I can not love Him à thousandth part so much as I ought myself. O, for an angel's tongue! O, for the tongues of ten thousand angels, to sound His praises.

If the same characteristic marked these men it was because they obtained it at the same source. A hearer of Griffin in New Jersey in 1829 gives us a description of his preaching and of the near-irresistible love which was its inspiration. The occasion was a very hot summer's evening and the preacher's text was 'The harvest is past, the summer is ended, and we are not saved':

I have heard many sermons from these words, all, I think, impressive, but this one from Dr. Griffin was beyond almost any sermon I ever heard. One felt as if he must cry out in amazement that any soul unprepared to die could be quiet and unconcerned. During most of the sermon his face was wet with tears, and for nearly an hour he spoke to us with such tender and appealing sentences that it seemed as if his hearers must cry out in an agony of fear and trembling . . . But what a climax the ending was! It was a wonder how he had endured the strain so long, and that he had not given up physically exhausted. The mental agony, the heart-breaking sympathy, were enough to break an angel down! When he fell on his knees as if he had been knocked on the head with an axe, with outstretched arms, tears coursing down his face, he cried out: 'Oh! my dying fellow sinners, I beseech you to give your hearts to the Savior now. Give your life to Jesus Christ. Do not put it off. Do not leave this house without dedicating yourself to His service, lest you be left at last to cry, "The harvest is past, the summer is ended, and I am not saved".'[1]

Griffin's married daughter, with whom he lived after returning to Newark in 1836, wrote of how in his old age the salvation of souls from eternal misery 'was the one subject that occupied his time, his conversation, and his prayers'. Arriving in Newark during the winter, he was not content to preach occasionally: 'Early in the spring he commenced a course of visitation, which occupied his mornings for several successive

---

[1] Quoted in Samuel B. Halliday, *The Church in America and its Baptism of Fire*, being an *Account of the Progress of Religion in America, in the eighteenth and nineteenth centuries* (New York, 1895), p. 93. The sermon will be found in *Life and Sermons*, vol. 1, pp. 437–53.

weeks. And who that marked his feeble footsteps as he bent before the chilling blast but felt that some mighty purpose moved his soul? These visits, these admonitions, these prayers of anxious love, can never be forgotten.'[1] 'There were more than forty individuals among his impenitent friends whom he bore on his heart before the Mercy Seat many times each day. And as he had opportunity, he failed not to warn every one of them with tears.'[2] In this manner, and in a spirit of joy and praise, Griffin spent the last months of his life in 1837. His wife died on 25 July, 'Great sinner, great sinner, great Saviour' being among her last words.[3] He followed on 8 November, in great calmness and gratitude: 'I know heaven must be a blessed place,' he said. 'God is there. Christ is there.'

We have only touched upon some of the features which characterized these five leaders. But we shall misinterpret both them and the whole age of revival in which they laboured if we fail to see that it was the grace and providence of God which made them all that they were. As Sprague observed at the conclusion of his *Life of Griffin*, they were men whose gifts received a 'holy impulse' from the influence of God's Spirit. Their public work was planned to coincide with 'a period of unrivalled interest; a period when great events were the order of the day, and the spirit of missions was breaking forth in one country, and the spirit of revivals in another, and in a third, a storm of atheistical fanaticism, that made the very foundations of society rock'.[4] What Sprague wrote of Griffin could be said of them all:

Had he lived at an earlier period, he would indeed have been remembered as a great man, and perhaps as an eminently devoted minister; and yet the monuments of his pious activity might have been comparatively few: his commanding energies might have been exhausted in prophesying to bones upon which the breath from heaven had not begun to fall, even to the time of his going down to the grave. But he came upon the stage at the very time when the preparation in providence seemed to have been completed for the introduction of a new order of things: the fields were white around him, and what he had to do was to take his sickle and go forth to the harvest.[5]

---

[1] *Life and Sermons*, vol. 1, p. 239.   [2] Ibid., p. 234.
[3] Ibid., p. 222.   [4] Ibid., p. 266–7.   [5] Ibid., p. 267.

9

'NEW MEASURES' AND OLD
REVIVALS?

Asahel Nettleton (1783–1843)
Reproduced by courtesy of
The Connecticut Historical Society,
Hartford, Connecticut.

9

Early nineteenth-century America was on the move to a degree undreamed of by previous generations. On 28 February 1795, 500 loaded sleighs were counted travelling westwards through Albany, New York, and 1,200 at another time that same winter. It was an era when maps went out of date within a few years. New towns sprang up almost overnight. For example, Rochester, New York, which in 1812 was unbroken wilderness, became by 1830 a marketing and manufacturing centre of 10,000 people. Roads, rivers, and canals speeded up the dispersal and relocation of people, but even more significant were the factors that helped the swift movement of ideas. Schools and colleges, the principal sources and disseminators of thought, were springing up everywhere. In the realm of theological education alone, seventeen seminaries came into existence between 1808 and 1827. Still more influential in the dissemination of ideas was the age of publishing which arrived with the new century. While the day of the 'penny press' had not yet come, gazettes and magazines – the majority with a religious content – were becoming commonplace. Every denomination had its opinion-moulding periodicals; the Presbyterians alone possessed dozens by the 1820s.[1] 'No less than 37 religious weeklies flourished in the United States' in 1837.[2]

[1] 'American Presbyterian Periodicals and Newspapers, 1752–1830', *Journal of Presbyterian History* (Philadelphia, Sept. 1963).

[2] A. L. Drummond, *Story of American Protestantism* (Edinburgh, 1949), p. 363.

The autobiography of Wilson Thompson, a Baptist preacher, gives us a glimpse of how quickly a new idea could now travel from one part of the country to another. In 1810 Thompson and his family left Kentucky, where they had belonged to the Regular Baptist churches which had originated in Virginia, for the largely unsettled forests of Missouri. Thompson had been a witness of the effect of revival on the Baptist churches of Kentucky, but he found very different spiritual conditions in his new frontier home on the other side of the Mississippi. There were few churches and his congregation was made up of small groups from settlements on creeks, separated by twenty miles of forest. Among such hearers at an open-air service in December 1812, he saw his first awakening in Missouri. People had assembled 'from different settlements, for twenty or thirty miles around . . . Solemnity, deep as death, was depicted on most of the countenances', and joy and serene peace was evident in believers:

I took for a text the saying of Paul: 'For the wages of sin is death, but the gift of God is eternal life through Jesus Christ' . . . At the close of this discourse the large congregation seemed deeply affected. I cast my eyes over them, and the general appearance was a solemn stillness, as though some unseen power was hovering over them. Every eye was set on me, and I felt mute with astonishment, and stood silent for some minutes. I believe there was not a motion nor a sound during the time, until, simultaneously, some twenty or more persons arose from their seats and came forward.

The Missouri settlers were responding to an altar call which he had not given. As the idea of the mourner's bench had reached England by 1807, it is hardly surprising that it was also to be found on this trackless frontier in 1812. A preacher with less experience in revival than Thompson might have welcomed this public demonstration of concern. Instead, he simply prayed and made it clear that he did not mean to adopt the innovation which he knew was already popular elsewhere. At the evening service the same day, Thompson says: 'No mourning benches were there for the seekers to exhibit themselves upon, but many mourning hearts were hiding from the public gaze in some dark corner, and there, in the secret breathing of desire, were seeking after the Lord, "if haply He might be found".'[1]

The transmission of an idea from one denomination to another failed in this instance, but it more often met with success, and nowhere more so than in central New York State. What happened there became a watershed in evangelical history and introduced the first major controversy on the meaning of revival between leaders who equally professed their belief in the work of the Spirit of God.

In the early nineteenth century the state of New York, with its 45,000 square miles, was realizing its potential for vast increase – both in its central area from Albany, on the Hudson, westwards into the Mohawk Valley, and in the western region proper, bordering the southern side of Lake Ontario and extending as far west as Lake Erie. From 1790 a large number of people began pouring into the region, including many from Connecticut and Vermont. By 1803 the counties of Cayuga and Onondaga alone had a population of around 30,000. Oneida County, which linked central and western New York, was to become still more important, especially after the completion of the Erie Canal in 1825.

There were so many New Englanders in central New York that men could speak of it as a colony of New England. In some senses it was, but its people were widely different from the largely homogeneous population, possessing common Christian beliefs, which had been found in New England a century earlier. Methodism, which had not found ready entrance in New England, was by this time well established in New York. So too were other Arminian groups, including the Freewill Baptists (from around 1780) and the 'Christians', a group that promised an end to all sects and denominations. Following the War of Independence, New England had been in a ferment both socially and religiously. Innovating religious parties, including the influential Unitarians (who were ministers of professedly orthodox Congregational churches until the early nineteenth century) and the more recent Universalists, were united in what one writer called 'an abhorrence of New England Puritanism'.

In western and central New York many of the Presbyterian

[1] *The Autobiography of Elder Wilson Thompson: His Life, Travels and Ministerial Labors* (1867; Springfield, Ohio, 1962), p. 121; see also p. 150.

and Congregational churches were linked by the Plan of Union of 1801, which brought both denominations together with the intention of furthering missionary expansion on the basis of a common adherence to the theology of the Westminster Confession.[1] It met with considerable success. Early in the Second Great Awakening, Cayuga and Onondaga Counties saw revival in 1797, and a movement affecting a much wider area began in March 1800. Thereafter, periodic revivals were noted in many places, including Jefferson County, on the frontier bordering the north-eastern corner of Lake Ontario. A revival is said to have swept over parts of that county in 1815, to be followed by others. New Presbyterian churches emerged here as elsewhere, including one at Sackets Harbor and one at Adams where the Rev. George W. Gale saw sixty-five converts at the opening of his ministry in 1819. B. B. Warfield wrote of this area: 'Seventy were added to the church at Sackets Harbor in 1820. In 1821 the whole region was stirred to its depths; from eight hundred to a thousand converts were reported from Jefferson County.'[2]

These records from an obscure corner of upstate New York would be of little consequence were it not for a now famous name, which was first heard of in Adams at this date. In 1821 Charles Grandison Finney was one of many to become a communicant member at the church in Adams pastored by Gale. From the outset, however, this tall, fair-haired, twenty-nine-year-old New Englander was no average person.[3] Finney

[1] The Plan aimed to remove competition between churches. Thereafter, newly established churches in New England would be Congregational and those in New York State Presbyterian, with some latitude permitted in local church polity for congregations of Congregational origin.

[2] *Perfectionism* (New York: Oxford University Press, 1931), vol. 2, p. 15.

[3] Finney (1792–1875) was born in Connecticut from whence his family had followed the emigration tide when he was about two years old. The main source of information about Finney is his own *Memoirs*, written between 1866 and 1868 and published posthumously in 1876 after revision and abridgement by J. H. Fairchild. Two versions of the *Memoirs* are now available. The best-known is the Fairchild text as found in *Memoirs of Rev. Charles G. Finney, Written by Himself* (New York: Fleming H. Revell, 1903). Recently, however, the original, unrevised text has appeared for the first time, G. M. Rosell and R. A. G. Dupuis (eds.) *The Memoirs of Charles G. Finney: The Complete Text* (Grand Rapids: Zondervan Publishing House, 1989). The latter volume, which includes valuable notes, shows the extent to which the *Memoirs* had

had already been in church attendance during his four years as a law apprentice in a local attorney's office and Gale had noted him as a forceful, independent individual whose influence 'stood in the way of the conversion of many'. After his conversion in October 1821 Finney was as decided for the gospel as he had formerly been for the world. Almost immediately, he began to study for the Christian ministry, at first informally under Gale and then, from June 1823, with a second teacher in addition to Gale, at the direction of the local presbytery. By then Finney was also helping Gale as an evangelist. He was licensed by the presbytery in December 1823 and soon after became a missionary in the north of Jefferson County, being supported by the Female Missionary Society of the western district of the state of New York. His ordination in the Presbyterian Church followed in June 1824.

For nearly two years Finney remained a frontier missionary, determined to preach wherever he could in scattered country congregations. The Fall of 1825 was a turning-point. On a visit to Utica in Oneida County he met Gale, who had relocated on account of ill health. Gale clearly had a high view of his ability and persuaded him to remain in this far more highly populated area, which was strategic for both central and western New York. So committed was Gale to enlisting Finney's help that for nearly three months at his new home in Western he gave up his own study and bedroom for the missionary and his wife, Lydia, who had also belonged to his former church at Adams. Here Finney was close to stronger churches and more influential ministers of his own Presbyterian denomination. In the remaining months of 1825 the church where Gale needed Finney's help at Western saw a powerful spiritual awakening, with some 140 professions of conversion. The 'Western revival' was to give its name to a wider movement of revival in Oneida County, which continued, it was said, up to the spring of 1827. Many men were engaged in the work but none was more

---

been revised and abridged by Fairchild. As a source it is, therefore, superior to the popular version. But as the popular version remains the one most generally accessible I will use it in the following pages, with the title *Memoirs.* When it is necessary to refer to the Rosell and Dupuis edition I give the title as, *Memoirs: Complete Text.*

suddenly prominent than Charles Finney who preached successively at Rome and Utica, the two largest towns of the county. Rome, with a population of some 4,000, saw an estimated 500 added to the churches – Baptist and Methodist as well as Presbyterian. According to one minister: 'Worldly business was to a great extent suspended. Religion was the principal subject of conversation in our streets, stores, and even taverns'.[1] At Utica Finney preached for months from the pulpit of the First Presbyterian Church while he stayed in the home of its pastor, Samuel C. Aikin. Before the end of 1826 the fame of Finney's evangelistic work was further spread by his acceptance of an invitation to the pulpit of the prominent Nathan Beman, minister of the First Presbyterian Church at Troy on the Hudson River, the largest church in the northern part of the state. At Troy too there were reports of remarkable revival.

The following year, 1827, saw the first public controversy between parties that both claimed to believe in revival. Towards the end of 1826 Finney met twice with Asahel Nettleton who was preaching at Albany across the Hudson from Troy. At these meetings Nettleton came to believe that he could make no headway in alerting the younger man to dangers of which he seemed to be heedless. Immediately after their second meeting Nettleton set out his concerns in a letter to Samuel Aikin of Utica dated 13 January 1827. The letter, which was not hostile to Finney personally, was meant for circulation among ministers. Its aim was to warn against 'the irregularities and confusion introduced into revivals at the West'.[2] 'Those ministers and Christians who have heretofore been most and longest acquainted with revivals', wrote Nettleton, 'are most alarmed.' It was by the avoidance of practices now favoured that 'the character of revivals, for *thirty years past,* has been guarded. If the evil be not soon prevented a generation will arise, inheriting all the obliquities of their

---

[1] From the account of Moses Gillet in *A Narrative of the Revival of Religion in the County of Oneida, Particularly in the Bounds of the Presbytery of Oneida, in the Year 1826* (Utica, N.Y., 1826), pp. 10–11.

[2] Dr David Porter writing to Gardiner Spring on the subject on 28 May 1827 (*Personal Reminiscences of Gardiner Spring*, vol. 1, p. 235). An abridgement of Nettleton's letter to Aikin is found in *Nettleton and his Labours*, pp. 342–55.

leaders, not knowing that a revival ever did or can exist without all those evils.'[1]

Finney saw Nettleton's letter and replied to it indirectly in a sermon on 'Can Two Walk Together Except They be Agreed?' which he preached first at Utica, then at Troy. The main purpose of the sermon seems to have been to show that the things that Nettleton and others had warned against in the recent revivals were also those to which worldly men were opposed, and therefore the state of heart of those who issued such warnings must be as cold as those of impenitent sinners. Men do not walk together 'except they be agreed'. This audacious interpretation of Nettleton's counsel, which was soon published, instantly heightened controversy and, as far away as Philadelphia, brought the comparatively unknown Finney to the critical attention of Ashbel Green in the columns of the June issue of the *Christian Advocate*. Nettleton, too, now went public for the first time in consenting that a long letter from him to Gardiner Spring, of 4 May 1827, which reviewed Finney's sermon, be published in the *Observer* of New York.

Prior to the outbreak of public controversy in 1827, there had been indications that disagreement existed. As early as 13 May 1825, a letter from Charles Sears to Finney had pin-pointed what later became a central issue. Sears had been a close friend of Finney in Adams and both men had been converted around the same time. In 1825 Sears was at Hamilton College where there had been a powerful revival. But news he heard of some aspects of Finney's work disturbed him. Nor were his feelings based on hearsay. He had recently seen a letter of Finney's to 'Brother Maynard' – a mutual Christian acquaintance – written in response to advice that Maynard had sought to give the young evangelist. Maynard pointed out the danger of using or aiming at excitement to promote results. Finney's reply was written, to Sears' dismay, 'in the language of very severe reproof'; it implied that the adviser's real problem was his own 'cold heart'. Rejecting this interpretation of Maynard's character, Sears wrote to Finney on 13 May 1825:

I confidently presume that when you demanded of Br. M. who he was that he should direct as to the particular degree of excitement that was

---

[1] *Nettleton and his Labours*, p. 348.

necessary and when you implied that God would manage such things and according to the best plan, you did not mean that everything in a revival was right, and that no degree of rant and passion could be wrong . . . my opinion is that in a revival of religion the great instrument of its progress is Prayer, that exhortation and warm and appropriate appeals be made to the understanding and conscience, that the truth should be exhibited in its most impressive light and if God does not bless that, it is because he has no intention to display his grace. But that excitements have been produced in ways different from this my own observation can well attest, and it is as much our duty to expose this counterfeit as to expose any other error that we discover in the religious creeds or practices of men. If you admit these principles (as I assume you do) under these Br. M. I am persuaded has the fullest justification, but if you do not admit them I shall have the unhappiness of differing from you, and I shall also take the liberty of expressing a very serious doubt of the genuineness of that revival which is conducted upon the principle that no degree of animal feeling is too great, and that every excitement, however raised, is to be cultivated and cherished.[1]

There is no record of Finney's reply to Sears but subsequent events make it clear that he was not listening.

In 1826 there were more indications of the coming controversy in an eighty-eight-page booklet, *A Narrative of the Revival of Religion in the County of Oneida*, compiled by three leading members of the Oneida Presbytery, John Frost, Moses Gillett, and Noah Coe. They believed that the revival was 'a work of divine power of what we have witnessed no parallel in this country, and such as we have seldom discovered in the history of the church': '*More than three thousand* are indulging hope that they have become reconciled to God through the Redeemer.'[2] But they also reveal that besides the inevitable opposition of Unitarians, there were misgivings among some of the orthodox: 'Some few individuals may have differed from their brethren, with regard to the propriety of some measures.'[3] What these 'measures' were is not stated, but comparison of the *Narrative* with accounts of earlier revivals reveal features that were new to Presbyterian, Congregational, and Baptist churches. Inquiry meetings, as we have seen, had long been

[1] Finney Papers, Oberlin College Library.
[2] *Narrative of the Revival of Religion in the County of Oneida*, p. 35.
[3] Ibid., p. 26.

used but only when the number seeking further help was too large to be dealt with privately.[1] In the Western revivals, by contrast, the inquiry meetings began to assume a special importance as a necessary part of revival and a means of conversion: 'Meetings of inquiry have apparently been a powerful means of bringing sinners to repentance . . . in these meetings of inquiry, it was not uncommon for two or three in every meeting to submit their hearts to Christ.'[2] Naming unconverted people in prayer meetings and references to 'the prayer of faith' were also noted, without criticism, by the authors of the *Narrative*. Although Finney was mentioned in various places by several writers as 'signally owned and blessed', he was not central to the different accounts submitted to the compilers by many churches. It is clear that revivals occurred in some parts of the county before he visited them or even where he never went. 'Much opposition has been made to this revival', reads the *Narrative*, but the impression left is that it was all without foundation.

Another publication from other orthodox ministers in Oneida soon followed which pointed to the possibility of a different conclusion. In May 1827 pastors of Congregational churches in Oneida published a *Pastoral Letter of the Ministers of the Oneida Association to the Churches under their Care*, a booklet containing twenty-two pages of close print. It was commonly supposed that the author was William R. Weeks, minister at Paris Hill and the scribe of the association. The *Pastoral Letter* makes it clear both that 'Revivals of Religion are a divine and glorious reality' and that such revivals had been seen among them in 'the past year': 'In most of our congregations, there have been, as we trust, instances more or less numerous, of souls converted to God, and brought to the saving knowledge of

---

[1] Thus Nettleton, during revival in Virginia in 1828, 'would not even hold "inquiring meetings" until the increase of the work made it impracticable any longer to see inquirers privately'; quoted in 'Revivals of Religion', *Miscellanies of Thomas E. Peck*, vol. 1 (Richmond, Va., 1895), p. 215.

[2] *Narrative*, pp. 13, 22 (and 30, 42 etc). Referring to the different use of inquiry meetings under the new-measures evangelism, Charles P. McIlvaine observed: 'I fear . . . inquiry was a very secondary matter on the part of the conductors, and the fanning of excitement and the inducing of those who felt little to *commit themselves*, in other words, to make some *profession*, were the engrossing objects' (Sprague, *Lectures*, appendix, p. 95).

the truth. And we desire to call upon ourselves, and upon all under our care, to rejoice in the grace of God which is manifested in the outpourings of his Spirit, wherever enjoyed.'[1]

Thus the *Pastoral Letter* was in no sense a denunciation of the Western revivals, still less of Charles G. Finney, who is not mentioned. But the pastors who supported the document were disturbed at the attitude (displayed in the *Narrative of the Revival of Religion* published by their Presbyterian brethren) which admitted no admixture of anything wrong or unscriptural, and their chief purpose was to draw attention to the danger of this lack of discrimination. In other words, they believed there was cause for the criticism of some things that had occurred and that such criticism was necessary, not to hinder revivals, but in their best interests:

If a revival is attended with faults and blemishes, it is not certain that there is no good in it. Nor if it is admitted to be a revival of religion, is it certain that no faults have attended it. And as it would be wrong to refuse to see the good because there are some evils, so it is doubtless wrong to shut our eyes upon the evils that exist, because there is some good . . . We are not required, indeed, to trumpet abroad every fault we see; and where no injury will result from concealment, then doubtless we ought to be silent. But where such faults accompany a revival, as are known to the public, such as are likely to operate to the injury of souls . . . silence would be criminal.[2]

The general points of concern in the *Pastoral Letter* can be seen from the following headings:

Condemning in the gross, or approving in the gross; Making too much of any favourable appearance; Not guarding against false conversions; Ostentation and noise; The hasty acknowledgement of persons as converted; (The strength of a church does not consist in its numbers, but in its graces . . . We fear that the desire of counting numbers is too much indulged, even by good people.); Suffering the feelings to control the judgment; Talking too much about opposition; Censuring, as unconverted, or as cold, stupid, and dead, those who are in good standing in the visible church; Praying for persons by name, in an abusive manner; Denouncing as enemies of revival those

---

[1] *Pastoral Letter to the Ministers of the Oneida Association to the Churches under their Care* (Utica, N.Y., 1827), p. 13.
[2] Ibid., p. 5.

who do not approve of everything that is done; Taking the success of any measures, as an evidence that those measures are right, and approved of God.

The *Pastoral Letter* concludes by emphasizing the necessity of distinguishing between revivals and abuses in revivals:

The evils which we have pointed out are by no means the necessary attendants on a revival of religion; and the idea that they are so, if it should prevail, must go towards destroying the character of revivals entirely. We hear of extensive and powerful revivals, in various parts of New England, and elsewhere, at the present time, and are assured by our brethren abroad that such evils do not accompany them, but are carefully guarded against, as tending in their opinion, more than anything else, to hinder a genuine work of the Holy Spirit.[1]

By the time the warning words of this *Pastoral Letter* were published in the early summer of 1827, the churches through the Mohawk Valley, from Utica to Troy, were caught up in controversy, with the lines drawn between those who feared that a significant change was occurring in the character of the revivals in western and central New York and those who did not. In an attempt to allay the division, a week-long convention of ministers from the area and beyond was held at New Lebanon in July 1827. The organizers of the meeting appear to have been Nathan Beman and Lyman Beecher. Present with Finney were some of his ministerial supporters from the West, while Beecher's side was represented by Heman Humphrey, William R. Weeks, and a few others. Before the convention met, Nettleton wrote down a number of reasons why he did not wish to attend and why he feared its purpose could not succeed. His statement included the following:

I have been compelled by ministers to talk and exhaust all my strength, and to spend nearly all my time, for about eight months, on this subject. I have done all that I can; and have been greatly blamed by many for what I have done. I have resigned the subject entirely to the management of settled pastors, whose business alone it is to determine the question, what measures shall be introduced into their churches . . .

I have no controversy with any man on the subject, and I fear, if I

[1] Ibid., p. 21.

attend, it will be construed into a personal controversy, and that it will be impossible to avoid it.

I fear that settled ministers at the East and South have not yet *felt* enough of the evils, to appreciate what has already been done; and that these ministers will be obliged to experience more of these evils, before they will take a decisive stand; and the sooner I withdraw, and leave the whole responsibility on them, the better.[1]

In the event, Nettleton was prevailed on by friends to attend some of the meetings of the convention although, as he had anticipated, the discussions were to prove fruitless. 'Had the friends of the new measures been kind enough to inform us of their determination not to renounce them it might have saved their brethren much painful anxiety', he wrote in New York on 6 December 1827.[2] These were among the final words that he put to the 104 pages of materials which were sent for publication that month in New York, entitled *Letters of the Rev. Dr. Beecher and Rev. Mr. Nettleton, on the 'New Measures' in Conducting Revivals of Religion'*.[3] Beecher's contribution was a lengthy letter on the dangers of fanaticism which he had written to Beman of Troy in January 1827. The unsigned preface, which is clearly not by Nettleton, states that its purpose was to leave a testimony so that, if the recent innovations should succeed, a later generation could know that it had been in spite of the warnings of an older generation of leaders, and that if the new practices should become generally acceptable,

if they induce desolation to the churches; if their pathway shall hereafter be traced by the burning of their progress; if their consequences should prove widely ruinous, and confessedly wrong in the end; if the worst anticipations of these letters should be at last realized, or, possibly, transcended, – *that it may be at least known*, though our heads should then be low in dust, and known by witnesses that we furnished, and that shall survive and faithfully interpret us, *that some were NOT their patrons.*

---

[1] *Letters of the Rev. Dr. Beecher and Rev. Mr. Nettleton on the 'New Measures' in Conducting Revivals of Religion* (New York, 1828), pp. 102–3.

[2] Ibid., pp. 22–3.

[3] The first eighty pages contain Nettleton's letter to Aikin of 13 January 1827 and his letter of 4 May 1827, to Spring, which reviewed Finney's sermon 'Can Two Walk Together Except They be Agreed?'.

The preface concludes with the hope that candidates for the ministry, especially, would become acquainted with the letters now published:

Lest, on the one hand, through ignorance or mistake, they become prejudiced against the very name of revivals; or, on the other, so wedded to incorrect principles, and that probably from profound ignorance of the true, that their future influence shall sweep us as with the spirit of the whirlwind, or the death-blast of the sirocco; till all that has been dreaded, as the legitimate result of erroneous principles, shall be visited upon the ruined churches of our land.

If 1827 was a year of controversy the year which followed suddenly seemed to bring it all to a surprising end. For the first time, Finney was now in the East and preaching in Philadelphia, America's second largest city. There, in May 1828, Lyman Beecher signed with Finney and others on the Finney side of the controversy what the Unitarian press called a 'treaty of mutual *silence*'. The signatories agreed 'to cease from all publications, correspondences, conversations and conduct designed and calculated to keep those subjects before the public mind' and 'to induce our friends on either side to do the same'. Nettleton was away in Virginia at this time and when he heard the news he must have been as surprised as William Weeks who 'was collecting facts and making preparations to publish them'.[1] By the time Weeks' work was published in 1848, he and Nettleton were dead and the whole controversy, far from having been settled in 1828, was proceeding to change the course of American church history.

*   *   *

We must now turn to analysis of the causes of the division sketched above. The simplest approach is to explain it in terms

---

[1] *The Pilgrim's Progress in the Nineteenth Century* (New York, 1848), p. 269. Weeks' work gives a detailed account of the whole controversy (pp. 207–418), using pseudonyms for the leading participants: 'Mr. Meek' represented Nettleton, 'Mr. Bold' Finney, 'Mr. Scribus' Aikin, 'Mr Fearless' Beman, 'Mr. Strangeways' Burchard, 'Mr. Thoughtful' Weeks, and so on. This valuable book clearly draws on information recorded twenty years before publication.

of a personal collision between Nettleton and Finney. A recent writer represents Nettleton as piqued by the sudden popularity of Finney which threatened his own reputation.[1] Personal allegations like this date back to the period itself – 'Mr. Nettleton has lost his mind'; 'He is not the man he was'; 'his character has sunk wonderfully'.[2] This line of argument is as inaccurate as it is simple. It does not begin to explain the controversy which is far more complex. Perhaps the first thing to be done in the interests of clarification is to set down some evidence to show that the issues in this controversy are not instantly apparent and straightforward.

While subsequent history has singled out Finney as the representative and prototype of the changes that gave rise to the controversy, the fact is that what was new did not so much derive from Finney as an individual as it did from the whole situation out of which he emerged. What was happening in the melting-pot of western New York and beyond in the 1820s was the result of a fusion of ideas and practices imported from New England and elsewhere. As we have seen, the churches belonging to the older orthodox tradition were by no means alone in this region. The Methodists, whose churches saw a sixteen per cent increase in 1816, were there and so were the Freewill Baptists who, for the first time, it is said, now shared in 'extensive revivals'.[3] With widespread spiritual hunger among the people, and the comparatively small number of ministers and churches (Presbyterians had 116 churches and eighty-two ministers in the entire region in 1818), a new order of itinerant missionaries was also in the field. The Female Missionary Society, which first supported Finney, was one among many evangelistic agencies. In 1826 Finney transferred to a more influential one, the Oneida Evangelical Association. His colleagues in that association were also prominent in the mid-1820s and in some instances were initially better known. The foremost among them were close to Finney. One of them, Jedediah Burchard, had been helping Gale at Adams in the

---

[1] Keith J. Hardman, *Charles Grandison Finney*, p. 124.
[2] *Letters of Beecher and Nettleton*, p. 22.
[3] Whitney R. Cross, *The Burned-Over District: The Social and Intellectual History of Enthusiastic Religion in Western New York, 1800–1850* (Ithaca, N.Y.: Cornell University Press, 1950), p. 11.

year of Finney's conversion and, although he had been only a student at the time, there is reason to think that he had considerable influence over Finney in his formative years as a Christian. In a letter of 1829 Finney spoke highly of Burchard and professed to 'love that man'.[1] Others of the same group – sometimes inaccurately called Finney's 'holy band' – included Daniel Nash, Horatio Foote, Luther Myrick, and Nathaniel Smith.

Nettleton, Weeks, and others, who were not willing to accept uncritically all that occurred during the Western revivals in Oneida County, have been often blamed for not providing more documented evidence against Finney. But the fact is that they were often unsure of who was primarily responsible for the various innovations that were being pressed on the churches by a large group of itinerants and their younger imitators who appeared in the wake of the revivals. George Gale thought that the latter were influenced 'more especially by the Rev. Mr. Nash'. Nettleton, recognizing Finney's gifts and earnestness, at first clearly hoped that he could be won over from the wilder element – 'the whole host of insurgents', as he called them in writing to Beecher.[2] He did not seem to regard Finney as *the* fountain-head of all that was wrong. Before his hopes were finally dashed, Nettleton wrote to Aikin at Utica on 13 January 1827:

The friends of brother Finney are certainly doing him and the cause of Christ great mischief. They seem more anxious to convert ministers and Christians to their peculiarities, than to convert souls to Christ . . . Brother Finney himself has been scarcely three years in the ministry, and has had no time to look at consequences. He has gone, with all the zeal of a young convert, without a friend to check or guide him . . . I believe him to be a good man, and wishing to do good. But nobody dares tell him that a train of causes is set in operation, and urged on by his own friends, which is likely to ruin his usefulness.

I wish I had health and strength to shew brother Finney my whole heart on this subject. I have long been wishing to correct some of his peculiarities, that I might invite him into my own field, and introduce him to my friends. Aside from feeble health, one consideration only has prevented me from making the attempt. Some of his particular

---

[1] Quoted in Hardman, *Finney*, p. 173.
[2] *Autobiography of Beecher*, vol. 2, p. 75.

friends are urging him on to the very things which I wish him to drop. I fear that their flattering representations will overrule all that I can say. And having dropped these peculiarities, his labours for awhile might be less successful; and then he would resort again to the same experiment.[1]

Who Finney's particular friends were at this date we do not know for sure, but they certainly included his three seniors, Jedediah Burchard (c.1790–1864), Daniel Nash (1771–1831), and Nathan Beman (1785–1871). Weeks wrote that Burchard claimed that 'the credit of the new measures' belonged to himself[2] and Burchard appears repeatedly in Weeks' narrative on the controversy published in 1848. Dr Beman of Troy was the most influential of Finney's ministerial supporters. He was patronizing new measures (and disrupting his congregation) before Finney first shared his pulpit in the Fall of 1826. 'I hope we look to God but we must have means', Beman wrote to Finney in September 1826. E. H. Gillett recorded that Beman, whom men nicknamed 'the War-Horse', was 'almost fierce in the construction of the "new measures" . . . By nature fitted to lead and unfitted to follow, he assumed a prominent position in the controversies with which the Church was agitated'.[3]

If Finney had been able to recognize wisdom in at least some of the warnings given by Weeks and his associates in their *Pastoral Letter*, and by others at the New Lebanon Convention, the subsequent course of events might have been very different. Instead, he believed, and was encouraged by others to believe, that the credibility of the Western revivals, and his own reputation, depended on an acceptance of the very things which the Congregational pastors of the Oneida Association regarded as dangers. From now on the new measures were to be defended by Finney as of the essence of revival, and by the

[1] The letter is reprinted in *Nettleton and His Labours*, pp. 342–55. Without offering the slightest reason, Hardman rejects Nettleton's profession of sincerity and talks of 'Nettleton's pretense of friendliness' (*Finney*, p. 115). Hardman claims that the Nettleton biography is 'flawed by a lack of historical perspective and objectivity' (p. 463) but again offers no evidence: 'Nettleton was wise enough to realize that although he could not bring down Charles Finney in fair combat, he could still undermine him by exaggerated and false reports' (p. 179). It is hard to imagine a less objective statement.

[2] *Pilgrim's Progress in the Nineteenth Century*, p. 463.

[3] *Presbyterian Church in U.S.*, vol. 2, p. 277.

stand he thus took the whole controversy became personalized around himself. If the measures were inseparable from the work of the Spirit, then to oppose them, or their defenders, was to oppose revivals, indeed, to oppose God. Finney so convinced himself of this that in the account of the Western revivals in his *Memoirs*, written forty years later, his ministry and the revivals had become one and he wrote of Weeks that 'he carried his opposition to those revivals to the day of his death'.[1] The identification of the revival with Finney was not made by the Presbyterian contributors of *A Narrative of the Revival*, even though they were then Finney's friends and supporters. One of the authors of the *Narrative* was the Rev. Israel Brainerd, and his daughter, Elizabeth, described how the identification first came about: 'At first all stood amazed and glorified God. At length persons of ill-balanced minds and scanty knowledge of Bible truth, began to glorify Mr Finney. To them it was plain *he* had caused the revival, he had converted souls; and as the work progressed and extended, it was believed it would never cease.'[2] The euphoria brought of success contributed largely to Finney's unwillingness to consider any criticism. Referring particularly to his seniors Nettleton and Beecher, he wrote in his *Memoirs*: 'their opposition never made me ashamed, never convinced me that I was wrong in doctrine or practice, and I never made the slightest change in conducting revivals as a consequence of their opposition. I thought I was right. I still think so. I thought their opposition was impertinent and assuming, uncalled for and injurious to themselves, and the cause of God.'[3]

If Finney had not so resolutely defended the new measures, their correctness might have been discussed apart from his own ministry. He was not, after all, their originator, for they were not new at all. They did not derive from Burchard, Beman, or

---

[1] *Memoirs: Complete Text*, p. 197. Joseph Brockway complained of this attitude in Beman and Finney in his booklet *A Delineation of the Characteristic Features of a Revival of Religion in Troy in 1826 and 1827* (Troy, N.Y., 1827).

[2] Mrs Elizabeth Thomson, 'Early Labors of President Finney', *New York Evangelist* (9 December 1875), p. 2; quoted in Finney, *Memoirs: Complete Text*, p. 143 n.

[3] *Memoirs: Complete Text*, pp. 239–40. Fairchild wisely dropped these words in his revision of the text.

anyone else in New York State. The encouragement of physical responses to preaching (such as falling to the floor); women speaking in worship; meetings carried on through long hours and on successive days (protracted meetings); and, above all, inviting individuals to 'submit to God' and to prove it by a 'humbling' action such as standing up, kneeling down, or coming forward to 'the anxious seat' – all came straight from the procedures that some Methodists had been popularizing for a quarter of a century. 'The anxious seat' was only the altar call and the mourner's bench under another name. Finney claimed that 'except in rare instances' he did not use 'the anxious seat' to promote revivals before the Fall of 1830.[1] But this is merely a quibble over the *kind* of public response he employed in his early years; that from the outset of his ministry he sought to make would-be converts visibly distinct is evident. In his first days as a missionary in Jefferson County in the summer of 1824 he told a congregation:

Now I must know your minds, and I want that you who have made up your minds to become Christians, and will give your pledge to make your peace with God immediately, should rise up; but that, on the contrary, those of you who are resolved that you will not become Christians, and wish me so to understand, and wish Christ so to understand, should sit still.' After making this plain, so that I knew that they understood it, I then said: 'You who are now willing to pledge to me and to Christ, that you will immediately make your peace with God, please rise up.'[2]

It may be thought that a calm discussion of the merits of different measures should have prevented division. Some ministers certainly thought that when they went to the New Lebanon Convention, which was intended to ease the controversy in July 1827. The problem, they hoped, was simply a

[1] *Memoirs*, p. 288.
[2] *Memoirs*, p. 63. See also pp. 116, 255 and 261, where those who would 'submit' were instructed to kneel down, but for such controversial points it is essential to read the *Memoirs: Complete Text*. It shows that Fairchild regarded the subject as extremely sensitive and he edited Finney accordingly, e.g. pp. 115, 320–3. Rosell and Dupuis observe that 'about 20 per cent of the text was omitted or changed. Some of this may have been in order to reduce the length of the book, but much of it was because of its controversial or embarrassing character' (p. xli).

question of methods and therefore there could surely be an accommodation between men who shared a common belief in revival. But such hopes were dashed, for, as Nettleton had begun to see, the difference was far more fundamental.

The issue began to clarify around the question of the relationship of emotion, feeling, and excitement to revival, the point that Sears had raised with Finney in May 1825. It was a question of being for or against, not emotion, but rather the adoption of means, in addition to preaching and prayer, to *promote* emotion. There was no disagreement over whether or not hearers under the power of the truth ought to feel and be disturbed and moved, but should methods not mentioned in Scripture be employed to induce a response in those hearing the gospel? Most of the new measures were deliberately calculated to have that effect. They included such things as denunciatory language designed to alarm, pointed remarks to particular individuals delivered in public, naming unconverted people in prayer, using inquiry meetings to make individuals pray or 'submit', and other similar practices.

Such practices were introduced in the Western revivals and, while they succeeded in heightening excitement, they inevitably confused the feeling that attends the powerful preaching of the truth in a revival with excitement that can be worked up where there is no revival. Nettleton and his friends did not deny the existence of revival but held that the results would 'have been equal, or even far greater, without the new measures'.[1] What they deplored was the deliberate use of emotion to increase the number of converts without regard to the danger of counting as converts the spurious as well as the true. As Weeks later wrote: 'We complain that the whole system of measures seems to be adapted to promote false conversions, to cherish false hopes, and propagate a false religion; and thus, ultimately, not only destroy the souls of those who are deceived by it, but to bring revivals, and experimental religion itself, into discredit.'[2]

*   *   *

[1] *Letters of Beecher and Nettleton*, p. 14 n.
[2] *Pilgrim's Progress in the Nineteenth Century*, p. 242.

At the heart of the matter lay a different doctrine of conversion. Gale, Aikin, and other Presbyterian ministers who were attempting to guide Finney failed to see it at the time. So did Beecher who wrote, 'It was not a question of orthodoxy, nor of the reality of revivals, but of wrong measures.'[1] But within a few years the matter was beyond dispute for most observers. Apart from the Utica sermon mentioned above, nothing of Finney's preaching was in print in the 1820s. There was therefore no proof that his teaching differed from that of other Presbyterian ministers. When he preached in Boston in the Fall of 1831, however, Asa Rand, a critical newspaper editor who was one of his hearers, took down a good deal of his sermon on 'Make Yourselves a New Heart' and published lengthy extracts, together, with comment, in a pamphlet. It was not so much Finney's text (Ezekiel 18:31) that was especially noteworthy, but the meaning he gave to the words made the real significance of the 'new measures' unmistakable. Speaking from Griffin's former pulpit, Finney told his Park Street congregation:

I will show you what is intended in the command of the text. It is that man should *change the governing purpose of his life*. A man resolves to be a lawyer; then he directs all his plans and efforts to that object, and that, for the time is his governing purpose. He directs all his efforts to *that* object and so has changed his heart . . . It is apparent that the change now described, effected by the simple volition of the sinner's mind through the influence of motives, is a sufficient change, all that the Bible requires. It is all that is necessary to make a sinner a Christian.[2]

Finney knew that for most of his hearers a major obstacle to accepting this simple account of conversion was what they had been taught about the character of man's fallen nature. If men needed only the inducement of motives in order to effect a change of nature, how was the doctrine of human depravity to be understood? Did the Holy Spirit do no more than persuade men by means of motives to obey the gospel? That was what Finney believed, and he made clear that the whole idea that an unregenerate man was governed by a fallen nature was wrong. Men, he declared, are not governed by natures, either fallen or

---

[1] *Autobiography of Beecher*, vol. 2, p. 75.
[2] Quoted in review in *Biblical Repertory and Theological Review* (1832), p. 295.

holy: 'A nature cannot be holy . . . The nature of Adam, at his creation, was not holy. Adam was made with a nature neither sinful nor holy. When he began to act he made it his governing purpose to serve God.' It was Adam's *will,* not his supposed nature, that controlled his actions and, Finney declared, what was true of Adam remained true for all men; a decision of the will, not a change of nature, was all that was needed for anyone to be converted.

That Finney was not being misquoted in Rand's review was clear from his own *Lectures on Revivals of Religion,* delivered in New York City in the winter of 1834–5 and immediately published. In these lectures Finney repeatedly argued that men must have the ability to commit themselves to Christ, otherwise God would never command it: 'When God commands us to do a thing it is the highest possible evidence that we can do it. He has no right to command unless we have power to obey.'[1] If the influences of the Spirit are 'indispensable to *enable* us to perform duty', the bestowal of them would be 'a mere matter of common justice'.[2] 'God is tyrannical if He commands that which is impracticable.' To speak of the inability of sinners on account of a fallen nature 'slanders God so, charging Him with infinite tyranny in commanding men to do that which they have no power to do'.[3] He criticized the idea that conversion involved an act of omnipotence, or creation, and warned against those who prayed as though they believed that the Spirit's influences were necessary to make the unconverted '*able* to obey their Maker'.[4] Regeneration he argued, was to be effected by 'argument'. 'Truth is the outward means, the outward motive, presented first by man [the preacher] and then by the Holy Spirit.'[5] 'God never did and never can, convert a sinner except with the truth. He may Himself directly communicate it to the sinner; but then the sinner's own agency is indispensable, for conversion consists in the right employment of the sinner's own agency.'[6] 'Men are to be converted, not . . . by a change wrought in their

---

[1] *Lectures on Revivals of Religion,* (New York and London, 1910), with introduction and original notes by W. H. Harding, pp. 116–17.

[2] Ibid., p. 116. [3] Ibid., p. 232. [4] Ibid., p. 357.

[5] Ibid., p. 195. [6] Ibid., p. 359.

nature or constitution by creative power, but by the truth
made effectual by the Holy Spirit. Conversion is yielding to the
truth.'¹ 'What is regeneration? What is it but the beginning of
obedience to God?'² 'WILLING to obey Christ is to be a
Christian. When an individual actually chooses to obey God,
he is a Christian.'³

Finney himself was deeply conscious of the radical contrast
between his own preaching and the orthodoxy of his day. By
1835 he was ready to tell his hearers that he was presenting
what was virtually a new theology of conversion: 'The truth is,
that very little of the Gospel has come out upon the world, for
these hundreds of years, without being clogged and obscured
by false theology.'⁴ And he made clear the very point that
Nettleton had been one of the first to suspect, that the new
measures were to be defended on the basis of a new theology.
If conversion was the result of the sinner's decision, and if the
inducing of that decision was the responsibility of a preacher,
assisted by the Holy Spirit, then any measure that would
bring the unconverted 'right up to the point of instant and
absolute submission' had to be good. For men to be converted,
he argued, 'it is necessary to raise an excitement among
them':⁵

The object of the ministry is to get all the people to feel that the devil
has no right to rule this world, but that they ought all to give
themselves to God, and 'vote in' the Lord Jesus Christ as the
Governor of the universe. Now, what shall be done? What measures
shall we take? Says one: 'Be sure and have nothing that is new.'
Strange! The object of our measure is to gain attention, and you must
have something new.⁶

Thus Finney was open in confessing that the purpose of getting
people to identify themselves publicly was to get them committed, 'to bring them' to submission. 'The anxious seat' or its
equivalent, was vital to evangelism. He held that the procedure
served to make conversions quick, as they ought to be. The
unconverted were to be plainly addressed and 'brought right
up to the single point of immediate submission . . . Then, if

¹ Ibid., p. 377.   ² Ibid., p. 383.   ³ Ibid., p. 424.
⁴ Ibid., p. 427–8.   ⁵ Ibid., p. 2.   ⁶ Ibid., p. 202.

they do not submit, the Holy Spirit forsakes them and their state is well nigh hopeless.'[1]

It may, however, be asked why Finney was dealing with the subject of conversion in his *Lectures on Revivals*. The answer is that to establish his view of conversion was essential to his whole case. If the conversion of one individual could be understood in the way he described, so could the conversion of hundreds. And when hundreds were converted it must mean a revival. So Finney's *Lectures* announced the startlingly novel principle that revivals, as individual conversions, were to be 'promoted' by the right use of *means*. Indeed, they were to be expected by no other way.

Revivals were formerly regarded as miracles . . . For a long time it was supposed by the Church that a revival was a miracle, an interposition of Divine power, with which they had nothing to do, and which they had no more agency in producing than they had in producing thunder, or a storm of hail, or an earthquake. It is only within a few years that ministers generally have supposed revivals were to be *promoted*, by the use of means designed and adapted specially to that object. It has been supposed that revivals came just as showers do, sometimes in one town, and sometimes in another, and that ministers and Churches could do nothing more to produce them than they could to make showers of rain come on their own town, when they were falling on a neighbouring town.

Many people have supposed God's Sovereignty to be something very different from what it is. They have supposed it to be such an arbitrary disposal of events, and particularly of the gift of His Spirit, as precluded a rational employment of means for promoting a revival . . . and they cry out: 'You are trying to get up a revival in your own strength. Take care, you are interfering with the Sovereignty of God. Better keep along in the usual course, and let God give a revival when He thinks it is best. God is a Sovereign, and it is very wrong for you to attempt to get up a revival.'[2]

The older belief in revivals is caricatured here. Evangelicals had always believed that divine blessing was related to the prayer and the preaching of the gospel. It was not to be passively awaited. Thus Ebenezer Porter said of the leaders of 1800: 'There was but one sentiment among the ministers of those times respecting the indispensable importance of using

---

[1] Ibid., p. 430.   [2] Ibid., pp. 13–15.

means for the conversion of sinners; though it was often said by cavillers against the Calvinistic doctrines that these rendered means altogether useless.'[1]

But the older leaders knew that, while obedience to scriptural duties should always mark the church, the *measure* of attendant blessing was in the hands of God who has put 'the times and seasons' in his own power (Acts 1:7). The times of great advance – to which they reserved the name of 'revivals' – were not explainable in terms of 'means', for means were *always* to be faithfully employed. Evangelicals had therefore asserted that such times came unpredictably, spontaneously, sovereignly.

This was what Finney was opposing. He boldly asserted that Christians were to be blamed if there was no revival, for God 'has placed His Spirit at your disposal'.[2] 'You see why you have not a revival. It is only because you do not want one.'[3] 'God has been for one thousand eight hundred years trying to get the Church into the work.'

> If the whole Church, as a body, had gone to work ten years ago, and continued it as a few individuals, whom I could name, have done, there might not now have been an impenitent sinner in the land. The millennium would have fully come into the United States before this day. Instead of standing still, or writing letters, let ministers who think we are going wrong, just buckle on the harness and *go forward*, *and show* us a more excellent way . . . If the Church will do all her duty, the millennium may come in this country in three years . . . If the Church would *do all her duty*, she would soon complete the triumph of religion in the world.[4]

Similarly, Finney insisted that if Christians had agreed in faith and prayer in asking for revival they would have it now: 'We must agree not only about *a* time, but it must be the *present* time.'[5] With such words he led his hearers to his conclusions:

> There is vast ignorance in the Churches on the subject of revivals. After all the revivals that have been enjoyed, and all that has been

---

[1] *Letters on Revivals which Prevailed about the Beginning of the Present Century*, p. 15.
[2] *Revivals of Religion*, p. 134.
[3] Ibid., p. 34.   [4] Ibid., pp. 345–6.   [5] Ibid., pp. 353–4.

said and written and printed concerning revivals, there are very few who have any real, consistent knowledge on the subject . . .

There is vast ignorance among ministers upon this subject, and one great reason of this ignorance is that many get the idea that they already understand all about revivals, when in reality they know next to nothing about them . . .

We see why revivals are often so short, and why they so often produce a reaction. It is because the Church does not understand the subject . . .

We see the guilt of ministers, in not informing themselves, and rightly and speedily instructing the Churches, upon this momentous subject. Why, what is the end of the Christian ministry? What have they to do, but to instruct and marshal the sacramental host, and lead them on to conquest? What, will they let the Church remain in ignorance on the very subject, and the only point of duty, for the performance of which they are in the world – the salvation of sinners? Some ministers have acted as *mysteriously* about revivals as if they thought Christians were either incapable of understanding how to promote them, or that it was of no importance that they should know. But this is all wrong. No minister has yet begun even to understand his duty, if he has neglected to teach his people to work for God in the promotion of revivals.[1]

It is clear that belief about conversion will determine what men believe about revival. If the Holy Spirit's aid is permanently available to all, if conversion is nothing more than the moment when the sinner, employing that aid, yields to the truth and makes his decision, and if there are measures such as the altar call calculated to induce it, then, certainly, the church is to be blamed if she does not achieve conversions and revivals. Finney, therefore, was quite logical in representing critics of the new measures as 'enemies of revivals'.

On the other hand, for Finney's opposers, the teaching that if a person can only be brought to will then he must be regenerate was a fundamental error. It rested on the assumption that there was no problem in man *deeper* than the will – no mind or nature at enmity with God that must first be renewed before there can be any saving response to the gospel. By asserting that man's only problem was his will, Finney had put himself among the Pelagians who denied the reality of man's ruined nature.

---

[1] Ibid., pp. 371–3.

Reviewing the controversy, Gardiner Spring wrote:

Men were instructed that all that is necessary in order to become
Christians is to *resolve to become Christians*, and that the purpose and
determination to become Christians are themselves the religion of the
Gospel . . . It was the teaching of some that the renovation of the
heart, instead of being the work of the Holy Spirit, is the creature's
work and that the power of the Spirit consists in *persuading the sinner
himself to perform* it. The principal advocate of these new measures
and these Pelagian errors was the Rev. Charles G. Finney.[1]

For Finney an appeal for a *public action* had become an
essential part of evangelism. He believed that all that was
needed for conversion was a resolution signified by standing,
kneeling, or coming forward, and because the Holy Spirit
always acts when a sinner acts, the public resolution could be
treated as 'identical' with the miraculous inward change of
sudden conversion'. The words just quoted are those of
Whitney Cross who goes on to observe: 'Managed by a Finney,
such a process might be sober, restrained and highly impressive. But it could also be a relentless mechanism forcing the
person to say he was converted and to imagine the corresponding inner transformation.'[2] This was the main reason for the
opposition to the innovations introduced into the Western
revivals. Weeks, who observed it at first hand, represented it in
dialogue form between 'Love-self' (representing the new
measures) and 'Thoughtful' (representing the old):

---

[1] *Personal Reminiscences*, vol. 1, p. 221. Long before Finney, Richard Baxter
represented the Pelagians as believing that 'the will of man is so free that he
can turn and become a new creature at any time'; *Practical Works of R. Baxter*
(London, n.d.), vol. 4, p. 658. Finney understood man's 'total depravity'
only as a voluntary condition. The assertion of the traditional evangelical
theology that the action of God renewing men within or opening the heart
(Acts 16:14) was necessary to 'make sinners *able* to obey the Gospel' he
specifically rejected (*Revivals of Religion*, p. 356). He argued this more fully in
his *Lectures on Systematic Theology*, rev. edn 1878), particularly pp. 282–300.
Thus, for example, he states: 'The sinner has all the faculties and natural
abilities requisite to render perfect obedience to God. All he needs is to be
induced to use these powers and attributes as he ought . . . God cannot do the
sinner's duty, and regenerate him without the right exercise of the sinner's
own agency.'
[2] *Burned-Over District*, pp. 181–2.

L.S. . . . In your method you spend your strength to little purpose. You press upon the sinner, it may be, his obligation to repent without delay; but you do not ask him whether he will comply. If he were disposed to say he would, I should infer, from your manner of talking, that you would rather not have him say it. You would dismiss him from the meeting, without his having said or done any thing, by which he should feel committed. Now, I would ask him to *do something* by which he should feel committed. If he can be led to take this step, whether it is taking the anxious seat, or rising up, or kneeling down, or whatever it may be, by which he shall pledge himself, he will feel that he is committed, and that he must go on . . . You would never do any thing to place him in this situation.

Th. No. It is not a process directed in the Bible; and that is a reason why I should regard it with suspicion . . .

L.S. 'I suppose no evangelical Christian now questions, but that preaching ought to produce its results *at the time*; and yet, according to general experience, it rarely does so.' And if you are not satisfied with the measures which have been contrived for the purpose of producing this result, it would seem to be right to call upon you to suggest others which you think better.

Th. Let Paul plant, and Apollos water; and let all pray God to give the increase. I have no doubt that every instance of the faithful preaching of the word produces some effect upon its hearers, at the time. But as it belongs to God to give it such effect as he pleases, it may be different in different individuals. The preached word may harden one; it may awaken another; it may produce conviction in another; and it may be the instrument of bringing another to submission. Is that what you mean?

L.S. No. I mean that a sermon addressed to sinners ought to bring them to repentance, at the time. And it ought to be *expected* to do it.

Th. On whom does the obligation rest? On the preacher, or on the hearer? or on some other being or agent?

L.S. The sinner is bound to repent now. And if the preacher does his duty, he may expect to see sinners brought to repentance immediately.

Th. There is a great deal of such talk, at this day, which seems to have very little definiteness. I do not believe the preacher can make the word preached by him effectual to the conversion of sinners. The Lord Jesus did not in all cases; nor the prophets, nor the apostles, nor was it required of them. If they faithfully preached the word, that was their duty. What effect it should produce was the divine prerogative to determine . . .

L.S. If you admit that it is the duty of every impenitent hearer to repent now, why not take some means to ascertain, at the close of the sermon, how many have done their duty?

[251]

Th. For the plain reason that the eyes of man cannot ascertain. God only looks on the heart. And more time is required for a sober, human judgment to be formed. 'By their fruits ye shall know them;' and there must be time for the fruits to appear.

L.S. You are so often hinting at false conversions, false hopes, and the like, that I begin to think you have not much confidence in the revivals of the present day.

Th. I confess I cannot have much confidence in those which are produced by new-measure influence. I think the new measures are usually found connected with radical errors in relation to what Christian experience is, and that the kind of experimental religion which these measures is adapted to produce, is not true Christian experience, but a dangerous delusion.[1]

This was the heart of the issue, which Nettleton, in his letter to Aikin of Utica, described as 'a civil war in Zion'.[2] But as we shall see, it was not as clear as this in 1827. It was 1835 before Finney openly denounced the orthodox side for their 'vast ignorance', and to those intervening years we shall have to return.

[1] *Pilgrim's Progress in the Nineteenth Century*, pp. 358–61.
[2] *Nettleton and his Labours*, p. 344.

10

ORIGINS OF A GREAT DIVISION

Princeton Theological Seminary

10

That Charles G. Finney took a considerable part in the great change which was occurring in Protestant America in the 1820s and 1830s, is indisputable. The interpretation of this fact, however, as has already been argued, is complex. Questions emerge from any discussion of Finney's part to which answers are not immediately apparent. For an illustration of this point we may turn to probably the most influential of Finney's books, his *Memoirs*. This autobiography is particularly full on the years considered in chapter 9, but it stands in marked contrast to my narrative on one important point. I represented Finney's doctrinal position as one that emerged gradually and, unlike the new measures, was not a subject of open public dispute until 1831. Only then did it become clear that his view of conversion was contrary to the one that had hitherto prevailed in the American evangelical and Calvinistic tradition.

But in his *Memoirs* Finney dates his breach with that tradition nearly ten years earlier, when he began studying for the ministry under his Presbyterian pastor, George Gale. The autobiography begins with the sentence, 'It has pleased God in some measure to connect my name and labors with an extensive movement of the Church of Christ, regarded by some as a new era.' What was new, he went on to say, had much to do with a rejection of the beliefs taught in the Presbyterian Church at Adams which he joined in 1821. Gale 'held to the old school doctrine of original sin, or that the human constitution was morally depraved', and Finney's studies under him 'were little

[255]

else than controversy' because: 'These doctrines I could not receive. I could not receive his views on the subject of atonement, regeneration, faith, repentance, the slavery of the will, or any of the kindred doctrines. But of these views he was quite tenacious; and he seemed sometimes not a little impatient because I did not receive them without question.'[1]

Once licensed and ordained as a Presbyterian minister, Finney, as he asserted, took every opportunity to oppose the traditional teaching. 'Wherever I found that any class of person were hidden behind these dogmas, I did not hesitate to demolish them, to the best of my ability.'[2] In his *Memoirs* Finney cited numerous examples from his early years of how he had been the means of delivering elders, ministers, churches, even a whole presbytery, from their Calvinistic beliefs. When he first went to the East and preached in orthodox Philadelphia in 1828, he sought to hunt out people 'from under' those peculiar views of orthodoxy in which I found them entrenched'.[3] 'Much of my labor in the ministry has consisted in correcting these views.'[4] The *Memoirs* – which deal most fully with the early period of his ministry – portray him as continually waging a crusade to change the doctrinal standards of the churches. Noting this fact, G. Frederick Wright, his sympathetic biographer, has written: 'Finney has left in literature a permanent record not only of his life, but also of his struggles to adjust the truths of Christianity into such a harmonious system of thought that no violence should be done to the dictates of reason. This, as he often said, was (after that of the actual conversion of souls) the great aim of his life.'[5]

However, Finney's record of himself as a doctrinal reformer of the churches from the outset of his ministry cannot be reconciled with the fact that no one, Nettleton included, observed it at that time. Even George Gale, who ought to have known him best, suspected no such revolutionary purpose. Gale's account of Finney as a student does not square with the latter's own account. Introducing Finney to Samuel Aikin of Utica in 1826, Gale: 'told him that Mr. Finney had some

---

[1] *Memoirs*, p. 46.   [2] Ibid., p. 59.
[3] Ibid., p. 242.   [4] Ibid., p. 257.
[5] G. Frederick Wright, *Charles Grandison Finney* (Boston, 1891), p. 314.

peculiarities, some things that were not practicable that I would alter, but many things [said against him] had little or no foundation, that he was a good man and God was with him.'[1]

The only tenable explanation for the disparity between Finney's account of his career and the perception of contemporary observers is either that the preacher was practising a massive subterfuge in the 1820s – assailing Calvinistic beliefs while successfully hiding what he was doing – or his *Memoirs* present a very loose and inaccurate reconstruction of the story as it concerns these years. The first alternative has to be rejected, although Finney cannot be cleared entirely from an element of the underhand. From his ordination in the Presbyterian Church in 1824, he was, in the eyes of that Church and the general public, committed to the Westminster Confession. He did not leave the denomination until 1836 and so there is point in Warfield's observation, 'Under its cover he for a dozen years flouted the doctrines he had been placed by it under obligation to propagate.'[2] In Philadelphia in 1828 Finney described himself as 'in the heart of the Presbyterian Church and where Princeton views were almost universally embraced'. That he should feel uneasy at the inconsistency of his position is understandable and he wrote from Philadelphia to Thomas Weld, one of his recent converts, 'here we are all hereticks . . . the churches are in a dreadful state . . . I am in a land where many would entangle me in my talk. Be careful what you do with my letters.'[3]

But the explanation cannot be that Finney was consciously and constantly playing a double part in the 1820s. The evidence points rather to the fact that the *Memoirs* give us no more than a loose reconstruction of his early career. The very date of the book points to that conclusion. Finney did not write

---

[1] *Autobiography of Rev. George W. Gale* (New York: n.p., 1964), pp. 269–72, quoted in Hardman, *Finney*, pp. 78–9.

[2] Warfield, *Perfectionism*, vol. 2, p. 38. On the principle involved here Horatius Bonar wrote: 'We live in a land, certainly, where any one may think what he pleases. And so long as a man does not offer himself as a teacher in a Church there is perfect liberty to believe and to teach what his own conscience or convenience dictates. But in *choosing an official creed he voluntarily curtails* this liberty.' *Memoir of G. T. Dodds* (London, 1884), p. 88.

[3] 27 March 1828; quoted in Hardman, *Finney*, p. 166.

it until 1867–68, forty years after the Western revivals, and he was said to have been without a diary on which he could depend. Thus it is not surprising if the autobiography, which was not begun until he was in his mid-seventies, should contain a number of inaccuracies and generally read back into the early years ideas that belonged to a later period. The seeds of Finney's ideas were no doubt present in the 1820s, but his portrait of himself in those years as a fully developed doctrinal reformer has to be taken with a huge pinch of salt. It was not only his critics who believed that his account of the 1820s, 'written in his old age, is more or less adjusted to his subsequent modes of thought';[1] Wright, his biographer, was of the opinion that 'Finney has accompanied his narrative by numerous doctrinal disquisitions, in which those familiar with the controversies of the time readily detect the result of subsequent years of reflection interjecting their later theology in the narrative of early experience.'[2]

Finney's failure to present an accurate account of how his doctrinal beliefs came to be formulated is liable to mislead the unwary reader of his *Memoirs* in one serious respect. The *Memoirs* supply not the slightest hint that his practices and views were derived or developed from contemporary teachers or influences. Rather the impression is left that they burst upon Finney's mind directly from Scripture and from heaven. It can be proved that they did not. Some of the most characteristic opinions he came to embrace such as his denial of the doctrine of imputation, his strong commitment to teaching on 'the prayer of faith', and his general antipathy to Calvinism, can be traced to Methodism and to ideas that spread far in the aftermath of the Kentucky revival.[3] Finney praised Methodism, in reference to what he regarded as the best evangelism, in his *Memoirs* and his *Lectures on Revivals of Religion*. This was also confirmed by one of his hearers as early as 1826. Joseph Brockway, a member of Beman's First Presbyterian Church in Troy, was convinced (and time would prove him correct) that

---

[1] *Perfectionism*, vol. 2, p. 15.   [2] *Finney*, p. 6.

[3] On Finney's rejection of imputation see *Memoirs*, pp. 56–7. His teaching on 'the prayer of faith' (prominent in his *Revivals of Religion*) probably derived from Daniel Nash, but it was also an error propagated in the Kentucky revivals.

his minister, aided by younger men, was carrying the church away from its doctrinal position:

He [Beman] had before said, in one of his lectures, that the only reason why the Methodists were so much blessed, and why they had grown up, as it were, in a day, to so great a people, was because they preached the simple truth of God. Mr. Finney, too, bears testimony to the same point, and says that there has been more of the spirit of religion among them, and they have done more good than all other denominations put together. I say then, let them go to the Methodists.[1]

But Finney differed from the Methodists in at least one major respect. While Methodist preachers were quite capable, as we have seen, of assailing Calvinistic belief, their primary interest was never theological. Sustained doctrinal discussion was neither their forte nor their interest. They attempted no major reformulation of Christian doctrine. Finney, on the other hand, had as much interest in theory as in practice, and he would, in due course, make *Lectures on Systematic Theology* his *magnum opus*. Unlike many of his imitators, he was an intellectual as well as an evangelist.

In the field of theology proper a significant part of Finney's thought came not from Methodism but from ideas from New England which were already in circulation when he first became a missionary in Jefferson County in 1824. The centre of this influence was at New Haven, and the principal advocate was Nathaniel William Taylor, pupil and assistant to Timothy Dwight. Taylor, an effective preacher and a firm believer in revival, was pastor of the First Church from 1812 and the foremost figure of the Yale Divinity School which was established in 1822. Among those converted under his ministry was Sereno E. Dwight, to whom we owe the most influential edition of *The Works of Jonathan Edwards* (his great-grandfather).[2] But while the younger Dwight was preparing Edwards's works for publication, Yale's professor of theology was moving in a

---

[1] *A Delineation of a Revival of Religion in Troy*, p. 59 n. Yet forty years later Finney blamed 'Methodist brethren' for encouraging 'a wild excitement' which made part of the western section of New York State 'a burnt district' before he preached there (*Memoirs: Complete Text*, pp. 78–9).

[2] 1834 and Banner of Truth, 1974.

very different direction. Taylor was convinced that, in the interests of evangelism, emphasis needed to be moved from the sinner's dependence on God (too exclusively stressed, he believed, in New England) to the accountability of sinners. Beecher and Nettleton agreed with him that there had been some tendency in New England to distort the biblical balance. They also agreed that evangelism could not exist without an insistence on the duties of immediate faith and repentance. The older Calvinism insisted both on the bondage of the unregenerate man and on his immediate responsibility to obey the gospel, holding both truths to be scriptural and not believing that men are called to harmonize them. Taylor, however, was convinced that his generation had to show the *reasonableness* of their beliefs. Questions affecting human responsibility 'he felt obliged to solve, under the alternative of giving up his faith'.[1]

The motives that moved Taylor included a desire to answer the attacks on Calvinism of the Boston Unitarians, his own inquiring and ambitious intellect, and his desire to advance evangelism. In short, the conclusion Taylor came to was precisely the one which we have seen was preached by Finney, namely, that man is not governed by a moral *nature*. If men have inherited a corrupt and depraved nature from Adam, it would mean, Taylor supposed, the necessity of a 'physical' regeneration prior to conversion. It would also mean that God had placed men in a condition in which they could not help but sin. This was the point that Boston's Unitarians urged against Calvinism and time and again Finney employed the same charge against orthodox men. For example, with terrible caricature, he claimed that William Weeks (whom he regarded as responsible for the *Pastoral Letter of the Ministers of the Oneida Association*) taught that 'God made men sinners' and had the right 'to send them to hell for the sins he had directly created in them, or compelled them to commit by the force of omnipotence'.[2]

The solution to the Unitarian charge, and the belief essential to evangelism, according to Taylor and Finney, was to assert that sin and guilt can *only* be attributed to men's voluntary

[1] Noah Porter, quoted in Sidney Earl Mead, *Nathaniel William Taylor, 1786–1858: A Connecticut Liberal* (Chicago: Archon Books, 1967), p. 64.
[2] *Memoirs*, p. 179.

What about the fall? man wasn't created with a fallen nature. Adam sinned. As a result, he was separated from God. How can we argue that we don't have a fallen nature when so is *Origins of a Great Division* so clear from Scripture that

choices. All that needs to be changed in the unconverted man is his will, not his nature. As Taylor's biographer observed, the doctrine of total depravity was central in the Unitarian attack on orthodoxy, and in departing from that doctrine Taylor and his New Haven colleagues were trying to 'restate Calvinism in more acceptable terms'.[1]

Taylor's formulation of his position clearly preceded Finney's by many years. While Timothy Dwight, who died in 1817, was still alive he was unhappy with the trend already apparent in Taylor. But men were slow to recognize the significance of what was being proposed, partly because of the mystifying language in which it was presented by its advocates. Taylor's biographer called it statements of doctrine 'that verged on incomprehensibility'. By the early 1820s, however, the ideas of Yale's first professor of theology were being understood and were passing into general circulation. By 1826 Yale divinity students were talking of the 'New Divinity' being taught by their professors, and the phrase stuck. So Taylor's teaching was in the air by the time Finney began his ministry. How it first came to his notice we do not know. Whitney Cross surmises that it may have been Jedediah Burchard (another New Englander) who provided the 'link between New Haven and new measures'.[2] What is certain is that the plan devised at New Haven and adopted by Finney was 'to make regeneration so easy that men may not be discouraged from attempting to do it'.[3] In 1827 Nettleton may have wondered whether Finney's commitment to new measures was connected with a departure from orthodox belief. By 1831, when Finney preached the sermon 'Make Yourselves a New Heart' in Boston, it was beyond doubt. The voice was Finney's, the thinking Taylor's, and the title of Asa Rand's review of Finney's sermon – 'The

---

[1] Mead, *Taylor*, p. 213. There was weight in the contemporary charge that the New Divinity men had been led 'toward a modification of the truth by undue efforts of policy . . . to make it palatable to men' (p. 229). Many of the 768 graduates from Taylor's classes 'became the leaders in the great surge of liberal thought that dominated Congregationalism during the next generation' (p. 163).

[2] *Burned-Over District*, p. 160.

[3] Samuel J. Baird, *A History of the New School, and of the Questions Involved in the Disruption of the Presbyterian Church in 1838*, (Philadelphia, 1868), p. 19.

New Divinity Tried' – gave an identification which could not fairly be disputed.

The doctrine of the atonement was not directly involved in this controversy, but, in passing, it should be noted that here too Finney's belief probably owed its origin to New England influence. In the late eighteenth century the so-called 'governmental' theory of the atonement (first advanced by Grotius in the previous century) was adopted by such men as Samuel Hopkins and Jonathan Edwards, Jr. They were followed by others, including Nathan Beman who published *Four Sermons on the Doctrine of the Atonement* in 1825. These sermons were later expanded into a book. According to this view, Christ's death was not a payment of debt on behalf of those whose sins he bore; it was rather an action to satisfy public justice, making it safe and possible for God to forgive those who repent and believe. So the act that secures forgiveness is man's, not Christ's. 'The atonement of itself does not secure the salvation of any', wrote Finney.[1] 'When a sinner repents that state of feeling makes it proper for God to forgive him.'[2]

Thus it may be seen that the new-measures movement, which appeared to have its origin in central New York, was in fact the result of a confluence of ideas arising from several quarters, and while Finney soon became their best-known

---

[1] *Lectures on Systematic Theology*, rev. edn (1878), p. 281.

[2] *Revivals of Religion*, p. 49. See also Finney's *Memoirs*, pp. 42, 49–51, etc. While he spoke of a 'vicarious' atonement he did not mean that Christ represented sinners as a substitute, suffering the penalty they deserved. *The Works of Jonathan Edwards* (1834; Edinburgh, 1974), vol. 1, p. cxciv; B. B. Warfield, *Studies in Theology* (1932; Banner of Truth, 1988), pp. 271–6, 288–97, 532–6; 'Beman on the Atonement', reviewed in *Princeton Theological Essays* (first series, Edinburgh, 1856) where the reviewer said: 'The particular error concerning the nature of the atonement inculcated in this book, has, we believe, done more to corrupt religion, and to promote Socinianism, than any other of the vaunted improvements of American theology, which, after all, are but feeble reproductions of the rejected errors of the sixteenth and seventeenth centuries.' It is probable that Finney was also influenced by the writings of Albert Barnes who in 1829 wrote the words almost exactly repeated by Finney later: 'The atonement, of itself, secured the salvation of no one' (words which Barnes misleadingly attributed to John Owen). Albert Barnes, *The Way of Salvation; A Sermon Delivered at Morristown, New-Jersey, Feb. 8, 1829: Together with Mr Barnes' Defence* . . . (Seventh ed., New York, 1836), pp. 29, 66–7.

representative, their beginnings came from a much wider context. Unless this is recognized the speed with which the change in evangelism occurred across the country would be inexplicable. Nathan Hatch writes: 'Charles Finney's "new measures" are best seen as an aftershock of a more fundamental reordering . . . To a remarkable extent Finney's experience and convictions resonate with the themes of insurgent Christianity that had flourished in New York's "Burned-Over District" . . . Finney's fifth column effort brought revivalism into America's citadel of theological orthodoxy.'[1]

* * *

We turn now to the divisions which were brought on by this controversy. The issue of the new measures divided many congregations. Beman's large church at Troy was split. So was the Bowery Presbyterian Church in New York City, where 'Finneyism was the talismanic rallying-word' between the two parties.[2] The party that withdrew from the Bowery church in 1829 became the starting-point for Finney's own pastorate in that city. The Presbyterian church at Rome – a centre from which Finney had worked in the Oneida revivals, supported by Moses Gillett, its minister – was also divided, with a pro-Finney party leaving Gillett to form another congregation. In his *Memoirs* Finney could not remember the reason for that division but it was clear enough in a letter written by one of the participants who justified it to Lydia Finney in 1831: 'Our former dear Pastor had relapsed into his Old School views and feelings, and you will readily perceive that we could not walk together because we were not agreed. Some individuals felt that something more *must* be done for the advancement of the Redeemer's kingdom.'[3] Similar trouble forced William Weeks to leave his church at Paris Hill where opponents, following Finney's lead and language, had dubbed him an 'anti-revival man'.

[1] *Democratization*, pp. 226, 199–200.
[2] *Life of Joel Hawes*, p. 140; Hardman, *Finney*, p. 183.
[3] Maria Roberts to Mrs Finney, 12 Jan. 1831; quoted in *Memoirs: Complete Text*, p. 635 n. See also pp. 544–5, 634.

Another notable instance of local disruption occurred in the German Reformed Church in Philadelphia which Finney used as a campaign base in 1828. He preached there regularly from 27 August 1828 to 5 January 1829. The result was division, with the minister of thirty years' standing, Samuel Helffenstein, being asked to leave. The majority wanted to call Finney to the pastorate. When he declined, and thoughts of securing Burchard or Beman were unfulfilled, the congregation fell away to a mere fifty-one members.[1] From that time the revivalism issue racked the German Reformed denomination for more than ten years, and the debate brought about one of the strongest reponses to the new measures in Dr John W. Nevin's *The Anxious Bench* (1843).

Finney was himself often responsible for the division of congregations, not only because of his general criticism of ministers,[2] but because of the very nature of his teaching on revival. If, as he taught, all faithful men were able to secure revivals, only one conclusion could be drawn on preachers who failed to do so. Elizabeth Thomson has recorded the effect of this new attitude which she saw popularized in Oneida county: 'What man had done [that is Finney in the Western revivals], man could do; therefore those staid pastors who had not wrought such revivals, must be at fault. The Church was suffering from the delinquency of its shepherds . . . Persons whom they had baptized in infancy, and received into the Church in maturer years, wrote anonymous letters to their pastors, asking them to create and continue a revival; or if not, to resign, and not to stand in the way of souls.'[3]

A typical illustration of how this spirit worked was recorded by a preacher in Wisconsin in 1847. One of his colleagues was Stephen Peet, a Congregationalist who had adopted the new views on revival. The senior man in this mission field com-

---

[1] 'If Papa Helffenstein can be peaceably and quietly disposed of', Finney wrote on 7 May, 1829, 'this church may yet be made the centre of revival operation'. For further detail, which Finney had forgotten by the time he wrote his *Memoirs*, see Marion L. Bell, *Crusade in the City: Revivalism in Nineteenth-Century Philadelphia* (Lewisburg, Pa., Bucknell University Press, 1977), pp. 65–7, 73.
[2] See below, pp. 281–2.
[3] *Memoirs: Complete Text*, p. 143 n.

plained that, despite Peet's many good qualities, his attitude on securing results dismayed those who had been labouring before him: 'Some young ministers and feeble churches who have been toiling hard and praying fervently have been cut to the quick by such a remark as this: "What have you been about all this time that you have not got a revival before now?"'[1]

Many controversies were thus introduced into particular congregations, but these were soon overshadowed by the major divisions affecting whole denominations. I shall leave the Baptists to another chapter and deal here with the Presbyterians and Congregationalists. From about 1828 men in the Congregational churches of New England divided over the views of Nathaniel Taylor and the New Divinity of Yale. Bennet Tyler resigned his pastorate in Payson's former charge at Portland to lead the opposition to the New Haven influence.[2] Through rival magazines and theological seminaries, the dispute was to rage in New England for years. So great was the rift, says Mead, that efforts to unite the two seminaries (Yale and East Windsor) 'just before the deaths of Taylor and Tyler in 1858, and again in 1864, completely failed'.

With few exceptions, the New England leaders most closely identified with revival appear to have taken the side of Tyler and Nettleton. The principal exception was Lyman Beecher. Beecher's break with Nettleton over this controversy is one of the surprises of church history. The friendship of the two men, as we have seen, was close and long-standing. They appeared in print together against Finney in 1827, and in a private letter Beecher wrote to a friend around this time he said of Nettleton: 'that such a man as he should be traduced, and exposed to all manner of evil falsely, in order to save from deserved reprehension such a man as Finney (who, whatever talents or piety he may possess, is as far removed from the talent, wisdom, judgment and experience of Nettleton, as any corporal in the French army was removed from the talent and generalship of Bonaparte), is what neither my reason, nor my conscience, nor

---

[1] W. W. Sweet, *Religion on the American Fronter*, vol. 3, p. 404.
[2] Tyler saw a republication of the records of earlier revivals as a vital part of the opposition to the changes now being promoted. See the preface to his *New England Revivals, as They Existed at the Close of the Eighteenth, and the Beginning of the Nineteenth Centuries*.

my heart will endure.'[1] In similar vein, Beecher had warned Finney at the New Lebanon Convention of July 1827 that if he attempted to come to Boston he would see there was a 'fight every inch of the way'.[2] Yet, as already noted, the next year saw Beecher pledge himself with Finney in their 'treaty of mutual silence'.[3] When Nettleton reopened the issue with Beecher in Boston in October 1829, and insisted upon its seriousness, the two men disagreed and parted permanently. Beecher asserted that Nettleton wanted him to 'denounce Taylor', and that he refused and 'playfully' said something like 'Taylor and I have made you what you are, and if you do not behave yourself we will hew you down'.[4] This was how Beecher recalled the disputed words in later years, but Nettleton did not so understand them. He saw Beecher as now sadly committed to Taylor, Finney, and the New Divinity. Subsequent events confirmed that he was right. In 1831 Beecher welcomed Finney to Boston and, falling over himself to retract earlier words, he wrote to his new associate, 'with very little difference, and that now on points of discretion unessential, you and I are, as much, perhaps even more, *one* than almost any two men whom God has pleased to render conspicuous in his church'.[5]

Beecher's view of Nettleton underwent a corresponding change. The editor of his *Autobiography*, Charles Beecher, asserted that 'party spirit supplanted brotherly love' in Nettleton.[6] Beecher himself wrote: 'When Nettleton wanted us to break fellowship with the New Measure men, and we would not, he became dissatisfied . . . Nettleton never did much good after he got crazy on that subject.'[7] 'He wanted the battle to go on. He was one of those that never can give up their own will. He had the notion that the New Haven brethren were currying

---

[1] The letter to John Mitchell was published in the *Christian Spectator* (18 Dec. 1827), *Memoirs: Complete Text*, p. 192 n.

[2] *Autobiography of Beecher*, vol. 2, p. 75.

[3] Finney denied the record of this pact when he saw reference to it in Beecher's *Autobiography*: 'I was not a party to the agreement entered into at Philadelphia' (*Memoirs*, p. 223), but here his memory is again at fault, for the document setting down their pact still exists and carries his signature. Beecher maintained the agreement better than Finney.

[4] *Autobiography of Beecher*, vol. 2, pp. 287–8.

[5] Hardman, *Finney*, p. 149.

[6] *Autobiography of Beecher*, vol. 2, p. 363.   [7] Ibid., p. 118.

favor with Finney . . . That was the origin of all his bitterness against Taylor.'[1] Beecher defended his own change with respect to Finney on the grounds that the evangelist had corrected the excesses of his new measures and that there had never been any serious underlying difference in beliefs.

Various additional interpretations have been advanced to explain how Nettleton and Beecher, once so close, could part in this manner. Some writers suppose that Beecher's interest had always been in using evangelism and revival to maintain 'the social order' and that he came to believe that Finney's work could be accommodated to the same purpose. More plausibly, others interpret Beecher as primarily wanting to maintain the wider evangelical unity of the Northeast over against Unitarianism and therefore he opposed such division as Nettleton's convictions were causing. Beyond question, there was a strong element of the pragmatic in Beecher. He had long given quiet support to Taylor as a theological reformer, provided his friend's speculations did not go too far and disturb the peace. As early as 1819 Taylor wrote to Beecher on the need to 'change the current of theological sentiment'. Referring to Jonathan Edwards, Taylor said in that letter: 'We may peradventure attempt to supply his defects and give to the world that desideratum which will show that good sound Calvinism, or, if you please, Beecherism and Taylorism, is but another name for the truth and reality of things.'[2]

Ten years later, when the outworking of the New Divinity was in full public view, Beecher was compelled to choose one way or the other. Friendship with Taylor came into it – in closeness it exceeded his relationship with Nettleton – but pragmatic considerations may well have weighed strongest. Beecher had been impressed, it would seem, by Finney at the New Lebanon Convention, and startled at subsequent signs of the influence and popularity of this new leader whom he had dismissed as a 'corporal'. The future could well be with this new school of younger preachers. Their growing success threatened Beecher's generation with the prospect of becoming yesterday's men, the more so if they were represented as opponents of revivals. If Finney could be moderated (and he

---

[1] Ibid., pp. 79–89.   [2] Ibid., vol. 1, pp. 284–5.

did moderate in some things from the time of his visit to Philadelphia), he could be valuable in serving the evangelism in which Beecher had long been a leader. In his *Autobiography* Beecher wrote of Timothy Dwight that ambition 'was his easily besetting sin'.[1] The orthodox men who parted with Beecher at this time feared that Beecher had not cast the beam out of his own eye.[2] Ambition and expediency are natural companions.

Beecher, as we shall further see, anticipated the success of the new movement correctly, although that success was to be more sweeping than he ever thought. Such was Finney's meteoric rise to fame that Beecher tended to become the tail to his kite. And Finney, far from thinking that he owed anything to Beecher, viewed him in his *Memoirs* with a degree of contempt. A more fitting memorial to the man is found in Gardiner Spring's *Reminiscences*, although Spring had taken the Nettleton side in the controversy. Two years after Beecher's death, Spring wrote: 'So long as an honest and earnest effort for the salvation of men is honored in the Church of God, will the memory of Lyman Beecher be a rich treasure to the American churches.' There, generously stated, was Beecher's strength. His weakness was his readiness to allow his beliefs to be swayed by factors other than adherence to the Word of God. The concern to be successful was too prominent a feature in his make-up.

I have dwelt on this particular division partly because Beecher's words after 1827 have often been used to discredit Nettleton and the position he represented. But those who have accepted the personal criticisms of Nettleton contained in Beecher's autobiography have overlooked an important witness on the other side, which reminds us that the division on the issues also ran into families. Defending Nettleton from the aspersions of his own father and younger brother, Edward Beecher wrote of him, and of the stand he took in the controversy, 'I was not surprised at his feelings. They grew out

---

[1] Ibid., vol. 1, p. 240.

[2] According to Joseph Brockway, Nathan Beman, who cannot be classified among the orthodox, believed that Beecher's initial criticism of the Western revivals was not on the grounds of principle: 'He has set himself up to oppose revivals, for fear they were getting unpopular' (*Delineation* p. 62 n.). Lewis Tappan wrote to Finney of Beecher in 1868, 'He believed in the doctrine of expediency to a criminal excess of thought' (Finney, *Memoirs: Complete Text*, p. xxxiii).

of his deep religious experience.'[1] In his book *The Conflict of Ages* Edward Beecher further observed that the view of his father, Taylor, and Finney 'denies what are the actual facts in all men, as stated in Scripture and revealed by experience – that is, real depravity, and strong sinful propensities, anterior to action'. The tendency of this denial was 'to sweep away the true and deep doctrine of depravity and Satanic influence, and to leave only a nominal and superficial depravity'. It was to the recognition of this fact that he attributed the 'earnestness and perseverance' of the opposition shown by Nettleton and the Old School divines, and he quoted at length, and with approval, Nettleton's conviction that the New Divinity teaching on depravity undermined the whole plan of redemption and endangered evangelical religion.[2] A candid acknowledgement from such a quarter – for Edward Beecher was not an Old School man – ought not to have been ignored as it has been by writers on this controversy.

*   *   *

The effects of the New Divinity, and the new evangelism which accompanied it, were even more disruptive in the Presbyterian Church. The Plan of Union had given New Englanders from Yale and Andover ready access to the pulpits of a denomination that was growing far more rapidly than their own. By the early 1830s, able spokesmen for the new views were to be found in a number of leading Presbyterian pulpits. They included Samuel Cox (1793–1881) in New York, and Albert Barnes (1798–1870) in Philadelphia. In 1831 Archibald Alexander of Princeton wrote that the 'new preachers' in the Church – ' a large portion of our younger theologians' – were preaching that

man is in possession of every ability which is requisite for the discharge of his duty. That it is as easy for him to repent, to exercise faith, and to love God, as to speak, or eat, or walk, or perform any other act . . . Nothing is more in the power of a man, they allege, than

---

[1] Sprague, *Annals*, vol. 2, p. 554.
[2] Edward Beecher, *The Conflict of Ages; or, The Great Debate on the Moral Relations of God and Man* (Boston, 1853). See review in the *British and Foreign Evangelical Review* (Edinburgh, 1854), pp. 309–10.

his own will; and the consent of the will to the terms of the Gospel is all that is required to constitute any man a Christian.[1]

From the beginning of the 1830s, Alexander, followed by other Princeton men, wrote persistently in an attempt to prevent a take-over of the Presbyterian Church by the new ideas. The Seminary's quarterly journal, *The Biblical Repertory*, was the main organ for their testimony. With the exception of an article on 'Regeneration', which critically reviewed a sermon by Samuel Cox on that subject in 1830, the first responses were more indirect and by means of historical theology. Thorough attention to Pelagianism, original sin, and imputation was given in successive articles in the *Repertory* in 1830 and 1831 from the pen of Archibald Alexander: 'It is attended with many advantages to bring into view ancient heresies, for often what modern innovators consider a new discovery, and wish to pass off as a scheme suited to remove all difficulties, is found upon examination to be nothing else than some ancient heresy clothed in a new dress.'[2]

From the summer of 1831, after the strength of the innovating party had just been demonstrated in the General Assembly of the Presbyterian Church, the opposition of Alexander and his colleagues became more direct. 'I had never suspected that the new men and new measures would so soon prevail in the supreme judicatory of our church', the professor wrote to a former student on 6 July 1831.[3] The next year the *Repertory*, for the first time, gave forceful criticism of Finney's views in 'The New Divinity Tried' in its April issue. The October 1832 issue, in a thirty-two page review of 'Sprague on Revivals', contrasted the old revivals with what was now being promoted. Sprague, a Princeton man, published an appendix in his *Lectures on Revivals* which was as long as the book itself, consisting of letters from some of the best-known evangelical leaders in six denominations. Practically all Sprague's correspondents were critical of what members of the New School were advancing in the name of revival. Samuel Miller followed with more strictures in his

[1] 'The Inability of Sinners', *Biblical Repertory* (1831); *Princeton Theological Essays*, first series (Edinburgh, 1856), p. 231.
[2] *Biblical Repertory* (1830); *Theological Essays*, op. cit., p. 97.
[3] *Life of Alexander*, p. 475.

Letters to Presbyterians in 1833. Two years later came the most important analysis of Finney's teaching and measures to be published in the 1830s. This was a ninety-seven-page article in two issues of the *Repertory*, which reviewed the preacher's volume of *Sermons on Various Subjects* and his *Lectures on Revivals of Religion*. The author was Professor Albert B. Dod of Princeton College: 'Let us not be deluded with the idea that opposition will exasperate and do harm,' wrote Dod. 'Under cover of silence and inaction which this fear has already produced, this fanaticism has spread, until now twelve thousand copies of such a work as these *Lectures on Revivals* are called for by its craving. And there is danger this spirit will spread still more extensively.'

During these years, church courts in the Presbyterian Church, from presbyteries to General Assemblies, were racked with charges and counter-charges on doctrinal issues. In Philadelphia, Barnes was suspended from his ministry for teaching on the place of the human will in regeneration which, it was claimed, was contrary to the Westminster Confession. When Beecher went from Boston to the Second Presbyterian Church of Cincinnati in 1832 a sustained attempt was made by the city's senior Presbyterian minister, Dr Joshua L. Wilson, to stop his ministry on account of error on the same point. Wilson also accused Beecher of 'aiming at popular effect'.[1] Beecher successfully evaded the charge that he was teaching error but in a manner that only increased the belief of Old School men that he was not being straight.[2] Beecher's *Autobiography* represents Wilson as an earnest evangelical man – he 'had revivals in which many were brought in' – who was suddenly put on the wrong side by misinformation fed to him by Archibald Alexander.[3] Wilson, it seems, did change his views on evangelistic practices; the reason, however, was not so much advice from Princeton as his own personal experience and observation. In the course of a letter to the Rev. R. J. Breckinridge of Baltimore he wrote in 1834:

[1] *Autobiography of Beecher*, vol. 2, p. 283.
[2] Evidence that their suspicions were not unfounded appears in Beecher's *Autobiography*. His family ridiculed the idea of strict adherence to the Confession, e.g., vol. 2, pp. 215–18.
[3] Ibid., p. 211.

You go the whole for camp-meetings, anxious seats and hasty admissions, that is, admissions of all instanter who convince you '*by words*' that God has converted their souls. I perceive, Dr Sir, you are on the same slipping path in which I unhappily trod before you and you are conducted exactly by the same guides. If you are a faithful minister of Jesus Christ, these movements will yet give you unspeakable distress and much trouble. But no man is prepared to take warning while he is in a fit of blind zeal.[1]

By this date New School men were clearly acting together across the United States. Cox of New York reported to Beecher in April 1834: 'Our heresy-phobia in this region is, I think, exhausting itself. Morbid in its original elements, it grows not to increasing strength but wanes toward extinction.'[2] The following year Beecher wrote to Albert Barnes: 'Every year of our action is telling powerfully in contrast with their accusations and growling. We wish to also avoid, if possible, what they so much desire, any doctrinal authoritative exposition of the Confession, either Old School or New.'[3]

At this time the Old School side were constantly accused of raising controversy over trifles and of suspecting brethren where no suspicion was justified. Finney complained in 1835:

Who does not know that ministers have been crying out 'Heresy,' and 'New Measures,' and talking about the 'Evils of Revivals,' until they have got the Church all in confusion? Oh, God, have mercy on ministers! They talk about their days of fasting and prayer, but are these the men to call on *others* to fast and pray? They ought to fast and pray themselves. It is time that ministers should assemble together, and fast and pray over the evils of controversy, for they have caused it. The Church itself would never get into a controversial spirit, unless led into it by ministers. The body of Church members are always averse to controversy, and would keep out of it, only they are dragged into it by ministers. When Christians are revived they are not inclined to meddle with controversy, either to read or hear it.[4]

[1] Quoted in W. W. Sweet, *Religion on the American Frontier*, vol. 2, p. 742.
[2] *Autobiography of Beecher*, vol. 2, p. 226.   [3] Ibid., p. 257.
[4] *Revivals of Religion*, pp. 226–7. Elsewhere, Finney claimed that the controversy was 'wholly groundless' (p. 346), that all accusations of error were 'slanderous', and that 'a great portion of the Presbyterian Church' needed to be brought to repentance on that account (p. 329). As early as 1827, Joseph Brockway accused the advocates of the new measures of a policy that hid 'the real state of things' and of a readiness to 'smother the facts', (*Delineation of a Revival*, pp. 49, 63).

This representation of the case is rather like that of an arsonist complaining of disturbances caused by fire brigades. The success of the misrepresentation was made the easier by the caution in revealing their beliefs that men such as Beecher exercised on the other side. But by the middle of the 1830s the Old School leaders were certain of the situation. In February 1836 Dr Leonard Woods of Andover (a friend of Nettleton) replied to W. S. Plumer, Presbyterian leader in the South: 'I believe what you say, that there is a perfect understanding among those in every part of our country who are opposed to Calvinism, and that they are acting in concert; that there is an alarming looseness among young preachers, and that there is a fixed determination to maintain a party holding loose opinions and that there must be a battle fought here, and there, and everywhere.'

Woods went on to refer to the opinions of three Congregational leaders recently deceased who 'were most deeply alarmed and distressed with the loose speculations which have come from the New Haven School and from Mr. Finney and others of that stamp. I know how they all felt, and what a full conviction they had that the notions which are peculiar to Dr. Taylor and Mr. Finney would undermine the fair fabric of our evangelical churches and spread a system far more unscriptural and pernicious than Wesleyan Methodism.'[1]

The uproar in the Presbyterian Church at this time could not continue. Archibald Alexander wrote to Plumer on 13 September 1837 of the crisis he believed was near:

I see dark clouds collecting. The new revival measures connected with the New Theology, are gaining strength and popularity every day. The stream is deepening and widening, and will shortly pour forth such a torrent as will reach over the whole surface of the land. Our Church cannot proceed much further under her present organization . . . it is necessary for our very existence that we should separate.[2]

In the following year the Presbyterian Church formally split into two, each side being known by the names with which they

---

[1] Quoted in E. H. Gillett, *Presbyterian Church in the U.S.*, vol. 2, p. 458.
[2] *Life of Alexander*, p. 477.

had become identified in the controversy, Old and New School.[1]

Prominent New School members at the General Assembly which saw the disruption of 1838 were Nathan Beman, Lyman Beecher, and N. W. Taylor. Speaking of that disruption in later years, Beecher is reported to have said, 'The Oneida revivals did it.'[2] What Beecher did not concede was the truthfulness of the statement of another contemporary, Samuel J. Baird: 'the practical system of Finney, Burchard, Myrick, and their compeers, was deduced from the theology of New Haven by a logic which no ingenuity can evade.'[3]

---

[1] According to Baird, *Religion in the United States of America*, Old School had 2,025 churches and 141,000 communicants and New School 1,375 churches and 102,060 communicants. See also George M. Marsden, *The Evangelical Mind and New School Presbyterian Experience* (New Haven, Conn., Yale University Press, 1970).

[2] Finney, *Memoirs: Complete Text*, p. 145 n.

[3] *History of New School*, p. 234.

I I

'THE ILLUSION OF A NEW ERA'

Ashbel Green (1762–1848)

I I

We now turn to the reasons why the New Divinity, coalescing with new measures, achieved such success in changing the understanding of evangelism and revival in the American churches. Before the 1820s the altar call, or its equivalent, was little known in most churches, yet William McLoughlin could write, 'after 1835 it was an indispensable fixture of modern revivals'. The same author says: 'Finney's revivalism broke "The Tradition of the Elders" (the title of one of his most pungent sermons) and transformed "the new system" from a minority to a majority religion. By mid-century it was in fact the national religion in the United States.'[1]

In these words McLoughlin, along with other modern authors, exaggerates the speed with which the old was replaced by the new. In later pages we shall see evidence that the change was in fact slower than such statements would suggest, for the present it is enough to refer to the statements of two eyewitnesses who looked closely at this very point in the year 1834. Andrew Reed and James Matheson were two senior British ministers sent to America in that year as deputies of the Congregational Union of England and Wales. In their brief they were asked to give special attention to the subject of revivals. On their return to Britain they published an extensive account and report of their findings and, even allowing for the

---

[1] *Modern Revivalism: Charles Grandison Finney to Billy Graham* (New York: Ronald Press, 1959), pp. 97, 66.

[277]

fact that the two leaders were only temporary visitors, their *Narrative* remains a valuable contemporary source. They came away convinced that in the thirty-one years which culminated in 1831, 'One of the most remarkable and extensive revivals ever known had passed over this people.'[1]

The Reed and Matheson visit coincided with the height of the controversy over new measures, the essence of which, in their judgment, consisted of 'the anxious seat' and the promotion of protracted meetings: 'These practices, have the countenance of many in the leading denominations; and of the ministers who use them, some are of excellent talent and undoubted piety.' But they did not record the innovations and injurious effects that followed them as integral to the whole revival period. On the contrary, they had only 'recently sprung up'.[2] 'They followed on the great revival of 1831; but they were the mere sediment of that flood of life, which went over the land, and blessed all things where it came.' Far from regarding the changes as now established in all the evangelical churches, they hoped that support for them was subsiding. 'Those ministers of most talent and character, who were carried away partially by the heat and interest of the period, are now reviewing their course . . . The leading ministers of the country, and amongst them the best friends of revival have entered their testimony against them.'[3]

If McLoughlin was faulty in his dating he is not, however, wrong in his main assertion. Reed and Matheson were premature in their optimism that the new evangelism had not come to stay. Certainly, before the end of the nineteenth century this form of evangelism and its attendant 'revivals' was so established across the United States that few could remember anything different.

We must look, then, for the principal reasons why such a major change in evangelicalism ever gained the credibility so thoroughly to displace what had gone before. The explanation is, in part, a general one. When any error in belief or practice gains swift popularity in the churches it will almost invariably

---

[1] Andrew Reed and James Matheson, *Narrative of the Visit to the American Churches* (London, 1835), vol. 2, p. 2.
[2] Ibid., p. 32.   [3] Ibid., p. 43.

be found to be connected with something conducive to it in the spirit of the age. The nineteenth century was an era of unparalleled activity. A nation awoke to what could be accomplished through human energy. What visitors called 'the American spirit'[1] – a consciousness of what could be done by action – was born. Successful achievements multiplied, including the steam-powered press and then steam-powered transport. The past paled beside the present and encouraged a general reaction against everything old. It seemed as though progress lay with accepting change and novelty in every sphere of life, and no one believed that more than the self-made men whom the spirit of democracy was bringing to the fore.

We have already noted a populist and radical element in society which affected the revival in Kentucky at the beginning of the century. At that date the same spirit was evident elsewhere. The Rev. Samuel Porter, for example, in a synod address at Pittsburgh in October 1811, said:

A spirit of innovation, hostile to all existing systems, has gone forth into the world, and is to be found in operation within the precincts of the Christian church. For the purpose of uniting in communion professing Christians of every species and description, and thereby to render the church perfectly analogous to the ancient Babel, those religious systems in which the church of Christ has expressed the sense in which she understood the Scriptures, and which men of superior learning and piety have long considered as necessary barriers between truth and error, are attacked, *in toto*, by men in our vicinity and elsewhere, who have sagacity enough to perceive that they stand in the way of the execution of their schemes; whilst others are engaged in brandishing their javelins at doctrines contained in those confessions of faith to which they profess adherence, as systems founded on the Word of God. Human nature, in avoiding one extreme, tends to the other; and the candid and well-informed will grant, that if a bigoted attachment to human system prevailed in some periods that have passed, the present tendency is to a lawless catholicism . . . The prevailing taste is so much in favor of a liberality in sentiment, which affects to look down on systems and confessions of faith as old-fashioned, musty, useless lumber, not calculated for this

---

[1] F. A. Cox and J. Hoby, *The Baptists in America; A Narrative of the Deputation from the Baptist Union in England, to the United States and Canada* (London, 1836), p. 380. 'As soon as a question is announced . . . the question is, "Well, what *action* shall be taken on this?"'

enlightened, refined philosophic age, that the man who aspires to celebrity and fame must endeavour to gratify that taste. Clergymen of ambition are under a strong temptation to sail with the wind and tide.[1]

By the 1820s and 1830s this same spirit had reached far greater proportions across the land. In a sermon on 'Religious Ultraism', preached in 1835, Sprague reflected on the effects of this new climate of opinion: 'In other days the Church has had more internal quietude . . . But now everything in the Church and the world seems to be in motion: the elements of social order, of civil society, are disturbed; and ten thousand tongues and hands are busy in an effort to break up the foundations of many generations.'[2] The spirit of the times as it was affecting the church, Sprague believed, was manifesting itself in the ascription of 'an unscriptural and disproportionate importance to human agency'.[3] It was representing man as 'a mighty agent rather than a humble instrument'.[4] It was giving rise to the error that 'all religion consists in excitement, in action', and was pushing 'a restless desire of change'. 'With persons who are the subjects of such a passion, the mere fact that a thing is old is enough to condemn it. They dislike old doctrines; they have no patience with old measures; and to use their own significant and stereotyped expression, they "wish to see things go ahead".'[5]

This ethos was simultaneously encouraging a new anti-intellectualism both in society and in the church. Important doctrinal distinctions, carefully stated in confessions and catechisms, were now treated as 'theological subtleties'. 'Down with them', Luther Myrick preached of all creeds. Joshua Leavitt, editor of the *New York Evangelist*, wrote to Finney of their common constituency, 'You know one half the good men do not know but that all doctrine is alike if only seasoned with a little "pious talk".' Their friend Lewis Tappan shared the same view, believing that the need was for 'ardent and practical

---

[1] *Old Redstone*, pp. 371–2.
[2] W. B. Sprague, *Religious Ultraism: A Sermon Delivered August 25, 1835, at the Installation of the Rev. John H. Hunter in West Springfield, Massachusetts* (Albany, N.Y., 1835), p. 43.
[3] Ibid., p. 11. [4] Ibid., p. 12. [5] Ibid., pp. 12–13.

men', not theologians; there was 'too much "theology" in the church now and too little of the Gospel'.[1] This was the popular mood, and when preachers played down any attachment to what Henry Ward Beecher called 'mouldy orthodoxy',[2] they had ready listeners. It is significant that in his criticism of the itinerants who carried the Western revivals to excess Weeks did not accuse them of preaching doctrinal error. Rather, he complained that doctrinal instruction of any kind was singularly lacking in their addresses; they majored in exhortation and story-telling, and took 'particular pains to render *orthodoxy* a term of reproach'. 'It has been a common thing to speak of *orthodoxy* in connection with being asleep, and of being awake as something in opposition to orthodoxy.'[3] Weeks blamed Finney in particular for this.

Another factor also showed how the new departure in evangelism reflected the spirit of the times. The office of the Christian ministry had hitherto been held with varying degrees of efficiency and usefulness, but no one had seriously questioned that pastors of local churches were the divinely appointed teachers and evangelists. But in the new age of democracy, now dawning, traditional positions and offices stood for far less, and half-educated, fast-talking speakers, claiming to preach the simple Bible, and attacking the Christian ministry, were more likely than ever to find a hearing. Ebenezer Porter, contrasting the position in 1832 with what he remembered in 1800, told his Andover students: 'Then there were no beardless oracles to stand forth, after a Christian experience, at best but very brief, and say of such venerable guides in the church as Mills and Hallock that they did not understand the subject of revivals and were behind the spirit of the age.'[4] Finney frequently criticized ministers of the gospel: 'His lectures were full of examples of revivals which had been killed by the inept practices of ministers unskilled in the science of revivalism.'[5] More than thirty years after the *Lectures*, when

---

[1] These Leavitt and Tappan quotations, from the years 1832 and 1831 respectively, are given by McLoughlin, *Modern Revivalism*, p. 76.

[2] *Autobiography of Beecher*, vol. 2, p. 359.

[3] Weeks, *Pilgrim's Progress in the Nineteenth Century*, pp. 240, 264.

[4] *Letters on Revivals*, p. 78.

[5] McLoughlin, *Modern Revivalism*, p. 94.

he wrote his *Memoirs*, Finney rarely mentioned ministers without some negative comment: 'I was from the very first aware that there was this wide gulf between myself and other ministers.'[1] In another age this would have told against him. It did not in the 1820s and 1830s.

A more particular reason why the change spread so fast and far was still more influential. It was the effective use of the same argument employed by Methodists for the camp-meeting procedures after the Kentucky revival, namely, the argument from success. It was claimed that employment of the new measures would guarantee success. Calvin Colton believed that, given the new understanding of the subject, the 'probabilities of the future uninterrupted march of American revivals from this time, amount to a moral certainty'.[2] No one pressed this expectation more than Finney. He affirmed, around the country, words we have already quoted from his *Lectures on Revivals of Religion*, that if Christians would only give themselves to the task they could convert the world and bring on the millennium in three months.[3] There is much of the same thing on revivals in his *Lectures*. 'We should expect their attainment to be connected with *great certainty* with the appropriate means'; measures were now in use such 'as are wisely calculated to secure the end'; 'The effect is more certain to follow' than any means used by the farmers in the world of nature; he held out the prospect of a revival that 'would never cease'.[4] 'Let loose from the chains of predestination,' Calvin Colton wrote in 1839, 'the scheme has been set on foot in America of converting the world *at once*.'[5]

The same promise of results was made by Finney with respect to the conversion of individuals. 'The prayer of faith,' he claimed, 'is always answered by the *specified* blessing prayed for.' Thus on the practical consequences of 'the prayer of faith' he asserted: 'We see that pious parents can render the salvation

---

[1] *Memoirs*, p. 89.

[2] Calvin Colton, *History and Character of American Revivals of Religion* (London, 1832), pp. 62–3.

[3] One of Finney's Rochester hearers noted the words in his diary on 28 November 1830. See Bell, *A Shopkeeper's Millennium*, pp. 3–4.

[4] *Revivals of Religion*, pp. 6, 209, 29, 134, 29.

[5] Quoted in Hardman, *Finney*, p. 186.

of their children certain. Only let them pray in faith and be agreed as touching the things they shall ask for, and God has promised them the desire of their hearts.'[1]

These were breath-taking claims for the new teaching, for they were easily verified or proved false. Initially, that proof might not have been clear for, while the Second Great Awakening continued and revivals were common, both new measures and old were marked with success. But even in its brightest periods the older approach to revival and evangelism never guaranteed a sure succession of spiritual harvests as did the advocates of the new measures. It was now claimed as proven that the use of 'the anxious seat', and its attendant teaching, *always* saw the multiplication of converts; and, the argument went, as such a result could not be without the working of divine power, God must be setting 'his seal to the doctrines that were preached and to the means that were used'.[2] What was indisputable was that making 'conversion' a matter of instant, public decision, with ascertainable numbers immediately announced in the religious press, produced a display of repeated 'successes' on a scale never before witnessed.

Numbers *seen* to be responding were claimed as more than sufficient evidence for the rightness of the changes in practice and teaching. If the argument for the new measures had been based on the testimony of Scripture or the witness of church history, the likelihood of the propaganda succeeding would have been small, but these were not the grounds on which the case for the new measures was based. The proof urged for them was much simpler: people had only to look at what could be seen across the country. This was the argument which William Weeks heard in Oneida County in 1826 and which he represented in the form of a conversation after a meeting where Mr Bold had preached:

Man. I call that *preaching*, gentlemen, don't you? Such preaching as that will promote a revival. This man is not one of your cold, theorizing, hair-splitting preachers. He has some *feeling*; and he makes his hearers feel too.

[1] *Revivals of Religion*, pp. 373–4; see also pp. 129–32.
[2] Finney, *Memoirs*, p. 221.

Thoughtful. I admit that he preaches much truth, and with a great deal of earnestness: but there are some things in his manner which I regard as very objectionable.

Wife. That is because you are in a cold, dead, and stupefied state yourself. You would feel differently, if you should only get waked up . . . The Holy Spirit gives his sanction to Mr. Bold, such as never was given to mortal man before. Revival upon revival follows him wherever he goes. How dare you find fault with a man whom the Holy Spirit approves?

Th. Where is the evidence that the Holy Spirit approves of this man?

Wife. His success in converting souls is the evidence. Wherever he goes the Spirit seems to follow him. And whenever he speaks it seems as if the Holy Spirit dictated every word he says.

Th. That is extravagant. Surely you cannot believe that the Holy Spirit gives utterance to such strange expressions as we hear from Mr. Bold.

Wife. Your being so cold is the reason why you are not pleased. If you once get your heart warmed, you will feel differently. But if you find fault with Mr. Bold's preaching and measures, what is that but to find fault with the Holy Spirit?

Th. It seems to me to be a very different thing. I cannot yet see that Mr. Bold is actuated by the Holy Spirit. I should not dare to ascribe to that blessed agent all his strange speeches. I do not see how you prove his success to be an evidence of divine approbation.

Wife. Why, does not every-body say that the Holy Spirit blesses these means, and therefore they must be right?

Th. Not quite every-body. There are some yet who think they must judge of things by the appointed rule, the law and the testimony.

Wife. Well, if you find fault with Mr. Bold's measures, when they are so successful, I must think you are more nice than the Holy Spirit.

Th. Do you think success is always a mark of the divine approbation?

Wife. Certainly.[1]

The argument from alleged success was one continually presented by Finney himself. He wrote:

I used to say to ministers, whenever they contended with me . . . Show me the fruits of your ministry.[2]

Instead of telling sinners to use the means of grace and pray for a new

---

[1] *Pilgrim's Progress in the Nineteenth Century*, pp. 235–6.
[2] *Memoirs*, p. 83.

heart, we called on them to make themselves a new heart and a new spirit and pressed the duty of instant surrender to God . . . Such teaching as this was of course opposed by man, nevertheless it was greatly blessed by the Spirit of God.[1]

God led me by his Spirit, to take the course I did . . . I never did or could doubt that I was divinely directed. That the brethren who opposed those revivals were good men, I do not doubt. That they were misled, and grossly and most injuriously deceived, I have just as little doubt.[2]

Much fault has been found with measures which have been *pre-eminently and continually* blessed of God for the promotion of revivals . . . TAKE CARE how you find fault with God.[3]

As noted above, Finney's claim that success proved the rightness of his cause could be tested by facts; the facts, however, reveal evidence contrary to Finney's thesis. In the early 1830s Finney repeatedly asserted that if preachers adopted his convictions there would be continuous revival. Many men did adopt them and the practices that went with them but the revival that 'would never cease' never came. On the contrary, the Second Great Awakening, which had begun under doctrinal preaching different from his own, came to an end and no protracted meetings could recall it. The excitement of 1831 seems to have been the point of termination. Sprague wrote in 1835: 'Look then at the cause of Revivals – a cause which, a few years ago, moved forward in our land with constantly increasing triumph; and united the labors, the prayers, the hearts, of almost all evangelical Christians. And what is the state of that cause now? The Ultraists themselves being judges, it is greatly depressed.'[4]

More important for our purpose is that Finney's own testimony on this point of historical fact is identical with that of Sprague. In the same year as Sprague expressed the above opinion Finney was giving his Lectures on Revivals of Religion in New York. After speaking of the year 1831, he went on, 'Ever

---

[1] Ibid., p. 189. See also p. 55 for the same argument used against Gale's teaching.

[2] Ibid., p. 222.

[3] *Revivals of Religion*, p. 212.

[4] *Religious Ultraism*, p. 31. The statement is in marked contrast to his *Lectures on Revivals*, 1832, pp. 3–4.

since the glory has been departing and revivals have been becoming less and less frequent – less and less powerful.'[1] The very construction of Finney's *Memoirs* points to the same conclusion. The little more than ten-year period prior to 1835 occupies 335 pages in the popular edition of that book, whereas the next thirty years of active ministry take up only 139 pages. Instead of writing an account of 'a new era of revivals', he confirmed that the period of revivals that had prevailed over the land through three decades was moving to a close by the early years of his ministry – the years of which he said, 'Certainly in no part of my ministry have I preached with greater success and power'.

Finney spoke similarly of the passing of revival in his *Letters on Revival* of 1845: there was a 'great falling off and decline in revivals';[2] 'I have observed, and multitudes of others also I find have observed, that for the last ten years revivals of religion have gradually been becoming more and more superficial.'[3]

So Finney's promise of continuous revival was, by his own admission, unfulfilled. In his *Lectures* of 1835–36 he accounted for this in terms of the opposition to which he had been subject. This explanation does not accord with the facts. Leaving aside his own ministry, there were preachers enough who believed his teaching that if you do not have a revival 'it is only because you do not want one',[4] but these men also proved that the belief was false. An example was Jedediah Burchard, Finney's early companion and possibly his mentor. Burchard was a leader in carrying what Sprague called 'religious ultraism' into Vermont. Prior to the 1830s, the gospel had advanced in that state without the new evangelism:

The display of fanaticism had been infrequent during the Evangelical Awakenings earlier in the century. A sense of propriety and an intense seriousness had characterized those under conviction. In 1830 and 1831, however, a new current overspread the Green Mountain country; in concert with much of interior America the 'Great Revival'

---

[1] *Revivals of Religion*, p. 329.
[2] Charles G. Finney, *Reflections on Revival* [the revised title of Finney's *Letters on Revivals*], comp. Donald Dayton (Minneapolis: Bethany House Publishers, 1979), p. 69.
[3] Ibid., p. 14.
[4] *Revivals of Religion*, p. 34.

permeated the region as no previous movement had done. In a single year the Congregationalists received over five thousand converts, while the Baptists numbered an increase of 2,726.

These upheavals were distinguished from others by the employment of 'new measures' – protracted meetings, anxious seats, and inquiry rooms as auxiliaries to the usual methods of conducting sessions.[1]

This work was carried on by 'revival men', itinerant evangelists who moved from town to town, of whom 'Jedidiah Burchard won greatest notoriety'. In 1834 and 1835 Burchard raised 'a great fire of religious fervor' in central and northern parts of Vermont:

After repeated prayers and appeals, by which he almost compelled multitudes to repair to the anxious seats, he asked again and again if they loved God. They were silent. 'Will you not say that you love God? Only say that you love or wish to love God.' Some confessed; and their names or numbers were written down in a memorandum book, to be reported as so many converts. It was enough to give an affirmative to the question: but many were not readily, and without continual importunity and management, induced to the admission. He would continue – 'Do you not love God? Will you not say you love God?' Then taking out his watch, – 'There now, I give you a quarter of an hour. If not brought in fifteen minutes to love God, there will be no hope for you – you will be lost – you will be damned.' A pause and no response. 'Ten minutes have elapsed, five minutes only left for salvation! If you do not love God in five minutes, you are lost forever!' The terrified candidates confess – the record is made – a hundred converts are reported.[2]

Burchard was not mentioned in Finney's *Memoirs*. His case is similar to those others whose careers began in the excitement of the new-measures controversy. Luther Myrick, ordained an evangelist by the Oneida Presbytery in 1827, was suspended by the same Presbytery in 1834. Jacob Knapp was another prominent leader in the new evangelism, who will be considered more closely in chapter 12. After being challenged for financial indiscretions in 1842, it is said that Knapp 'seldom ventured into New England' in the remaining thirty years of his

---

[1]   David M. Ludlum, *Social Ferment in Vermont 1791–1850* (New York, AMS Press, 1966), p. 56.
[2]   F. A. Cox and J. Hoby, *Baptists in America*, pp. 180–1.

life.[1] Asa Mahan, the contemporary of these men, was to write in his autobiography, that of all the evangelists of the 1830s who were inspired by Finney, 'I cannot recall a single man, brother Finney and Father Nash excepted, who did not after a few years lose his unction and become equally disqualified for the office of evangelist and pastor'.[2] Evangelical authors in Vermont observed that ultraism had first appeared among them in 1829 and become prevalent after 1832. Rufus Babcock, a Baptist, in the *American Quarterly Register*, August 1840, affirmed that its influence had 'divided associations and churches – alienated friends, and stopped the mouth of prayer or destroyed its vitality. This, we believe, is the principal cause of the spiritual death that has reigned so long and so fearfully among the churches in Vermont.'

*　　　*　　　*

Finney's claim that the truth of his teaching was proved by its success must come back to his own ministry for its best support, but even here it would be an understatement to say there is reason for serious misgivings. That he was used in true revival was never questioned by any of his Old School contemporaries. Gardiner Spring, for example, wrote of the revival in which Finney was first prominent and in which his new measures were first employed:

There is no doubt that there was a powerful work of grace during the years 1826 and 1827, in Central and Western New York. It is no evidence of its spuriousness that it was mingled with human imperfection, and sometimes accompanied by irregularities and extravagance which filled the minds of men with solicitude, and even gave the enemy occasion to blaspheme.[3]

This recognition by those who were critical of the new teaching must not be forgotten. At the same time, it was their belief that the permanent results were considerably fewer than had initially been claimed. In the course of time, Finney himself admitted this. Joseph Ives Foot, a Presbyterian minister, wrote

---

[1] McLoughlin, *Modern Revivalism*, p. 144.
[2] Ibid., p. 132, quoting from Asa Mahan, *Autobiography* (London, 1882), p. 229.
[3] *Personal Reminiscences*, vol. 2, p. 215.

in 1838: 'During ten years, hundreds, and perhaps thousands, were annually reported to be converted on all hands; but now it is admitted, that his [Finney's] real converts are comparatively few. It is declared even by himself, that "the great body of them are a disgrace to religion".'[1] Finney's words were spoken in a lecture in the Fall of 1836 and were first published in the pro-Finney *New York Evangelist*. A similar statement was made directly by Finney later. After he came to believe in 'entire sanctification' or 'Christian perfection', Finney claimed that the reason for his frequent disappointments in former evangelism was due to the absence of this belief from his ministry: 'I was often instrumental in bringing Christians under great conviction, and into a state of temporary repentance and faith but, falling short of urging them up to a point where they would become so acquainted with Christ as to abide in him, they would of course soon relapse again into their former state.'[2]

Among the facts that compelled retractions from Finney one in particular deserves to be mentioned. We noted above his teaching in 1835 that 'pious parents can render the salvation of their children certain'. Finney and his first wife were married in 1824 and had six children. Thirty-two years later, as his first biographer reported, Finney was preaching on the training of children one Sunday at Oberlin, when he stopped and exclaimed, 'Brethren, why am I trying to instruct you on the subject of training your children in the fear of God when I do not know that a single one of my children gives evidence of having been converted?'[3] One can admire Finney's sincerity and believe, with his biographer that the position was later different, but how does this confession harmonize with his claim that the truth of his teaching was proved by its success?[4]

We have seen that the most significant single reason for the spread of the new evangelism was the scale and the immediacy

---

[1] *Literary and Theological Review* (March 1838), p. 39, quoted in Warfield, *Perfectionism*, vol. 2, p. 23.

[2] *Lectures on Systematic Theology* (Oberlin, 1851), p. 619. This work was first published in two volumes (1846–7).

[3] G. F. Wright, *Finney*, p. 268.

[4] Yet Finney never renounced the teaching. When Gardiner Spring heard Finney on 'the prayer of faith' in 1831, it 'startled me and I saw that it might lead to the wildest fanaticism' (*Personal Reminiscences*, vol. 1, p. 226).

of the results it claimed to have secured – a claim supported by the numbers who responded to the altar call. But how did that claim convince if evidence existed to disprove it? This brings us to a final reason why the new thinking came to prevail. It is that, ultimately, the facts were suppressed and a serious distortion of them came to be believed by a later generation. There is weighty evidence for that assertion.

At the outset of the new-measures controversy, questions of historical fact were in dispute. Old School leaders protested that the innovators were falsely claiming to have the support of some of the best-known leaders in revivals. For example, in his Boston sermon of 1831 on 'Making a New Heart', Finney professed that his teaching was in succession to that of Jonathan Edwards and Edward Griffin. This led *The Biblical Repertory* of Princeton to demand, 'We wish to know on what principle such statements can be reconciled with honesty.'[1] Many years later Finney was to admit the wrongness of his appeal to Edwards and Griffin but not before his claim to represent the true tradition of revival had been endlessly repeated.[2] Calvinistic beliefs, he argued, crippled true gospel ministry and made evangelistic success practically impossible.

We have seen how this argument (an echo of the Kentucky controversy) was first raised in Presbyterian and Congregational churches of the Northeast at the time of the Oneida revivals. Accordingly, it was argued that those who were critical of the new measures were against evangelism; they were 'anti-revival' men. All the orthodox, regardless of their record of usefulness, were so designated. Warfield complained of the 'undeserved contempt' Finney showed for William Weeks whose 'memory has been sedulously defamed ever since'.[3]

---

[1] *Biblical Repertory* (1832), p. 286.

[2] His admission was not explicit but in his *Lectures on Systematic Theology*, revised edition, 1878, p. 289, he openly criticized Griffin's doctrine and in his *Memoirs*, p. 317, he conceded that Edwards 'held the contrary' to 'my views on the subject of the divine agency in regeneration'. The misrepresentation of these two men gives weight to Nettleton's statement that one reason why he allowed his letter to Samuel Aikin of 13 January 1827 to be circulated was that his name was being falsely claimed in support of the new measures – a claim repeated by E. N. Kirk in his *Lectures on Revivals* (Boston, 1875), p. 52.

[3] *Perfectionism*, vol. 2, p. 30. Hardman continues the misrepresentation in *Finney*, pp. 95–9 and *passim*.

Sprague regarded Weeks as 'an able and faithful minister of Christ', but to John Frost, Finney's supporter, he was 'the *Orthodox Devil* on Paris Hill'.[1] Archibald Alexander, himself a child of revival, received similar treatment. In his *Lectures on Revivals of Religion* Finney alluded to such men as Alexander of Princeton and Ebenezer Porter of Andover as 'ancient men, men of another age and stamp from what is needed in these days, when the Church and the world are rising to new thought and action'.[2] He complained: 'It is as dangerous and ridiculous for our theological professors, who are withdrawn from the field of conflict, to be allowed to dictate, in regard to the measures and movements of the Church, as it would be for a general to sit in his bed-chamber and attempt to order battle.'[3] Alexander's biographer observed that 'at no time was he so much aspersed' as during the new measures and New Divinity controversy:

> It was even said that he was utterly unacquainted with the phenomena of religious revival . . . It may be safely asserted that there was no man in the Church who had studied more closely this whole subject . . . In regard to revival measures, he freely expressed the results of his long observation, when opportunity was given in public or private, but in such a way as to show how tenderly he distinguished between the genuine work of Divine grace, and the excesses of rash and fanatical instruments.[4]

Next to Alexander, there was probably no one of the older generation whose life showed greater commitment to the advancement of preaching and revival than Ashbel Green. But Green's opposition to Finney and the New School singled him out as a special target for animosity. Finney repeated with obvious approval what a new convert had said to him: 'If Dr Green had only told us this that you have told me we should all have been converted immediately. But my friends and companions are lost.'[5] The spokesman was clearly one of those referred to by Sweet: 'Wherever Charles G. Finney went he always left behind him scores of young men "emancipated from

---

[1] W. H. Sprague, *Annals*, vol. 4, pp. 473–6; and *Memoirs: Complete Text*, p. 206 n.

[2] *Revivals of Religion*, pp. 214–15.   [3] Ibid., p. 329.

[4] *Life of Alexander*, pp. 426–7.   [5] *Memoirs*, pp. 264–5.

sin and Calvinism".'[1] Attacks of this kind on Green were too much for the usually placid and moderate Samuel Miller of Princeton, who wrote to a friend in 1837:

When I think of the character of such a man as Dr Green, who has been laboring without weariness for the Presbyterian Church for fifty years, and who has probably done more for promoting her essential interests than any other man now living; and when I reflect on the manner in which he has been spoken of and treated by men of yesterday, who would find it very difficult to point to any services to our beloved Zion, and who scarcely know enough of her history to understand what others have done; I scarcely know how to express my indignation.[2]

These quotations reveal the degree to which historical fact was involved in the controversy. They also show how concerned those on Finney's side were to represent critics as men with no real zeal for the gospel.

But we have not yet dealt with the charge that there was an actual suppression and distortion of evidence. That becomes clear at a much later date, especially in Finney's *Memoirs*, written between 1866 and 1868, where all that happened before the revivals of Finney's early ministry was entirely ignored. The so-called 'new era' in revivals was dated not from 1798 or 1800 but from 1825! In his *Lectures* of 1835 Finney had told his hearers only of 'the last ten years in which there has been such remarkable revivals through the length and breadth of the land'.[3] His *Memoirs* elaborated that statement in such a way that the uninformed reader was left with no idea of the general prevalence of revival *before* Finney, even in the very areas where he later laboured.

If such a major omission should be defended on the grounds that it lay outside Finney's own memories, the same cannot be said of the time of his conversion. At that date (1821) revival had been widespread in parts of New York State for several

[1] William Warren Sweet, *Revivalism in America, Its Origin, Growth and Decline* (Gloucester, Mass.: Peter Smith, 1965), p. 160.

[2] Samuel Miller, *Life of Samuel Miller* (Philadelphia, 1869), vol. 2, p. 229. For an interesting comment by Finney on the doctrinal reason for New School dislike of Green, see Samuel J. Baird, *History of New School*, p. 488.

[3] *Revivals of Religion*, p. 314.

years, including George Gale's church at Adams, to which Finney belonged. It is impossible to escape the conclusion that Finney was consciously passing over what he knew would undermine the doctrinal thesis that his *Memoirs* were intended to prove. He claimed that at the time of his conversion Calvinistic teaching was regarded 'as highly orthodox', so obviously he could not concede the long-continued existence of revivals under that teaching. To have conceded that would have been to have abandoned one of the main parts of his polemic. So, although it is known that dozens were brought into the Adams church under Gale's ministry in 1821, Finney was at pains to deny that there was any success in his pastor's ministry in those years: Gale, he says of that time, did not know the gospel 'as an experience'; 'As far as I could learn his spiritual state, he had not the peace of the Gospel when I sat under his ministry.'[1] These words are at odds with known facts, including the testimony of Gale's own autobiography which was unpublished in Finney's lifetime.

We have seen instances where lapses in Finney's *Memoirs* can probably be put down to a failure of memory but his treatment of Gale cannot be so explained. Why should Finney have consistently misrepresented the spiritual standing of the pastor who befriended him at his conversion, more than forty years before the *Memoirs* were written? I believe the answer is that, while Finney had nothing personal against Gale, he had much against the place where Gale was trained for the ministry, Princeton Theological Seminary. Princeton epitomized the orthodoxy against which Finney crusaded and he could not allow it the possibility of any success. Instead, he said that the teaching Gale had received 'crippled' him and would have permanently 'ruined' him as a minister if he had not later been delivered from it with Finney's help.[2] So Finney alleged, but his assertions were propaganda rather than facts.

Furthermore, Finney even suppressed his own testimony when it would have been relevant to include it. We have given above his admissions from the years 1836–46 on the failures occurring during his ministry in the revival period. His *Letters on Revival* (1845) were especially frank. In those pages he says:

[1] *Memoirs: Complete Text*, pp. 56–8.   [2] Ibid., pp. 57, 154.

'When I first began to preach I was without knowledge and without experience on the subject of revivals. I can see that in some things I erred in manner and spirit; which things I want to point out both by way of confessing my own faults and as a warning to others.'[1] There are many things in these *Letters* that might well have been written by any Old School leader. Finney urged the need for caution against fanaticism,[2] against using premature pressure for response,[3] against fault-finding with churches and ministers:[4] 'impulses' were not to be confused with the leading of the Spirit,[5] and a greater teaching content was needed in preaching.[6] By 'means and measures' it was possible to promote 'a certain kind of excitement' which is called 'a powerful revival of religion, but certainly not a revival of pure religion'.[7] There are 'spurious revivals' in which 'many supposed converts are numbered, when in reality there is not a genuine convert among them'. 'Efforts to promote revivals of religion have become so mechanical, there is so much policy and machinery in them, so much dependence upon means and measures, so much of man and so little of God, that the character of revivals has greatly changed within the last few years, and the true spirit of revivals seems to be fast giving way before this legal, mechanical method of promoting them.'[8] 'Those ministers who have witnessed none but the later revivals of which I speak are almost afraid of revivals. They have seen the disastrous results of modern revivals so frequently.'[9] He complains of ' a strong and ultra democratic tendency of mind, anti-conservative in the extreme and strongly tending to misrule'.[10]

These quotations are a sample of the strong and valuable words Finney wrote in 1845. But concessions of this kind, well calculated to ease controversy, wholly disappear from the *Memoirs* of twenty years later. And his admission of the transitory impression made on too many hearers of his

---

[1] *Reflections on Revival*, p. 11.　　　[2] Ibid., p. 13.

[3] Ibid., pp. 18–20.　　　[4] Ibid., pp. 54–6.　　　[5] Ibid., p. 25.

[6] Ibid., p. 79.　　　[7] Ibid., p. 60.

[8] Ibid., p. 102. 'The more I have seen of revivals, the more I am impressed with the importance of keeping excitement down as far as is consistent with a full, thorough and powerful exhibition of truth' (pp. 41–2).

[9] Ibid., p. 15.　　　[10] Ibid., p. 53.

preaching similarly disappeared from editions of his *Lectures on Systematic Theology* after the second printing of 1851. Finney knew in the 1840s that there was reason for the alarm which others had raised before he saw any need for it. At that date he owned the lack of knowledge that had marked his early ministry. He recognized that success had been exaggerated and that damage, even 'disastrous results', had sometimes followed the undue pressing of 'measures'. There was confirmation enough of that fact in relation to the Western revivals. In 1828 J. H. Rice passed through areas in central New York where Finney and other 'revivalists' had been prominent two years earlier. Rice wrote to Archibald Alexander: 'I saw in Troy and Utica, how the raging flame had passed through the garden of the Lord, and everything looked black and desolate.' Andrew Reed was in the same area in 1834 and had extended discussion with ministers in Utica on the subject. He no doubt had this region in mind when he reported in his *Narrative*:

There has certainly been good done where there has been much evil; for with this evil, there has still been a large portion of divine truth. But I fear not to say, that where there has been the largest infusion of the New Divinity into the New Measures, there has been the greatest amount of unwarrantable extravagance. There have been great excitement – much animal emotion and sympathy – high resolves, and multiplied conversions; but time has tested them, and they have failed. Many see this.[1]

There was therefore good reason for Finney to repeat his acknowledgements when he came to write at length of that early revival period in his *Memoirs*. But he did nothing of the kind. It was as though his *Letters on Revival* had never been written, and it has been through his *Memoirs*, together with his *Lectures on Revivals*, that posterity has judged his work.

There were probably two reasons why Finney suppressed in the 1860s what he had said in the 1840s. The first was the shock of a discovery he made when he visited Britain in 1849, where he experienced a very cautious welcome among evangelicals. In Birmingham, for example, one of his hosts was the Rev. John

---

[1] *Visit to the American Churches*, vol. 2, pp. 74–5. See also vol. 1, pp. 340–1, and Cox and Hoby, *Baptists in America*, pp. 255–6.

Angell James who had written the preface to a British edition of Finney's *Lectures on Revivals* published in 1839. But James' reservations had increased since that date and in the intervening years he had publicly repudiated his recommendation of the *Lectures*.[1] Finney rightly referred to James as 'the principal dissenting minister in Birmingham' and recorded in his *Memoirs*: 'the ministers were not prepared to commit themselves to the work of promoting a general revival of religion which should morally renovate the whole city as we have seen revivals sweep through and renovate our American Towns and Cities from time to time.' The explanation for this reserve was that after 'the report of our great revivals from 1825 onwards' reached Britain, the good that might have also been done by his ministry in Britain was counteracted by the effect of critical reports received from the United States. In particular, he alleged, such had been the success of his *Lectures on Revivals of Religion* in Britain that Nettleton had crossed the Atlantic 'it would seem for the purpose of counteracting the influence of those lectures'. So 'the good brethren on that side of the ocean' were 'frightened out of the revival movement'.[2]

This representation of events was absurd and Fairchild was right to take the above quotations out of the *Memoirs* as they first appeared. Nettleton's only visit to Britain had taken place three years *before* Finney ever gave his lectures in New York. But what was indisputable was that Finney was taken aback by his transatlantic visit of 1849, and by the fact that, following his visit, British opposition to his ministry increased rather than diminished. The main reason for the increase was that British evangelical leaders had seen something of the injurious effects of the new teaching. But Finney took an entirely different view: 'I have never doubted that had it not been for the misrepresentations of opposers on this side of the Atlantic a most sweeping and far reaching revival would at that time have swept not only over Birmingham, but also over all England, Wales and Scotland.'[3]

Among these 'opposers' he included 'Dr Hodge of Princeton', which brings us to the second and main reason for

---

[1] *Memoirs: Complete Text*, p. 487 n.
[2] Ibid., p. 496.   [3] Ibid., p. 497.

the contrast between the admissions he made in the mid-1840s and his silence on the same things twenty years later. It was doctrinal. Finney was sincere in believing Calvinism to be not only a threat to his reputation but, more seriously in his eyes, the main obstacle to effective evangelism. In the 1840s he had admitted mistakes in practice but not mistakes in theology. His Preface to his *Lectures on Systematic Theology* of 1846, had begun with the words, 'To a great extent the truths of the blessed gospel have been hidden under a false philosophy.' The pages that followed were a full-scale defence of the New Divinity.

But in the 1860s Finney knew that it was not from theological lectures that the verdict of history would be drawn. The popular mind was far more likely to be impressed by easily read narratives and especially by narratives that were pre-eminently records of success. So nothing was to be allowed in the *Memoirs* that would weaken the impression. There would be no concessions or admissions. There would be no hint of the influence of Old School preachers in revivals, for it might introduce doubt over the case he meant to prove. In the great purpose he had in view in 1866–8 everything that did not serve to strengthen his doctrinal crusade was put aside. The autobiography that at first sight seemed to be the artless record of the life of an evangelist was actually governed in its whole construction and presentation by one overriding polemic.[1] The thousands who have accepted it at face value have unwittingly accepted a reconstruction of history.

While Christians in the 1830s and 1840s were not carried away by the new teaching to the extent that McLoughlin and others claim, there can be no question that by 1900 the impression was almost universal that Charles Grandison Finney had *introduced* revivals in nineteenth-century America and that his usefulness so exceeded that of all who went before him that there was little evangelistic endeavour before him that

[1] There is enough in the commonly known abridged version of the *Memoirs* to raise this suspicion; in the complete restored text it is unmistakable. When the preparation of an autobiography of Finney was first under discussion, Truman Hastings advised, 'The work, I think should contain a full "diagnosis" of the Theological Night Mare, under which the Churches were prior to the advent of Mr Finney'. Introduction to *Memoirs: Complete Text*, p. xxvi.

deserved serious attention. The belief has been repeated so often that it is commonly regarded as an unquestionable fact. Billy Graham, for instance, writes of Finney: 'Through his Spirit-filled ministry, uncounted thousands came to know Christ in the nineteenth century, resulting in one of the greatest periods of revival in the history of America.'[1] Another modern writer claims: 'When Charles Finney was converted and filled with the Holy Ghost the American churches were in a sickly state. Most churches were either Hyper-Calvinist or Universalist . . . apathy prevailed.'[2]

In conclusion, the reasons why the new measures came to be accepted may be summarized as follows. First, the claim that they were justified by massive success appeared so feasible that biblical warrant for their use seemed to be unnecessary. Scripture was not the decisive criterion. Had it been so it would have shown the importance of Sprague's observation that 'there is scarcely a more uncertain test than that of mere numbers'.[3] Secondly, all Christians rightly want to *see* success, and the new measures seemed to offer that possibility in a way not known before. Thirdly, the introduction of the new measures in a time of real revival gave weight to the claim that their 'successes' were due to divine blessing. And, finally, the illusion was ultimately accepted because the alleged successes received far more publicity than did the evidence of harm done to the life of the churches. Nettleton spoke of the results of the new evangelism as constituting 'the illusion of a new era'.[4] Unlike the writings of the evangelical leaders of the Second Great Awakening, Finney's *Memoirs* have not been out of print since the first edition of 1876.

---

[1] Foreword to Lewis A. Drummond, *Charles Grandison Finney and the Birth of Modern Evangelism* (London, 1983), p. 6.
[2] Homer Duncan, *Prepare Now* (M C International, 1981), pp. 218–19.
[3] *Lectures*, p. 14.
[4] Letter to John Frost, 15 February 1827, Oberlin archives.

THE BAPTISTS IN TRANSITION

The Triennial Baptist Convention, Philadelphia, 1814, first
national body of Baptists; convened to advance foreign missions.

12

It has been argued in the preceding pages that the ultimate success of the new views of evangelism and revival owed much to the loss, sometimes even the suppression, of earlier history. Among the Baptists, as with other denominations, the impressiveness of the claims made for the new depended in no small part on an acceptance of the charge that the preceding eras had been largely a story of hyper-Calvinistic barrenness. So effective was the propaganda in most Baptist churches that by the twentieth century their real history was almost entirely unknown. The doctrines of grace which had built these churches, Thomas J. Nettles remarks, 'like a puff of smoke in a strong wind . . . vanished in American Baptist life.'[1]

Part of this loss of history, however, has to be attributed to the shortage of published records. There was no general history of the Baptists in America until David Benedict's two volumes appeared in 1813. Benedict was brief on individuals and on doctrines, and complained of 'the want of materials'[2] even on the Great Revival of 1800–1803. After Benedict nothing major seems to have been published until 1860 when W. B. Sprague issued the massive volume on the Baptists in his monumental series, *Annals of the American Pulpit*. Sprague presents personal portraits, which were lacking in Benedict but, while he showed in over 850 pages that American Christians of Baptist persuasion were possessors of a noble heritage, he also had to

[1] *By His Grace and for His Glory: A Historical, Theological, and Practical Study of the Doctrines of Grace in Baptist Life* (Grand Rapids, Mich.: Baker Book House, 1986), p. 223.
[2] *Baptist Denomination in America*, vol. 2, p. 164.

acknowledge in his Preface: 'In regard to not a small number of deceased ministers of highly respectable standing in their day, after pursuing my inquiries to a great length, I have been forced to the conclusion that, though their record is doubtless in heaven, they have left no record on earth out of which it is possible to frame such memorials as they were entitled to.'[1] It was almost the end of the nineteenth century before further general Baptist histories were written, by which time there were very few alive who remembered the preaching that was common before the 1830s.[2]

We have already touched on earlier Baptist history, chiefly as it related to Virginia and Kentucky, but a brief general overview may help at this point. In the first hundred years after the first settlement of America only seventeen Baptist churches were formed. The advance came in the eighteenth century when Baptist churches spread largely from two main starting-points: from 'the Welsh tract' near Philadelphia, and from New England, where their first prominent leader was Isaac Backus (1724–1806) who travelled over 67,000 miles from his church base at Middleborough, Massachusetts. Before the end of the eighteenth century there were Baptist pastors of eminent ability in most of the major cities, and in a number of instances records exist of the powerful revivals they witnessed. These witnesses included Richard Furman of Charleston, John Davis and Absalom Butler of Baltimore, John Williams and Archibald Maclay of New York, and Samuel Stillman and Thomas Baldwin of Boston. As the pages of Sprague's *Annals* show, many Baptist pastors were involved in the ingathering of the Second Great Awakening and nothing else can explain the great numerical growth which their churches experienced. As Robert G. Torbet observes, 'Without a doubt, the Great Revival of the early nineteenth century provided the dynamic for growth and spiritual vigour among Protestants generally'.[3]

---

[1] *Annals*, vol. 6, p. vi.

[2] Thomas Armitage's *History of the Baptists* (New York, 1887), reflected the changed theological climate. Albert Henry Newman's *A History of the Baptist Churches in the United States* (1894), presented a good objective history and some perceptive doctrinal comment but, as he noted, the differences between Calvinism and Arminianism were no longer considered an important issue. See Newman's *History*, sixth ed. (Philadelphia, 1915), pp. 499–500, 531–4.

[3] *A History of the Baptists*, rev. ed. (Valley Forge, Pa.: The Judson Press, 1965), p. 302.

From the records in Sprague's volume, it can be clearly seen that the personal lives of the early Baptist pastors and preachers had the same spiritual characteristics as marked the men of other denominations who were their fellow-labourers. They shared a common firm commitment to doctrinal Christianity with 'their pious and beloved Pedobaptist brethren' (to use a phrase of Benedict's) which, in their case also, was combined with a concern for real communion with God. Richard Furman's description of John Gano might have been applied equally to many others: 'Having discerned the excellence of Gospel truths, and the importance of eternal realities, he felt their power on his own soul . . . he excelled in the pathetic, – in pungent, forcible addresses to the heart and conscience'.[1] Of another preacher it was said: 'In preaching, he placed great reliance on the sensible presence of his Master, and, sometimes, when his feelings were warmed and quickened by a powerful divine influence, he delivered himself with an energy and a pathos that were quite irresistible'.[2] Describing John Williams of New York, Charles Sommers said: 'He was a most diligent student of the Bible, and his great object in preaching seemed to be, not only to bring out the mind of the Spirit, but to bring it in contact with the thought and feelings of his hearers in all its divine power . . . His prayers were remarkable specimens of the simplicity as well as fervour of devotion. I think it must have been difficult for any man – no matter how wicked he might have been – to have heard him pray without being impressed with the thought that he was in actual communion with God.'[3]

John Leland described their common view of what a preacher should be when he wrote: 'It is of primary importance that the preacher should be clothed with the garment of salvation; that he should be filled with a sense of the immense worth of the truth, the guilt, depravity and danger man is in; the unsearchable love of Christ in the bloody purchase, and his ability and willingness to save redeemed penitents. Without this robe, he will preach a distant Jesus, by an unfelt gospel, and with an unhallowed tongue.'[4]

---

[1] *Annals*, vol. 6, p. 66. [2] Ibid., p. 110.
[3] Ibid., p. 362. [4] *Writings of Leland*, p. 679.

What we know of the personal lives of these men provides repeated instances of their experience of the efficacy of prayer. For instance, Isaac Backus was called to assist in the healing of a rift between two Christians which had destroyed the peace of a church. All previous attempts at reconciliation had proved useless and when Backus joined in a long night of discussion and pleading it looked as if the result would be no better. As the dawn of a new day approached, it is recorded: 'Mr Backus rose up, saying, "Let us look to the throne of grace once more;" and then kneeling down he prayed. The spirit and tone of his prayer were such as to make everyone feel that the heart-searching God had come down among them. The result was, the contending parties began immediately to melt, and the rising sun saw the rupture healed and closed up for ever.'[1]

There is a similar testimony on how a prolonged and severe drought came to an end on a memorable day during the ministry of Stephen Gano. On that day, his son-in-law wrote, he prayed in such a manner for the end of the drought 'that some of the younger portion of his audience, on leaving the church, remarked one to another, "We must hasten home; for, after such a prayer, the rain will overtake us." And so it came to pass – the rain came pouring down in less than an hour.'[2]

These men believed in the reality of prayer, and Sprague has given us enough information on the way their lives ended for us to judge that they died as they had lived. At Richard Furman's death, says a friend, as he was making his way 'through the dark valley', he told those beside him, 'I am a dying man but my trust is in the Redeemer: I preach Christ to you dying, as I have attempted to while living.' He asked that the Twenty-Third Psalm should be read 'and before the reading of it was concluded his heart had ceased to beat.' One of the sayings of Samuel Stillman in his advancing years was, 'Heaven is not far off when we feel right', and his final words as he left this world were, 'God's government is infinitely perfect.' The dying Samuel Jones confided in a friend, 'When alone, I tune like a nightingale at the prospect of death.' Observing the serenity of William Elliot as he approached death, a visitor commented, 'You enjoy yourself very well, don't you?' 'Oh no,' Elliot

[1] Hovey, *Memoir of Backus*, p. 276.
[2] *Annals*, vol. 6, p. 232.

replied, 'I don't enjoy *myself* at all, but I never enjoyed the *Lord* so well in all my life.' On being asked how he was at the end, Andrew Broaddus said, 'Calmly relying on Christ', and the last words he was heard to whisper were, 'Happy! Happy! Happy!' Oliver Hart, another of this same company of men, called on all who were with him to help him praise God and on being told that he would soon be in the company of saints and angels he ended his course with the exclamation, 'Enough, Enough!' Of Morgan Rhees, who died 'in the triumphs of faith' at the age of forty-four, it was said, 'his departure seemed rather a translation than a death.' The aged Andrew Marshall, when approaching death, asked a friend to carry this message to relatives in New England: 'Tell them that I am yet in the land of the *dying*, but am bound to the land of the *living*.'[1]

In Sprague's records, from which all the above words except the last are taken, there is another characteristic of the Baptist preachers which repeatedly appears and is too important to omit, namely, their catholicity of spirit. Had this not been so they might well have been forgiven for no group suffered more from nominal Christians of other denominations than the Baptists did on account of their convictions. But most of their leaders emphasized the great things which they had in common with all true Christians and not what had led them conscientiously to form churches of Baptist persuasion. Lewis Lunsford, John Williams and John Leland, leaders in the revival of the 1780s in Virginia were all marked by this spirit. So were other leaders elsewhere. No one thought it strange, for instance, that Richard Furman's funeral sermon should be preached by a Presbyterian or that the epitaph of Benjamin Foster, one of the early pastors of the First Baptist Church of New York, should be written by another Presbyterian. The much-used pastor of the First Baptist Church of Philadelphia, William Staughton (1770–1829), explained their common perspective in the words: 'The points in which we differ from our Christian brethren of other denominations, compared with those in which we all agree, bear no greater proportion to each other, than does the trembling lustre of a star to the meridian blaze of the summer sun.' Of all these men it could be said, as it was said

[1] Benedict, *Fifty Years Among the Baptists*, p. 54.

of Abel Woods, they 'embraced in cordial fellowship all who bore the image of the meek and lowly Jesus'.[1]

This catholicity brought help to other Christians, as we noticed earlier with respect to Presbyterians in Virginia. It also strengthened the Baptists themselves. A striking instance of this can be seen in the influence of Baptist links with the College of New Jersey at Princeton. Just as Presbyterian graduates of Princeton took a vision of experimental preaching and of revival into their ministries, so did young men of Baptist conviction who trained there. Hezekiah Smith, pastor of the First Baptist Church of Haverhill in New England for forty years, was at Princeton in the presidency of Samuel Davies. He lived to see the Second Great Awakening and died in the midst of a revival. Newman wrote of Smith, 'He was the foremost Baptist pastor of the time and he was instrumental in the conversion of thousands.'[2] Henry Smalley, a graduate of Witherspoon's era, served the Cohansey Baptist Church, Cumberland County, New Jersey, from 1790 until his death in 1839. We read that 'While the growth of his church was, for the most part, gradual, there were several revivals which brought considerable accessions to it.' Better known than Smalley was the Hon. Joseph Clay, a Princeton graduate and a judge, who became a Baptist preacher in 1804 and spent most of the seven remaining years of his life itinerating in different parts of the country.

Perhaps Princeton's most important Baptist graduate of the eighteenth century was James Manning. After leaving Princeton in 1762, Manning spent his life in Rhode Island where, aided by the Philadelphia Association, he founded another college which, as Brown University (1804), became the premier Baptist institution of its kind. A revival experienced by Rhode Island College, Manning's church, and the Congregational church at Providence, Rhode Island in 1774–75, contributed to the ethos in which this new venture was born. Many of the Baptist leaders threw their weight behind the college, none

---

[1] See *Annals*, vol. 6, pp. 128, 132, 183, 192, 250, 315–16, 342. On the same point see Francis Wayland and H. L. Wayland, *A Memoir of the Life and Labours of Francis Wayland*, (New York, 1867; New York, Arno Press, 1972), vol. 1, pp. 83–4.

[2] *Baptist Churches in the United States*, p. 261.

more so than Manning's fellow Princetonian, Hezekiah Smith. Preachers trained at the college included Thomas Ustick and William Rogers (both to be leaders in Philadelphia), William Collier, John Sterry, Zenas Leonard, Lucius Bolles, Charles Screven, Adoniram Judson (pioneer missionary to Burma), and Joshua Bradley (author of *Accounts of Religious Revivals in Many Parts of the United States from 1815 to 1818*).

Enough of the lives of these men has been recorded to show that they belonged to the same common tradition that had given rise to Princeton. While they valued education, academic distinctions were not their first priority. Screven, for example, was made a Doctor of Divinity by Brown University but a friend wrote of him: 'All saw that his ruling passion was that of a true minister of the Gospel, – to save souls. The College gave him its highest titles, but in his humble efforts to bring sinners to God, for a third of a century, a monument has been erected which will stand when academical honours are forgotten.' The same writer went on to quote characteristic words from Screven: 'Our religion is a system of love and good will. It manifests not only the unspeakable love of God to a fallen world, but also tends to fill the hearts of men with holy affections towards their Creator and one another. The man whose heart is a stranger to compassion, or cannot adopt the language of "being affectionately desirous of you", is a most unsuitable person to dispense that Gospel every sentiment of which emanates from love . . . The celestial flame of love must mingle with all our preparations, and burn on every acceptable sacrifice.'[1]

In order to judge the extent of the doctrinal change which subsequently occurred in the Baptist churches we need to remember the Calvinistic commitment of these men. The point has been noted earlier in these pages. Both the 'Welsh tract' preachers, who adopted the Philadelphia Confession, and their New England brethren, held to the same school of belief or – in Asbury's critical words, 'what they think is the good old cause'. While they allowed a difference among themselves on the extent of the atonement, there was no difference on the sovereignty of divine grace. On this the Confession drawn up

[1] *Annals*, vol. 6, pp. 441–2.

by Isaac Backus was entirely at one with that of the Philadelphia Association. The words of the Backus Confession on conversion governed all their thinking:

The Holy Ghost, and he only, can and doth make a particular application of the redemption purchased by Christ, to every elect soul. John 3.5 and 16.7–15. The Spirit of God applies his redemption by convincing us of our sinful, lost and miserable condition, and then discovering the glorious Saviour, as he is offered to us in the Gospel, in his suitableness and sufficiency, and enabling us to embrace him with our whole souls, whereby he is made unto us wisdom, righteousness, sanctification and redemption. John 16.8 and 1.12, 1 Cor. 1.30.[1]

These words state the essence of the difference between the Baptists as a whole and the distinct and numerically weaker, Freewill Baptists. The doctrinal commitment of the best-known Baptist pastors is constantly apparent in the pages of the sixth volume of Sprague's *Annals*. Oliver Hart was 'a fixed Calvinist. The doctrines of *free efficacious grace* were precious to him.' John Gano embraced the doctrines 'which are contained in the Baptist Confession of Faith, and are commonly styled Calvinistic.' Benjamin Foster was said to be 'strictly Calvinistic and full on the doctrine of salvation by free grace.' Lewis Richards's beliefs 'were decidedly Calvinistic, without, however, the least approach to Antinomianism.' Ambrose Dudley was 'a thorough Calvinist'; Andrew Marshall, the eminent black preacher of Savannah, 'was of the old Calvinistic order'; Abel Woods regarded his salvation 'as a wonder of free and sovereign grace'. It is needless to extend the list any further for the fact is beyond all dispute.

As a representation of the preaching of this generation of men let us take the testimony of Archibald Maclay of New York whose congregation, formed in 1809, seemed to have been an overflow from that of John Williams, with which it came to share in the same spiritual prosperity. Maclay wrote of his ministry in the time of revival around that date, when 'not less than five hundred were brought out of darkness into God's marvellous light' and 'eighteen brethren were licensed to preach':

[1] *Memoir of Backus*, p. 335.

In my ministry it has been my aim to keep back nothing profitable to my hearers, but to declare unto them 'all the counsel of God'. The leading theme of my preaching has been Christ crucified, as the only Saviour of lost sinners. I have shown the universal and total depravity of man; that every unconverted sinner is under the dominion of a carnal mind, which is at enmity to God and not subject to his law; that a change of heart, a heavenly birth, is absolutely necessary to see the kingdom of God and enter therein; that the same power that created the world, and raised our Lord from the dead, must quicken the sinner dead in sins, and make him alive to God; that if saved from sin and hell, it must be by free, sovereign, efficacious grace, through faith in the Lord Jesus Christ; and that nothing can meet the necessities of a sinner awakened to a sense of his guilt by the teaching of the Holy Spirit, but what satisfied divine justice, the full atonement of Jesus Christ.[1]

*   *   *

How these beliefs came to be attacked, and ultimately overthrown, among the very churches which owed their existence to their proclamation, has to be one of the strangest stories of church history, although it closely parallels what we have already noted in other denominations. Prior to the 1830s there were a few ineffectual attempts made to change the common creed of the Baptist churches. In 1815 a judge who was an influential member of a church in Woodford County, Kentucky, published a pamphlet in defence of Arminianism, but, although he gained some local support, three Baptist Associations 'passed judgment against it' while none gave it support.[2] More serious was the case of Henry Holcombe, pastor of the First Baptist Church of Philadelphia, who is alleged to have published Arminian views in 1823. In the ensuing dispute a sizeable number seceded from the congregation, affirming that the pastor and those adhering to him 'had erred and abandoned the grounds on which the church was

---

[1] Humphrey, *Revival Sketches*, pp. 227–8. These words are very similar to the testimonies of other preachers of the revival period, e.g. John B. Preston: 'The truths which have been most evidently blessed in this revival, have been the divine holiness and sovereignty, the grace of the gospel, and the sinner's total depravity and dependence' (p. 173).

[2] *Annals*, vol. 6, p. 157.

originally constituted'. The charge was incontestable and the minority group was granted a charter by the Philadelphia Baptist Association.[1]

By the 1830s, as a result of the influences we have already seen operating in other churches, a readiness to accept change was also appearing among the Baptists. The autobiography of Wilson Thompson, quoted earlier, provides a typical example of the new voices that were being heard. On a visit to Cincinnati in the late 1820s Thompson heard a fellow Baptist pastor, Jeremiah Vardaman, deliver an hour-long address to students at a seminary in which he dismissed 'the foundation of the whole Calvinistic creed' with 'burlesque, ridicule and sarcasm'. Thompson was not altogether surprised, for on the previous evening he had heard Vardaman leading what were claimed to be revival meetings and a 'great work among the Baptists'. When Thompson had gone to the church where the meetings were taking place – a Baptist cause where he had often preached himself – he was asked to do so again that night. He accepted the invitation and his address was followed by that of another visiting preacher so that there was no time for Vardaman to speak as usual. From his view of the congregation, which was supposed to be in a state of revival, Thompson could see none of the solemnity which was usual on the faces of people at such times. Vardaman, however, was determined that the service should not be closed: and the older man tells us what followed:

Mr Vardaman then arose and said in a dull, low manner that he very much regretted the unprofitable manner in which the evening had been wasted. It was now too late to do anything to profit, and the people must wait until another opportunity. All at once he raised his voice and said: 'Late as it is, I feel such an agonizing of soul for these poor mourning sinners, who feel as if this might be the last hour that salvation would be offered to them, that I cannot dismiss them until I have given them one more opportunity to come forward for me to pray for them'.

'All the people seated on those long benches fronting the pulpit', said he, 'will please leave them for the mourners to occupy, while I come down to pray for them. All who desire salvation will come to

---

[1] Marion Bell notes how in course of time 'Holcombe's heresy became an accepted part of church theology'. *Crusade in the City*, p. 73.

these seats. I have prayed for such hundreds of times, and never without more or fewer being converted while I was praying; therefore, come without delay'.

We went down. He started a song and, as many voices joined in the singing, the spacious house was filled with melody. Every few minutes he would raise his voice and tell the mourners to 'come on,' and 'not confer with flesh and blood;' 'this might be the night that would seal their eternal doom;' 'come and receive offered mercy.' Again, he would order runners to go up every aisle and lead the mourners to these benches. Yet, with all this, they came but slowly. He stepped upon one of the long seats, and turning his eyes upward and raising his hand with his arm stretched out above his head, he roared at the top of his voice, in an authoritative manner: 'Stop, Gabriel, stop; don't speed your golden pinions again, nor attempt to take the news to the throne of God, until you can report at least fifty humble mourners on these anxious benches seeking the salvation of their souls amid the prayers and songs of God's elect.'

When he had given this command, he raised his right foot and hand and stamped with his foot on the bench, at the same time striking the back of it with his open hand, making a startling sound through the spacious house. This he repeated three times, in rapid succession, and then followed a general movement through the house. He stepped down from the seat, telling them to sing with more animation, and not to pause between the songs even for one minute. His runners now began to lead in the mourners very fast. They were handed up to him; he would slap them on the shoulders and halloo, 'Glory to God,' and motion them to the seats. The seats were soon filled, and no more came. He ordered the singers to stop singing, and commanded every person in the house to go upon his knees. He knelt, and in that position surveyed the congregation; and again, in an authoritative manner, cried: 'Go down upon your knees, I say; young men, down upon your knees! "It is written, unto Me every knee shall bow."' When he had spent some time in this way, and had got all that would obey him on their knees, he pronounced some very heavy invectives on the others, and then said: 'Let us all pray.' He went on to give a history of his coming to Cincinnati; of the cold state he had found the city and the church in; how he had proceeded since he came; how many he had baptized; and the great work that was going on with increasing power. This historical account made up his prayer.

He then called upon the singers to assist him, and he commenced singing the hymn, 'How happy are they who their Saviour obey,' etc. They all joined in the singing, and he passed between the benches where the mourners had been placed, and stooping down to each one he would, in a low whisper, converse a short time with them, and in many cases he would rise up erect, clap his hands together, and shout 'Glory to God, here is another soul born for heaven.' In this manner he passed between all the mourners' benches. I had not seen one among the whole number that I thought looked like a contrite mourner, such as the Saviour pronounced blessed, at least as far as I could judge from the appearance of those even who were on the anxious benches.[1]

By the time of Vardaman's death in 1842 he was said to have baptized 'a greater number than any Baptist minister in the United States'.[2] Even so, he does not appear to have been among the foremost who were introducing these changes among the Baptist churches. Frank G. Beardsley accords that honour to Jacob Knapp and Jabez S. Swan whom he names as 'pioneer evangelists of the denomination'.[3] According to McLoughlin, Jacob Knapp 'was almost as well known as Finney by 1840. He claimed to have conducted 150 separate revivals and to have converted 100,000 persons by 1874, the year he died.'[4] These claims for Knapp, made by Beardsley in 1904 and McLoughlin in 1959, must be subject to some doubt for they probably rest too heavily on Knapp's own statements as published in his *Autobiography of Elder Jacob Knapp* in 1868. But Knapp's book certainly proves that he was among the first of the Baptist practitioners of what he called 'the new method of presenting the gospel'.[5]

Jacob Knapp, a native of Otsego County, New York, became a pastor in 1825. In the 1830s, as he heard the news of the work done by evangelists through 'protracted efforts', he came to look upon 'the past eight years of my ministry as comparatively wasted'.[6] In 1833 he left his pastorate and, modelling himself on Finney and Burchard, he found that his work among the Baptist churches had immediate success: 'It was thought by some, who were counted reliable judges, that not less than two

---

[1] *Autobiography of Thompson*, pp. 312–21.

[2] Sprague, *Annals*, vol. 6, p. 426. It is impossible to reconcile what J. M. Peck (quoted by Sprague) said about Vardaman's attitude to new measures in evangelism with Thompson's eyewitness account.

[3] *History of American Revivals* (Boston, 1904), p. 164.

[4] McLoughlin, *Modern Revivalism*, p. 140.

[5] *Autobiography of Elder Jacob Knapp* (New York, 1868), p. 68.

[6] Ibid., p. 28.

thousand souls were converted during these eighteen months.'[1] From that point, he said, he came to regard his mission as the conversion of the Baptists to the new views. It was a task that would have daunted other men: 'Among Baptists, at the time when I started out, there was no one man who stood forth as a champion and exemplar of revival measures. I felt that I was entering upon a path that had not been trodden before me.'[2] Elsewhere he said of his early labours, 'Notwithstanding this success, my work was looked upon with suspicion, and scarcely alluded to in the public prints. I was forty years ahead of the times.'[3]

Knapp claimed to be the first to introduce 'the anxious seat' to the churches of his denomination in New York City in 1835. This was not without opposition from the 'hyper-Calvinists' who believed in 'fossilized mummies' instead of 'God's methods'. Hitherto, he claimed, 'hyper-Calvinistic tenets constituted the staple of pulpit ministration' in Baptist Churches and 'prevailed throughout the States of New York, New Jersey, Pennsylvania, Delaware and Maryland'.[4] He found the same type of 'old fogies' in other denominations – people such as the Congregationalists in North Rutland, Jefferson County, New York, who 'would invite neither Finney nor Burchard to labor with them'.[5]

At one point, at least, Knapp went beyond his New School Presbyterian models: he believed in the instant baptism of converts. This posed a problem for Baptist churches, for along with all evangelical churches, they had hitherto required time to elapse before professed converts were received into membership. Formerly, writes Knapp, those seeking membership were first required to 'go before the deacons, or a committee, for examination, and then must wait a while before they related their experience to the church'. It was in the congregation once led by Dr Maclay in New York City that Knapp first devised an expedient to meet this hindrance. He arranged for a group of members to meet in the basement of the Baptist Tabernacle, night by night, at the same time as he counselled 'the anxious' above:

[1] Ibid., p. 30. [2] Ibid., p. 41.
[3] Ibid., p. 50. [4] Ibid., pp. 38–9. [5] Ibid., p. 62.

As fast as they found peace in believing with all their hearts, I sent them below to present themselves to the church. Sometimes there were thirty or forty persons who thus presented themselves on an evening. On one occasion, the lamented Deacon Colgate, in his humorous way, took me to task for sending the converts faster than the church could receive them. Brother Everts and myself baptized ninety-six in one day; and so the work went on for ten weeks, day and night, without any cessation . . .[1]

As I continued to labor other ministers caught the spirit of evangelism. Many of them went forth from their own immediate fields to assist neighboring pastors, and adopted the measures which had proved so successful with evangelists. Thus the work extended all through the United States. Converts were multiplied by tens of thousands; while those churches which did not sympathize with these new measures died out, and those ministers who opposed the progress of evangelical effort are forgotten, or are remembered only as men who misinterpreted the signs of the times.[2]

*   *   *

Summarizing the message of Knapp's *Autobiography*, R. Jeffery, one of his contemporaries, wrote in the Preface to that volume: 'Among the agents whom God has employed for the bringing about of this marked and blessed change in the spirit of our churches, Jacob Knapp occupies a place of indisputable preeminence . . . Posterity will speak of Elder Knapp as the pioneer and champion of modern evangelism.'[3] This is an extraordinary claim, that it was the new men such as Knapp who introduced evangelism and 'revivals' among the Baptists in the 1830s and subsequently. Along with many others of a later generation, Frank Beardsley accepted the claim and helped to teach subsequent generations to regard it as authentic history. But what Beardsley wrote in his *History of American Revivals* in 1904 was not consistent on this subject. He acknowledged, briefly, that 'Baptists shared to no inconsiderable extent in the Awakening of 1800', while also asserting that 'many' of their churches 'were at a standstill and in many instances were dying out'.[4] His explanation for their allegedly

---

[1] Ibid., p. 108.   [2] Ibid., p. 47.
[3] Ibid., p. xi.   [4] *American Revivals*, pp. 163–4.

poor condition is similar to ones we have often encountered:

As a class [the Baptists] did not favor special efforts to promote revivals of religion. The cause is not far to seek. With the exception of the Freewill Baptists, who were Arminian in theology and the ardent friends of revivals, the Baptists as a rule were tinctured with the hyper-Calvinism of the period, which looked askance upon all human attempts to effect the regeneration of men. God's sovereignty rendered inconsistent any man-made attempts for the salvation of others. It was presumptuous to undertake anything of the kind. Regeneration was a divine work to be wrought independently of any human agency. The salvation of sinners being determined by God's electing grace, human efforts looking to that end were not only needless but useless. God knew who would or would not be saved, and in his own good time, and in accordance with his own good purposes he would gather the elect into his kingdom. The strength of the church was to 'lie still'.[1]

We have seen this same charge laid against all the older evangelical denominations prior to the advent of Finney. In the case of the Baptists a host of writers agree with Beardsley's main contention. They treat hyper-Calvinism and historic Calvinism as one and the same thing. Thus George Washington Paschal calls teaching in the Philadelphia Confession of Faith 'hyper-Calvinistic' and treats its influence as hostile to evangelism.[2] The article on 'Evangelism' in the *Encyclopedia of Southern Baptists* states that Finney 'has tremendously influenced Baptists as well as other evangelicals ... . With his legal logic and Scripture texts, he refuted the extreme Calvinism which denied use of one's will and repentance or use of one's efforts to win others to Christ'.[3]

This viewpoint is incompatible with the facts of history. As noted above, Baptist churches were marked by aggressive evangelism long before the new era of the 1830s – the era which the Baptist historian David Benedict called 'the age of excitements'. The 'quarter of a century' *before* the 1830s Benedict referred to as, 'This golden age of our denomination,' and said of it, 'the increase of our communicants was often a matter of

[1] Ibid., pp. 163–4.

[2] G. W. Paschal, *History of North Carolina Baptists* (Raleigh, N.C., 1955), vol. 1, pp. 529–30; vol. 2, p. 497.

[3] *Encyclopedia of Southern Baptists* (Nashville, Tenn.: Broadman Press, 1958), vol. 1, p. 415.

astonishment to our people at home, and our friends abroad'.[1] Far from regarding the new era in which Finney and Knapp became prominent as a great advance, Benedict, writing in the 1850s, believed that it marked a downturn:

In the early part of the present century, and up to the age of excitements, which, as I have already stated, had a paralyzing influence on the better feelings of Christians, conversions and additions among our people, were in many cases of the most exhilarating and encouraging nature ... During all this time scarcely any of the new measures of more modern times were adopted ... as a general thing, the old way of conducting meetings, whether in seasons of revival or declensions, was pursued, and all attempts to produce a high state of feeling among the people were carefully avoided. Depth of feeling was the main thing desired by our most efficient men, whether in the pulpit or the conference room. They also made much dependence on the silent workings of the divine Spirit on the hearts of the people.[2]

There is a great weight of evidence to sustain the assertion that definite Calvinistic beliefs did not inhibit evangelism among the Baptist churches before the 1830s. Some of that evidence has to do with home missions. The Baptists who evangelized Mississippi, for example, and drew up Articles of Faith for the Mississippi Baptist Association (1806), held 'the theology of the magisterial Calvinistic Reformers with a Baptist ecclesiology attached'.[3] The same theology was held by the Baptist leaders of 1800 in Boston, New York and Philadelphia (Thomas Baldwin, John Williams, William Rogers and William Staughton) who pioneered Baptist concern for foreign missions and sent 'frequent and large' help to William Carey in India.[4] In this connection it is noteworthy that when Adoniram

---

[1] *Fifty Years Among the Baptists*, p. 201.

[2] Ibid., p. 201.

[3] Joe B. Nesom, 'The Faith of Ezra Courtney, Pioneer Missionary in the South', *The Founders Journal* (Cape Coral, Fla., Winter 1993), p. 21.

[4] S. Pearce Carey, *William Carey* (London, 1923), p. 131. Woodward's *Surprising Accounts of the Revival of Religion in the United States*, 1802, includes a letter of Carey's to Rogers which reads: 'The glorious work going on in America, the establishment of missionary societies, and the like, call for our most lively thanks, and have given us great encouragement' (p. 69). Carey acknowledged the receipt of six thousand dollars from American Christians in the years 1806–1807. See Francis Wayland, *A Memoir of the Life and Labours of Adoniram Judson* (London, 1853), vol. 1, p. 29.

Judson and Luther Rice transferred from the Congregational churches of New England and became the foremost Baptist foreign missionaries, there was no question of any change in their theology save on the single point of baptism. Judson had been a class-mate of Gardiner Spring at Andover and in 1810 was invited to become a colleague of Griffin's in Park Street, Boston. 'I shall never live in Boston,' Judson told his sister, 'I have much further to go'.[1] He was to carry the same message as Griffin preached to Burma and to give the churches of that land the same creed which later generations so confidently asserted to be contrary to evangelism.[2]

It is not to be denied that hyper-Calvinism had some existence in the United States at the beginning of the nineteenth century but its features can be readily recognized and they were not those of any of the Baptist leaders. Hyper-Calvinism was a form of rationalism which deduced from the doctrine of the sovereignty of God 'that all men were not under obligation to repent of their sins and believe the gospel'.[3] In upholding one truth it thus denied another. Instead of teaching man's duty, its tendency was to encourage a form of passivity under the impression that this was more honouring to God. No Calvinistic confession had ever upheld that error. The Baptist leaders believed as much as the Presbyterians that 'God requires us to labor, and to use the means which he has appointed; and it is only in connection with those efforts that we are authorized to expect those influences of the Spirit without

---

[1] Wayland, *Memoir of the Life and Labours of Judson*, vol. 1, p. 23. Judson was a pupil of Griffin's and it is said that 'his eloquence and oratory were a transcript of Dr Griffin's' (p. 17).

[2] Ibid., vol. 2, p. 383–84. 'Art. IV. God, originally knowing that mankind would fall and be ruined, did, of his mercy, select some of the race, and give them to his Son, to save from sin and hell. Art V. The Son of God, according to his engagement to save the elect . . . made an atonement for all who are willing to believe.'

[3] Benedict, *Baptist Denomination in America*, vol. 2, p. 373. Benedict contrasts that error with the conviction of Samuel Stillman, the Boston leader. I am of the opinion that the necessary documentation does not exist to show how far hyper-Calvinism had some presence among American Baptists at this period; it is enough to show that it was never the dominant form of belief. Too often it is assumed that the experience of the Baptist churches in America ran parallel to that of the Baptist churches in England with respect to hyper-Calvinism.

which all our efforts will be in vain.'[1] They were persuaded that Christ authorized them to 'invite sinners indiscriminately to repent and believe'.[2]

Evidence that the Baptist leaders were not hyper-Calvinistic can be readily found. We read for example, of William Elliott (1748–1830):

The doctrine of election was a theme on which he delighted to dwell, both in preaching and in conversation; yet he held it in connection with the sentiment that the sinner is accountable to God, and justly condemned for his impenitence. He had no fellowship with the doctrine that the man who does not love our Lord Jesus Christ is so much of a machine as not to be blameworthy.[3]

John Leland, the veteran evangelist whom we first met in Virginia – a member of that group described as 'possessed with a burning zeal for the salvation of their fellow-men' – was of precisely the same view. It is well represented in the record of a conversation between Leland and a local physician which was told by G. N. Briggs, one-time Governor of Massachusetts. At the time it occurred the physician had only recently become a Christian and was eager for more teaching:

They both stopped, and, after some conversation, the Doctor told him that he should be glad to have his views upon two or three points of religious doctrine. First, as to the Sovereignty of God. This was with Elder Leland a favourite theme, and one in which his head and his heart had been engaged for sixty years. He proceeded, and occupied several minutes in repeating appropriate passages of Scripture, and commenting upon them in a most lucid manner, until the Doctor said

---

[1] Seth Smith, quoted in Sprague, *Annals*, vol. 6, p. 399.

[2] Francis Wayland and H. L. Wayland, *Memoir of Wayland*, vol. 1, p. 197. Wayland states this over-against the view of a member of his congregation – 'so far as a good man could be, a thorough fatalist' – who denied that preachers should invite sinners. This individual is one of the few clear instances of hyper-Calvinism that I have come across in the early part of the century. By the mid-nineteenth century hyper-Calvinism had developed in a number of Baptist churches. Poorly trained pastors over-reacted to the rise of Arminianism and this led to an opposition to missionary endeavour. But in contrast to this later condition, which existed in some areas, Newman is right to assert, 'At the beginning of the present period nearly all of the churches were friendly to the foreign missionary cause' (*Baptist Churches*, p. 437).

[3] Sprague, *Annals*, vol. 6, p. 238. See also *Writings of Leland*, p. 68.

he was entirely satisfied with those views. 'Now', said he, 'please let me know what you think of the free agency of man'. With no less authority from Scripture, and no less potency of reason, he made this point equally satisfactory. 'Now, Elder', said the Doctor, – 'one more solution, and I shall be entirely satisfied – will you tell me how you reconcile these two great and important truths'. 'Doctor', said he, 'there was once a mother, who, while busy with her needle, was teaching her daughter to read. The child at length came to a hard word, and asked her mother what it was. "Spell it, my child", said she. The child made an effort, but did not succeed. "Mother", said she, "I can't spell it". "Let me see it then". She handed her the book, and the mother, after puzzling over it for some time, returned it to the child, and said, – "Skip it then".'[1]

Such was Leland's way of expressing the need to hold two complementary truths which it is not part of our duty to reconcile. Francis Wayland, Baptist leader in the Northeast, said exactly the same.[2] Now these were men who lived to see the new era of Finney and Knapp and, given they were not hyper-Calvinists, it might be supposed that they would have welcomed it. On the contrary, their reaction matched that of the Old-School leaders among the Presbyterians and Congregationalists. Leland often spoke with dismay of the changes that he saw in his later years, and he especially deplored the emphasis on what could be achieved through man's efforts. He wrote to an old friend in Kentucky in 1830:

A new order of things has taken place in the religious department, since I began to preach. Then, when I went to meeting, I expected to hear the preacher set forth the ruin and recovery of man, and labor with heavenly zeal to turn many to righteousness. His eyes, his voice, and all his prayers, and deportment, gave evidence that his soul travailed in birth for the salvation of his hearers. But now, when I go to meeting, I hear high encomiums on Sunday-schools, tract societies, Bible societies, missionary societies, anti-mason societies etc., with a strong appeal to the people to aid with their money those institutions which are to introduce the millennium; assuring the people that 'every cent may save a soul'.[3]

Elsewhere Leland said: 'In barbarous times, when men were in

---

[1] Ibid., p. 181.
[2] *Memoir of Wayland*, vol. 1, p. 125.
[3] *Writings of Leland*, p. 602.

the dark, it was believed that the success of the gospel was according to the outpourings of the Holy Spirit, but in this age of light and improvement, it is estimated according to the pourings out of the purse.'[1] 'In the course of life I have been announcing Christianity for more than fifty-five years, having more reverence for that preaching which shows how the Lord draws sinners, than I have for that which shows sinners how to drive the Lord.'[2]

In a direct reference to what Finney and others were teaching, Leland wrote in 1832:

In these days of novelty we are frequently addressed from the pulpit as follows: . . . 'Profane sinners, I call upon you to flee from the wrath to come – come this minute and give your hearts to God, or you will seal your own damnation – God has given you the power, and will damn you if you do not use it – God has done all he can for you and will do no more – look not for a change of heart; a change of purpose is all that is necessary . . . My hearers, you may have a revival of religion whenever you please . . .'

Had I the spirit of infallible orthodoxy, I could fix a standard of orthodoxy; but as I have no claim to that high attainment, I shall only remark that, 'I have not so learned Christ – I do not understand the scriptures in that light – it is not the voice of my beloved,' it sounds like the voice of a stranger and I dare not follow it.[3]

Leland died in 1841. The last entries in his short autobiography, 'Events in the Life of John Leland', were written in 1835 and included the following:

I have been preaching sixty years to convince men that human powers were too degenerate to effect a change of heart by self-exertion; and all the revivals of religion that I have seen have substantially accorded with that sentiment. But now a host of preachers and people have risen up, who ground salvation on the foundation I have sought to demolish. The world is gone after them, and their converts increase abundantly. How much error there has been in the doctrine and measures I have adopted, I cannot say; no doubt some, for I claim not infallible inspiration. But I have not yet been convinced of any mistake so radical as to justify a renunciation of what I believed, and adopt the new measures.[4]

---

[1] Ibid., p. 524. [2] Ibid., p. 617.
[3] Ibid., p. 668. [4] Ibid., p. 39.

As far as the Northeast was concerned, no Baptist leader was better qualified to speak on these issues than Francis Wayland (1796–1865), president of Brown University and biographer of Judson. Born in New York, where his parents were members of the congregation of the Rev. John Williams, Wayland trained at Andover, heard the preaching of Nettleton, and succeeded Samuel Stillman as pastor of the First Baptist Church in Boston in 1821. In that situation he was surrounded by many who knew the history of the Second Great Awakening, their number including Thomas Baldwin (pastor of the Second Baptist Church) with whom he boarded for his first eighteen months in the city. From 1823 Wayland joined Baldwin in producing the American Baptist magazine, the premier Baptist magazine in the United States. In 1826, at the age of thirty-one, he was called to the presidency of Brown, and in that position of widespread influence he remained until 1855. After that date his work was by no means done for the years 1857–58 found him occupied temporarily as the pastor of the First Baptist Church of Providence ('no part of my ministerial life was so full of enjoyment'[1]) and he was to remain busy with his pen until his death. Wayland was never primarily an educationalist. His greatest concern was for the preparation of men for the ministry and his views on their training were akin to those of Archibald Alexander of Princeton whom he admired.[2] His convictions on revival, which were formed in his early years, remained with him all his life. He rejoiced to see an awakening at Brown in the winter term of 1847, 'when religion took precedence of all else within the walls of the university', and, more widely, eleven years later in the whole area.[3]

After forty-five years as a teacher and preacher Wayland published his *Notes on the Principles and Practices of the Baptist Churches* in 1857. Few living Baptists were better placed than he was to compare existing conditions with those prior to the era when, through Knapp and others, the Baptist ministry were supposed to have 'caught the spirit of evangelism'. Wayland's writings are far from supporting that contention. He observed:

Those who remember the Baptist preachers forty or fifty years since, will, I think, call to mind the fact that Christ Jesus was, in a particular

[1] *Memoir of Wayland*, vol. 2, p. 227.   [2] Ibid., p. 177.
[3] Ibid., pp. 64, 209–27. See also his letter in Sprague, *Lectures*, appendix, pp. 9–15.

manner, the burden of their discourses. The character of Christ, his wonderful love, his sufferings and death, his character as prophet, priest and king, his teachings, his example, his infinite excellency, the glory which he was shortly to bestow upon the believer, his nearness to us at all times, specially in the hour of trial and death, were frequently the subject of their discourses. Thus, the late John Williams, the first pastor of Oliver-street church, speaking to a friend on the morning of his sudden death, said 'I love President Edwards, *he always speaks so sweetly of Christ.'* . . .

From the manner in which our ministers entered upon their work, it is evident that it must have been the prominent object of their lives to *convert* men to God . . . They were remarkable for what was called experimental preaching. They told much of the exercises of the human soul under the influence of the truth of the gospel. The feeling of a sinner while under the convicting power of the truth; the various subterfuges to which he resorted when aware of his danger; the successive applications of truth by which he was driven out of all of them; the despair of the soul when it found itself wholly without a refuge; its final submission to God, and simple reliance on Christ; the joys of the new birth and the earnestness of the soul to introduce others to the happiness which it has now for the first time experienced; the trials of the soul when it found itself an object of reproach and persecution among those whom it loved best; the process of sanctification; the devices of Satan to lead us into sin; the mode in which the attacks of the adversary may be resisted; the danger of backsliding, with its evidences, and the means of recovery from it . . . these remarks show the tendency of the class of preachers which seem now to be passing away.[1]

In assessing what made the older generation the preachers that they were, Wayland pointed to 'a simplicity of reliance on the power and grace of Christ to aid them, and render their work effectual, which have not been so apparent in later times'. This was related, he argued, to a conscious weakness which cast them on God in earnest prayer. A pastor of the Old School, he explained, was not commonly professionally trained for the ministry and apart from the Bible he might have had little accumulated knowledge but, 'trembling and fearing', he went to preach, believing in the promised aid of the Holy Spirit:

His knees smite one against another, as he ascends the pulpit stairs. In a voice scarcely audible, he calls upon God for his blessing upon

[1] *Notes on the Principles and Practices of the Baptist Churches* (New York, 1857), pp. 21, 41–3.

the congregation. He commences his sermon. His own voice seems strange to him. Gradually he forgets himself, and loses his fears. As a prophet from God he delivers his message. The powers of his mind begin to react. He is transported beyond himself. He would that the whole world were present to hear the story of redeeming love. He pours out his soul in earnest entreaty. He warns the ungodly, as though he and they were already in view of the judgment-seat. Words, burning and impressive, come unbidden to his bursting heart. The time will not allow him to say half that fills his soul. He sits down, and thanks God for fulfilling his promise.[1]

Wayland believed that in the 1850s men of this spirit were no longer common in applying for the gospel ministry:

Formerly we were obliged to repress the earnestness with which men were pressing into the ministry. Now we are unable, with every inducement that can be presented, to urge men into it. The number is diminishing, and men frequently ask, Is the quality improving? It is said that this deficiency in ministers is owing to the fact that we have few revivals now in comparison with former years. But why have we so few revivals? We are under a system which was intended to increase the *efficiency* of the ministry. It would seem, then, that while we have been laboring to improve the ministry, we have decreased its number and diminished its power.[2]

What is not in dispute in the authors we have considered in this chapter is that the Baptist churches were experiencing widespread change by the middle of the nineteenth century. The issue is, Was it a transition from un-evangelistic hyper-Calvinism to a more biblical position, or was it a descent from orthodoxy to Arminianism? The evidence points clearly to the latter. The Baptist churches were being affected by precisely the same influences as the Presbyterian and the Congregational. This subject came up in a valuable series of letters between Wayland and J. W. Alexander after the latter had published the biography of his father, Archibald Alexander. Both men observed a general weakening in doctrine and spirituality; Wayland noted, in particular, 'the tendency to treat lightly and seldom the doctrine of depravity, and to

---

[1] Ibid., p. 25.
[2] Ibid., pp. 39–40. Improved ministerial training is the system to which Wayland referred. 'Since the year 1820,' he said, 'we have established ten theological seminaries.'

generalize the atonement of Christ, until it fades away into an undefined and inoperative idea'.[1] Benedict, writing at about the same date, spoke more fully on the same point. 'In my early days', he wrote, 'the Associated Baptists were all professedly Calvinistic in their doctrine.' Since then a major change had occurred:

The kind of preaching now much in vogue . . . would have been considered the quintessence of Arminianism, mere milk and water, instead of the strong meat of the gospel . . . At present, the modes and manners, and the eloquence of their ministers, engage more of the attention of the people, than their doctrinal expositions; and most of all, they look for attractions which are pleasing to young people, and which will collect large assemblies, and enable them to compete with their neighbours in numbers and style. With this end in view, nothing that will sound harsh or unpleasant to very sensitive ears must come from the preachers; the old-fashioned doctrines of Predestination, Total Depravity, Divine Sovereignty, etc., if referred to at all, must be by way of circumlocution and implication . . . As a general thing, now, our people hear so little, in common conversation, in their every-day intercourse with each other, on the doctrinal subjects, before, at the time and after they become church members, and are so much accustomed to vague and indefinite references to them, that, different from former years, they have but little desire to hear them discussed. Indeed, many of them would sit very uneasy under discourses in which the primordial principles of the orthodox Baptist faith should be presented in the style of our sound preachers of bygone years.[2]

This state of things was affecting the South as well as the North. James Petigru Boyce was a student under Wayland at Brown during the time of revival there in 1847.[3] After further study at Princeton Seminary, Boyce settled in his native South in 1851 and soon became a leader among the Baptist churches. His views were decidedly old school and he shared the catholicity of the earlier Baptists to the extent of calling the Westminster Confession 'our Confession'.[4] In 1856 he complained that 'the

[1] *Memoir of Wayland*, vol. 2, p. 177.
[2] *Fifty Years Among the Baptists*, pp. 138, 142–3.
[3] John A. Broadus, *Memoir of James Petigru Boyce* (New York, 1893), pp. 50–1.
[4] J. P. Boyce, *Abstract of Systematic Theology* (Baltimore, 1887; Escondido, Calif.: den Dulk Christian Foundation, n.d.), p. 339.

distinctive principles of Arminianism have also been engrafted upon many of our churches', and that 'some of our ministry have not hesitated publicly to avow them'.[1] Among those sharing Boyce's concern was Patrick Hues Mell who was to serve as President of the Southern Baptist Convention for seventeen years. In his second charge at Oglethorpe, Georgia, Mell found 'a number of members drifting off into Arminianism'. In a preface to a work which he published in 1850, 'to counteract the tendencies in our midst to Arminianism', he wrote: 'I have been pained to notice, for some years past, on the part of some of our ministers, in some localities in the South, a disposition to waive the doctrines of Grace in their public ministrations. While some have been entirely silent about them and have even preached, though not ostensibly, doctrines not consistent with them, others have given them only a cold and half-hearted assent, and some few have openly derided and denounced them.'[2]

The speed at which altar-call evangelism spread among the Baptists appears to be a subject which has remained unstudied. It had not captured anything like the majority of the churches in the 1830s[3] but there can be no doubt that, with the Baptists

[1] J. P. Boyce, *Three Changes in Theological Institutions* (Greenville, S.C., 1856), pp. 33–4, quoted in Nettles, *By His Grace*, pp. 194–5.

[2] P. H. Mell, *A Southern Baptist Looks at Predestination* (Cape Coral, Fla., n.d.), p. 15. Repr. from *Predestination and the Saints' Perseverance, Stated and Defended from the Objections of Arminians, in a Review of Two Sermons, published by Rev. Russell Reneau.*

[3] Cox and Hoby found the use of the 'anxious-seat' 'customary' among the Freewill Baptists and make some comment on its use elsewhere (*Baptists in America*, pp. 152, 165, 169, 180–81, 263, 336–7, 457–9). An American Baptist pastor, visiting England in 1839, was too sanguine in reporting: 'There had, indeed, been much discussion, about what were termed "*new measures*": and some men had adopted what he should consider, very extravagant measures; but these were principally among the Presbyterians; and there had not been much trouble about them among the Baptists' (Rev. W. Hague, of Rhode Island, on 'The Religious State of America' in *The Northern Baptist; a Magazine Intended for the Use of the Poorer Classes*, London, 1839, p. 174). We read of strong but unsuccessful 'objections' to some of Knapp's methods in Boston in 1842 (Martin Moore, *Boston Revival of 1842*, Boston, 1842; Richard Owen Roberts, Wheaton, Ill., 1980). 'Have no revival expedients', Wayland counselled a younger minister, 'that is devices to commit the people; to hold them up before the people for effect' (*Memoir of Wayland*, vol. 2, p. 210). McLoughlin is right in saying that revivalism eventually became more pervasive among the Baptists than among the Presbyterians (*Modern Revivalism*, p. 136).

also, it was the alleged success of the new evangelism which hastened both its adoption and the gradual doctrinal shift to justify it. Benedict writes:

At length *protracted meetings* began to be much talked of far and near, and so many reports were circulated concerning the wonderful effects of them, that by many they were thought to be the very thing for promoting religious revivals . . . In process of time the Baptists became a good deal engaged in these peculiar gatherings, and many of them seemed much pleased with them. The *revival ministers*, as they were called, soon became very popular; they were sent for from far and near, and in many cases very large additions were made to our churches under their ministrations. But in some cases, the old ministers and churches demurred . . . they were jealous of these wonder-working ministers, and of a new machinery in the work of conversion . . . To see converts coming into a church by the wholesale was a pleasing idea to many members . . . But another class of members had fearful forebodings for the future.[1]

Wayland viewed the change that was taking place in the membership of the churches with deep concern. Too many had entered the churches under laxer standards and the ministry had a concern not to offend the worldly in their midst to a degree unknown fifty years earlier. The great interest in numbers which had been engendered in the evangelical churches was having far-reaching consequences. The modern view, wrote Wayland, was that the older 'sort of preaching must have been distasteful and almost incomprehensible to men of the world, intelligent or irreligious. They would never come to hear sermons on experimental religion, and earnest calls to repentance. To gain these, we must of necessity modify our preaching, and deliver discourses in which both church and congregation will readily sympathize.'

Against this view, Wayland argued that true biblical preaching would never leave unbelievers comfortable in the presence of true Christians. To make no clear distinction between them, to preach generalities so that 'both parties like it equally well' might increase the number of church goers but it would not advance the gospel:

But it will be said, Are we then to drive away all but the children of

---

[1] *Fifty Years Among the Baptists*, pp. 202–3.

God? I reply, *Is there any Holy Ghost?* If we preach in such a manner that the disciples of Christ are separate from the world, prayerful, humble, earnest, self-denying, and labouring for the conversion of men, the Spirit of God will be in the midst of them, and souls will be converted. The thing will be noised abroad. There is never an empty house where the Spirit of God is present. You could not keep men away from church where souls were asking what they should do to be saved, and where converts were uttering the new-born praises of the King of Zion. There are two ways of seeking to fill our houses of worship. Which is to be preferred? Which looks most like fidelity to the Master?[1]

Enough has been given in this chapter to show that, as with other denominations, the burying of a noble history was accomplished by a caricature of its real nature. The representatives of the old, who lived to see and to oppose the changes in the churches, were commonly regarded as men whose views would never live again and whose ministries would therefore have nothing to teach posterity. That is not how these men themselves thought. They could pray, as did Francis Wayland: 'O God of eternity, this is not our cause; it is thine. We are nothing. Thou art all.' Wayland lived long enough after the publication of his last book relevant to the state of the churches, *Letters on the Ministry of the Gospel* (1863), to know that it did not receive a good reception. 'He was charged with painting a gloomy picture of the present piety and activity of the churches and ministry.'[2] The Rev. William McKenzie, a close friend, visited him not long before his death and has recorded how the old man, with tears on his face, spoke with sadness of this fact. But then, clasping his hands and looking upwards, he exclaimed: 'My God, thou knowest *all* things – thou *knowest* I have spoken the *truth* in regard to the condition of religion

---

[1] *Principles and Practices of Baptist Churches*, p. 47. He noted another example of the way in which an accommodation to the world was affecting the churches: 'We select our music and hire our performers for the sake of pleasing those who spend their evenings at the opera' (Ibid., p. 38). A certain kind of singing in the church was 'an abomination to God' (*Memoir of Wayland*, vol. 2, pp. 221–2). Reed and Matheson on their visit to Congregational churches were dismayed in some places at the way praise was being entrusted 'to a band of singers', while the congregation became spectators and auditors rather than participants (*Visit to the American Churches*, vol. 2, pp. 114–15).

[2] *Memoir of Wayland*, vol 2, p. 283.

among us; but my dear brethren will not receive it from thy unworthy servant.' Then, turning to his friend, he added, 'We must not expect to be above our Lord. Perhaps, when I am in my grave, God will show them that I was right'.[1]

[1] *Memoir of Wayland*, vol. 2, p. 283.

13

JAMES WADDEL ALEXANDER AND THE NEW YORK AWAKENING OF 1857–58

James Waddel Alexander (1804–1859)

13

The third marked era of general revival in American history, in succession to the First and Second Great Awakenings, was unquestionably the movement which occurred in the years 1857–58. Men old enough to remember the beginning of the century had no hesitation in recognizing the same phenomenon that they had seen in their youth. Heman Humphrey, for example, called it 'this most remarkable revival'.[1] In its extent the new work appeared to exceed all that had gone before. A writer in *The Presbyterian Magazine* for June 1858, under the heading 'Thoughts Concerning the Present Extraordinary Revival of Religion', spoke of it as extending from the Atlantic to the Pacific and from the Northern Lakes to the Gulf of Mexico: 'It is not confined to a single section of the country, nor to a single Christian denomination; but, with some exceptions, it extends to all'.[2] Looking back to the same event, the biographers of Francis Wayland wrote of it as a time of 'universal revival'[3] and the biographer of John L. Girardeau recorded, 'About this period revivals occurred over practically the whole country'.[4]

Those who comment on a revival close to its occurrence are generally inclined to over-state its significance in comparison with other movements of the Spirit of God which they

[1] *Revival Sketches*, p. 278.
[2] *Presbyterian Magazine* (Philadelphia, 1858), p. 248,
[3] *Memoir of Wayland*, 1867, vol. 2, p.223.
[4] George A. Blackburn, *The Life Work of John L. Girardeau* (Columbia, S.C., 1916), p. 100.

themselves did not witness. But it is noteworthy that J. Edwin Orr, who gave much time in the second half of the present century to the study of revivals, came to the conclusion towards the end of his life that 'the Awakening of 1857–58 was the most thorough and most wholesome movement ever known in the Christian Church'.[1] If the validity of that judgment is subjected to discussion one of the first obstacles to be encountered is the fact which Orr observes, 'in 125 years no definitive history of the 1857–58 Awakening has been written'.

All that we can hope to do in this concluding chapter of historical narrative is to give a view of the work as it occurred in New York, the city for which the fullest details are available. In so doing we cannot miss what was characteristic of the work as a whole for, as the writer of 1858 already quoted says, 'If any one great centre can be designated the radiant point from which this mighty movement has proceeded, it is the principal commercial metropolis of the United States, the city of New York.'[2] As a guide to this theme we can do no better than to turn to material provided by the life and work of James W. Alexander, pastor of the Nineteenth Street Presbyterian Church.

James Alexander's name has already been before us in these pages as the biographer of his father, Archibald Alexander, but the eldest son of Princeton Seminary's first professor merits attention in his own right and not least for his relationship to the awakening which happened less than two years before his death. Timothy L. Smith, a modern writer, suggests that James Alexander, whom he calls 'a very conservative Old School Calvinist', was brought to participate in the revival only because he was 'pulled along by the popular tide'.[3] That suggestion is far removed from the facts. Prior to 1857 no preacher in New York had done more to keep the necessity of faith in the power of the Holy Spirit before his people. It is significant that the man perhaps best remembered in connection with the revival, Jeremiah Calvin Lanphier, who started

[1] J. Edwin Orr, 'The Event of the Century': The 1857–58 Awakening: a Startling Update. Unpublished MS.

[2] *Presbyterian Magazine*, op. cit., p. 248.

[3] *Revivalism and Social Reform, American Protestantism on the eve of the Civil War* (New York: Harper, 1957), p. 69.

the Fulton Street Prayer meeting in September 1857, had been a member of James Alexander's church for eight or nine years prior to that summer.[1] Lanphier's views on prayer and on the special work of the Spirit were the same as those he had been taught from the Nineteenth Street pulpit. During the revival it was Alexander's tracts that were most widely distributed in the city and Samuel I. Prime, one of the first recorders of the *annus mirabilis*, singles them out for their efficiency and direct usefulness.[2] When sermons by twenty-five of the city's preachers were published in 1858, with the title, *The New York Pulpit in the Revival of 1858*, it is a sermon by Alexander that the publisher put at their head, and one of the last things from Alexander's pen was a Preface to a book of his tracts issued under the title, *The Revival and its Lessons*.

The truth is that Alexander had long since come to the same settled convictions on revivals as those which his father had met among the hearers of Samuel Davies. At this point, as at many others, there is a close resemblance between James Alexander and his father. Even the outward course of their lives ran somewhat parallel. Both were Virginian born. Both were converted in their teens and ordained in their early twenties. Both had for their first charge the congregation at Prince Edward – scene of the awakening of 1788. In that first pastorate James even boarded in the same home in which his father had boarded thirty years earlier and it was in that home that he was later to marry a Virginian girl as his father had also done before him. In their Christian calling the two men had to face the conflicting claims on them made by the pastorate and the seminary. As we have seen, Archibald, after two pastorates, was committed to Princeton after 1812. James, at Princeton from the age of eight to twenty-three, served churches in Virginia and New Jersey from 1827 to 1832 before returning to

[1] Lanphier's contemporaries spell his surname with either an 'n' or an 'm' but his autograph puts the matter beyond doubt. See T. W. Chambers *The Noon Prayer Meeting of the North Dutch Church, Fulton Street New York* (New York, 1858), p. 33. Lanphier had transferred to this congregation on being appointed as its missioner in the down-town area where the church was located.
[2] *The Power of Prayer; Illustrated in the Wonderful Displays of Divine Grace at the Fulton Street and Other Meetings in New York and Elsewhere in 1857 and 1858* (New York, 1859; Edinburgh: Banner of Truth Trust, 1991), p. 208.

a professorship in Princeton College. From there he accepted a call to Duane Street Church in down-town New York in 1844. In 1849 he was reluctantly constrained back to Princeton as the colleague and successor of Samuel Miller whose health was rapidly failing. As James Alexander and Miller spoke and prayed together near their parting, the elder 'deplored the absence of religious revival in the country'. Shaking James' hand at their last meeting the dying man apologized for his feeble grip and added, 'Christ's hand is never cold'.[1] James Alexander loved Princeton and nowhere more than the home of his parents both of whom were still alive at this date and with whom his bachelor younger brother, 'Addy', also lived. The latter's biographer, describing visits made by James prior to his return in 1849, says, 'under his father's roof, his spirits rose, his merry face beamed, and his sonorous voice rang from cellar to tile'.[2] But a yet greater love was to prevail and when James was recalled to his New York congregation in December 1850 he accepted. There he remained until shortly before his death (only eight years after that of his father) in 1859 at the age of fifty-five.

While James Alexander was close to his father, he never surrendered his own judgment and he came his own way to his convictions. In his teenage years and before he discovered himself to be a lost sinner, he opposed Calvinism and 'the doctrine of Rom. 9.15 with all the enmity of a rebellious heart'.[3] So he wrote in his *Forty Years' Familiar Letters*, sent to his friend, John Hall, who published them after his death. These two volumes exceed in value any biography of him that could ever have been written. In his earlier years as a Christian, James Alexander had to think through the charge – then growing in popularity – that Calvinistic belief was necessarily a hindrance to evangelism. Biographies of such men as Edwards, Whitefield, Davies and Brainerd helped him to reach the opposite conclusion. Among other influences which confirmed to him

[1] H. C. Alexander, *The Life of Joseph Addison Alexander* (New York, 1870), vol. 2, p. 671. J. A. Alexander, James' younger brother, regarded the 1840s 'as about the golden age of Princeton' (p. 593).

[2] Ibid., p. 603.

[3] *Forty Years' Familiar Letters of James W. Alexander*, ed. John Hall (New York, 1860), vol. 1, p. 32.

his father's theology were Puritan books and living examples of the old faith which he saw in his first years in the ministry. Among the latter none was more notable than James Pollock, 'a poor dyer and broken-down invalid', who in an anguish of physical sufferings, as Alexander writes to Hall on one occasion, 'was illuminated by the fire of Christian animation beyond anything I ever saw, and he poured forth, in the broadest Scotch dialect, the strongest Calvinism of Paul, every point of which seemed in his soul to be turned into rich experience . . . He declared to me that under agonies of bodily pain his views of Christ and of the sovereign, distinguishing grace of the plan of salvation, had wholly neutralized his sense of suffering'.[1]

While Alexander became firmly convinced in his doctrinal position it was equally true that he was marked by a catholicity of spirit and by a breadth of esteem for all fellow Christians. He had an aversion to controversy and deplored the spirit in which it was too often conducted: 'At judgment I heartily believe that some heresies of heart and temper will be charged as worse than heavy doctrinal errors'. Praise for other sections of the Christian church is often found in his letters to Hall. He prized a number of Baptist and Episcopalian authors and he admired Methodist zeal. During a revival in Trenton, New Jersey, in 1833, he writes of his Methodist neighbours: 'They seem disposed to attempt the conversion of every soul in Trenton. God grant them success. I cannot but say God is with them of a truth, though we have lost a number of hearers'.

In accordance with this spirit we are not surprised that James Alexander took a moderate position on his first encounter with the new-measures controversy which was at its height during his years at Trenton. Writing to Hall in 1831 he mourned the 'theological warfare' that was prevalent and commended the writings of Archbishop Leighton: 'particularly his commentary on 1 Peter, which I am now concluding for the second time. He was a hater of polemics and shared the usual fate of all moderate men'. Alexander saw points to commend in the New School brethren and believed that the issues were not of such a nature as to require a division. His first reference to

[1] *Familiar Letters*, vol. 1, p. 248.

Finney is in a letter of 14 April 1831, and in this letter he expressed the view that both sides were too ready to follow the example of their leaders. There were those that said:

'Our fathers did so and so, and we must do so too.' The others say: 'Mr Finney does so and so, and we must do so too.' I freely confess that I have much doubt respecting 'anxious meetings', as they are commonly called, especially as I have sometimes seen them conducted. There is a certain stage in an awakening when they are indispensable; i.e. where the number of seeking souls is great; but many of my brethren use them as a *means of awakening*. How far is that correct?

Alexander was clearly still formulating his opinions. A few months after the above letter he was in the Troy Presbytery and in the midst of what he calls 'the furnace of the new measures controversy'. But he still counselled forbearance and was not provoked even when he heard 'the curious argument' (which he knew to be absurd) that Nettleton had 'ceased to have revivals' as soon as he opposed Finney. In this same spirit he wrote to Hall on 27 March 1832:

I wish all parties would read what Edwards says hereupon, in his work on Revivals. I dare not condemn a multitude of things, which I would as little dare to do. There is, it seems to me, an inordinate stress laid by both parties upon mere *measures*, as unreasonable as argument about mere ceremonies. On one hand a truly superstitious reliance is placed on certain methods of conducting meetings, etc.; on the other, certain measures are denounced as if they were absolutely antichristian. One man has anxious meetings, another anxious seats, a third calls them out in the aisle, a fourth invites them to his study, a fifth visits them at home. Here are diversities of method, but no ground, I think, for violent controversy. Various methods have been blessed, to my knowledge, in various revivals, and new ones are yet to be invented. On this subject I think our old men are too tenacious.

Alexander was determined to be cautious and 'to study the matters in debate a little more impartially and deliberately'. He was slow in coming to the conclusion that the new measures were not simply a mistake about methods, rather they were the direct result of the Pelagian belief about human nature which supposed that regeneration could take place by human decision. Described by a friend as 'one of the kindest and noblest' of

[336]

men[1], it went against the instincts of Alexander's nature to believe that a crusade against orthodoxy was underway, led in several instances by men who, by denominational affiliation were expected to be upholders of the Westminster Confession. By 1835 his concern was deepening. Writing to Hall on Finney's 'Lectures on Revivals', when they were appearing in serial form in *The New York Evangelist* in that year, he regretted that the lecturer 'betrays throughout a polemical attitude, and evidently is fuller of animosity against the foes of revival-measures, than of direct zeal for the saving of souls'.[2] In the autumn of 1836 a crisis meeting took place in the study of Charles Hodge at Princeton in which Presbyterian Old School leaders debated the seriousness of the position. There was disagreement between those still counselling moderation and those who believed that firm and decisive action was needed. It is a striking evidence of the regard with which the thirty-two-year-old James Alexander was held by those present that it was his words which finally brought the meeting to a harmonious conclusion, leading to the united Old School action the following year which we have already noted above.[3]

When we find Alexander settled in his New York pastorate his views on the controversy are definite and the spiritual scene in the city deepened his impression of the harm done ten years earlier in the name of evangelism. 'Revivalism [i.e. the excitement which had attended the introduction of the new measures] is no more', he writes, but its spirit remained and could be seen 'even in good men, in making all religion consist in evangelical *effort*. Some are very busy saving souls, with all the dialect and levity and coarseness of Maj. Downing'. People had acquired 'a craving for effect' and a desire for speedy results which made everything else subordinate to that end: 'The Gospel is not attractive enough for people now-a-days. Ministers must bait their trap with something else. The old-fashioned topics are seldom heard'.

---

[1] *Life of J. A. Alexander*, vol. 2, p. 841.

[2] *Familiar Letters*, vol. 1, p. 227. I am assuming Finney is the person whose name has been removed from the text of this letter, as also on p. 250 (after Alexander had heard him preach). Another and more favourable comment on Finney's preaching can be found in vol. 2, p. 278.

[3] Baird, *History of New School*, p. 510.

In a letter to Hall of 31 December 1846, Alexander writes: 'there was great interest under the Finneyitish revivals, but it was not evangelical, and I am working among its bitter fruits every day. There is a wonderful vitality and permanency in experience which is built on the preaching of Christ. The style of sermons in the Scottish Free Church seems to be the thing.[1] When the new-divinity converts grow cold, they are colder than ice, nothing but a biting censoriousness. I had no idea, even in Jersey, of the modifications wrought in the city by the overwrought revivalism of past years'. On another occasion, speaking of the religious degeneration in the city, he says he had lived to see fulfilled 'predictions made by Nettleton which at the time I thought absurd'.[2]

But Alexander is far from laying the blame for conditions wholly upon others. The people had seen little evidence of the older evangelicalism for some years. In a city whose population was to reach around 800,000 by 1858 only Gardiner Spring's church remained a dominant influence among the Presbyterians. (In the 1850s, remarkably, Spring was in the same pulpit as he was in 1810 and Alexander could write in 1851: 'Dr Spring told me he lately sat at his sermon desk from 9 a.m. to 7 p.m. without dinner; but he felt worse for it. His morning services are overcrowded, which can be said of no other Presbyterian assembly here'). Alexander was often left longing 'for a generation of the old sort of preachers'. 'The savour of old-schoolism is not good here. Many have not seen old-schoolism allied to any zeal, and have all their early associations connected with new measures. Such a character as McCheyne would be to them as out of character as a Centaur, Sphynx, or a Griffin'. In despondent moments he feared it could never be otherwise: 'Old-schoolism has no good chance in New York, where the warp is Dutch and the woof Yankee'.

At the same time as Alexander was writing such words there were some Presbyterians who were inclining to the view that revivals were so liable to do harm as well as good that a period

[1] He is thinking of preaching such as that of Robert M'Cheyne whose life by Andrew Bonar was published in Philadelphia in 1844. On that book Alexander writes to Hall: 'What zeal and faith! what proof that Old Calvinism is not insusceptible of being used as an arousing instrument!'

[2] *Familiar Letters*, vol. 2, p. 169.

without them would be no great loss. Even Charles Hodge sometimes gave the impression that he was inclined to that view. His volume, *The Constitutional History of the Presbyterian Church in the United States*, published in 1839, gave so much attention to the excesses which arose during the First Great Awakening, that it was liable to undermine all belief in revival. Archibald Alexander disagreed decidedly with his younger colleague's evaluation of the Great Awakening and did what he could to counter the danger which he saw in his *Biographical Sketches of the Founders and Principal Alumni of the Log College, together with an Account of the Revivals of Religion under their Ministry* (1845). James Alexander held the same high view of revivals as his father. To lose faith in the special and extraordinary work of the Spirit of God because of the excesses of mere excitement was a capital mistake. Revivalism was not to be confused with revival. So he told his New York hearers:

The agency of the Holy Spirit has been cast into the shade: new and dangerous views of regeneration have become common; while the tendency has been away from dependence on God, and towards a religion of human fabrication. Even the traditionary reverence of our people for revivals has been played upon by the adversary, and we have had the name without the reality . . . At the same time that we were doing away with the true glory of revivals, even the sovereign agency of the Holy Spirit in changing the depraved nature, we were in some places laying mighty stress upon certain external means and measures . . .[1]

His main concern, however, was to emphasize the positive. Jeremiah Lanphier was no doubt in his place as usual when, for example, Alexander preached on 'Our Modern Unbelief' in February 1852. It was a subject often on the preacher's mind. What could be done to counter the fast-spreading rationalism in the city where newcomers, generally unsympathetic to America's spiritual history, arrived at the rate of as many as 1,800 in one day? 'The living cargoes, which are poured in on us day by day, from Ireland and the European continent . . . are increasingly making their influence felt on our manners, our morals, our religion . . . We are in the midst of a gradual and silent but tremendous revolutionary movement.' In this ser-

[1] *The New York Pulpit in the Revival of 1858* (New York, 1858), pp. 27–8.

mon he argued for positive action against the invasion and diffusion of infidelity through gospel effort and the spread of the Bible. But the 'chief hope' lay in the Holy Spirit himself:

Who can tell how far the revolutionary atheism of France might have become the established religion of America, if it had not pleased God to make our country the theatre of mighty and extensive revivals? Perhaps I address some who love to recall these awakenings as the scenes in which they were made to know Christ. Such will join in testifying, that the progress of convincing and converting grace did not wait for the tedious preparative of philosophic reply and formal argument, but went forth to consume at once and forever the difficulties of the sceptic and the cavils of the deist, as the flame of a conflagration reduces combustible obstacles in its rapid and blazing career. All other means together will not do so much to rid our land of antichristian scoffing, as would one general communication of power from on high.[1]

Unlike his father, J. W. Alexander had not been converted at a time of revival, but in subsequent years he had seen something of that power. In his first pastorate in Virginia he lived among 'the fruits of the great revival' of forty years earlier and he knew of the awakening which Nettleton had seen in another part of that state in 1828. His letters speak of news of 'great revival' in several places in 1831 and of 'a wonderful work of grace' in his own town of Trenton (scene of his second pastorate) in 1833. In 1837 he aided a friend in New Brunswick and reported to Hall: 'That ultra-old school town is shaken by a great awakening'. Alexander's second teaching spell at Princeton coincided with the first special work of grace to have been seen there since 1815. His nephew wrote of it: 'The whole college now became aroused. From one hundred and twenty to two hundred now attended the prayer meetings . . . Some of the worst men on the role appeared to be converted'.[2]

*　　　*　　　*

In New York Alexander found conditions different from

---

[1] J. W. Alexander, *Discourses on Common Topics of Christian Faith and Practice*, (New York, 1858), pp. 46–7.

[2] *Life of J. A. Alexander*, vol. 2, p. 672.

anything he had known before and if his past experiences gave him reason to hope they also made him cautious. Amid the confused views of revival that existed there it was quite possible that mere excitement could be confused with a true movement of the Spirit. The spiritual life of his congregation seems to have grown slowly until the spring of 1856 when he saw brighter signs than ever before. When he invited 'those willing to be guided about seeking salvation' to his home, more than forty came. 'It is a remarkable coincidence', he adds, in narrating this to Hall, 'that the meeting of Presbytery was almost a Bochim, and from beginning to end exhibited tenderness, humility, and affection on the part of ministers'. In the summer of that year, while Addy was staying in his brother's New York home, and writing his commentary on Acts, James was giving mid-week lectures to his people from the same book – lectures, his nephew says, which 'were now at the zenith of their popularity, from which they never declined'. Alexander sensed a quickening and, as he writes to Hall, had he been prepared to 'press measures' he did not doubt they would 'work': 'You or I could get up a stir in one week which would fill a column of tabulated statistics'. That was the last thing he wanted:

I am dreading, beyond expression, the rise of a fanatical breeze among my church members, and shall humbly endeavour to suppress rather than arouse human passions . . . The way I am taking would be deemed a quenching of the Spirit by sundry of my brethren. But I distrust everything in revivalism which is not common to it with the stated, continued, persistent presentation of the gospel . . . New-measure people undertake to use instruments, and often kill the child. In spiritual as in natural travail, I suppose there must be waiting.[1]

In the midst of these labours Alexander's health, never strong, visibly weakened and a throat condition gave him special trouble. Medical opinion faced with such cases proposed the customary voyage to Europe as the best means to secure 'permanent relief'. It was his second trip across the Atlantic and he and his wife were to be away from May to October, 1857. When he returned at the end of October it was, in his own words, 'to find as it were a pall of mourning over every house'.

[1] *Familiar Letters*, vol. 2, p. 223.

During his absence the inflation and 'money mania' of recent years had been followed by a general financial collapse. Ten thousand factory workers in the city stood idle and on October 14 a crisis of panic occurred which 'prostrated the whole monetary system of the country, virtually in one hour'. 'Like a yawning earthquake', wrote Heman Humphrey, 'it shook down the palaces of the rich, no less than the humble dwellings of the poor, and swallowed up their substance. Men went to bed dreaming all night of their vast hoarded treasures, and woke up in the morning hopeless bankrupts.'[1]

Something similar had happened in 1837, but in 1857 there was a marked difference. Alexander writes:

Visitations of this kind – the remark is common concerning pestilence – often produce a hardening effect. In the present instance, it pleased God, in his marvellous loving-kindness, by the ploughshare of his judgements, to furrow the ground for the precious seed of salvation and to make distresses touching worldly estate to awaken desire for durable riches and righteousness . . . From the very heart of these trials emerged spiritual yearnings, thirstings and supplications after the fountain of living waters.[2]

The day after his return from Europe Alexander wrote to Hall, 'there is a marked reviving of spiritual interest during the six months of our absence'. The way in which that interest developed no one could have predicted for it followed no known precedent, at least not on the scale that was soon seen. Lanphier had quietly begun a noon-time prayer meeting in the lecture room of the North Reformed Dutch Church in Lower Manhattan on 23 September, 1857. The first week only six attended. The next week the number reached twenty and the following, forty. During October the meetings, previously held weekly, became daily. By the time the new year began a second room had to be used simultaneously to accommodate the numbers and in February a third. By then a number of similar

---

[1] *Revival Sketches*, pp. 277–8.

[2] *The Revival and its Lessons*, p. 6. Alexander's private life was in accord with this teaching. One of his prayers in 1859 included these words: 'Oh, my ascended Lord and Master! be pleased to anoint me afresh for my ministry, send me some new and special grace, and cast me not aside as a useless instrument' (*Life of J. A. Alexander*, vol. 2, p. 826).

meetings had begun elsewhere in the city and so marked was the turning to prayer that the *Daily Tribune* of 10 February, 1858, reported, 'Soon the striking of the five bells at 12 o'clock will generally be known as the "Hour of Prayer"'.

In mid-March Burton's theatre, capable of holding 3,000, was crowded for a prayer meeting and by April scores of buildings – including printers' shops, fire stations and police stations – were open for the same purpose, necessitating a weekly bulletin with information on the locations of these simultaneous gatherings. In their form they all followed the simple pattern and the catholic breadth of concern which Lanphier had long witnessed at the Nineteenth Street Church. 'In order to mighty and unexampled revival', writes Alexander in his tract *Pray for the Spirit*, 'what we especially need is for the whole church to be down on its knees before God.' The headings of the material in this tract give us a good idea of the faith in which Lanphier shared and to which he led others:

1. *There is such a thing as the pouring out of the Holy Ghost.*
2. *The influence of the Spirit of God is exceedingly powerful.*
3. *The Spirit whom we seek is the Author of Regeneration and Sanctification.*
4. *The Holy Spirit sends those gifts which are necessary for successful work.*

Prayer meetings had been common enough before 1858 but that such gatherings should become the place of conversion for many was previously little known. 'From the mingled motives in which religious concern has its beginnings', writes Alexander, 'numbers of worldly visitors entered the doors. Conversion after conversion was reported. Men who had felt the emptiness of earthly things, and smarted under losses, came hither for consolation.'

On 1 March 1858, Alexander reported to Hall: 'the tidings of revival on every side certainly tends to set people a-thinking about their souls; which is a point gained. I feel it overshadowing my own mind, and opening ways of address to the careless'. On April 2, he wrote further:

Though I have aimed to keep down and regulate excitement among us, and have no additional service but an exhortation on Monday to such as seek instruction on points connected with conversion, I perceive such a degree of inquiry as has never met me in my ministry. The number of declared inquirers is not more than twenty five, and

[343]

most of these have dates a good way back; but the feelings of communicants and the indescribable tone of assemblies, are new to me. From the start I have held myself ready to adapt measures to emerging demands; I however feel glad I have pursued the repressive method; which, by the way, has lost me sundry good opinions even among my own flock. Study I cannot, being run down by persons, many of whom I never knew, in search of counsel. The uptown prayer meetings are very sober and edifying. I am told the general tendency in all is to increased decorum. The openness of thousands to doctrine, reproof etc., is undeniable. Our lecture is crowded unendurably – many going away. The publisher of Spurgeon's sermons, says he has sold a hundred thousand. All booksellers agree, that while general trade is down, they never sold so many religious books. You may rest assured there is a great awakening among us, of which not one word gets into the papers; and that there are meetings of great size, as free from irreverence as any you ever saw. I have never seen sacramental occasions more tender and still than some meetings held daily in our part of the town. The best token I have seen of revival was our meeting of Presbytery. I never was at such a one. Brethren seemed flowing together in love, and reported a great increase of attention in all their churches – and this within a very few days. The inquiring condition among ourselves is strange, and all but universal; God grant it may be continued or exchanged for true grace in them all.

By Spring of 1858 much news of the awakening was appearing in both the religious and what had formerly been the secular press. *The Presbyterian Magazine* for May, quoting the *New York Christian Advocate*, said that 'no important part of the Northern States, at least, remained unaffected by it'. By June figures of 50,000 conversions in New York and 200,000 across the Northeast were in circulation. There was also a growing discussion on where and how the revival had started and Lanphier's noon-day prayer meeting became famous. With reports of this kind Alexander was not in sympathy. He was content to speak of 'remarkable increase' and to add, 'the statistics of conversion are sometimes unsafe; where there is so much room for mistake and exaggeration, it may be wisest to venture no figures'. Instead of treating the Consistory room of the North Dutch Church as the starting point – as popular opinion was inclined to do – he believed that when Lanphier and 'a few like-minded servants of God' first met

Revival was already begun. God had already poured out the Spirit of grace and of supplications. We doubt not there was a simultaneous effusion, on other groups and in other places. Prayers long treasured up were beginning to receive copious answer; prayers, of which we have thought, may have been offered by those venerable ministers of Holland, whose portraitures still adorn the walls of the Consistory-room. It has been questioned who first conceived the project of these meetings. The problem is unprofitable; human plans looked forward to no such results; let God have the glory!

Gardiner Spring was entirely of the same mind as he made clear as the closing speaker at a service to mark the first anniversary of the Fulton Street prayer meeting. He concentrated his remarks on the words of a text read earlier in the meeting: 'In that day, the loftiness of men shall be bowed down, and the Lord alone shall be exalted':

This is the thought which has an effect upon this meeting and has an effect upon the church of God . . . We want nothing but to behold the glory of God and to see him exalted by all, and everywhere, to be happy. When I read the descriptions of the heavenly world, I see nothing so prominent as these two great truths: Man abased and God exalted . . . 'Behold! what hath God wrought?' Look back during the past year. Who has wrought what has been done? One of my brethren inquired, 'Where has been the motive power?' His object was wise and good in making the inquiry. But I must not inquire of laymen, nor of ministers. There was a motive power above; and we shall be lifeless as mere corpses, inanimate dead remains lying dead in the grave, until the Spirit of God moves. I look back over the past year, around these congregations, and there is no question so appropriately presents itself to my thoughts. Oh, look at it! We love to look at the works of man, and they are interesting when they exhibit human ingenuity, invention and perseverance. But this work of God – oh, this wondrous work of God, for which all other works were made . . . The object of this meeting to-day is to give the God of heaven all the praise. 'Oh, praise him sun and moon, and all the stars of night. Praise him, ye ministers of his that do his pleasure. Praise him young and old; young men and maidens, and little children praise him; and let the whole earth be filled with his praise.' And to this poor, aged, hard heart, I would say, 'Bless the Lord, O my soul'.[1]

By the time of this anniversary meeting the revival was passing in New York and with it Alexander's own life. The European

---

[1] Chambers, *Noon Prayer Meeting*, pp. 266–68.

visit had not restored his health and the probability is that the added joys and labours of 1858 had shortened his days. By the winter of 1858–59 his forty-years correspondence with John Hall was tailing away. 'Writing which was a solace has become a very burdensome task,' he tells his friend in April 1859. On 9 May 1859, he preached his last sermon to his people then left for rest in Virginia, passing through his beloved Princeton for the last time on the way. According to his nephew, J. W. Alexander's diary later revealed that he was passing through 'a season of profound nervous and mental depression' but in Virginia 'the declining slopes of the hill were at length irradiated with heavenly sunshine' and 'the cloud was now forever rolled away'. He died on 31 July 'with his countenance visibly illumined with the hope of a blessed immortality'.[1] The words of prayer which he had written when he was twenty-six, in his unsurpassed translation of Paul Gerhardt's hymn, 'O Sacred Head! sore wounded', were answered:

> Be near when I am dying
> O show Thy cross to me!
> And for my succour flying,
> Come, Lord, to set me free.
> These eyes, new faith receiving,
> From Jesus shall not move,
> For he who dies believing,
> Dies safely through thy love.

*　　　*　　　*

We noted at the beginning of this chapter that no definitive history of the awakening of 1857–58 has been written. The books that were published on the subject at the time were largely collections of anecdotes. Now, almost a century and a half later, various obstacles stand in the way of the preparation of any definitive account. But there is one which deserves particular mention. Revivalism had so spread across the United States by the time of the awakening of 1857–58 that it is sometimes impossible to judge how far alleged results should be given the credit which reporters expected. Two different

---

[1] *Life of J. A. Alexander*, vol. 2, p. 871.

influences might be found side by side and both at work. A readiness in certain quarters to broadcast the numbers of converts was one illustration of this factor. It is also apparent from various records of the time that there was no longer a common understanding of what constitutes revival. One writer in the Philadelphia *Press*, for example, in April 1858, believed that the 'last quarter-century' had brought such a 'cultivation' of revivals that the period presented 'a succession and general distribution of spiritual refreshings'.[1] Others spoke similarly. But the view of Heman Humphrey, reporter of the Second Great Awakening, was decidedly different. He believed that by 1845 'there were few powerful revivals, and for some years these sacred visits seemed to be becoming less and less frequent'.[2] Prime's book *The Power of Prayer* registers the same view. Before 1857: 'Men were hardly aware what a low, lax, state of religious feeling prevailed. There was outward attention to religion, but the power, the vitality was gone'.[3] This was also Alexander's view on the pre-1857 situation. On a visit to Newport in 1854 he wrote: 'With no disposition to judge harshly, but all the reverse, I am led to think that what we regard as experimental piety is at a low ebb in New England. The revival day has gone by. I hear of no savoury old-time Christians'.[4] Similarly, speaking of the new conditions in New York in 1858 he said: 'This great interest in things divine and eternal, did not "come with observation". There had been no pomp of preparation. Indeed the foregoing season has been one of remarkable aridity and dearth; so that multitudes of the younger professing Christians had never seen what is called a Revival'.[5]

Here, then, is a major discrepancy in judgments. The only explanation for it is that two different standards of assessment were in operation. What some had become used to claiming as 'revivals', others regarded, in Alexander's phrase, quoted

[1] Quoted by W. C. Conant in his *Narratives of Remarkable Conversions and Revival Incidents* (New York 1859), p. 359.

[2] *Revival Sketches*, pp. 275–6.

[3] *Power of Prayer*, p. 39.

[4] *Familiar Letters*, vol. 2, p. 200.

[5] *Revival and Its Lessons*, p. 9. Other New York preachers confirm this. R. D. Hitchcock spoke of the revival as following 'a season of comparative declension, lasting for nearly thirty years, during which the power of the gospel seemed somehow to be strangely hindered'. *New York Pulpit*, p. 357.

above, as 'the name without the reality'. In 1858 all the classic marks of a true spiritual awakening were present – hunger for the Word of God, for prayer and for serious Christian literature; a sense of wonder and profound seriousness; the same work evident in many places at once; joyful praise and readiness to witness; a new energy in practical Christian service; the recovery of family worship and family religion; and an observable raising of the whole moral tone of society. Prime's book sums up the characteristic features, as seen in New York, in the sentence: 'The early dawn of the revival was marked by love to Christ, love for all his people, love of *prayer*, and love of personal effort'.

Nevertheless, along with all these things there was an admixture of ideas and practices, drawn from more recent evangelical history, which gave some observers at the time reason to fear that the permanent spiritual results might not be as large as some too-confidently predicted. All revivals are inevitably mixed, but the spread of the methods of the new evangelism prior to the awakening introduced factors which require us to be especially discerning in reading the history. The very fact that the total number of converts was set at estimates as different as 300,000 and one million shows the need for caution.

Despite this qualification, the great fact which stands out in the general awakening of 1858 is that its salient features were utterly different from the results of human efforts. We have earlier noted McLoughlin's claim that the high pressure evangelism of the altar-call was 'the national religion' by the mid-century. In accordance with that thesis he concluded that the 1857–58 awakening was 'best explained as the acceptance of mass evangelism by urban businessmen seeking God's help in time of trouble'. It was nothing more than organized religious excitement.[1] This assertion ignores a multitude of testimonies to the contrary by eyewitnesses. Alexander acknowledges that there were some in New York in January 1858 who believed in using 'blast bellows to get up artificial heat',[2] but the idea that the awakening was brought about by

---

[1] Quoted by Edwin Orr in his MS. 'The Event of The Century'. See also McLoughlin, *Modern Revivalism*, p. 163.

[2] *Familiar Letters*, vol. 2, p. 275.

such efforts he would have regarded as ludicrous. It was perfectly clear to him and to many others that what was happening could not possibly be put down to revivalism nor could it be harmonized with the new views on promoting revivals. On this point Alexander wrote in his Preface to *The Revival and its Lessons*:

The work of grace in which we rejoice was not the result of any human project, concerted arrangement, or prescribed plan. It was not an excitement foreseen, predicted and made to order . . . And this is of the greatest importance to record, for the silence of such as stigmatize the entire proceedings as the creations of ingenious artifice working on overheated fancy . . . even when the holy elevation of feeling was at its height, it was, in the circle open to our survey, entirely free, on the one hand, from the machinery of religious manoeuvre, and on the other hand, from manifestations of unruly enthusiasm.

Prime's *Power of Prayer* drew the same lesson:

In no former revival was there such abnegation, on the part of Christians, of themselves; such distrust of all mere human agencies and instrumentalities . . . There were no revivalists; no revival machinery . . . The 'anxious seat', and the labor of peregrinating revival-makers were all unknown . . . The union prayer meetings all over our country have not been appointed to create religious feeling, but rather to give expression to, and increase the religious feeling already existing. The appointment of these meetings was to *meet* the *demand* of religious interest already existing, not to *create* that *demand*. There is a wide difference between the two things, which has a significant and emphatic meaning. The revival was nowhere attended by any special measures intended and adapted to produce intense excitement on the subject of religion.[1]

As the *New York Christian Advocate* commented on the 'divine visitation to the whole land', it had 'arisen amid the ordinary means of grace'.[2] And the visitation had come mysteriously and simultaneously in so many places at once. From Charleston to Boston, Christians were united in a common testimony: 'Awed by the manifest presence of God which we have felt to be around us, conscious that it has arisen from no measure of ours,

[1] *Power of Prayer*, pp. 27–30, 36. It is no wonder Finney was critical of Prime's book. See his *Memoirs: Complete Text*, p. 574 n.
[2] Quoted in *Presbyterian Magazine*, 1858, p. 191.

nay, more that it has come in spite of our coldness, of our inaction, and of our indifference, – it is natural that we should stand half-fearful, lest our hands should disturb, rather than advance the work – least of all presuming that we can direct its progress.'[1]

*   *   *

If the awakening of 1857–58 was proof that the distinction between revival and revivalism is a real one, the personal ministry of J. W. Alexander was also proof of something else. Since the 1830s, as we have seen, the cry against Calvinism was that in terms of evangelistic effectiveness it could not be compared with the new views, and that evangelism was alien to its true ethos. Alexander's many published sermons and tracts show the absurdity of that claim. He never denied that orthodoxy may be found where there is lack of warmth and zeal towards the unconverted, but such a failure was not due to the truth, it only showed the need for Christians to be elevated to a greater measure of life.[2] When revival came and his people were ready to respond, as never before, to his call to give to everyone 'tidings of that rich gospel feast which awaits their acceptance',[3] there was not the slightest question of any need of a change of theology. But so evident was the evangelistic force of Alexander and his school in 1858 that those accustomed to caricature Calvinism were left to protest that he was changing his position. *The Independent,* a paper unfavourable to Old-School belief, drew attention to one of his sermons in which he said that everyone will be saved who 'yields to the moving of the Spirit, takes God at His word, and makes the universal offer his own particular salvation'. Henry Ward Beecher claimed that such a statement represented the theology of 'Taylor, the

---

[1] 'The Religious Awakening of 1858', *The New Englander*, August, 1858, quoted by J. D. Hannah, 'The Layman's Prayer Revival of 1858', *Bibliotheca Sacra* (Dallas, Jan-Mar. 1977), p. 71.

[2] *Sacramental Discourses*, 1860, pp. 284–85 (reprinted as *God is Love*, Banner of Truth, 1985). 'Without this elevation within the church,' he adds, 'no measures however well-chosen or diligently plied are likely to have much effect'.

[3] *Revival and Its Lessons*, p. 190.

theology of New England, but it is not the theology of Princeton'.[1]

The point which Beecher and his fellow critics missed was that Alexander, and the Old School generally, had been preaching this long before 1858, just as Whitefield and Davies had preached it in the previous century. And the words of Beecher quoted above continued to misconstrue the difference between Calvinism and Arminianism. Arminians held that the proclamation of grace is to be universal. Calvinists believed that no less strongly. In the words of Alexander: 'The provision of grace leaves nothing wanting for the worst conceivable case . . . Were all the sons and daughters of Adam, who have been, are, and shall be, to gather in one numberless mass, with the Cross for its centre and object of desire, there were enough for all. Yea, though all worlds were peopled with sinners, here were enough for all.'[2] Calvinists further agreed with Arminian brethren that the same promises of salvation go out to all men in the gospel, and that *nothing* is required of men in order to their salvation other than an acceptance of Christ: 'Believe on the Lord Jesus Christ, and thou shalt be saved' (Acts 16.31).

But if Christ calls all men to himself, and if their coming is by faith, then, according to Arminianism, God must give grace to all men sufficient to enable that response. Calvinism asserted that the reason men do not respond lies in their sin but that God distinguishes between men who are equally undeserving by giving saving grace to those whom he has chosen. How God's willingness that all should be saved is to be harmonized with this particularity and sovereignty they did not explain, for the very good reason that Scripture itself does not explain it. The attitude of an Old-School preacher in this regard is well stated in John Kennedy's description of consistent biblical preaching:

While never losing sight of God's sovereignty in dispensing his grace, he never hesitated to proclaim his good will to all. He believed on the

---

[1] The incident is discussed by T. L. Smith, *Revivalism and Social Reform*, p. 90. So far was Alexander, in fact, from Taylor and New Haven that he could write, 'the Newhavenites, while they confess the divinity of Christ, and the agency of the Holy Spirit, do (in their *system*) deny all that makes these doctrines indispensable' (*Familiar Letters*, vol. 1, p. 168).

[2] *Discourses on Common Topics of Christian Faith and Practice* (New York, 1858), pp. 230–1; from a sermon preached in 1854.

same authority the electiveness of God's covenant purposes, and the indiscriminateness of his gospel calls . . . He makes much more than others of God's will . . . He is therefore quite prepared to find mysteriousness investing in it; and its incomprehensibleness is to him but an evidence of its divinity. He cannot reconcile the good will declared to all, with the saving love confined to the elect; but he takes the revealed will of God as it is given to him. He would have others, he would have all, to come in; for the salvation he himself has found is sure and free. In Scripture light he sees the will of God in its relation to the chosen, and in its bearing upon all. The one melts his heart, the other enlarges it.[1]

With such words Alexander would have heartily concurred. His theology put no restrictions on the calling of all men to the obedience of faith. His tracts showed great wisdom in leading seekers through difficulties and doubts. His knowledge that God himself had to be working if the response of hearers was to be saving, led him to put no qualifications or conditions in their way. In the words of one of his contemporaries: 'God needs to do a great deal *to* sinners, in order to turn them; but God is requiring nothing *of* sinners but that they return'.[2]

It is important further to add that while the Old School believed that the relationship between regeneration and faith was a relationship of cause and effect, the cause, as far as our consciousness in conversion is concerned, is not immediately known. Regeneration as the act of God occurs in the unconscious depths of our being.[3] We know it only by its effects.

---

[1] Kennedy is describing the preaching of the Scottish evangelist, John MacDonald. I quote from Spurgeon's review of Kennedy's biography of MacDonald (*The Apostle of the North*) in C. H. Spurgeon, ed., *The Sword and the Trowel* (London, 1866), pp. 154–5. Spurgeon commends this doctrine and says, 'Would to God all our pulpits gave forth such a testimony to a full-orbed gospel!'

[2] A. Moody Stuart, *Recollections of the Late John Duncan* (Edinburgh, 1872; repr. Banner of Truth as *The Life of John Duncan*, 1991), p. 219.

[3] Alexander says: 'Regeneration itself indeed is not gradual; the transition from death to life is instantaneous; but we are not competent to judge of that single instant. Too great stress has undoubtedly been laid on the marked character of the first exercises supposed to be saving; and the error has operated in twofold evil, by darkening the views of the desponding, and

Though the convert may not be aware of it at the time, yet in his first true desires for Christ, and in his first glimpses of the Saviour's divine glory, he has already passed from death to life. He knows that his faith and his submission to Christ are his own free acts but more has happened than he knows. In the words of Archibald Alexander on the rebirth: 'The soul, though operated on by an almighty power, is conscious of no restraint, unless it be the sweet constraint of the love of Christ. There is indeed an irresistible drawing towards Christ, but the more powerful it is, the more freely does the soul seem to act. Under the sweet influence of grace, the affections spontaneously go forth to him.'[1]

In the hands of critics the profound issues involved in such beliefs may be made to contrast with the supposed 'simplicity' of other views. But when the two positions were put to the test as they were in the harvest of 1857–58 we are not surprised that Alexander was able to play the part that he did, nor that it was the sermons of the like-minded Spurgeon which were in such demand.

When Alexander taught at Princeton he had urged his students to recognize that 'to declare God's truth so as to save souls, is a business angels might covet', and he encouraged them to pray, in the words 'of the sweet psalmist of early Methodism', for grace

> To spend, and to be spent for them
> Who have not yet my Saviour known;[2]

In his own life, and especially in its closing years, that prayer was wonderfully heard.

---

making the self-deceiver more presumptuous. It is not by any single moment, even though it were the best, that we can judge of the genuineness of piety. Judged thus, the stony ground hearers, believing and rejoicing, would have been unblamable.' *Revival and its Lessons*, pp. 117–18.

[1] Archibald Alexander, *Practical Sermons*, (Philadelphia, 1850), p. 562.

[2] J. W. Alexander, *Thoughts On Preaching* (1864; Banner of Truth, 1975), p. 105.

14

OLD AND NEW, PAST AND FUTURE

Room in Consistory Building of the North Reformed Protestant
Dutch Church, New York, where the prayer meetings began on
September 23, 1857, with J. C. Lanphier seated

14

Christianity in America has moved on from the period we have considered in these pages and in doing so it has very largely discarded the viewpoint which has been our theme. Even by the end of the nineteenth century it was a near universal opinion that the controversy over revival and new measures in the 1830s was of little relevance to the modern church. The whole subject was regarded as a closed and unimportant chapter of history. In so far as any view was held on the matter, most people supposed the debate would never have arisen if the opponents of the new measures had possessed a better understanding of the Bible's teaching on human responsibility. Few writers referred to the issue without expressing opinions such as those of Arthur S. Hoyt, author of *The Pulpit and American Life*, who believed that 'Men of the theology of the Alexanders and Hodges discredited his [i.e. Finney's] work because of his doctrine of human responsibility'.[1]

The real convictions of opponents of Finney passed almost wholly out of sight. Why Archibald Alexander believed that acceptance of 'the new religion' would mean that glory had departed; why Nettleton thought acceptance would be 'ruinous to the cause of revivals'; why John W. Nevin held that if the old orthodoxy lost the struggle, the failure would shape the 'entire complexion and history' of the churches in time to come – these were all questions which became incomprehensible to the later generation. Nevin wrote in 1843: 'The march of New Measures

---

[1] *The Pulpit and American Life* (London, 1921), pp. 159–60.

at the present time may well challenge our anxious and solemn regard. It is an interest of no common magnitude, portentous in its aspect, and pregnant with consequences of vast account'.[1] Such statements, or any explanation why they were made, are nowhere to be found in the later writers on revivals in America. None of the popular revival histories which were selling from the 1870s onwards suggest any idea of a crisis or watershed in the 1830s. No mention of it is to be found in H. C. Fish's *Handbook of Revivals*, 1873; in E. N. Kirk's *Lectures on Revivals*, 1875; in James Porter's *Revivals of Religion*, 1878; in G. W. Hervey's *Manual of Revival*, 1884; or in Frank Beardsley's *History of American Revivals*, 1904, to name but some of the books which appeared.

As we have seen, many of the writers on revival *before* the 1870s spoke very differently. The preachers and authors who had known the Second Great Awakening left a testimony which can never be harmonized with the thinking of most of these later revival writers. The first historians of the earlier revivals, such as W. H. Foote on North Carolina (1846) and Virginia (1850), and Joseph Smith on Western Pennsylvania (1854),[2] shared fully in the apprehensions of those who feared where the new evangelism was going to lead. Writing as early as 1832, Ebenezer Porter of Andover believed that if the Old-School apprehensions 'prove wellgrounded, another century will disclose the calamitous results'.[3] Heman Humphrey in his *Revival Sketches and Manual*, 1859, does not so much as mention Charles G. Finney though he characterizes the innovations he popularized as tending to 'weaken the churches instead of strengthening them'.[4] But all these were books which were to gather dust on library shelves while Finney's *Memoirs* (1876) was to remain in print for more than a century to come.

All this is a reminder that history can be read in different ways. But the fact that these earlier and later writers should be so near-uniform in their disagreement can only be explained in one way: their doctrinal and theological presuppositions were not the same. The difference between them is general as well as particular. It is not simply a difference of detail. The whole

---

[1] *The Anxious Bench*, third ed. (Reading, Pa., 1892), p. 24.
[2] See *Old Redstone*, pp. 15–16, 175, 224 etc.
[3] *Letters on Revivals*, p. 148.   [4] *Revival Sketches*, p. 210.

ethos has changed. The older generation, while prizing the work of the Spirit of God in history, never gave their interest in that work priority over the work of the same Spirit in inditing the truth in Scripture. For God works in accordance with his Word. Without Scripture there is no 'sword of the Spirit'. The test whether experience is of the Spirit of God or of 'another spirit' is whether or not it brings greater understanding of the Bible and a closer obedience to it. So the foremost role of the church is always to teach and preach the Word and the work of evangelism and the ingathering of souls is never to be considered as in tension with the maintenance of true doctrine. Another way of stating this would be to say that the ultimate end of all things is the glory of God, and that glory is not given to him other than by men and women being brought to comprehend the truth.

This standpoint is well stated by Dr Thomas Murphy at the conclusion of his fine volume, *The Presbytery of the Log College; or, the Cradle of the Presbyterian Church in America*, a book which deals largely with the First Great Awakening in the Middle Colonies. In drawing lessons in his conclusion, Murphy's principal appeal to his younger brethren centres around the following:

Be it, therefore, the inflexible purpose of every Christian, every church and every body of churches to cling with a grasp that will not be relaxed to the truth, the truth alone, to the whole truth – to the truth in doctrine, in worship and in practice. We can afford to be branded with old-fogyism: if old-fogyism can do what this history shows has been done, we may well be proud of the name. We may well say, especially to those who are near the commencement of their course, Cling to the truth, pure and simple – to the truth, and not to mere feelings, impressions, sentiments; to the truth, and not tampering with falsehood; to the truth: it is heaven-born; to the truth: it is from God, and he knows best what we should believe and what do . . . to the truth: it is sure to bring the rich blessings of its Author.[1]

When Murphy wrote these words in 1888 he knew that their emphasis was not that of the spirit of the church at large. We have already noted how, earlier in the century, a new evangelical synthesis was developing, disinterested in doctrinal distinctives, unsympathetic to credal statements of Christianity and opposed to Calvinism. Strangely, perhaps, this spirit

[1] *Presbytery of Log College*, p. 467.

gained strength through the circumstances connected with the 1858 revival. For one thing, that revival encouraged, as do all revivals, a greater catholicity and communion between true Christians. Churches rejoiced that former differences could be laid aside as they engaged in a common purpose. Their knowledge that the Spirit of God was at work in many denominations showed up the wrongness of narrow party interests. In accordance with this spirit the Evangelical Alliance gained many to its cause (on both sides of the Atlantic), and there was, henceforth, a new readiness among Christians to support wider, non-denominational interests.

In all this there was much that was good. Denominations had too often contended over issues which had little long-term significance for the spread of the gospel. Secondary truths had been sometimes wrongly treated as though they were fundamental. But this new spirit could too easily merge with a low view of doctrine as such and with the idea that efforts to advance the faith were far more important than the need to understand and believe it in its fullness.

Another factor emerging from the 1858 revival also worked in the same way. The extent to which it was a 'layman's revival' has probably been exaggerated, but there is no question that workers such as Jeremiah Lanphier did immense good and they well illustrated how much could be done by earnest Christians who were not ordained by the churches to any teaching office. There was a scriptural balance that needed to be recovered. The preacher is not the beginning and end of Christian witness. But in some quarters the balance was now thrown too far the other way. If laymen could effectively conduct prayer-meetings, why could they not also be the evangelists? Perhaps the foremost public spokesmen for the church did not need to be ministers at all. So attractive did this view quickly become that in the 1860s when D. L. Moody asked a ministerial friend, 'What do you think about my being ordained? he got the reply, 'Don't. If you are ordained you will become one of us. Now you are a preaching layman and that gives you an advantage'.[1]

[1] J. C. Pollock, *Moody Without Sankey*, (London: Hodder and Stoughton, 1963), p. 58.

The idea of lay ministry, separate from church office, had appeared in the eighteenth century but it received far less support because a good understanding and knowledge of the truth was then commonly regarded as paramount in those who stood in public to teach and preach. They were expected to show sound evidence that they were prepared of God for such labour: 'For the priest's lips should keep knowledge, and they should seek the law at his mouth: for he is the messenger of the Lord of hosts' (Malachi 2.7). The pastors of the New Testament, the successors to that work, were regarded as men appointed to their office by the churches and not by themselves. This high view of the ministry of the Word was far more susceptible to change in a situation in which the evangelical synthesis of belief, consisting of only a few 'fundamentals', was regarded as all that was necessary. 'Teachers' could now multiply as they had never done before. And whereas the older generation had regarded nothing as more profound and demanding than the gospel itself, the 'evangelist' was now encouraged to think that his was a work requiring little or no understanding of theology.

This danger was foreseen by some at the time of the 1858 revival. In his 'General Reflections' at the conclusion of his work *The Noon Prayer Meeting*, Talbot Chambers wrote:

Fervent exhortation and conversational appeals are of inestimable value in supplementing and carrying out the instruction of the pulpit, but they cannot take its place . . . The usefulness of the union prayer meeting presupposes previous indoctrination of men by the ministry. Take away that groundwork for its exercises, and although feeling may be excited even to a violent pitch, it will be the rapid blaze of stubble leaving the field 'burnt over' and hopeless, whereas the excitement which is based upon truth, will last as long as the material upon which it rests.[1]

---

[1] *Noon Prayer Meeting*, pp. 305–6. J. W. Alexander had the same concern, *Familiar Letters*, vol. 2, p. 283, and so did C. H. Spurgeon who disagreed strongly with those who minimized the instrumentality of preaching in revival: 'The outcry against the "one man ministry" cometh not of God, but of proud self conceit, of men who are not content to learn although they have no power to teach'. *Metropolitan Tabernacle Pulpit*, vol. 8 (London, 1863), p. 195. For an incident in which Spurgeon declined to lead a prayer meeting for revival see G. Holden Pike, *The Life and Work of Charles Haddon Spurgeon* (Banner of Truth, 1991 repr. vol. 2, p. 50).

Such warnings as this proved ineffective to resist the sea-change which was taking place in views on the importance of Christian doctrine. The serious issues controverted in the 1830s were not settled, they were simply passed by. We have noted something of the change as it was going on among the Baptists but the same thing was now gathering pace among Presby-terians. In 1871 Old and New School churches reunited. In contributing to a volume commemorating that event, the Rev. John Hall spoke for the past in saying, 'old Calvinism was the form of doctrine most effective in producing revivals and saving men'. But his words fell by the wayside. The accepted view was that 'New School' men were now as orthodox as the 'Old'.[1] The truth appears to be rather, as Timothy L. Smith says, that Presbyterianism generally was now adopting what he calls 'Revivalistic Calvinism', which was 'paradoxically enough, almost Arminian on matters of election and free will and leaned well toward "new measures"'.[2]

In contrast with the early part of the century the orthodox seminaries were now noticeably silent in opposing the thinking which was allowing revivalism to take over evangelicalism. This was partly because they were occupied with other concerns, most notably with how conservative Christianity was to meet the attack of Higher Criticism on the Bible. At the level of scholarship, the world-wide debate was not about revival or evangelism, it was about such things as the authorship of the Pentateuch and of Isaiah. Further, orthodox seminary pro-fessors did not want to contend on such matters with earnest fellow Christians such as Moody when an assault on the very foundations of the faith had to be met from another direction.

Another point is relevant here. At an earlier date, the seminary leaders – the Alexanders, the Griffins, the Porters – had all served in pastorates. They had personal experience of the work in which the church had to succeed on its front line.

[1] *Presbyterian Reunion, A Memorial Volume, 1837–1871* (New York, 1870), compare pp. 11, 48.

[2] *Revivalism and Social Reform*, p. 32. The contrast between the end of the nineteenth century and the beginning can be seen when it is remembered that in 1811 the Presbyterian Church in South Carolina suspended a minister for teaching, among other things, that 'faith precedes regeneration' (Foote, *Sketches of N.C.*, pp. 459, 472).

They were themselves evangelists and physicians of souls and their opposition to the new measures arose directly out of that fact. Their assessment of priorities was not affected by the latest books from Germany; it rested directly on the Bible itself. In contrast, the church of the later nineteenth century, deeply conscious of the high profile which the world gave to the claims of 'scholarship', now tended to put its own professional scholars into the seminary leadership roles and the course was set for these institutions to be seen primarily as educational establishments. Even at Princeton Seminary the original vision of a place that would be 'a nursery of vital piety as well as of sound theological learning . . . to train up . . . friends of revivals of religion' was dimmed. Theology and evangelism were parting company.

We have argued that the change traced in these pages was closely related to the issue of Calvinistic belief. That point now needs to be stated more exactly. It is not that every point of so-called Calvinistic belief is equally vital to the prosecution of evangelism and the conversion of sinners. Belief in predestination, for example, will comfort Christians but it is not a prerequisite for evangelism. Nor is preaching on the extent of the atonement essential for evangelism; evangelism calls men to come to Christ not because they have been saved but so that they may be saved. The seeking soul is not, after all, to be presented with systems of theology.

But there are aspects of biblical doctrine which are directly related to evangelism. These have to do with the real condition of human nature and the work of the Holy Spirit in regeneration. Here lies the difference between Arminian and Calvinistic teaching which has immediate consequences in practice. Arminianism treats believing and regeneration as amounting to the same thing. The gospel is to be preached to all men, the same light comes to all who hear it, and those that believe are born again. According to this view, the truth heard is the means of regeneration. But if this is so, why is it that among a congregation hearing the same gospel truth some respond and others do not? There are only two possible answers to that question: either man is not so 'dead in trespasses and sins' as Scripture represents and the difference can therefore be explained solely in terms of human choice, or there is a work of

[363]

the Spirit *additional* to the outward hearing of the message – a work which lies behind the will, giving men a new nature. The latter, the Old School believed, is the biblical position. Men not only need the light of the truth, they need the capacity to *see* it; they need a removal of the enmity which causes them by nature to 'receive not the things of the Spirit of God' (1 Cor. 2.14); they need to be *made* willing. The voice of the preacher leads people to the exercise of faith, but the *ability* to believe comes only as 'the dead hear the voice of the Son of God' himself (John 5.25). This is a voice which the unsaved do not hear (John 10.16–27); it is the 'calling' which brings faith and justification (Rom. 8.30); and it is much more than the outward hearing of the words of the gospel. Regeneration is the putting forth of creative power in the implanting of a new nature. There can be no *exercise* of faith until men hear the gospel (Rom. 10.14) but it is the power of the Holy Spirit with the gospel which first gives men a believing nature. Salvation is through faith, not *because* of it. Men are not renewed because they believe, rather they 'see' and 'hear' because they are reborn (John 3.3; Acts 16.14; Eph. 2.4–9).

All this was already clear in the teaching of Jonathan Edwards, 'The heart can have no tendency to make itself better, until it first has a better tendency'. Ebenezer Porter speaks of all 'those revival preachers' of 1800 being agreed 'that means have no independent efficacy to renew the hearts of men . . . that man does not gradually become holy, by the influence of means, – regeneration being an instantaneous and not a progressive work; that his renovation is not produced by any direct instrumentality of means, it being a supernatural work, not effected, like ordinary events, by the laws of nature'.[1]

---

[1] *Letters on Revivals*, p. 16. Porter says that any idea of regeneration without special, divine influence was unknown among 'revival preachers' in 1800 and he contrasts this with the change which had occurred by 1830 (p. 172). In the above discussion confusion arises because 'regeneration' – re-making alive – is sometimes used in different senses, i.e., sometimes in the wider sense referring to what is involved in conversion as a whole, and sometimes in the specific sense of the act of God in implanting new life. In the broader sense the Word of God plays an essential part; in the narrow and particular sense it plays no part. It is simplest to speak of conversion as a process in which man is active and regeneration as a single and immediate act of God in which man receives a new nature. Spurgeon, using the language of Old-School belief,

It was this teaching, as we have seen, which gave rise to the charge that Calvinism denied human responsibility. For, it was claimed to be self evident that men cannot be responsible to do what they are unable to do. The idea that the preacher can call sinners to faith while also teaching that faith is beyond their powers was held up to ridicule. But to this the older evangelicalism replied that the Scriptures constantly teach both responsibility *and* inability. 'I well recollect', says Nettleton dryly, 'a celebrated preacher in one of His discourses used this language: "*Come unto me*, all ye that labour and are heavy laden and I will give you rest." In another discourse this same preacher said: "No man *can come unto me* except the Father which hath sent me draw him". Now what think you, my hearers, of such preaching? What would you have said had you been present and heard Him? Would you have charged him with contradicting himself?'[1]

It was enough for the older generation to preach that man *ought* to repent and believe the gospel and to insist, with Scripture, that it is *only* their sin which prevents them from doing so. But here was the very difference which, as we have seen, had immense practical consequences. The New School believed that if Calvinism's doctrine of man's sinful nature, and consequent inability, was removed from the evangelist's message, then faith and regeneration would be seen to be simple. An immediate response to the message would thus be made far more likely. In Baird's apt phrase, already quoted, the plan was 'to make regeneration so easy that men may not be discouraged from attempting it'. And to that theory, the altar call and other methods of securing public response were added, being 'nothing more than the effort to secure action – however small – which would place men in the way of repentance and faith'.[2] So

---

says, 'Regeneration is an instantaneous work. Conversion to God, the fruit of that work occupies all our life but regeneration is effected in an instant'. *New Park Street Pulpit*, vol. 4 (London, 1859), p. 293. One great benefit from the new-measures controversy was that it led to clearer exposition of this subject, e.g. Charles Hodge, *Systematic Theology*, vol. 2 (London and Edinburgh, 1874), p. 700 ff. and W. G. T. Shedd, *Dogmatic Theology*, vol. 2, (Edinburgh, 1889), p. 490 ff.

[1] *Nettleton and his Labours*, pp. 215–16.
[2] *The Pulpit and American Life*, p. 159.

wrote one apologist for the new measures. What the physical action of standing, kneeling, or coming to the front, had to do with regeneration no one ever attempted to make clear. It was enough that these things were visual proofs that something could be *done* at once.

It was in this context that many of the best men stated the case against the altar call. Their arguments may be summarized as follows:

1. They alleged that the call for a public 'response' confused an external act with an inward spiritual change. This confusion was inevitable because the encouragement given to aid a response was that the two things – coming forward and becoming a Christian – were so closely related as to be virtually identical. The hearer was given the impression that answering the public appeal was crucial because salvation depended on that decision. 'It is not uncommon,' wrote John Nevin of preachers practising this measure, for them 'to throw in occasionally something like a word of caution with regard to this point . . . As a general thing, even the cautions that are interposed are in such a form as to be almost immediately neutralized and absorbed by representations of the opposite character. The whole matter is so managed as practically to encourage the idea that a veritable step towards Christ at least, if not actually into His arms, is accomplished in the act of coming to the anxious seat . . . Indeed I do not see well how the measure could be employed in any case with much effect without the help of some such representation'.[1]

2. They argued further that this procedure had inevitable serious consequences. Those who come forward and who experience no saving change are liable either to go back to the world, hardened in the idea that 'there is nothing in it', or they may go on to join the church, assured that they have done all that was required. Thus the anxious seat, in the words of Samuel Miller, favoured 'the rapid multiplication of superficial, ignorant, untrained professors of religion'.[2]

3. It was claimed by those supporting the altar call that 'a sinner who is not humble enough to take the step is not humble enough to be saved'.[3] On the contrary, the Old School argued

---

[1] *The Anxious Bench*, p. 70.   [2] Sprague, *Lectures*, appendix, p. 41.
[3] James Porter, *Revivals of Religion* (New York, 1878), p. 279.

that it was entirely unsafe to suppose that it was spiritual influence which brought people forward. Those most likely to make an immediate public reponse were 'the forward, the sanguine, the rash, the self-confident'. No *spiritual* power was necessary to secure a *physical* response.

4. There was agreement on all sides that many who went forward in response to the appeal subsequently showed that they remained unconverted. But, it was said, 'If only *some* souls are saved by the use of the new measures, we ought thankfully to own their power, and give them our countenance'. Conversion is so important that if any cases prove genuine is that not enough to justify the method? This argument was very widely used. R. L. Dabney reports an example of it from a conversation between a new-measures evangelist and one of his hearers. Surely the preacher could not be blind, said his hearer, to the failure of many of the professed conversions? 'Of course not; we are not fools', replied the evangelist. 'Why then', asked the enquirer, 'do you employ these measures?' The answer was: 'Because a few are truly converted, and make stable, useful Christians; and the rest when they find out the shallowness of their experience, are simply where they were before'.[1]

This reply, as Dabney says, rests on a number of fallacies. The lapsed who were once held up before public view as converts are not where they were before; they are likely to be more careless and more indifferent. Furthermore, in their lapse the reputation of the gospel has been brought down in the eyes of the world. On the other hand, those who were saved did not owe their conversion to their public response. They were people in whom God was working, and whose consciences had become tender, so that, hearing that coming to the front was their duty, they responded. Whatever they were told, their conversion was not the result of that action. It was the work of the Holy Spirit and of gospel truth. So even in these cases nothing was gained by the unbiblical measure, and much harm would have been avoided had it not been used. After witnessing the new evangelism in central New York State, in 1828, the moderate J. H. Rice wrote to Archibald Alexander, 'From the little that I

---

[1] *Discussions*, vol. 3 (Banner of Truth, 1982 repr.), p. 17. See also Dabney's important treatment in *Discussions*, vol. 1, pp. 565–74.

saw, I would say that if good is done by these irregular means, it is done at frightful expense. It is like slaying hundreds to save one'.[1]

5. The altar-call evangelism not only confused regeneration and faith but it also confused the biblical doctrine of assurance. When people were told that *all* that was needed to be saved was an act of the will – 'submitting' to Christ, deciding for Christ – then, when willingness was 'proved' by a public response, assurance of salvation tended to be seen as an automatic consequence. Did Jesus not say, 'him that cometh unto me I will in no wise cast out'? And did people not come to the front in order to come to Jesus?

The older Methodism, even when it first introduced the altar call, had safeguarded against this danger by insisting that assurance was always a matter of the witness of the Spirit of God. Their preachers did not promise 'eternal security' to all who made a decision. But the anxious-seat evangelism wanted to do away with any doubts in those who made the public response. The whole strength of its appeal, as already said, lay in its suggestion that a response would ensure salvation. To have conceded that there was no sure connection between answering a public appeal and being converted would have been to undermine the whole system. It would also have made impossible the proclamation of the large 'results' claimed by the new evangelism.

Sprague and the older generation argued that if being saved became identified with performing a bodily act, and if hearers were told that it was 'as easy to change one's heart from the love of sin' as to perform that act, then multitudes would be encouraged in a false assurance.[2] This point, as others, was never answered.

The relation of the public appeal to assurance was not an argument about whether saving faith carries assurance with it. That was not in question. The weakest true believer, resting on the promises of Christ, has sure grounds for assurance. But the issue was whether every person who is ready to *profess* faith has, at once, sufficient reason to tell themselves and others that they have become Christians. The Old School believed with

---

[1] *Memoir of Rice*, p. 338.   [2] *Lectures on Revivals*, pp. 225-6.

Ebenezer Porter that, in regard to conversion, 'the work may be done in a moment, and God may see it to be done effectually'; but, the Andover professor adds, 'the proof to ourselves and to other men that it is done is not the work of a moment nor of a day'. At the beginning of the Second Great Awakening, says the same writer, 'ministers urged it as the immediate duty of all men publicly to profess Christ; but to have themselves, and to exhibit to others, *evidence of real friendship to Christ*, they deemed indispensable to consistency in this solemn transaction'.[1] So would-be converts were never encouraged to make instant profession. About six months would pass, Porter says, between hopeful conversion and a public profession of faith.[2] 'In the revivals of 1800 etc. it is a prominent fact that ministers used great caution in giving opinions concerning the spiritual state of living individuals, which they might apply to themselves'. Phrases such as 'hopefully renewed', or 'hopefully born of God', were then commonly used of professed converts, whereas by 1832, says the same writer, he heard of 'conversions', 'wonderful conversions', which were only supposed to have happened 'yesterday afternoon' or 'last evening'.

Such were the main arguments against the altar-call evangelism. And behind them lay a major difference over the preaching of the gospel itself. Against the New School charge that insisting on human depravity and inability hindered evangelism, the preachers of the earlier generation emphasized that such preaching was vitally related to the true presentation of the gospel. If we are to follow their thinking on this point, the Old School preaching has to be distinguished from the caricature which Finney and others fixed to it. That there were cases which did resemble the caricature cannot be doubted.

---

[1] *Letters on Revivals*, p. 84, italics mine.

[2] To the common objection that apostolic precedent on the day of Pentecost is against any such delay (Acts 2.41), Porter replied: 'Without spending time to controvert the premises often assumed in regard to this matter, I will barely say, that, as to any number of individuals who have recently professed religion, let me be assured, on divine authority (as I am, for example, with the Pentecost converts), that they "believed," that "the Lord added to the church," – that "they continue in the apostles' doctrine and fellowship," – and that "they shall be saved;" let me have this assurance, and I can have no apprehension that any mistake has been committed. But who will undertake to give me this assurance?' (Ibid., pp. 146–7).

There were some who gave too little emphasis to human responsibility. When any school of belief has a general following over a lengthy period there will always be adherents who are not its genuine representatives. So when Calvinism was the traditional belief it was inevitable that there would be lesser and ill-equipped preachers who might speak of human inability in such a way as to make it an excuse for lethargy. But that was not what happened where inability was preached biblically and in the power of the Holy Spirit. It was then an awakening truth, a truth calculated to bring home to men a realization of the full extent of their need. Man is more lost than he understands and the older evangelicalism believed that the first objective in gospel preaching was to bring men to despair of themselves. To tell men the worst about themselves is not to hinder conversion. On the contrary, the real impediment to conversion is the absence of conviction of sin. The preacher's first duty is to address that fact by awakening the conscience to the meaning of sin, and to sin understood not simply as wrong action requiring forgiveness, but as an evil principle governing man's very heart. A sinner's knowledge of his own inability is therefore part of the knowledge which leads him to recognize that what he needs is a new nature. This was the reason why Nettleton and his brethren believed that the new-measures evangelism, which assured men that the decision which would put everything right was in their own hands, was 'in direct opposition' to 'the progress of conviction'.

The proclamation of the truths respecting man's fallen condition can be no hindrance to evangelism. On the contrary, as Nettleton says: 'It is only when, without seeking the special and peculiar working of the Spirit, man is trying to work upon his fellow men, by the power of mere motives, that these truths seem to be hindrances.'[1]

Forty years after Nettleton, another evangelical leader, Dr John Kennedy in Scotland, made the same point in his criticism of Moody's superficial treatment of regeneration. Kennedy argued that the securing of mass consent in evangelistic campaigns was only possible where the full biblical teaching on depravity and regeneration is kept out of view.

---

[1] *Nettleton and his Labours*, p. 231.

Because, he wrote: 'To be sensible [i.e. conscious] of the power of spiritual death is to feel oneself entirely at the disposal of Him who "will have mercy on whom He will", and who alone can, by His Spirit, cause a dead soul to live. Such a case would become utterly unmanageable by human hands. The most urgent pressing of belief in gospel propositions would not help such a soul. Plying such an one with all the skill an evangelized rationalism could bring to bear upon him, would be weak against his difficulties. Such a case must, therefore, if possible be prevented . . . There must be a shorter and easier method of converting men.'[1]

The debate here, it should be noted, was not about whether conversion is effected simply through divine sovereignty *or* through preaching. That was obviously not the issue. No one could fairly accuse the Old School of not treating preaching as of momentous importance. The issue was what constitutes gospel preaching. Behind the different answers to that question lay a different view of conversion itself. The Old School teaching represented conversion as a much bigger thing than did the teaching it opposed. Conversion meant not simply a change of status (forgiveness instead of condemnation for the believer), it also meant a stupendous moral change, taking its subject from a life of disobedience to a life of holiness, from a life of self-centredness to one of glorifying God. To be converted, therefore, meant not only to escape *the punishment of sin,* it was to be delivered from *the power of sin* itself. The regenerate man is the man in whom sanctification has become a reality.

The new-measures evangelism in its concern to get men to receive forgiveness passed over what they regarded as a separable issue, namely, the transformation of his moral nature. Time was to prove the force of John Nevin's complaint, 'Conversion is everything, sanctification nothing'.[2] In contrast,

---

[1] J. Kennedy, *A Reply to Dr Bonar's Defence of Hyper-Evangelism* (Edinburgh, 1875), pp. 27–8. For further discussion on Moody see below, pp. 398–408.

[2] *The Anxious Bench*, p. 60. J. C. Ryle's volume, *Holiness*, 1877, enlarged 1880, in addition to expounding Scripture is a masterful demonstration of how nineteenth-century deviations in doctrine had led to impoverished spirituality. The problem of the holiness movement to which Ryle was opposed was brought on by superficial views of conversion. See particularly his lengthy footnote in the chapter on 'The Cost'.

the old evangelicalism saw the moral character of God, and the holiness and obedience which he requires, as part of gospel preaching. Men have to know what they have fallen from, and what they are called to. Let gospel hearers attempt to change themselves in accordance with what God demands: let them attempt to 'enter into life' by keeping the commandments (Matt. 19.17); for in so doing they will learn the depth of their plight. Gospel preaching must begin, as John the Baptist's heralding of Christ began, with ethical demands – demands intended to convict, to humble and, in God's time, to lead to the certain conclusion that there can be no relief except in Jesus Christ and that by a rebirth wrought by divine power.

Such preaching did not deny that faith alone is all that is needed to bring men to peace with God. Nor did it tell anyone to 'wait for regeneration'. Every sinner, as soon as he hears the promises of the gospel, has all the warrant he needs to trust in Christ, but God's usual way is to lead men to that point through a painful discovery about themselves. Preaching does not regenerate, but in the hand of God it has a key role both in the 'legal conviction', which is generally preparatory to regeneration, and in setting forth the Saviour in whom alone the penitent and the believing find rest. Thus Griffin can say, 'Though the Word of God in the shape of motives has an important instrumentality in carrying on the preparatory work in the conscience, and in *occasioning* the *exercises* of the new heart, it is in no sense instrumental in *changing the disposition* [i.e. in regeneration itself].[1] As we have seen, Finney and his school accused the older evangelicalism of cutting the nerve of evangelistic preaching by insisting that regeneration lay in the hands of God. Part of the reply of the other side was that the new views seriously misunderstood the relationship between preaching and conversion. This is a point that we cannot pursue further but it would appear from the evidence of history that Nettleton's charge that the new approach would militate against conviction of sin was correct. It was as evangelicalism increasingly came to accept the appeal system that the phenomenon of conviction of sin gradually disappeared.

[1] *Lectures in Park Street*, p. 157. Further on this, see John Owen, *Works*, vol. 3, pp. 228–42.

Griffin, describing the preaching in the revival in Connecticut at the beginning of the Second Great Awakening, says:

Little terror was preached, except what is implied in the doctrines of the entire depravity of the carnal heart – its enmity against God – its deceitful doubtings and attempts to avoid the soul-humbling terms of the gospel – the radical defects of the doings of the unregenerate, and the sovereignty of God in the dispensations of his grace. The more clearly these, and other kindred doctrines were displayed and understood, the more were convictions promoted. By convictions, are meant those views and feelings which are caused by uncovered truth, and the influences of the Spirit antecedent to conversion.[1]

This was precisely the kind of preaching that was almost to pass away before the end of the nineteenth century and hand-in-hand with its passing went a sense of sin. As a final example of what this difference meant in practice an illustration from the life of B. M. Palmer is noteworthy. At a time of revival in Savannah in the early 1840s a young man was attending Palmer's church and eventually, with considerable unease and irritation, he complained to the preacher of the teaching he was hearing:

You preachers are the most contradictory men in the world; you say, and you unsay, just as it pleases you, without the least pretension to consistency. Why you said in your sermon that sinners were perfectly helpless in themselves – utterly unable to repent or believe and then turned round and said they would all be damned if they did not.

On hearing these words, Palmer tells us that he judged it best to reply 'in an off-hand sort of way, and with seeming in-differences so as to cut him off from all opportunity to coquette

---

[1] *New England Revivals*, Bennet Tyler, p. 66. D. M. Lloyd-Jones is correct in saying the 'great evangelical preachers three hundred years ago in the time of the Puritans, and two hundred years ago in the time of Whitefield and others, always engaged in what they called a preliminary "law work"' (*Romans, Exposition of Chapters 7.1–8.4*, Banner of Truth, 1973, p. 114). Archibald Alexander says that 'legal conviction' had been the mark of all revivals prior to his day, and he takes care to assert that the preparatory work must *not* be understood 'in the sense of disposing the person to receive the grace of God. The only end which it can answer is to show the rational creature his true condition, and to convince the sinner of his absolute need of a Saviour' (*Thoughts on Religious Experience*, pp. 17–8). The Old School leaders were also careful not to represent conviction as any stereotyped experience which was required to be of a certain depth or duration in time.

with the gospel'. So, according to his biographer, he responded:

Well, my dear E——, there is no use in our quarreling over this matter; either you can or you cannot. If you can, all I have to say is that I hope you will just go and do it.

As I did not raise my eyes from my writing, which was continued as I spoke, I had no means of marking the effect of these words, until, after a moment's silence, with a choking utterance, the reply came back: 'I have been trying my best for three whole days and cannot.' 'Ah,' responded Palmer, raising his eyes and putting down his pen, 'that puts a different face upon it; we will go then and tell the difficulty straight to God'.

We knelt down and I prayed as though this was the first time in human history that this trouble had ever arisen; that here was a soul in the most desperate extremity, which must believe or perish, and hopelessly unable of itself, to do it; that, consequently it was just the case for divine interposition; and pleading most earnestly for the fulfillment of the divine promise. Upon rising I offered not one single word of comfort or advice . . . So I left my friend in his powerlessness in the hands of God, as the only helper. In a short time he came through the struggle, rejoicing in the hope of eternal life.[1]

*   *   *

Several definite conclusions can now be drawn on the subject of revival. Until about 1830 it would appear that one single definition of that phenomenon prevailed. A revival was a sovereign and large giving of the Spirit of God, resulting in the addition of many to the kingdom of God. Such was the definition of Edwards and Davies and, though the word 'revival' does not appear to have been used in print before Cotton Mather's *Magnalia Christi Americana* of 1702, the phenomenon was understood in the same way long before that date. Robert Fleming (1630–1694), for example, speaks of one revival in the 1620s as an 'extraordinary out-letting of the Spirit' and of another as 'so convincing an appearance of God and downpouring of the Spirit'.[2]

In 1832, preceding Finney by three years, an American Presbyterian minister and writer by the name of Calvin Colton

---

[1] *The Life and Letters of B. M. Palmer*, T. C. Johnson, 1906 (Banner of Truth, 1987), pp. 83–4.
[2] *The Fulfilling of the Scripture* (Glasgow, 1753), pp. 398–9.

went into print with the novel theory that genuine revivals could be classified into two different types: the old and the new. The old, he wrote, which came mysteriously and unexpectedly 'directly from the presence of the Lord', with overwhelming effect, were, 'till a few years past . . . the more ordinary character of revivals in America'.[1] 'Churches and Christians waited for them, as men are wont to wait for showers of rain'. The new, he believed, were the same in character and nature, but they had only begun to occur in recent years because previously men had not learned 'how, as instruments, to originate and promote them'. The reason this second type of revivals had not been known before was simply that the use of *means* in order to the promotion of revivals had not previously been studied. But now, Colton assured his British readers, there were scores of ministers and thousands of influential Christians in America 'who *believe* in revival and they believe too, that man may be the successful instrument of originating them – they see it is the fact – their own experience has proved it'.[2]

Here, then, was the issue which we have followed through these pages. Not one but two types of 'revival' were now said to exist and from this point onwards uncertainty on the subject multiplied. This can be seen, for example, in the reports of the two English Baptists, the Rev. F. A. Cox and the Rev. J. Hoby who went to the United States as a deputation from the Baptist Union of England in 1834. With some hesitations, at the conclusion of their volume *The Baptists in America; a Narrative*, they speak of 'three classes of revivals'. 'The first, and the worst', they write, 'are nourished by *injudicious camp-meetings*,' being particularly objectionable when 'held in districts considerably pervaded already by regular churches'. 'The second class of revivals, comprehends those which are, if we may so express it, constructed *upon the basis of protracted meetings*, and sustained by means of direct efforts of an exciting and agitating description . . . What appears to us of very questionable propriety in the *management* of these meetings is the direct call for instantaneous avowals at the *anxious seat*.' 'The third class of revivals is

---

[1] *History and Character of American Revivals of Religion* (London, 1832), p. 4.
[2] *American Revivals*, p. 87.

that of an *improved state of things* – it may be a very rapidly improved state of things – arising out of prayer meetings, conversations, inquiry, and an increased regard to the ordinary system of means, *with* or *without* protracted meetings.'[1]

These words are helpful in showing the various ways in which the word 'revival' was in use in 1834–35 but they deal with description rather than with analysis and spiritual definition. How the use of the word continued to broaden can be seen in the contrast between Porter's *Letters on the Religious Revivals*, first given as addresses to the students of Andover in 1832, and the addresses of E. N. Kirk, given in the same place in 1868. Porter knew only the traditional definition. Kirk thought that, because revival means an influence of the Spirit of God for the advancement of true religion, the word could be used of practically all true advances which the church has ever made in the world. So he includes such 'politico-religious movements' as Israel's deliverance from Egypt, and movements 'to the production of moral change' such as the work of Benedict and Bernard in the Medieval church or the more recent anti-slavery struggle. These he called 'indirect revivals'. In 'direct revivals' he included 'the silent growth or quickening of personal piety', 'the quickening of a community of believers' and 'conversions, accompanying efforts and prayers for conversions'.[2]

It may be argued that any attempt to define 'revival' is pointless for the word itself is not scriptural and indeed, as J. W. Alexander says, 'may not be wisely chosen'.[3] But rightly or wrongly, it *was* chosen, and its sense was commonly recognized over a long period of time. An understanding of the way in which that sense became confused is essential if we are to follow what has happened in history.

The crux of the issue with respect to definition has to do with Calvin Colton's distinction and with the question, Can an outpouring of the Spirit of God occur either sovereignly at God's giving or can it also be obtained by the use of the appropriate means? But the implication of the question is momentous, as both Colton and Finney saw. For if revival is something which can be secured by the fulfilment of conditions

---

[1] *Baptists in America*, pp. 508–9.
[2] *Lectures on Revivals*, pp. 12–14.   [3] *New York Pulpit*, p. 14.

then there is no reason at all why it should not be permanent.[1] And as revival became permanent the 'unpromoted', older revivals of former years would no more be needed.

It is amazing how long the argument for achieving permanent revival was persisted in when the very facts of history were teaching the opposite. Despite the work of so many revivalists from the 1830s onwards, spiritual awakening did not continue, and when in 1857–58 there was a renewed consciousness of divine power, enlarging the church in a marvellous way, it bore no relation to any theory about fulfilling conditions. Those most closely associated with the Fulton Street prayer meeting believed that the unusual spirit of prayer had been *given* to them. Finney, never lacking in boldness, denied this understanding of what happened in 1857 and claimed the New York prayer meetings proved all he had said on the use of means. In a letter written in England on 17 January, 1859, he wrote: 'The present great work in America is a striking exemplification of the justness of the views expressed in my lectures on revivals; so many of which have been published in this country'.[2]

Unlike Finney, Colton did not continue in the belief which he had been among the first to uphold. How he came to see his mistake we are not told but it seems that further experience was used to awaken him to question what he had regarded as indisputable. On returning from London to the United States he went to 'pastoral labours' in 'the western parts of New York' – the very area with which he had formerly been so impressed. Once there he seems to have seen more success, though we cannot be sure whether this was the time to which he refers when he writes, 'I have myself organized from ten to fifteen churches, giving them creeds drawn up by my own hand'. It was certainly not long before he was 'shaken' and 'disturbed', for his recantation of new-measures revivals was published in 1836. The influences which Colton had previously attributed to the Spirit of God he had come to believe were explainable on a purely natural level. He was now so shocked by things which he found in the Presbyterian Church that he decided to become an Episcopalian. Indeed he lectured his former colleagues on the

[1] *American Revivals*, pp. 62–3; 198–9 etc.
[2] Published in the *British Standard* and reprinted in *The Revivalist* (Louth, Lincolnshire, 1859), p. 32.

evil effects of 'special efforts', 'protracted meetings', 'novelties', 'rash experiments', 'sallies of fanaticism', 'over-heated excitements', 'spurious excitements' and 'religious mania'.[1]

In arguing that the two classes of 'revival' were one in kind and nature Colton had done the very thing which Nettleton had most feared: he had identified an honoured term, and what it stood for, with what could be induced by human energy. He had confused the work of the Spirit with human manipulation. But Colton's subsequent recantation seems to have passed with little notice and an indiscriminate use of the word 'revival' became normal in religious vocabulary. The ultimate result was that when the country all-too-slowly awoke to the damage done by the revivalism, it had no time for revival at all. R. L. Dabney, who well understood the distinction between the two things, wrote of 'Spurious Religious Excitements' in 1887: 'The ulterior evils of these rash measures are immense. A standard and type of religious experience are propagated in America, as utterly unscriptural and false as those prevalent in popish lands . . . Spurious revivals we honestly regard as the chief bane of our Protestantism. We believe that they are the chief cause, under the prime source, original sin, which has deteriorated the average standard of holy living, principles, and morality, and the church discipline of our religion, until it has nearly lost its practical power over the public conscience.'[2]

A. B. Strickland, writing in 1934, believed that 'the word "revival" must be stripped of those connotations which have put it into disrepute' but he did not know how that was to be done.[3] William L. Sperry, Dean of Harvard Divinity School, voiced what was the common sentiment by 1944, when he wrote: 'We are tired of religious revivals as we have known them in the last half century . . . Among all but the most

[1] I am quoting from a review of Colton's *Thoughts on the Religious State of the Country: with Reasons for preferring Episcopacy* (New York, 1836) in the *Biblical Repertory*, 1836, pp. 390–414. The Princeton review was unusually biting, believing that Colton never knew what Presbyterianism was, but perhaps it was unfair to say Colton was 'one who could play the zealot when fanatical excitement was the order of the day, who could try to import new measures and new nonsense into England, while they were in vogue at home; but now when the tide has changed, can change his course'.

[2] *Discussions of R. L. Dabney*, vol. 3, pp. 13–19.

[3] *The Great American Revival*, p. 227.

backward churches it is now agreed that education ought to be, and probably is, the best way of interesting our people in religion . . . Our efforts therefore have been turned from the religious revival.'[1]

Since that date many books from secular publishing houses have dealt with revival in America. Sadly the vast majority are based on the persuasion that all claims for the supernatural in revival have long since been discredited. After all, every intelligent person ought to know that the 'revival' methods for ensuring results run parallel to the manipulative methods of groups and organizations which have no religion at all. From that starting point, the total history of all revivals has been re-written. The divine has been obliterated, and revival and revivalism are regarded as one and the same.

But the difference between the two things is real and immense. The phenomenon of true revival retains the same mystery that belongs to the supernaturalism of the New Testament. No one can say why three thousand were converted in Jerusalem on the day of Pentecost and not in Athens or Rome, or why one preacher was greatly used in one place and not in another. Christ traced such things to the throne of God (Matt. 11.25). It is with reference to God's acts in history that the Scriptures say: 'How unsearchable are his judgments and his ways past finding out!' (Rom. 11.33). As these pages have shown, the vast and sudden spreading of the gospel which we call revival follow no observable plan or pattern. With respect to time and place and instrumentality, all attempts to account for them in mere human terms soon break down. No one can say why Whitefield saw only one Great Awakening though he was preaching for nearly twenty years after its conclusion. No one can explain why the same prayerful efforts, even under-taken by the same people and in the same place, were attended by such different results at different times.

A memorable illustration of this common fact occurred in Charleston, South Carolina, under the ministry of one of the South's most eminent preachers, John L. Girardeau. Girardeau's black congregation saw remarkable revival after

---

[1] W. L. Sperry, *Religion in America* (New York, 1946), pp. 161–62, 171, quoted by McLoughlin, *Modern Revivalism*, p. 462.

weeks of earnest prayer in 1858. Of this event and what followed, Girardeau's biographer writes:

Dr Girardeau frequently referred to this as the Lord's mercy in gathering His elect for the great war was so soon to sweep so many of them into eternity . . . After the war another great effort was made to secure a revival of the same kind. A sunrise prayer-meeting was organised for the sole purpose of praying for such a work of grace, and although the people went into it with great enthusiasm and with high expectations, after several months of earnest and persistent effort many of them began to cease their attendance. Some with stronger faith continued for a year before becoming discouraged and finally giving up hope. In speaking of this great struggle, Dr Girardeau was accustomed to say, 'God is sovereign'.[1]

In contrast with this, revivalism contains no real element of mystery: psychological pressure, 'prayer' used to create expectancy, predictions of impending results, the personality of the 'revivalist' pushed to the fore, the 'appeal' – these, and kindred things, are generally enough to account for the extraordinary in its success. The observation of Dr Kirk was not missed by many others: 'I have known an evangelist who seemed to be conscious of considerable tact in manipulating an audience. His aim seemed to be to get his hearers on their feet, for any one of twenty reasons'.[2] Revivalism is marked by the predictable, indeed so much did this become the case that its very promoters found nothing incongruous in announcing beforehand when 'revivals' would take place.

When the evangelistic campaign of the American revivalist, the Rev. James Caughey, in Sheffield, England, in 1859, was reported as a 'Pentecost' and a great revival, the *Wesleyan Times* believed that it proved the truth of the claim that revival could be secured through special efforts. Caughey, in that paper's view, proved that the promotion of revivals was a fact and it regretted that because so few other preachers followed him the result was 'the limitation of the revival here to the one place in which he happens to be at work'. In similar vein the *Wesleyan Times* added, 'In commenting upon the labours and successes of Mr Caughey, we have always said, that there is no reason but

---

[1] George A. Blackburn, *The Life Work of John L. Girardeau* (Columbia, S.C., 1916), pp. 100–1.
[2] *Lectures on Revivals*, p. 298.

the unfaithfulness of others, why similar scenes should not be witnessed wherever God has established a Christian church.'[1]

The very thing that was here being claimed as supernatural – that Caughey could bring revival – was in reality proof to the contrary. A true awakening has never been dependent on the presence of one particular preacher. This brings us to the most serious and to the ultimate difference between revival and revivalism. The ethos of one is that of concern and praise for the glory of God. The spirit of revival is the spirit of profound humility – churches and the wider communities around them find reason to 'cease from man'. The work of the Spirit of God is always to make men want to sing with Samuel Davies,

> Great God of wonders, all thy ways
> Are matchless, godlike and divine

To the extent that the promoters of revivalism were true Christians they also knew something of the impulse to put God's glory first, but we fear it is not untrue to say that the tendency of their work was generally in another direction. Awe, meekness and reverence were not part of the new ethos. The centre of gravity for Christian work was changed. The older generation had always spoken of their work as that of seeking 'the glory of God in the salvation of sinners'. Now the objective was simply 'soul-winning'. Even prayer ceased to be thought of primarily as worship and became rather the best means for the fulfilment of human need. As a witness to this change the words of E. N. Kirk on this point are impressive for his life work had been more closely connected with the new rather than with the old. In his *Lectures on Revivals*, published in 1875, he wrote of 'intense desire for the manifestation of the Redeemer's glory in the conversion of men' as essential to revival and went on:

This seems to have been supreme in the hearts of the apostles . . . to them it had become insupportable, that the world remained so ignorant of him, and either so indifferent or so opposed.

So far as we can judge, it would seem that a Revival springing from such a lofty impulse would have a much higher tone than those which are mainly the result, so far as the inspiring motive really operating is concerned, from a regard supremely to man's salvation, in itself

---

[1] Quoted in *The Revivalist*, 1859, p. 75. The contents of this magazine show the techniques of revivalism very well.

considered. And it may not be a sound judgment, but it has much in its favor, that this is the chief preferableness of the Revivals of the Edwardean type over our Revivals, and of the Calvinistic type over the Arminian type. Both classes of motives are pure: but the former is not only highest, it also includes and insures, the existence of the latter. Men of the stamp of John Howe, Richard Baxter, John Flavel and John Owen, who dwelt, like the attendant angels, in the very presence of infinite glory, reflected like Moses, that glory in all their ministrations. The human spirit was frequently over-awed, not by the greatness of these men, but by the reverent sense of God's holy presence. Our present ministry does certainly move on a lower plane, manifesting much less than theirs of the sublimer religious sentiments.[1]

The date at which these words were published should be noted: by the phrase 'our Revivals', Kirk is referring to organized special meetings. This definition was fast taking over from.the traditional understanding of the word.

There is, however, an important qualification to be remembered at this point. While we believe the distinction between revival and revivalism is a clear distinction, describing different things, this is not to say that in practice the two things are always easily distinguished. The difference, as far as our perception is concerned, can never be an absolute one. We cannot speak of true revivals as though they always result in unmixed blessing while revivalism can only be associated with spiritual damage. If the matter had been so simple then last-century evangelicalism would never have taken the course that it did. Because the subjects of revivals are always erring, fallible men, and because the tares that grow besides the wheat cannot be recognized with absolute certainty (Matt. 13.29), it would be entirely wrong to suppose that periods of true revival are not also times of danger. To ignore that is to ignore a major lesson of history.

Similarly, it would be foolish to argue that wherever earnest gospel work is attended by any errors or by any unwise methods, there *cannot* be true revival. As we have seen, when the exponents of the new measures first appeared they were fellow-workers in a spiritual harvest. And there were not a few who used the public appeal and the anxious seat without

[1] *Lectures on Revivals*, p. 228.

intending to manipulate people. They simply did not think out the spiritual implications of their actions.[1] Revivalism, after all, as a fully-developed, recognizable system, did not appear overnight. Its strength and its ultimate general ethos grew slowly. Even Dr Kirk, towards the end of his long ministry, confessed to uncertainty whether the theory which lay at its centre – the belief that we can fulfill conditions to bring revival – was true or not. Speaking of proponents of that teaching, he says, 'I am not of them, nor yet prepared to oppose their view'.[2]

The above qualification is important. Calvinists have sometimes been inclined to deny God's sovereignty by imagining that his working is always in proportion to the doctrinal correctness of the earthen vessels which he employs. But such is God's mercy that his blessing may also be found even among 'wood, hay, and stubble',[3] as was the case in Corinth (1 Cor. 3.12). Nettleton and his fellows were right not to think of denying that Finney had seen revival.

But this same qualification is misused (as Finney misused it on a grand scale) when it is employed as an argument to show that, *because* God has granted his blessing, therefore the 'wood, hay and stubble' cannot be errors at all but must represent a cause which he honours. Our understanding of God's ways in history is far too fallible to make providence the test of what is truth. In the end, while evangelicalism was seeking to guard faith in Scripture, it was her readiness to be impressed by pragmatic arguments, and by alleged success, by quantity rather than quality, that did so much to deprive her of true authority and strength.

---

[1] A notable example of this would be Daniel Baker, the Southern evangelist who knew true revival. He was clearly uncertain on how far to adopt the new methods and there were those that regretted that he did so at all. See George Howe, *History of the Presbyterian Church in South Carolina*, vol. 1 (1870), pp. 540–41, and Douglas Kelly, *Preachers with Power: Four Stalwarts of the South* (Banner of Truth, 1992), pp. 43–6.

[2] *Lectures on Revivals*, p. 286. On the practice of a preacher calling some hearers apart for special instruction Kirk says: 'In certain cases it seems to be precisely the step that an enlightened zeal in a pastor would take. But as soon as it is used mechanically or superstitiously, as a part of Revival-routine or machinery, it becomes decidedly mischievous' (p. 296).

[3] As R. L. Dabney shows, the words apply directly to errors of belief. *Discussions*, vol. 1, pp. 551–74.

There remains a final argument to be stated supporting the belief that the old definition of revival is the true one, by contrast with the new. The old taught that revival was the extraordinary and not the normal condition of the church. The new by asserting that revival ought to be the normal, and that it would be if only the right steps were taken, was not only propagating an illusion, it was depreciating the *place* and *importance* of the normal. According to its theory, an absence of revival necessarily meant disobedience and declension. As McLoughlin says, 'If Finney's theology was correct then there was no choice but between feast or famine in religion'.[1]

This view had very far reaching consequences. It made 'special efforts' the hall-mark of evangelism for the next hundred years and in so doing it inevitably induced discouragement over all that was not 'special'. For in the special, supposedly, lay the only hope. Built into this error was an unscripturally exaggerated view of revival. According to the older belief, revival meant a larger degree of the influences of the Spirit of God but it never asserted an absence of those influences at other times. It never supposed that there could be no effective evangelism without revival. To have done so would have been to deny Scripture. The Spirit is given to the church 'for ever' (John 14.16). He is her constant helper in all her life and service. In a time of revival, conversions appear on a larger and wider scale but they are the same as conversions that are seen in other times.

This is not to deny that there are eras of serious spiritual declension, eras when the influences of the Spirit of God seem to be largely withdrawn, but there can be an attitude which belittles periods of non-revival which comes close to belittling God himself. His providential care and love for his people are never in suspense. At all times he 'worketh all things after the counsel of his will' (Eph. 1.11). In periods of trial, of suffering and of sifting, God is as truly present with his church as in her days of prosperity. Further, the idea that there can be no real improvement or advance without revival, is quite the opposite of the teaching of Christ where he would have us understand

---

[1] *Modern Revivalism*, p. 149. Similarly, James Douglas, *The Revival of Religion* (London, 1839), wrote: 'we may lay it down as a maxim . . . that when there is no revival, there must be decay' (quoted in *The Northern Baptist*, London, 1839, vol. 2, p. 225).

that, as in nature, the law of slow and gradual growth is the norm in his kingdom (Matt. 13.31–33).

The men of the Old School, while believing in revival as fervently as they did, and knowing that there are seasons when believers have special reason to plead, 'It is time for thee, Lord, to work: for they have made void thy law' (Psa. 119:126), nevertheless knew no biblical reason to be cast down by the normal. Fruitfulness and blessing are possible at all times. The duties of labour, prayer and evangelism are constants. The Old School men kept the possibility of great effusions of the Spirit before them but they never supposed that without revival all labour was futile.[1] They believed that God would grant his blessing in the measure that was appropriate – whether in its heightened form – gloriously advancing his kingdom – or in quieter ways. They also sought to remember that the prayers and work of one generation are generally far more closely intertwined in God's purposes in another than we can readily recognize. 'One soweth and another reapeth' is a law in Christ's kingdom (John 4.37). Thus the larger fruitfulness of revival periods is itself connected to the labour and perseverance of the church in preceding years. So J. H. Rice could truthfully say of the revival at Prince Edward, Virginia, in 1828: 'Much that our valued friend, Mr Lyle, did in the way of sowing seed, is now springing up, and producing a glorious harvest'.[2] Similarly, J. W. Alexander could write of the sixty-one new members he received at one communion in 1858 that they were made up chiefly of 'persons with whom I have been dealing for years'.[3]

In these pages we have followed the lives of some Christians during both days of awakening and at other times. Their lives in all seasons speak to us of the high privileges to which Christians can rise in this world. Their testimony and the

[1] Isaac Watts, among the older writers, had warned against dependence on times of special blessing for such times 'are rare instances, and bestowed by the Spirit of God in so sovereign and arbitrary a manner, according to the secret counsels of his own wisdom, that no particular Christian hath any sure ground to expect them', *A Guide to Prayer* (London, 1810, 15th ed.), p. 194.

[2] *Memoir of Rice*, p. 343. Matthew Lyle (1767–1827) was converted in the revival of 1789 and spent all his ministry in Virginia, often afraid that he was accomplishing little.

[3] *Familiar Letters*, vol. 2, p. 279.

fragrance of their lives comes down to this day. Their pulpit oratory came from their hearts, and from the reality of living near to God. They themselves loved the Saviour whom they preached and hated the sin against which they warned. Personal religion, with devotion to Scripture and to prayer occupied a great part of their lives. Payson's testimony is representative of them all: 'I was never fit to say a word to a sinner, except when I had a broken heart myself, when I was subdued and melted into penitence, and felt as though I had just received pardon to my own soul, and when my heart was full of tenderness and pity'.

Why the spirit of this school of men so largely passed away is a subject that needs far fuller discussion than it has ever received. In part the answer has to be theological. The sublime truths relative to the conversion of sinners, worthy of the attention of angels, came to be regarded as commonplace. The interest in theological training shifted elsewhere. 'Scholarship' assumed a priority never given to it in Scripture. The older generation had not, in the first place, been concerned with the ability of a candidate for the ministry to prove his general learning. They wanted more. They looked for evidence of 'divine unction'. Speaking of this subject in 1857 a writer reported the words of 'one of our most eloquent preachers, now in glory': 'After listening to a popular discourse, delivered by a young licentiate, and expressing admiration of his pulpit talents, he closed his remarks by asking, "Do you think he can pray down the Holy Spirit?"'[1] Dr Kirk was referring to the same kind of thing when he wrote:

The old preachers of the law used to make the services of the sanctuary the opening of the grand assizes of the judgment. We have no more of that now, but a good deal of dilettantism in its place. We live too far from Sinai and from Gethsemane, busied with our alphabets and the questions of grammar and metaphysics.[2]

* * *

Our need of revival is indeed very great today. Once more men claim, as Voltaire claimed two centuries ago, that the world is

[1] 'On the Manner of our Preaching', *Presbyterian Magazine*, 1857, p. 21.
[2] *Lectures on Revivals*, p. 275.

seeing the twilight of Christianity. But it is not any kind of revival that we need. Before his death in 1963 Dr A. W. Tozer had come to this conclusion: 'A widespread revival of the kind of Christianity we know today in America might prove to be a moral tragedy from which we would not recover in a hundred years'.[1] With thankfulness we can believe that another kind of Christianity is reappearing in the English-speaking world and that in connection with a history which had been long largely forgotten. Contact between the bones of a prophet and a corpse was once God's way of bringing a man back to life (2 Kings 13.21) and handling the records of which we have sought to make use in these pages can have similar effect.

It may be that a generation of freshly-anointed preachers is already being prepared. Whether that is so or not, when such men are sent forth by Christ we can be sure of certain things. They will not be identical in all points with the men of the past, but there will be a fundamental resemblance. They will be hard students of Scripture. They will prize a great spiritual heritage. They will see the danger of 'unsanctified learning'. While they will not be afraid of controversy, nor of being called hyper-orthodox, they will fear to spend their days in controversy. They will believe with John Rice that 'the church is not purified by controversy, but by holy love'. They will not forget that the wise, who will shine 'as the stars for ever and ever', are those who 'turn many to righteousness' (Dan. 12.3). They will covet the wisdom which Scripture attributes to the one 'that winneth souls' (Prov. 11.30). But their cheerfulness will have a higher source than their work. To know God himself will be their supreme concern and joy. They will therefore not be strangers to humility. And their experience will not be without trials and discouragements, not least because they fall so far short of their aspirations. If they are spared to live as long as John Leland they will be ready to say with him at last: 'I have been unweariedly trying to preach Jesus, but have not yet risen to that state of holy zeal and evangelical knowledge, that I have been longing after'. Whether their days be bright or dark they will learn to say with Nettleton that 'the milk and honey lie beyond this wilderness world'.

[1] *Leaning into the Wind* (Wheaton, Ill.: Creation House, 1984), p. 18.

When Archibald Alexander died in 1851, an incident occurred in the Synod of Virginia which provides us with the right note both to part company with the men we have followed in these pages and to aid us as we look to the future. About the time that reports of Alexander's burial at Princeton reached the Synod, a debate was in progress on the needs of the Seminary at Hampden-Sydney where Alexander had once served. William Foote believed he knew the Seminary's greatest need and he shared his convictions with his brethren by means of recounting a dream he had enjoyed the previous night. 'It seemed,' he told the Moderator, 'you led us all, in solemn silence, to the graveyard at Princeton, New Jersey; and knocking at the gate, demanded of those assembling for a funeral, some of the previous dust lying there'. First the body of Samuel Davies was claimed, then that of another Virginian, Samuel Stanhope Smith, and finally that of Alexander himself: 'We must have Alexander, for he was ours; we loaned him, but never yielded him. They resisted,' Foote continued, but 'you took him'. Then Foote went on to describe the home-coming of this procession:

As we entered your native country, Moderator, you told the excited citizens that you had got the giants of the last generation. And at old Cumberland, you said we must pause for the night, and there we talked over the revivals after revivals for a hundred years, and spirits of the dead mingled with us, and the eternal world brooded over us.' Then in the speaker's dream, the procession passed away, followed by all his own generation, and then a new vision came in view – the future, 'full of brightness and glory and gospel success'. There came upon the stage some like Davies laying the foundations of churches, whose lips were touched with a live coal from God's Altar; some like J. B. Smith, wonderful in revivals and raising ministers of the gospel; and some like Alexander, fit to mould a host of ministers of the gospel![1]

Such was William Foote's dream of the future. But it was not only a dream.

[1] *Life of Alexander*, pp. 634–7.

APPENDICES

James Caughey preaching at Kingston Chapel (Wesleyan
Methodist Connexion), Hull, 1843

One

REVIVALISM IN BRITAIN

One of the earliest British publications to introduce the word 'revivalist' was Hugh Bourne's *History of the Primitive Methodist Church* in 1823. The link between Bourne's usage of the word and the United States is not hard to trace for it was Lorenzo Dow, on a visit to England in 1805–7, who encouraged Bourne and William Clowes, two English Methodists, to adopt the practice of the camp-meeting. Confronted with this novelty, the Methodist Conference of 1807 ruled: 'It is our judgment, that, even supposing such meetings to be allowable in America, they are highly improper in England, and likely to be productive of considerable mischief; and we disclaim all connexion with them.'[1] The response of Bourne and Clowes to this decision led to the formation of their own denomination, the Primitive Methodists. This fast-spreading group was marked by earnest evangelism and simple godliness. Their work was attended by true revival in various places but it was marred by the

---

[1] H. B. Kendall, *The Origin and History of the Primitive Methodist Church*, (London, n.d.), vol. 1, p. 77.

admixture of revivalism which had been present from the outset and which served to create general suspicion in other denominations. John Angell James, the Congregationalist leader, was undoubtedly referring to the Primitive Methodists when, in an article in 1828 'On the Revivals of Religion in America', he said: 'Let us divest our mind of all that prejudice against the thing itself, which may have been produced by the noisy and disorderly scenes with which supposed Revivals have been attended amongst certain persons in this country. Unhappily the practices of some injudicious and ill-taught professors of religion, have brought an ill savour upon the very name Revival. We must distinguish, however, between the thing and the abuse of it.'[1]

James was a foremost evangelical leader but it was clear that, with others in Britain, he was poorly informed on what was happening in the States. In an Introduction to Sprague's *Lectures on Revival*, in a second British edition of 1833, he appeared to see no conflict between Sprague and Calvin Colton (whom he quotes)[2], and, later, no serious conflict with Finney himself for whose *Lectures on Revivals* he wrote an introduction in the British edition of 1839. In recommending Finney's *Lectures* James qualified his words with certain 'cautions', but time proved he was too unsuspecting.

On 22 July 1839, James wrote in the course of a letter to Sprague: 'I am glad to say that our churches are beginning to enter with considerable spirit into the subject of revivals. Protracted meetings are now becoming very common. Dr Redford about two years ago set the example, and has been followed by many of his brethren, with considerable success. Finney's Lectures has been extensively read, and will be more so by our ministers, and has helped on the movement.'[3]

---

[1] *Discourses Addressed to the Churches* (London, 1861), p. 446. Originally published in the *Evangelical Magazine* for 1828.

[2] Ibid., pp. 489–521.

[3] R. W. Dale, *Life and Letters of John Angell James* (London, 1861), p. 355. In a further letter to Sprague later the same year, James says of Finney's works: 'They should be read with caution, for there is a strange mixture of good and bad; but really he is a most extraordinary writer. There is great want of unction and tenderness in his words, but they are moulding the taste of many at this time . . .' (p. 357).

Four years later, writing to another American, James expressed a less sanguine view:

Our body [i.e. the Congregationalists] has been made a little uneasy by the rising up in some quarters of a tendency to what is known I believe with you by the designation of self-conversionism. I think Finney's books have done a little harm in this country, and I regret I ever gave a recommendation to his lectures, though what I wrote was as much in the strain of caution as of commendation. The sentiment here that has given uneasiness is a virtual denial of the Spirit's work in conversion . . . God brings the sinner under the power of the word, and then the truth converts him; and there is no other influence exerted by the Spirit upon the mind of the converted man than upon that of the unconverted one. Dr Wardlaw and the Committee of the Scotch Congregational College expelled eleven students lately for this heresy. America gets the blame for this, and by participation we. I who have recommended American theology come in for a share. I do not think it has spread very widely here, but it is usually connected with revivalism, which makes it seductive and mischievous.[1]

Events were to prove that James was much too optimistic about the limited spread of the new influence. Partly through literature, such as Finney's, and partly through visitors from the States, revivalism seems to have spread widely in England and, to a lesser extent, Wales, in the 1840s. It made a considerable inroad into Wesleyan Methodism, the denomination which had succeeded in keeping Dow and camp-meetings out of their churches in 1807. One indication of this was what the biographer of the Methodist leader, Jabez Bunting, called 'a very lamentable division' in the Society at Derby in 1831. In a comment on this split, Bunting wrote: 'About 300 have left, and formed themselves into a new sect called *Arminian Methodists*. The leaders of the party are factious enthusiasts, who . . . say it is wrong to pray for faith, because we all have it, and can experience it if we will.'[2] The 'Derby Faith' people were

[1] *Life of James*, p. 420.
[2] T. P. Bunting, *The Life of Jabez Bunting* (London, 1887), p. 633. Bunting was decidedly against any idea of setting the time when people are converted (p. 178), and would clearly have had John Wesley's support (Luke Tyerman, *The Life and Times of John Wesley*, London, 1890, vol. 2, pp. 130–31). It would appear that early-nineteenth century American Methodists, very conscious of the presence of an opposing tradition, often took their Arminianism further than did their British counterparts.

[393]

[handwritten note:] Would it be fair to suggest that revivalism moved to an easy believism after Charles Finney introduced the anxious seat?

expelled by the Wesleyan Methodist Conference in 1832. Prior to this, six local preachers had been suspended and censured in the Wolverhampton Circuit for representing 'man's free-agency to believe in Christ unto pardon and sanctification "at any moment" or "whenever *he pleases*".'[1] The editor of Bunting's correspondence speaks of 'revivalism' as the real issue at stake.[2] But dispute on the subject was to continue, and in no small part due to the Rev. James Caughey (c.1810–97), an American Methodist of more regular character than Dow, who was evangelizing and promoting revivalism chiefly among Methodists in the Midlands of England from 1841 to 1847. The correspondence of Jabez Bunting reveals why the visitor's high-pressure methods produced much disquiet. A Canadian Methodist (from Britain) had warned Bunting in 1839 concerning Caughey's anticipated visit, 'By him there is no doubt the Protracted Meeting will be introduced at home'.[3] With the 'protracted meeting' came the anxious seat and much else. By 1844 enough alarm was raised over Caughey's efforts to lead to an attempt to restrain him at the annual Conference. It failed, apparently because, as one minister thought, 'some of the simpletons who countenance Caughey cannot or will not see the tendency of their own proceedings'.[4] In January 1846 another minister, serving in a circuit where Caughey had been active, wrote to Bunting:

A long conversation with Dr Newton last Friday has convinced me that the Conference must *legislate* in reference to American innovations . . . A class of men exists among us who if not efficiently superintended will soon bring the *regularly instituted ordinances of God into utter contempt. These men are always boasting of their doings and making little or nothing of sound and wholesome preaching – and in spite of the fearful declensions taking place in certain circuits which some time since*

[1] W. R. Ward, ed., *The Early Correspondence of Jabez Bunting 1820–1829*, (London: Royal Historical Society, Camden 4th series vol. xi, 1972), p. 211.

[2] Ibid., pp. 211–2.

[3] W. R.Ward, ed., *Early Victorian Methodism: the Correspondence of Jabez Bunting, 1830–1858* (Oxford University Press, 1976), p. 236. This appears to show that the Congregationalists had preceded the Methodists in this practice. That 'promoting revivals' and holding 'protracted meetings' had also become popular among the Baptists is clear from the pages of *The Northern Baptist*, vol. 2 (London, 1839).

[4] *Early Victorian Methodism*, pp. 31–5.

*were made red hot with the ism – go on in their own ways, no man
forbidding them . . .*

I glory in real revivals of experimental and *practical* Christianity,
but I abhor self-sufficiency and absurdity. O how frequently I long
and sigh for the orderly and solemn services of *London* Methodism![1]

Another Methodist preacher passed on to Bunting information
received from North American colleagues on the influence of
Caughey and revivalism as they had seen it:

Amongst other things Mr Hetherington expresses his surprise that
Mr C, should produce so much *effect* in this country. He did not
produce so much in America where these proceedings are more
common. Religion, Mr H. says, is generally so low (that is in true
experience) in the States, that these extraordinary proceedings are
necessary at intervals to impart even the appearance of life; that there
are many such parties there as Mr C. and many more able and
striking than himself even in his own way; that the same people are
converted again and again; and that if all the announced conversions
could be found, the entire population of the States, would be
converted in four years; that they proceed at intervals to this
'converting work', as deliberately and mechanically, as a builder to
raise a house: and nowhere is true and fervent piety more scarce, than
where these proceedings are most frequent.[2]

At the Methodist Conference of 1846 Bunting moved and
carried a resolution that the American bishops be requested to
recall Caughey, but such was 'the prevalence of the Caughey
influence' that the preacher continued to linger on the British
side of the Atlantic. He left during 1847, then returned in 1857
when one of the American bishops expressed regret that
English Methodism 'might possibly suffer some degree of
inconvenience' from his proceedings.[3] It is clear that the vast
success claimed for Caughey's work did much to mute wider
criticism of his ministry. Figures announced for his work in

---

[1] Ibid., pp. 338–39.   [2] Ibid., pp. 340–41.

[3] Ibid., p. 419. Bishop Simpson explained that as Caughey 'was merely a
local Preacher' he was not under his jurisdiction but 'he had enjoined upon
him not to engage in any services in this country but such as he might be
invited to conduct by the official members of this Conference, though he
feared with no good effect'. Details of Caughey's work in England will be
found in *The Revivalist* for 1858–60.

Sheffield, August 1857 to May 1858 were: Converts 'out of the world', 3378; converts 'in the church', 742; 'sanctified', 1889.[1] These figures appear to have been arrived at by the numbers, and the type of persons, who answered his appeals to go to the front. In his eagerness to get such a public response Caughey would sometimes walk the aisles and shout, 'Come out, man! and save your soul now'.[2]

Among other notable American revivalists in Britain at this period were Walter and Phoebe Palmer. They appear to have been ignorant not only of evangelicalism in Britain but even of the Methodism which they claimed to represent. A reporter of the Palmers' work in Glasgow in January 1860 said that the preacher insisted 'we must come to Christ that we might have life', and informed his readers that 'the course adopted is to invite anxious inquirers forward to the communion rail'. But in the John Street Church this posed a major problem:

When the moment arrived for inviting the seekers of mercy to come forward for counsel and prayer, Dr Palmer appeared to be a little embarrassed. The absence of communion rails staggered him not a little. He had been accustomed, he said, in the sweetest spirit, to call penitent seekers forward ... At Hamilton, America, in a church where no rail existed, and where previously there had been no 'revival', the front pews were moved at the request of the Palmers, and in less than three weeks, availing themselves of the provision thus made, between five and six hundred persons, respecting whom their pastor wrote some months afterwards that he had never known converts so steadfast, professed to find a pardoning God.

These statistics, plus words from Mrs Palmer who told the congregation that she 'thought that Methodist churches should be erected for the salvation of souls', were enough to secure the necessary change in John Street Church. Before the next service front pews were removed and the same reporter noted, 'Our American Evangelists, with all their modesty and simplicity, are divinely great and powerful'.[3] Here was

---

[1] *The Revivalist*, 1860, p. 92. Our copy of this magazine is faultily bound and it is more likely this page reference belongs to the year 1858.

[2] Carwardine, *Transatlantic Revivalism*, p. 120. A full discussion of Caughey will be found in this volume.

[3] *The Revivalist*, 1860, pp. 41–2.

full-blown revivalism. Elsewhere in Scotland similar things were beginning to be practised.[1]

But the evangelism associated with revivalism was by no means prevalent in Britain in the early 1860s. No well-known British leader endorsed it and even denominations noted for evangelistic zeal now acted publicly against the innovaters. The Primitive Methodist Conference of 1861 directed 'station authorities to avoid the employing of Revivalists, so called', and the Wesleyan Conference of the following year resolved to close their doors to the Palmers.[2] An example of how some once favourable had grown cautious can be seen in a Primitive Methodist publication of 1862. In that year John Simpson brought out a little book *Revivals: Their Features and Incidents*, which was published by the Primitive Methodist Conference Offices. Its first chapter contained these rather surprising words:

When a great revival is genuine, that is, when it is obviously Divine in its origin – as its character, and more especially its fruits, never fail to indicate – we hail it as a 'time of refreshing from the presence of the Lord' . . . But thoughtful minds cannot investigate the history of churches in modern times without entertaining strong fears as to the soundness of many so-called revivals, and the means to secure and promote them. The 'revival meeting' seems to be fast undermining faith in the ordinary and every-day instrumentality . . . Let faith and expectation be directed to the ordinary means. Exercise as much faith and hope in the circuit ministers – yea, in the earnest local preachers, as in the professional revivalist . . . Is the 'special effort' associated with more facilities for the reconciliation of the sinner than the ordinary effort? Are an excited prayer meeting and a penitents' form necessary to the conversion of a sinner? If so, tell us why? Are not reconciliation to God and faith in the Lord Jesus Christ the only

---

[1] In Berwick, for instance, in 1861, the Rev. John Cairns spoke of the presence of 'considerable religious feeling' and went on: 'I should rejoice to speak of the movement in unqualified terms; but being in the hands of the Primitive Methodists, it has all the typical characters of their religion, and especially their revival religion – boisterous singing, the anxious seat, women and children praying, and services protracted to midnight. Still, good is being done, and some young people connected with my congregation have, I hope, received saving impressions.' A. R. MacEwen, *Life and Letters of John Cairns* (London, 1895), p. 477.
[2] *Transatlantic Revivalism*, p. 185.

necessary requirements of the Gospel? And may not a man become reconciled to God, and receive the 'truth as it is in Jesus', while he sits in his pew, or reclines on his couch, or plies his trade, or walks in the street?[1]

The writer goes on to draw the lesson of the 1859 revival in Scotland, Wales and Ireland and refers to S. I. Prime (who, as we have noted above, made the same point in his book, *The Power of Prayer*): 'We have not seen, in any of those parts of the world we have named, the employment of either professional gentleman or ladies to get up the awakening, nor anything which characterises revival meetings in general . . . the awakening seems to have come upon the churches unawares, to have taken them by surprise. Hence, like the movement across the Atlantic, it was not "got up"; no revival-mongers were employed.'[2]

*   *   *

With lessons such as this being drawn it is probable that the high-pressure evangelism associated with the planned 'revival meetings' would have waned in Britain had it not been for the visit of another American. D. L. Moody (1836–99), whose first missions in the United Kingdom were in the years 1872–75,[3] was a very different figure from the earlier transatlantic visitors. As a Christian – 'unworldly, unaffected, unambitious'[4] – he appealed to all sections of the churches, the more so as he was waging no crusade against traditional doctrine. A hearer of Finney in Manchester, England, in 1860 said that his address was 'in substance a mere tirade against Calvinism. I came away with a worse opinion of revivalists than ever'.[5] Nothing like that was ever heard from Moody who had no pretensions of being a teacher. He announced himself

---

[1] John Simpson, *Modern Revivals: Their Features and Incidents* (London, 1862), pp. 10–14.

[2] Ibid., pp. 17, 19.

[3] Moody made five visits in all to Britain but these years, and 1881–83, were those of his major campaigns.

[4] William G. Blaikie, *An Autobiography* (London, 1901), p. 331. Moody spent 'most of the winter' of 1873–74 in Blaikie's Edinburgh home.

[5] Quoted in C. G. Finney, *Memoirs: Complete Text*, p. 612n.

on his first visit to Britain as 'plain Dwight L. Moody, a Sabbath school worker'. Unlike other itinerants, Moody had no plans 'to awaken excitement or sensation'.[1] He differed also from predecessors in his deference to the counsel of local ministers with whom he aimed to work as fully as he could. The love of God in Christ, the substitutionary atonement, an infallible Bible, were at the heart of his message. Such was the acceptance which Moody came to enjoy on both sides of the Atlantic that David Breed, writing in the *Princeton Theological Review*, could later say: 'Mr Moody, of course, was the first of the lay evangelists of this period – first in time, character and influence. And the whole Protestant Church on both sides of the Atlantic believed in him'.[2]

Certainly Moody gained near unanimous support in Britain and in him revivalism was met at first with tolerance and then with an enthusiasm new to the country. In part this was due to his personality, and in part to the low-key way in which he sought for immediate public decision. Aware that the altar-call had never been accepted in Britain, Moody substituted an invitation to go to the inquiry room. As this novelty was not accompanied by any instantly apparent doctrinal deviation, it was commonly regarded as simply a matter of method, and few recognised the long-term change which was being introduced into evangelism. It may well be that Moody himself was unconscious of how the practice of calling for instant physical action at the close of a service was related to theological belief. He had grown up as a Christian in the ethos created by New-School evangelism and he never seems to have doubted the view of conversion which that school popularised. Thus, preaching in England on John 3:3 he could say, 'Regeneration is coming to Christ as a poor, lost, ruined sinner, and taking life from Him'; and in Scotland, 'You believe and then you are regenerated'.[3] As in the United States, this 'coming to Christ'

---

[1] The opinion of 'an Edinburgh divinity professor' quoted in J. C. Pollock, *Moody Without Sankey*, p. 109. It can be accepted only with qualification.

[2] 'The New Era in Evangelism', *Princeton Theological Review*, (Philadelphia, 1903), p. 229.

[3] Quoted in J. Kennedy, *Hyper-Evangelism: 'Another Gospel', Though a Mighty Power, A Review of the Recent Religious Movement in Scotland*, (Edinburgh, 1874), p. 16. Moody also used the words so often heard in America since Finney, 'God would not call men to believe, unless they had the power to do so'.

and 'believing' was all-too-easily confused with answering the evangelist's appeal to stand up and to go to the inquiry room. Moody clearly saw no real difference between an altar-call and the inquiry room for there were occasions when he would invite would-be converts to come to the front with such words as, 'Anyone who wants to take Christ as their Saviour, you all come forward now, so we can pray for you'.[1] It should also be noted that while, as quoted above, Moody may not have intended 'to awaken excitement', the way in which music was now coupled with the appeal to come to Christ had a very powerful emotional effect. The *Daily News* reported:

Concluding his sermon abruptly Mr Moody called for a moment or two of silent prayer. Presently, while all heads were bowed, the faint notes of the organ, scarcely louder than the silence, were heard, and before one could decide whether it was actual music or not, Mr Sankey, in the softest pianissimo, was singing
Come home, come home
You are weary of heart
. . . come home,
and at the end of each verse the well-trained choir, in little more than whispered melody, took up the refrain, 'Come home, come, Oh, come home'. Organ, soloist and choir in the most skilful manner, gradually increased their force of sound until the last verse poured forth in full volume. It is difficult to describe the effect the music had on the faces of the congregation who, still retaining their bowed position, were with one accord looking with transfixed eyes towards the platform.[2]

Further on Moody see: Weisberger, *They Gathered at the River*; McLoughlin, *Modern Revivalism*; and Marcus Rainsford, *The Fulness of God and Other Addresses* (London, 1898), which contains 'Gospel Dialogues Between Mr D. L. Moody and Rev Marcus Rainsford'. Those who would be converted were told: God 'has given us all He has to give; and the sooner we take it the better . . . When God gives a command, it means that we are able by grace to do it' (p. 245).

[1] See W. R. Moody, *The Life of Dwight L. Moody*, (London, n.d.), pp. 138–9, 196, 215, 223–4. Moody's son and biographer saw nothing wrong in believing that to be a Christian is to experience 'the regenerating work of God's Spirit by a definite acceptance of Christ' (p. 38). See also *Moody Without Sankey*, p. 115 and George E. Morgan, *R.C.Morgan: his Life and Times* (London, 1909), p. 217.

[2] Reported in *The Guardian*, 17 March 1875, quoted in John Kent, *Holding the Fort: Studies in Victorian Revivalism* (London: Epworth Press, 1978), p. 217.

Moody met with some resistance in Scotland,[1] most notably from Dr John Kennedy of Dingwall ('the Spurgeon of the Highlands'), and in England where *The Record*, the chief organ of Anglican evangelicalism, was cautious in accepting all that was being claimed for the work of the visitors. The representatives of the older Anglican evangelicalism, as John Kent has written, 'disliked revivalism as a system' and 'distrusted the revivalist as a professional . . . Revivalism looked like a short cut as far as they were concerned.'[2] Nonetheless, *The Record* came to give its support to Moody, and any disagreement which remained in Britain was soon forgotten.

We have already suggested some reasons why Moody succeeded in disarming criticism where Finney, Caughey and others had failed. Most were content to accept him for what he was. His strength was in his spirit, his Sunday-School simplicity, and his 'superabundant' anecdotes. 'Story by story, Moody worked his way through from Genesis to Revelation, turning the gospel which was the core of Protestantism into popular drama. It was a Bunyanesque performance, but this was a Yankee Bunyan.'[3] It was also a 'Bunyan' thin in teaching (a factor which partly explains why future Higher Critics of Scripture could be sympathetic to his work). Moody's practice as an evangelist was somewhat akin to the counsel he gave to youth workers when, 'he urged them to have done with colourless catechisms and tedious verse-learning, and to act on the belief that children could trust Christ as a Friend'.[4] Yet, in justice to Moody, the opinion of the Rev Alexander MacRae should be added. MacRae believed that Moody's emphasis was

---

[1] George Adam Smith, an eye-witness of the Edinburgh meetings, refers to 'the novel inquiry meetings, then exciting much jealousy' (*The Life of Henry Drummond*, London, 1905), p. 62. Morgan says, 'The inquiry meetings – regarded at first with a little misgiving – became a mighty power' (*R. C. Morgan*, p. 173). Smith's lengthy account of 'the Great Mission, 1873–1875' (pp. 54–100), though written from an entirely different standpoint from that of John Kennedy, confirms that there was good reason for the latter's concern. From this date onwards, 'deciding for Christ' became a part of the language of British evangelicals.

[2] *Holding the Fort*, p. 125.

[3] Weisberger, *They Gathered at the River*, p. 215.

[4] *Moody Without Sankey*, p. 68. Moody was sometimes known to speak highly of the Shorter Catechism.

needed in Scotland because 'the strictly orthodox character of the preaching of that period . . . failed because it was not evangelistic, not sufficiently personal, pointed, and urgent in seeking to lead souls to Christ.'[1]

The Calvinistic ministers who gave Moody such large support in Scotland no doubt thought that they could redress any danger from the occasional lapses in his teaching or methods when he was gone. The same consideration existed in England where *The Record*, speaking of Moody's teaching, 'even suggested that it might be altered, a view which implied little knowledge of either the American revivalists or the theological position which they inherited.'[2] But there was clearly another reason for a general reluctance to offer public criticism. British evangelicals believed in revival. The awakening of 1859, along with the hope of further revivals, remained in many minds. It was significant, therefore, that the first news which the British public at large had of Moody and Sankey was of 'the Great Revival' attending their Edinburgh mission of November 1873 to March 1874. W. G. Blaikie, a Free Church professor and editor whose judgment carried weight, wrote of 'The Revival in Scotland' and believed, 'It is revival without revivalism'.[3] Of the religious weeklies which took this view, the foremost was perhaps *The Christian*, originally founded in 1859 as *The Revival*. R. C. Morgan, its owner, believed that the numbers responding in the Scottish capital, and subsequently in Glasgow, showed that it was the same as the work of God in New York in 1858. Certainly the two cities were deeply stirred. Even the Assembly Hall of the Free Church of Scotland in Edinburgh was turned into an inquiry room on one occasion. With blessing

---

[1] Alexander MacRae, *Revivals in the Highlands and Islands in the 19th Century* (Stirling and London, n.d.), p. 16.

[2] Kent, *Holding the Fort*, p. 147. One certainly gains the impression that British evangelicals of the last century knew little of the far-reaching changes taking place in evangelism in the United States.

[3] *The British and Foreign Evangelical Review* (London and Edinburgh, 1874), vol. 23, pp. 477–92. Blaikie conceded that 'the absence of deep conviction of sin is in many cases characteristic of the present work', but urged that there ought 'to be tenderness of judgment towards those who are manifestly influenced by a true and fearless zeal for bringing as many souls as possible under the influence of God's grace'. 'The massess are the masses, and it is better they should be saved somewhat roughly than not saved at all'.

on this scale evangelicals elsewhere were scarcely disposed to retain any reservations they might have had. In the opinion of Morgan, 'If the stately Scottish city, with its historical inheritance and its noble literary and scientific associations, could thus esteem the American evangelists . . . they were worthy of honour in any city of the world.'[1] People began to speak of the 'greatest revival since Wesley'.[2] In view of the success, any expression of doubt could appear like opposition to God himself. This was the point of John Kennedy's question to his colleague in the Free Church of Scotland ministry, Horatius Bonar (who supported Moody): 'Why will Dr Bonar and others fear only the danger of not countenancing what is a work of God? Is there no danger on the other side? Their one fear tends to make them tolerant of all that accompanies what they regard as a work of grace'.[3] On the same point Kennedy – who was quickly charged with being 'against revival' – says in his reply to Bonar's defence of Moody: 'I am quite persuaded that many, who took an active part in the movement, had previously no

---

[1] *R. C. Morgan*, p. 196.

[2] *Moody Without Sankey*, p. 96. Perhaps what happened in Scotland contained elements of true revival, but the words of John Nevin, though spoken in the American context are relevant, 'No one whose judgment has been taught by proper observation will allow himself to confide in the results of a revival, however loudly trumpeted, in which the anxious bench is known to have played a prominent part' (*The Anxious Bench*, p. 76). Blaikie believed that a prior work in 'our godly families and godly congregations' had prepared the way for Moody's reaping in Edinburgh where there were 1,400 professed conversions. It is impossible to believe that there were not private discussions on Moody's advocacy of the public appeal and there are indications enough that Moody was not entirely deferential to the advice of ministers. He understood the psychological importance of immediate success. A comment of D. W. Whittle, his close colleague, is significant: 'I think M. in having before him just the one thing of the success of his immediate work, may be in danger of sacrificing principle and that he magnifies those things that have immediate effect . . . His heart is in the triumph of Christ's cause' (*Moody Without Sankey*, p. 168). Moody's strength and weakness lay close to each other.

[3] *A Reply to Dr Bonar's Defence of Hyper-Evangelism* (Edinburgh, 1875), p. 12. Perhaps the *Life and Letters of John Cairns*, p. 721, provides an example of this. In a private letter during a later Moody mission he says: 'The only feature that all might not approve of has been the coming forward of persons to be prayed for. Yet I have become so used to this, and everything else is so decorous that I am satisfied and even thankful.'

sympathy with the kind of teaching I assailed, and, if it lacked the recommendation of seeming success, would not tolerate it even now. But there is a strong tendency, on the part of the soundest, to glide into what they see to be effective, and owing to their sanguine estimate of its results, to adopt it as their own.'[1]

Dr Kennedy took care not to deny 'a genuine work of grace' accompanying Moody's preaching in Scotland[2] but he believed, as Nettleton had believed with Finney, that the good would have been accomplished and the harm avoided if the teaching had been sounder and the appeal system avoided. Most evangelicals, Calvinists included, thought that they could help Moody as a temporary visitor, without giving any long-term support to his system or methods. Like Breed, quoted above, they sought to distinguish between Moody and the 'Moodyism' of which Breed said he did not approve. Thus a writer commending Moody and Sankey in Spurgeon's magazine, *The Sword and the Trowel*, added the reservation, 'I do not, of course, commend myself to every method our brethren use'.[3] But just as it was a major misjudgment for Breed to believe in 1903 that 'Moodyism is a thing of the past', so it was a serious mistake for British ministers to think that Moody's methods, with their seemingly instant results, would not influence public opinion to a degree which would later be impossible to change. From the 1870s, decisionist evangelism, claimed to be proved by 'the Moody revival', became a permanent part of the British scene. Men such as the Bonar brothers, who had been strong opponents of Finney's teaching, by giving unqualified support to Moody, unwittingly aided the advance of a movement that was changing evangelicalism on both sides of the Atlantic.

*   *   *

[1] *Reply to Dr Bonar*, p. 6.

[2] The sub-title of his first pamplet, *'Another Gospel', Though a Mighty Power*, was therefore unfortunate. In those pages he said: 'I carefully refrain from forming an estimate of the results of this work, as these are to be found in individual cases . . . I most persistently continue to hope that good was done; for even were I persuaded that Satan was busy forging counterfeits, I cannot conceive what would induce him to do so, unless he was provoked by a genuine work of grace which he was anxious to discredit and mar' (p. 7).

[3] *The Sword and the Trowel*, 1875 (London), p. 190.

It remains to say something more on opposition to revivalism in Britain. As in America, it is noticeable that it was mainly those who both believed in revival, and were of Calvinistic belief, who were most prominent in their resistance to the new influence.[1] Certainly that was the case prior to Moody. In his *Memoirs* Finney claimed great success for his teaching in Wales; but, if he knew, he did not mention that those longest acquainted with revivals in that land were united in their alarm. The Rev John Owen, for example, in his *Memoir of the Rev Daniel Rowlands*, wrote of the great revival period which turned the Welsh people to the gospel in the eighteenth century:

In these revivals there was only the ordinary means employed . . . There was no praying for individual conversions . . . Nor was there any particular system adopted for carrying on the work, as in America some years ago; which had the appearance of making too much of human agency. According to some of the accounts given, there seemed to be there a sort of forcing system, as if the work could be propelled and urged on by a systematic plan of acting – a kind of *opus operatum*. But there was nothing of this nature, as far as the writer knows, adopted in the Welsh revivals. They were effects produced under the ordinary means . . . And there was no officious interference with those apparently impressed. They were generally left to make their own case known, and to offer themselves as members. There is human agency and there is a divine operation. The declaration of the truth and prayer belong to man; but the conversion of souls belongs wholly to God . . . The forcing system, as to individuals, is calculated only to increase the number of unsound professors.[2]

John Elias, another Welsh leader and preacher, who was an old man by the time Finney's new teaching first reached Wales, spoke still more strongly of its dangers. He was convinced that it would drive away the old dependence on the Spirit of God which had so marked the Welsh Calvinistic Methodist churches. Among a number of references to this subject in his letters there is this clear reference to Finneyism in 1838:

---

[1] Hence such remarks of Finney as: 'London is, and long has been, cursed with hyper-Calvinistic preaching' (*Memoirs: Complete Text*, p. 506.)

[2] *Memoir of Daniel Rowlands* (London, 1848), p. 127. The danger of the false or of the purely natural was emphasised by Rowlands. Revivals are not the cause but they may be the occasion of errors: 'Wherever God builds a church, Satan is sure to build a chapel by its side.'

I hear that unsound and slight thoughts of the work of the Holy Spirit are entertained by many in these days, and that he is grieved thereby. I heard a man this week assert in a speech that 'Influences are inseparably connected with all truths, so that if the truth be set forth sufficiently clear, accompanied with strong reasons and earnest persuasions it will prevail with all.' If so, nothing more is wanted but that we be strong and eloquent speakers, persuasive, eloquent and clever; and we shall then overcome the world! Is there not here a want of perceiving the corruption, obstinacy, and spiritual deadness of man, and the consequent necessity of the Almighty Spirit to enlighten and overcome him?[1]

The most outspoken opponent of revivalism in England was C. H. Spurgeon – the preacher whose sermons had such an enormous sale in New York in 1858 when he was only twenty-four years old. Nurtured in the same literature as the Old-School preachers in America, Spurgeon held the same general convictions as they did on revival as the extraordinary work of the Spirit of God. At a time when thousands were being helped by his ministry he was emphatically against the idea that any power to convert men lay in the hands of man. He told his people in a sermon of 1857 that it was folly to speak of 'a great Evangelist in America', and to claim, as he had heard a person do, 'That man, sir, has got the greatest quantity of converting power I ever knew a man to have'.[2] In a sermon of 28 March 1858, Spurgeon informed his people of the awakening in New York but he prefaced his words with this comment: 'As you are

---

[1] Edward Morgan, *John Elias: Life, Letters and Essays* (1844 and 1847; Banner of Truth, 1973), p. 259. There is most valuable information in this volume on the nature of true evangelistic preaching, pp. 349–372. For information, but weak analysis, on the introduction of revivalism into Wales see Richard Carwardine, 'The Welsh Evangelical Community and "Finney's Revival"', *Journal of Ecclesiastical History*, Oct.1978, pp. 463–80. Carwardine names Benjamin Chidlaw (an emigrant to Ohio re-visiting his homeland) as the first to introduce new measures in North Wales (1839).

[2] *New Park Street Pulpit* vol. 3 (London, 1858), p. 197. His thought is the same as that of John Leland, 'A great preacher of the gospel of humiliation and self-abasement, is a monstrous character' (*Writings of Leland*, p. 617);and of John Elias: 'It cannot be too deeply impressed on our mind, that the most eminent ministers are but instruments, and the most excellent preaching but means, and that the Holy Spirit only can do the work. Surely we are nothing, and are unable to do anything' (*Life, Letters and Essays*, pp. 329–30).

aware, I have at all times been peculiarly jealous and suspicious of revivals. Whenever I see a man who is called a revivalist, I always set him down for a cypher. I would scorn the taking of such a title as that to myself.' Without naming Caughey, he went on to make a clear reference to him and the heralded statistics of a 'revival' in 'a certain place in our own country' (Sheffield): 'All that I call a farce. There may be something very good in it; but the outside looks to me to be so rotten, that I should scarcely trust myself to think that the good within comes to any great amount.'[1]

Throughout his ministry Spurgeon continued to encourage faith and prayer with respect to true revival and also to warn against revivalism. 'If you want to get up a revival, as the term is, you can do it, just as you can grow tasteless strawberries in winter, by artificial heat. There are ways and means of doing that kind of thing, but the genuine work of God needs no such planning and scheming.'[2]

But while Spurgeon did not give great weight to special evangelistic efforts, he believed in their occasional usefulness. From the outset of Moody's work in Britain in 1873 he gave the American warm support and distinguished his labours from revivalism.[3] His longest printed comment on Moody occurs in a review, published in his magazine in 1876, of a book on *D. L. Moody and his Work* by W. H. Daniels. While Spurgeon was obviously far from the view that the country had just experienced 'the greatest religious revival since Wesley', he believed there had been unusual blessing in some parts. In that same article he repeated a testimony to the evangelists 'that all was orthodox and straightforward' and noted, with evident approval, Daniels' reference to Moody's 'Calvinistic theology'. In the very same volume of *The Sword and the Trowel* there is a strongly

---

[1] *New Park Street Pulpit*, vol. 4 (London,1859), pp. 161–2. The statistics Spurgeon gave from 'the Rev. Mr. So-and-so' were, with minor inaccuracy, those of Caughey announced for the days Jan. 27–29, 1858. See the *The Revivalist* for that date under the title 'The Great Sheffield Revival'.

[2] *Metropolitan Tabernacle Pulpit*, vol. 17 (London, 1872), p. 499.

[3] *The Sword and the Trowel*, 1874 (London), pp. 112–17, 137–39. J. C. Ryle took the same view, see *Holiness* (London: James Clarke, repr.,1952), p. 304.

critical review of Finney's *Memoirs* which had just been published.[1]

How far Spurgeon ever revised his view of Moody's beliefs we cannot say. He was clearly disturbed by the subsequent evidence of the coalescence of revivalism with Moodyism and was often to speak of the danger of the superficiality which he saw spreading in evangelicalism. He also recognized in the 1880s that Calvinistic belief, far from advancing as he had thought in the 1870s, was being very widely abandoned. In the last decade of his life, and against the current of popular opinion, he insisted that a doctrinal recovery would be essential to revival in the future. From Spurgeon's many words on this theme we give the following:

Possibly, much of the flimsy piety of the present day arises from the ease with which men attain to peace and joy in these evangelistic days.[2]

A woman said to one of our brethren a little while ago, 'If what you preach is true, I am a lost woman.' He said, 'I am sure it is'; and she replied, 'I have been to the Revivalists and have been saved ten times, and it has never been any good; it has been of no use whatsoever.'[3]

What mean these despatches from the battlefield? 'Last night 14 souls were under conviction, 15 were justified, and 8 received full sanctification'. I am weary of these public braggings, this counting of unhatched chickens, this exhibition of doubtful spoils. Lay aside such numberings of the people, such idle pretence of certifying in half a

---

[1] Ibid., pp. 84–87, 213–218. As far as London (where Moody had preached March–July 1875) was concerned, Spurgeon believed that 1875 had been 'a year of revival which did not revive the churches, and of mass meetings which have left the masses very much as they were . . . had a hundredth part of what has been proclaimed with flourish of trumpets turned out to be true, we should have commenced this new year in very different circumstances' (Ibid., p. 1). The review of Finney says: 'At the risk of being charged with blasphemy for daring to question the orthodoxy of the man who claimed divine inspiration for his views, fidelity to our convictions of what we believe the Bible teaches inspires the necessary courage, and we gravely question whether the supposed benefit of Mr Finney's labours has not been greatly overestimated.' The reviewer was Spurgeon's close friend, V. J. Charlesworth.

[2] *C. H. Spurgeon Autobiography*, vol. 1 (Banner of Truth, 1962), p. 54.

[3] Quoted by G. H. Pike, *The Life and Work of Charles Haddon Spurgeon* (London: repr. Banner of Truth, 1991), vol. 6, p. 225.

minute that which will need the testing of a lifetime . . . Flowing tears and streaming eyes, sobs and outcries, and crowds after meetings and all kinds of confusions may occur, and be borne with as concomitants of genuine feeling, but pray do not plan their production (1879).[1]

We have had plenty of revivals of the human sort, and their results have been sadly disappointing. Under excitement nominal converts have been multiplied: but where are they after a little testing? I am sadly compelled to own that, so far as I can observe, there has been much sown, and very little reaped that was worth reaping, from much of that which has been called revival. Our hopes were flattering as a dream: but the apparent result has vanished like a vision of the night. But where the Spirit of God is really at work the converts stand: they are well rooted and grounded, and hence are not carried about by every wind of doctrine (1881).[2]

Today we have so many built up who were never pulled down; so many filled who were never emptied; so may exalted who were never humbled; that I the more earnestly remind you that the Holy Ghost must convince of sin, or we cannot be saved . . . We cannot make headway with certain people because they profess faith very readily, but are not convinced of anything. 'Oh, yes, we are sinners, no doubt, and Christ died for sinners': that is the free-and-easy way with which they handle heavenly mysteries, as if they were the nonsense verses of a boy's exercise, or the stories of Mother Goose (1883).[3]

I would condemn no one, but I confess I am deeply grieved at some of the inventions of modern mission work (1888).[4]

Things are allowed to be said and done at revivals which nobody could defend. Do you notice, at the present time, the way the gospel is put? I am uttering no criticism upon anyone in particular, but I continually read the exhortation, 'Give your heart to Christ' . . . . If, for a moment, our improvements seem to produce a larger result than the old gospel, it will be the growth of mushrooms, it may even be of toadstools; but it is not growth of trees of the Lord (1890).[5]

It is a proof of the strength of the tide away from the old evangelism that these and many similar words from Spurgeon received little attention, even from men supposedly under his

---

[1] *The Sword and the Trowel*, 1879, pp. 503–5.
[2] *Metropolitan Tabernacle Pulpit*, vol. 27 (London, 1882), p. 531.
[3] Ibid., vol. 29 (London, 1884), p. 126.
[4] *An All-Round Ministry*, (Banner of Truth repr. 1965), p. 297.
[5] Ibid., p. 376.

influence. Even his own students were enthusiastic in taking up the methods of public appeals and inquiry rooms. There were no public appeals at the Metropolitan Tabernacle before Spurgeon's death in 1892 and he was against any regular use of inquiry meetings[1]. Things soon slid after his death and under A. C. Dixon, one of his successors whose father had advised him, 'Have as many prayer-meetings and revivals as you can', there was full-blown revivalism.[2]

In his support of Moody and his work, especially in the years of the evangelist's greatest influence in the United Kingdom, Spurgeon differed with his friend John Kennedy of Dingwall whom we have quoted above. Their difference illustrates how hard it may often be to judge whether the merely human –

[1] For Spurgeon and inquiry meetings see: *The Sword and the Trowel*, 1874, p. 191 (compare pp. 143–46 where there seems to have been at least a touch of revivalism at the Tabernacle while C. H. S. was ill in France); *The Sword and the Trowel*, 1875, p. 382n.; *All-Round Ministry*, pp. 372–3; and *Metropolitan Tabernacle Pulpit*, vol. 21, p. 339, where, in a defence of Moody's preaching of justification by faith, he says: 'It is not *every* faith that saves, but only *the* faith of God's elect. It is a small matter to go into an inquiry room and say, "I believe"; such an avowal as that proves nothing at all, it may even be false. It will be proved by this – if you have rightly believed in Jesus Christ you will become from that time forward a different man from what you were before.' His theological difference with Moody is clear in the way he speaks of regeneration, 'Wherever there is faith in Jesus Christ a miracle of purification *has been* wrought in the heart' (Ibid., p. 437, my italics).

It should be remembered that Spurgeon did not exercise dictatorial powers at the Tabernacle. In a letter to two Sunday School classes, written in February 1874 when he was ill in France, he said, 'I confess I am sorry the [Shorter] Catechism is still not the text-book, for I believe it is a good grounding, and keeps you near the most important subjects. Discussions on new theories of the day drive away the Spirit of God; the old wine is best'. *The Sword and the Trowel*, 1874, p. 194. On the point of baptism the catechism was revised in accordance with Spurgeon's convictions.

A recent biographer of Spurgeon advances the view that Spurgeon did not give invitations to receive Christ by coming to the front because the architecture of the Tabernacle did not lend itself to it (Lewis Drummond, *Spurgeon, Prince of Preachers*, Grand Rapids, MI: Kregel, 1992, p. 657). This is to overlook several facts but chiefly that when the Tabernacle was being built, according to the preacher's own wishes, in 1860, the practice was foreign to British evangelicalism and that for theological reasons which Spurgeon well understood and adhered to all his life.

[2] I have sought to treat this subject much more fully in *The Forgotten Spurgeon* (Banner of Truth, 1972).

revivalism – preponderates over the divine. Kennedy's main call was that there should be no announcement of revival until the fruit was clear. When he was attacked as 'an enemy of the gospel', Spurgeon defended his character and his 'zeal for the truth' but thought he was being too cautious.[1] Spurgeon was also concerned not to be silent while Moody and Sankey were being attacked in England by non-evangelicals: 'We do not want our friends to stand in the front of the battle, and to be looked upon as targets.'

The great lesson that emerges is the same one we have already seen in the parallel developments in America: once methods to induce and multiply a public response to the gospel are introduced it becomes very much harder to distinguish between the genuine and the merely temporary. If the apparatus for decisions is established, and the immediate public visibility of professed converts is encouraged, then the sheer weight of numbers 'responding' comes to be taken as indisputable proof. What is least important, because it is no real evidence of any divine power, becomes the great subject of interest and attention. Instead of warning against the superficial, the new evangelism came to regard the institution of the public appeal as no small part of its strength.

How disastrously that could affect a true revival was demonstrated in the last general revival to be seen on mainland Britain, the Welsh revival of 1904. If there was some lack of discernment in 1873–74, the position was far worse in Wales in 1904. At the latter date popular opinion, encouraged by the Welsh press, made Evan Roberts the 'inspired revivalist'. Roberts had very little theology and no previous experience of revival. Supported by his influence, the numbers of converts were not only published as in the worst type of revivalism but, we read in *The Welsh Religious Revival, 1904–5*:

Churches that were anxious to create the Revival fervour were encouraged to invite raw converts to hold Revival meetings. Their names were announced and particulars of their conversions given; the pulpit was thrown open to them, and their presence constituted in the minds of many the high-water mark of the Revival . . . Some of the finest elements in our Christian religion, so far from being strength-

---

[1] *The Sword and the Trowel*, 1875, p. 142.

[411]

ened in this Revival, were actually discouraged. So great was the passion for results that men forgot what was due to reverence and even to decency . . . It is possible to sacrifice too much for the sake of results, and such results are seldom enduring.[1]

But the same writer went on to show that this did not mean there was no true revival in Wales in 1904–5. The position seems to have been rather as the Rev Peter Price, another Welsh minister, described it at the time:

I can claim that I have had as good an opportunity as most people to understand what is really going on in South Wales; and I have come to the conclusion that there are two so-called Revivals going on amongst us. The one, undoubtedly from above – divine, real, intense in its nature . . . a Revival which is of God – of God alone – yea a most mighty – an almighty Revival . . . I understand that there are several would-be originators of the Revival; but I maintain that the human originator of the true Revival cannot be named. And this, to me, is one of the proofs that it is of divine origin. I have witnessed indescribable scenes of this real Revival, effects that can never be put down on paper . . . But there is another Revival in South Wales – a sham Revival, a mockery, a blasphemous travesty of the real thing . . . it is this mock Revival – this exhibition – this froth – this vain trumpery which visitors see and which the newspapers report. And it is harmful to the true Revival – very harmful. And I am horrified lest people who trust to what they see at Evan Roberts's meetings and to newspaper reports should identify the two Revivals – the true and the false – the heavenly fire and the *ignis fatuus*.[2]

Revivalism in Britain thus reveals the same truth that we have seen in the case of the United States. Whenever wrong methods are popularised, on the basis of a weak or erroneous theology, the work of God is marred and confused. Dependence on men, whoever they are, or upon means, is ultimately the opposite of biblical religion. But where sound theology is weak it is quite possible for success to appear to lie in the very things which ought to have been avoided rather than approved. It was no coincidence that Arminianism advanced in Britain at the same time as revivalism. The idea that conversion is man's work

[1] J. Vyrnwy Morgan, *The Welsh Religious Revival, 1904–5: A Retrospect and a Criticism* (London, 1909), p. 140.
[2] Letter to the *Western Mail*, Jan. 31, 1905, quoted in *The Welsh Religious Revival*, pp. 141–44. *Ignis fatuus* = a foolish, delusive fire.

became endemic to evangelicalism and, just as men forgot that regeneration is God's work, so belief in revival as the work of the Spirit of God disappeared. The most popular evangelical slogan of the early twentieth century, 'The Evangelization of the World in This Generation',[1] was a direct product of Finney's theology.

This change did not take place without unease in those who remembered earlier times. In that connection the words of several older preachers at meetings held in Aberdeen in 1909 to commemorate the revival of fifty years earlier were significant. While being thankful for the work of Moody, they spoke of a sense of sin being present in '59 which had not been seen to anything like the same extent since. Some feared it was a feature 'dying out' of English and Scottish Christianity. Dr S. R. MacPhail believed that 'revival times are special sovereign visitations' and he spoke of missing the type of conversion which was then common: 'Instead of the too frequent forced rising to be prayed for so common at present, persons in those days either remained after meetings dispersed because they could not go, or they went out and returned either to the same place or to a place set apart'.[2] Another speaker referred to his memory of Moody's visit to Glasgow in 1874 and continued: 'Its effects were great; but if I may venture on a comparison, I hardly think, in the retrospect, that it came up to the standard of 1859. I will not give this as a reason, but I state this as a fact worth considering, that *conviction of sin* was deeper and keener in the former work than in the latter . . . the former work had a broader and stronger foundation. I have felt so at least. We were in 1859 all Simon Peters falling at Jesus' knees and crying: "Depart from me, for I am a sinful man, O Lord!"'[3]

It is noticeable that the speakers at this Aberdeen Commemoration spoke of revival according to its earlier definition. What they had seen fifty years earlier was 'an extraordinary

[1] Originally the watchword of the Student Volunteer Movement (1888). William Robertson Nicoll believed that the phrase was born of 'a young impatience', and commented: 'This feverish, superficial conception of things springs from that "irreligious solicitude for God" to which Christian men are strangely addicted, and more than ever in this pragmatic age'. T. H. Darlow, *William Robertson Nicoll, Life and Letters* (London, 1925), p. 372.

[2] *Reminiscences of the Revival of '59* (Aberdeen, 1910), pp. 15–6.

[3] *Reminiscences*, pp. 34–5.

diffusion of spiritual influence'; a work 'with so little of man's organizing and so much of the almighty power of the Holy Spirit'; 'It was the secret inspiration of God, who was pouring out the spirit of grace and supplications'.[1] The change in terminology was also noted: 'We do not hear much about Revivals in modern ecclesiastical phraseology. The word has fallen into disuse, if not disrepute.'[2]

With this understanding of history we know that Moody himself had great sympathy for not long before his death in 1899 we read that his thoughts went back, not to the great mission meetings in Britain of 1873–75, nor to similar work in the States, but to his youth. 'I would like,' he said, 'before I go hence to see the whole Church of God quickened as it was in '57.'[3]

Almost another half century was to pass after the Commemoration meetings of 1909 before, in the ministry of Dr Martyn Lloyd-Jones, a powerful witness was again raised in Britain on the danger of the modern evangelism and for a true theology both of salvation and of revival.[4]

[1] *Reminiscences*, pp. 38, 43, 64.

[2] *Reminiscences*, p. 24.

[3] Quoted by J. Edwin Orr, *The Fervent Prayer: the Worldwide Impact of the Great Awakening of 1858* (Chicago, Ill.: Moody Press, 1974), p. 198.

[4] See, for example, his chapter, 'Conversions: Psychological and Spiritual' in *Knowing the Times: Addresses Delivered on Various Occasions* (Banner of Truth, 1989).

Two

REVIVALS IN THE SOUTH

The limited material available to me in the preparation of this volume has meant that there has been comparatively little mention of revivals in the Southern States, particularly after 1800. But the sources which I have seen warrant the impression that much remains to be rediscovered and that a volume worthy of the theme may yet appear. The subject is all the more deserving of attention because writers have sometimes created the impression that the South knew little or nothing of the revivals which occurred in the North. Finney, for example, in his influential *Memoirs*, speaks of 'the great revival' which 'prevailed throughout all the Northern states' in the winter of 1857–58, and continues; 'Slavery seemed to shut it out from the South . . . the Spirit of God seemed to be grieved away from them. There seemed to be no place for him in the hearts of the Southern people at that time.'[1] Nearly fifty years after Finney wrote, F. G. Beardsley repeated the same assertion.[2] These claims were no doubt sincerely made but they only show how

[1] *Memoirs*, pp. 442, 444.
[2] *History of American Revivals*, pp. 227–8.

common the lack of information has been.

Such sources as we have seen suggest that when revival became uncommon in the North after 1831, the position was different in the South. Not only was the 1858 awakening quite as extensive in the South as in the North but, prior to that date, local revivals clearly occurred in many places. Ernest Trice Thompson, the most exact of modern historians of Southern Presbyterianism, recorded:

Throughout the ante-bellum period Presbyterian churches in the South looked to revivals as a time of ingathering, though in all churches there were long seasons of drought . . . 'From 1832 down to 1860,' writes Johnstone in his *History of Transylvania Presbytery*, 'our churches had varied success and prosperity, many of them being at different times more or less favored with spiritual revival.'[1]

Statistics which Thompson quoted included the following: In 1842 the Synod of Kentucky reported that revivals had added from twelve to fifteen hundred to the denomination. In 1845 the Presbytery of South Carolina noted 'considerable additions in twelve or thirteen churches', in four or five of which they believed that 'the Holy Spirit has been poured out in his awakening and reviving influences'. In 1852 the Synod of Memphis testified that God had graciously poured out his Spirit upon thirteen of their churches 'and many, very many have been added to the church . . . all classes seem to share in the rich blessing'.[2]

George Howe, the historian of Presbyterianism in South Carolina, made reference to several places in that state, in this period, where the church 'has enjoyed rich effusions of the Holy Spirit', and 'the gracious presence of its great Head'. They included Charlotte (1848 and 1852), Williamsburg (1848–9), Hopewell, Pee Dee (1850 and 1852), Darlington (1848 and 1850), and Bethesda, York (1852 and later).[3]

A church historian for Alabama refers to the years 1852–61

[1] *Presbyterians in the South*, vol. 1, pp. 466–7.
[2] Ibid., pp. 467–8.
[3] George Howe, *History of the Presbyterian Church in South Carolina* (Columbia, S.C. 1883), vol. 2, pp. 514, 632, 638, 679. Howe points out that evangelical doctrine, with its distinctive and vital Calvinistic features, marked the ministry of so many of the pastors of this period.

as the 'Golden Age of Revival' but gives few details.[1] In the case of Virginia we know a good deal more of revivals in local congregations which began around 1850. John Bocock has written a graphic account of what was seen in his pastorate at Providence Church in Louisa County when 'the heavens were opened'. Of a service at an October communion season he writes:

> The discourse was poor enough, no doubt, but the text was a two-edged sword. It was in the hands of the Spirit of God, standing between the earth and the heaven. He was not visible, like the angel whom King David saw by the threshing floor of the Jebusite. But we could *feel* his presence. The death-like awe of silence and solemnity sometimes seemed as if it was the hem of the robe of his glory waxing all but visible.[2]

In 1850 the ministry of Robert L. Dabney, the thirty-year-old pastor of the congregation of Tinkling Spring, in the Shenandoah Valley, was attended by the first awakening that had been known in the church for twenty years.[3] Further up the valley at Lexington, a more extensive work had begun suddenly in October 1849. The main instrument of the latter was Dr William S. White, the local minister, who had settled in the town in 1848. His biographer says that White 'believed in revivals, worked and prayed for them', and that 'his harvest seasons were more abundant in the last nineteen years of his ministerial life than in the first nineteen'.[4] The work of 1849 began while White was away from Lexington and the first he heard of it was from a passer-by from whom he asked for news as he neared home. 'All I know is that there is a great revival of

[1] James Williams Marshall, *The Presbyterian Church in Alabama*, ed. Robert Strong, (Montgomery, Ala.: The Presbyterian Historical Society, 1977), p. 129.

[2] C. R. Vaughan, *Selections from the Religious and Literary Writings of John H. Bocock* (Richmond, Va., 1891), p. 402.

[3] Thomas Cary Johnson, *The Life and Letters of R. L. Dabney* (1903; Banner of Truth, 1977), pp. 112–14. Howard Mc Knight Wilson, *The Tinkling Spring: Headwater of Freedom: a Study of the Church and her People 1732–1952* (Fisherville, Va.: Tinkling Spring and Hermitage Churches, 1954), pp. 290–1.

[4] H. M. White, *Rev. William White and His Times (1800–1873), An Autobiography*, ed. H. M. White (1891; Harrisonburg, Va., Sprinkle Publications, 1983), p. 144.

religion in your church', was the reply. Through November and into January 1850 there were to be prayer meetings or preaching every night. In 1854–55 White saw a yet more powerful work of the Spirit, 'in which the town, the College, and the Military Institute shared about equally'.[1] On one Sunday in his own congregation fifty-five young people were received into membership, singing as they rose in the midst of 'an immense audience':

> Jesus, I my cross have taken,
> All to leave and follow thee,
> Naked, poor, despised, forsaken,
> Thou my all from hence shall be.

'This was a scene not to be described', writes White. 'My faith is scarcely strong enough to warrant the expectation that I shall live to see another like it. But be this as it may, the recollection of this will go with me through life, and cheer me in death.'[2]

There are records of the same kind of thing elsewhere in Virginia. Towards the close of 1851 there was an awakening in Richmond, affecting the First and Second Presbyterian Churches and probably others. Referring to that event, the biographer of one of the ministers involved wrote in 1899: 'The blessed fruits of this revival are found to this day. It has been a common experience to the children of those who were associated in this work to meet godly women, full of all the sweet graces of the Spirit and abounding in love and good works, who trace to this time the beginning of their Christian life.'[3] Notes in synod reports list other places in Virginia which saw similar blessing about this time.[4]

The few published records of individual churches in various parts of the South that we have seen are probably only indicative of how much more there is to be uncovered. The history of the Midway Congregational Church, Liberty County, Georgia, for example, contains a whole chapter on 'Revivals', listing their occurrence, along with various details,

---

[1] Ibid., p. 153.   [2] Ibid.,p. 154.
[3] P. H. Hoge, *Moses Drury Hoge: Life and Letters* (Richmond, Va., 1899), p. 113.
[4] Some are quoted in *Presbyterians in the South*, vol. 1, pp. 467–8.

in 1827, 1832, about 1834, 1836, 1841–2, 1848, and about 1853–55. Comments on these events by one who remembered them included the following:

> The very ground to me seemed holy. I remember one cold night the whole congregation were on their knees supplicating mercy for themselves and others . . . That revival was deep, pungent, powerful, and lasting; though it was noiseless, and hardly heard of at the time beyond the precincts of the village. It began and continued under the ordinary means of grace . . . there was a general noiseless religious awakening throughout the community that told in time. The precious seed yielded its fruit in God's own way and time.[1]

The biography of Daniel Baker (who, after the general revival of 1831, gave much of his life to itinerant preaching) provides information on revivals in a number of different places in the South – at Frankfort, Kentucky, 1835; in Washington County, Texas, 1840; in Indiantown, South Carolina, 1853; in Providence Church, North Carolina, 1853, and elsewhere.[2]

If the records of other denominations in the South could be examined they would no doubt confirm that these times of refreshing were often seen between 1831 and 1858. The latter year saw revival in every southern state, 'as far south as New Orleans, as far West as Houston, Texas'.[3]

The Presbyterian Magazine for June 1858, under a heading 'Revivals in Southern States', listed a number of places 'mentioned merely as specimens', and spoke of two hundred thousand conversions.[4] Bishop Candler believed that the results of this year of grace were 'in proportion greater in the South than in any other section'.[5] That, of course, cannot be proved but the records that exist in some places suggest that it is possible. For example, in the small town of Natchez, Mississippi, on 2 September 1858 it was reported that 600

[1] James Stacy, *History of the Midway Congregational Church, Liberty County, Georgia* (Newnan, Ga., 1903; rp. 1951), pp. 254–58.
[2] William M. Baker, *The Life and Labours of the Rev Daniel Baker* (Philadelphia, n.d.), pp. 198–9, 251–4, 449, 483–4.
[3] *Presbyterians in the South*, vol. 1, p. 470.
[4] *The Presbyterian Magazine* (Philadelphia, 1858), pp. 253–4.
[5] Warren A. Candler, *Great Revivals and the Great Republic* (Nashville, Tn., 1924), quoted by J. Edwin Orr, *The Fervent Prayer: the Worldwide Impact of the Great Awakening of 1858* (Chicago: Moody Press, 1974), p. 29.

people had been added to the churches. This figure represented one-tenth of the total population, 'a larger proportion than reported for any other city in the United States'.[1] From the records of the First Presbyterian Church in Natchez we learn that the first signs of something unusual had been the attendance at a daily 5 pm prayer meeting which began on 5 April 1858. Then from 23 May preaching services were commenced twice daily in the church at 8 am and 6 pm. Apart from an interruption of six days in August, when gas lighting was being installed in the building, these services continued until 6 November.[2]

It is interesting to note that the sequence of events in this Natchez congregation exactly parallels what happened else-where. No instance known to us is more striking than that of Zion Church, the largest in Charleston, South Carolina. It was constituted mainly of black people for whose sake – his 'brothers in black' – John L. Girardeau, the pastor, had declined attractive calls elsewhere. The regular congregation was estimated at between 1,500 and 2,000 people. Here also in 1858 special prayer meetings were begun 'that constantly increased until the house was filled'. At that point some of Girardeau's church officers counselled the starting of special preaching services, but 'he steadily refused, waiting for the outpouring of the Holy Spirit. His view was that the Father had given to Jesus, as the King and Head of the church, the gift of the Holy Spirit, and that Jesus in his sovereign administration of the affairs of his church, bestowed him upon whomsoever he pleased, and in whatever measure he pleased. Day after day he, therefore, kept his prayer addressed directly to the mediatorial throne for the Holy Spirit in mighty reviving power.' Then, at one of these evening prayer meetings the preacher received the most distinct conviction that their prayers were heard and he announced, 'The Holy Spirit has come; we will begin preaching tomorrow evening'. But when the congregation was dismissed they would not depart, nor did they till Girardeau had proclaimed Christ to them until midnight. 'A noted evangelist

---

[1] *Presbyterians in the South*, vol. 1, p. 470.

[2] J. Julian Chisolm, *History of the First Presbyterian Church of Natchez, Mississippi* (Natchez, Miss.: McDonald's, 1972), p. 42. New members in this congregation numbered 155, including seven black.

from the North, who was present, said, between his sobs, to an officer of the church: "I never saw it on this fashion".' Girardeau spoke of what began that night as 'the most glorious work of grace I ever felt or witnessed. It began with a remarkable exhibition of the Spirit's supernatural power. For eight weeks, night after night, I preached to dense and deeply moved congregations.' Even when the revival itself was over, he writes, 'The work grew steadily until it was arrested by the war'. As with so many others, he always believed that this great ingathering was the merciful work of God prior to the conflict which was so soon 'to sweep so many of them into eternity'.[1]

We have seen above that in the North, after the early 1830s, as revivalism increased so the phenomenon of revival as it had been previously known became uncommon. In the South, on the other hand, where there was far less acceptance of new-measures and revivalism, the old phenomenon continued to be more generally known. This was demonstrably the case among the Presbyterians where there was near unanimous opposition to revivalistic practices. What was written of Dr William H. Barr of South Carolina was true of so many others: 'He was decidedly opposed to what he was in the habit of calling "mechanical means" to get up an excitement at religious meetings – and he seriously distrusted the genuineness of conversions where such means were used . . . But it is not true that he was opposed to revivals.'[2] Precisely the same could have been said of Thomas Smyth, the Presbyterian leader in Charleston where new measures had evidently been adopted in a number of churches of other denominations. The strength of Girardeau's ministry among the blacks owed much to a revival that attended the earlier ministry of Smyth in the same city in 1846. Smyth's work, it is said, 'contrasted with the other churches of Charleston, which resorted to various mechanical methods of stirring up a revival, such as sunrise prayer meetings, exhorting in the aisle, anxious benches, inquiry meetings, and hasty baptisms'.[3]

[1] *Life Work of John L. Girardeau*, pp. 79–80, 101–2.
[2] Howe, *Presbyterian Church in South Carolina*, vol. 2, p. 740.
[3] Benjamin Rice Lacy, *Revivals in the Midst of the Years* (Hopewell, Va.:Royal Publishers, 1968), p. 107.

The leaders of the congregations to which we have referred above were united in their understanding of the difference between 'getting up a revival' and an effusion of the Spirit of God accompanying the 'regular ordinances' of the church. Their witness on this point, and their opposition to the thinking which was beginning to identify 'protracted meetings' (i.e., special evangelistic services) with revivals, was clear and definite. At the Midway Church, in Georgia, we read that there was 'the entire absence of anything like religious excitement, periodic protracted services, anxious seats and all the modern methods of church machinery and mere human appliances. These things were looked on with extreme suspicion.' It was held that 'it is the absence of spiritual life, and not the absence of church machinery' which explains the lack of spiritual power in congregations, and that the periodic use of artificial means to promote 'life' has the opposite effect: 'There is such a thing as "Reviving a church to death", as a Baptist brother once said of a certain community in Georgia, in which he lived.'[1] Girardeau of Charleston, Dabney of Tinkling Spring, and White of Lexington, to mention but a few, could all have written the same. White, at the end of his life, far from thinking that their stand against new measures had been overdone, felt that they had not wholly escaped the same influence which made those measures dangerous:

We were careful not to hurry young converts into the church, seldom or never admitting them under one or two months. About this time we adopted the plan of taking persons recently converted, or supposed to be so, under the care of the session as candidates for church membership. In some cases persons held this position for several months before they were admitted, and some, after trial, were advised to withdraw their application.

Notwithstanding these precautionary measures, candor compels me to confess that sufficient pains were not taken in many cases to secure

---

[1] *History of the Midway Congregational Church*, pp. 203–5. Speaking of the Midway people, Stacy further said: 'They looked upon home training, prayer at the family altar and in the closet, and the regular Sabbath ministration of the word, as the means of building up the church. They sowed every day with the expectation of reaping every day'. See also pp. 218, 261.

a more thorough work of grace before admission to the Lord's table. I am painfully conscious of having too often sought to convince inquirers that they had valid ground to hope they had been accepted of God. They were not sufficiently left to their own exertion and the guidance of the Spirit. They had too much of human help . . . Had I my time to live over, I would trust less to my own exertions and more to the work of the Spirit.[1]

It would appear that, in the decades following the Civil War, revivalism became far more general in the South and that revivals were remembered only in the minds of an ageing generation of Christians. Writing on 'Machine Revivals' in 1876, a Southern editor complained:

We have no idea that the Pentecostal season was preceded by flaming handbills announcing to Jerusalem that Peter would preach on such a day . . . or that the apostles took lessons in advertising themselves and their mighty work from some Jewish Barnum; or that the numbers of conversions day by day was heralded by Roman couriers . . . through the length and breadth of the land.[2]

It is also a confirmation of the theme of this book that it was a dwindling number of Calvinistic preachers in the South, towards the end of the last century, who warned that the innovations in evangelism and worship, instead of being proved by their 'success', were forerunners of spiritual barrenness. The words of T. E. Peck, spoken at the fiftieth anniversary of the Theological Seminary at Columbia, South Carolina, were those of a man who could remember a different day. They remain a witness to our present need:

Our people are too ready to concede that our forms of worship are 'bald'. They are too ready, when God's ordinances fail of their appropriate effect, to resort to devices of human wisdom, instead of humbling themselves before the Holy Ghost in earnest prayer for his quickening power, which alone can make ordinances efficacious for salvation. The true glory of Christian worship consists in the presence and power of the Holy Ghost . . . One thing, we confess, that

---

[1] *White and his Times*, pp. 148–9.
[2] *Southern Christian Advocate*, 11 July 1876, quoted by Weisberger, *They Gathered at the River*, p. 227.

commends Presbyterianism to us is that it cannot be worked by mere human wisdom or power; that it must either have the power of the Spirit to work it, or be nothing.[1]

---

[1] *Memorial Volume of the Semi-Centennial of the Theological Seminary at Columbia, South Carolina* (Columbia, S.C., 1884), p. 30. One of the best summaries of the traditional view of revivals will be found in Peck's article 'Revivals of Religion', *Miscellanies of Rev. Thomas E. Peck* (Richmond, Va., 1895–97), vol. 1, pp. 206–24.

TITLE INDEX

Books and magazines are listed below in title order, except in the case of Biographies and 'Works', where the name of the subject or author is given first in Bold Type. Fuller bibliographical details (publishers, dates etc.) are supplied in the first footnote reference. For older titles the publisher's name is unstated. Ibid references are not listed since where they occur they will follow a 'named' entry.

Green, Ashbel (1762–1848)
The Life of Ashbel Green, J. H. Jones
114n, 115n, 136n
Griffin, Edward D. (1770–1837)
Life and Sermons of Edward Griffin,
W. B. Sprague 195n, 202n,
210n, 221n, 222&n
The Great American Revival, A. B.
Strickland 113n, 155n
*The Great Awakening in the Middle
Colonies*, C. H. Maxson 184n
The Great Awakening in Virginia,
Wesley Gewehr 80n, 81n
The Great Revival 1787–1805, John B.
Boles 115n, 150n, 156n, 164n,
168n, 190n
The Great Revival 1800, W. Speer 133n
The Great Revival in the West 1797–1805,
Catherine Cleveland 154n, 155n,
168n, 172n
Great Revivals and the Great Republic,
Warren A. Candler 419n
A Guide to Prayer, Isaac Watts 385n

Handbook of Revivals, H. C. Fish 358
Hawes, Joel (1789–1867)
The Life of Joel Hawes, E. A.
Lawrence xiv, 214n, 263n
Hill, William
Journal 92n
*History and Character of American Re-
vivals of Religion*, C. Colton 282n,
375n, 377n
History of American Revivals, F. G.
Beardsley 312n, 314–15&n, 358,
415n
*History of the Baptist Churches in the
United States*, A. H. Newman 302n,
306n, 318n
History of the Baptists, T. Armitage
302n
History of the Baptists, R. G. Torbet
302n
History of the Baptists in Virginia, R. B.
Semple 65&n, 66n, 68, 76n, 78n,
82n, 87–8n, 181n
*The History of the Episcopal Church in
Connecticut*, E. E. Beardsley 114n

*History of the First Presbyterian Church of
Natchez*, J. J. Chisholm 420n
*History of the Methodist Episcopal
Church*, Nathan Bangs 69n, 70n,
80n, 83n, 85n
*History of the Midway Congregational
Church, Liberty County, Georgia*,
James Stacey 419n, 422n
History of the New School . . . S. J.
Baird 261n, 274n, 292n, 337n
History of North Carolina Baptists,
G. W. Paschal 315n
*History of the Presbyterian Church in
America*, Richard Webster 12n,
13n, 14n, 22n, 25n, 38n, 44n, 47n
*History of the Presbyterian Church in the
U.S.*, E. W. Gillett 53n, 54n, 57n,
240n, 273n
*History of the Presbyterian Church in
Kentucky*, R. Davidson 116n, 147n,
148n, 149n, 153n, 167n, 168n,
182n, 183n, 189n
*History of the Presbyterian Church in
South Carolina*, George Howe 383n,
416n, 421n
*History of the Primitive Methodist
Church*, Hugh Bourne 391
History of Western New York, J. H.
Hotchkin 123
Hoge, Moses (1752–1820)
Life of Moses Hoge, J. B. Hoge 180n
Life and Letters of Moses Hoge, P. H.
Hoge 418n
Holding the Fort . . . , John Kent
xviiin, 400n, 401n, 402n
Holiness, J. C. Ryle 371n, 407n
Hyper-Evangelism: 'Another Gospel' . . .
John Kennedy 371n, 399n, 404n

The Independent [New York] 350

James, John Angell (1785–1859)
Life and Letters of J. A. James, R. W.
Dale 296n, 392n, 393n
Jarratt, Devereux (1733–1801)
Life of Devereux Jarratt 63n, 68n,
84n, 85n, 86n
Journal of Ecclesiastical History 406n

GENERAL INDEX

Wherever additional information on a topic is included in a foot-note, the page number is followed by '&n' (e.g. 350–1&n). Abbreviations used are: GA – Great Awakening (1740s), SGA – Second Great Awakening (c.1800), NS – New School, OS – Old School.

Adams Church, Jefferson County 228–9, 293
Adherents, definition 10n; *see also* Church Membership
Aikin, Samuel C., pastor of First Presbyterian Church, Utica 230; and the New Measures Controversy 230, 239, 244, 290n
Alexander, Archibald, early life and spiritual experience 93–5; early ministry 105, 135; and Princeton Theological Seminary 134, 135–6, 388; decried by Finney 291; on fanaticism in the Kentucky revival 171–2; legal conviction 373n; on the Hampden-Sydney revival 100–1; and revivals in New England 200; on young ministers 8; opposition to the New Divinity 269–70, 271, 273, 357
Alexander, James W., early life and influences 333–5; health problems 341, 345–6; and the *1857–58* Revival in New York 342–53, 385; catholicity of spirit 335; on defining Revival 376; developing attitude to Finney 336–7; on the English language xx; importance of teaching ministry 361–5; and New Haven theology 350–1&n; and the New Measures 335–8; and Samuel Miller 334; tracts 333, 343, 350; visits to Europe 341
Alexander, Joseph Addison 334&n, 341

Altar Calls *see also* Anxious Seat; Inquiry Room; New Measures 185–8, 190, 213, 226, 242, 249, 277, 348, 365–6; arguments against 366–9; Baptists 325–6; in Britain 396, 399, 400
Amelia County, Va., conversions under Methodist preachers 70–3
Andover College 134, 195–6, 273, 317
Anglican Commissary of Virginia, complaints against Samuel Davies 10–11, 26–8
Anglicans *see also* Church of England; and the War of Independence 76; attacks on Baptists 66, 68; complaints against Samuel Davies 10–11, 26–8
Antinomianism, arising from the Kentucky revival 188
Anxious Seat *see also* Altar Calls; Inquiry Room; New Measures; 242, 246, 278, 283, 313, 325n, 336, 366, 375, 403n
Arminianism *see also* Calvinism; Methodism; Methodists; among Baptists 227, 309–26; reaction amongst Baptists 315–28; compared to Calvinism 178–9, 188–9, 351, 363; growth in Britain 412–13; growth of influence in western New York 227; in Kentucky 177–90; in Virginia 6n, 68–74
Asbury, Francis [first Methodist

Howe, John 382
Hoyt, Arthur S., on Finney's opposers 357
Hughes, James, Principal of Miami University 54
Humility, a mark of faithful preachers 217–19, 386
Humphrey, Heman, president of Amherst College 132; on the *1857–58* Revival in New York 331; apprehensions concerning the new evangelism 358; on the financial panic of *1857* 342; on lack of spiritual power 115–16; New Lebanon Convention 235; on revival at Yale 133–4; on the SGA 118, 121–2, 131, 133–4, 138; on spiritual leaders in the North East 193; on the state of religion in the *1840s* 347
Hurst, Bishop, on the revival at Yale 133
Hypocrites, false professions and errors of judgement 83 *see also* Converts, lapsed; Converts, numbering

Immigration, effect of influx from non-Protestant countries 339–40 *see also* Migration, westward
Imputation, doctrine of, *see* Original Sin
Independents, their condition in England in the *1750s* 15
Inquiry Meeting (Inquiry Rooms), as used by Finney and others 233; as used by Moody 399, 400, 401n, 402; as used by Nettleton and others 216, 233n; Spurgeon's attitude 410&n
Inter-denominational Activity in the SGA 131–2

James River, Va., Baptists 65, 67, 78, 80–2
James, John Angell, on New Measures and revivalism in Britain 392–3; repudiates his preface

to Finney's *Lectures on Revivals* 295–6, 392n, 393;
–on revivals and Primitive Methodists 392; on Samuel Davies 3
Jarratt, Devereux, rector of Bath Parish, Dinwiddie County, Va., 64, 83–6; complains of Baptists 68; complains of Methodists 84–7; danger of Pride in young preachers 86; letter to John Wesley 64n, 72–3; and Methodists in Virginia 68–73, 84–7; on Presbyterians 63–4
Jay, John, American ambassador in London 114
Jefferson, Thomas, unbelief not openly avowed 114–15
Jefferson County, NY, in the SGA 228
Jeffery, R., on Jacob Knapp 314
Johnes, Timothy, minister at Morristown, NJ, 46–7, 49, 57
Johnston, Tom (Secretary of State for Scotland in the 1940s) xx–xxi
Jones, Charles Colcock, and Davies' ministry to slaves 12n
Jones, Samuel, Baptist 304
Judson, Adoniram, missionary 316–17, 317n

Kennedy, Catherine, wife of William Tennent 58
Kennedy, John, ministers changed by Holy Spirit 108; resistance to Moody 370–1, 401&n, 403–4, 410–11; on Sovereignty and Responsibility 351–2
Kentucky, altar calls 185–8; camp meetings 151–4, 164–5, 166–9, 174–5, 183–7, 188, 190; denominational fragmentation 173–6; emotionalism and physical phenomena 163–70, 182–3; poor ministerial leadership 148; populist elements 175–7, 279; positive comment 173; Presbyterians 416, 419; response to physical phenomena 165–72; SGA 149–59, 163–90; state of religion before the SGA

145–50

Kirk, E. N., on new preachers 386; observation on revivalism 380; understanding of revival 376, 381–2, 383&n

Knapp, Jacob, Baptist preacher of the New Measures 287, 312–14, 316, 319, 321, 325n

Lacy, Drury, Presbyterian 103

Lane Seminary, Cincinnati, presidency of L. Beecher 195

Lanphier, Jeremiah C. 332–3, 333n, 339, 342–3, 344, 360

Leavitt, Joshua, editor *New York Evangelist*, on doctrine 280

Lee, Ann, Shaker prophetess 171, 173n

Lee, Jesse, Methodist preacher, altar calls and numbering of converts 185; on revival in Virginia 79–80

Lee, John, on revival in Prince George County, Va., 80

Leland, John, Baptist preacher in Virginia 81–2, 303, 305, 318–20, 387

Leonard, Zenas, Baptist 307

Lexington Presbytery, Va., 105

Liberty Hall 167

Licensing of Dissenting Preachers 10

Litchfield, Conn., ministry of Lyman Beecher 195; revival 211

Lloyd-Jones, D. Martyn 414; Holy Spirit and evangelism xvi; preliminary 'law work' 373n; on Samuel Davies 3

Log Colleges 13–14; Fagg's Manor 3–5, 13, 36; Neshaminy 13, 37

Love, evidenced in revival 24–8

Lunenburg County, Va., conversions under Methodist preachers 72

Lunsford, Lewis, Baptist preacher, Morattico, Va., 65, 81, 305

Lyle, John, Presbyterian, an 'anti-revival' man 168, 182; on emotionalism in Kentucky 165, 167, 168; on revival at Cane Ridge, Ky., 153–4&n

Lyle, Matthew, seed sown 385&n

M'Cheyne, Robert Murray 30n, 338&n

M'Culloch, William, of Cambuslang 23

Macdonald, John, fresh baptisms of the Holy Spirit 108; on Sovereignty and Responsibility 351–2

McDowell, James, Governor of Virginia 137

McGee, John, Methodist preacher in Kentucky 164, 182

M'Gready, James, Logan County, Ky. 54, 130, 149–52, 154, 164, 171, 182, 189; conversion experience 150; and prayer for revival 130

McIlvaine, Charles Pettit, Bishop of Ohio, revival at Princeton 141

McKendree, William, presiding elder, Kentucky Methodist District 155; on Baptists and revival in Kentucky 154–5; on growth in congregations due to revival 156

Maclay, Archibald, Baptist pastor, New York 302, 308–9

McLoughlin, William, on altar calls and revivalism 277, 348, 384; on Jacob Knapp 312

McMillan, John, pastor in Western Pennsylvania 49–50, 51–2, 53–4, 56, 57, 134; and the Princeton revival 47–8

M'Nemar, Richard, and the Kentucky revival 166–7, 169–70, 175, 178; becomes a Shaker 170

MacPhail, S. R., on Moody's missions 413

MacRae, Alexander, Moody needed in Scotland 401–2

Macurdy, Elisha 54, 55

McWhorter, Alexander, minister at Newark, NJ., 37–8, 47, 49, 57, 202

Mahan, Asa, loss of unction by the New Measures preachers 288

ford 65; on revival in Virginia 81;
on John Taylor 146; on David
Thomas 65–6
Seven Years War *1756–63 see* Old
French and Indian War
Shadford, George, Methodist mis-
sionary in Virginia 71&n, 73
Shakers, gains from Kentucky re-
vival 170–1, 172, 173
Shedd, W. G. T., on theological
education 39
Shepard, Samuel, Lenox, Mass., on
sovereignty of God in revival 128
Shorter Catechism, interest of new con-
verts 103; at the Metropolitan
Tabernacle 410n; Moody's inter-
est 401n
Simpson, Bishop, warning con-
cerning the revivalist James
Caughey 395n
Smalley, Henry, Cohansey Baptist
Church 306
Smith, Hezekiah, First Baptist
Church of Haverhill 306
Smith, John Blair, president of
Hampden-Sydney College 36, 78,
95–8, 100–2, 107–9; on hasty pro-
fession of faith 106
Smith, Joseph, apprehensions con-
cerning the new evangelism 358;
ministry in Western Pennsylvania
50–1, 52–5, 57
Smith, Nathaniel, one of Finney's
'Holy Band' 239
Smith, Robert, father of John Blair
Smith 36–7, 47, 48, 98–9; on de-
cline in religious thought 114
Smith, Samuel, son of Robert Smith,
36
Smith, Seth, Old School Presbyte-
rian on the work of the Spirit in
regeneration 318n
Smith, Timothy L., revivalistic
Calvinism 362
Smith, William, son of Robert Smith
36
Smyth, Thomas, Presbyterian leader
in Charleston 421

Society for Promoting Religious
Knowledge 12
Sommers, Charles, on John
Williams of New York 303
South Elkhorn Baptist Church and
Association 146, 154–5
Sovereignty of God, Finney's
attitude 247; and Responsibility
128, 317–9, 351–2; in revival 21–2,
127–8, 201–8, 247–8, 345, 379–80,
383, 385
Sperry, William L., 'tired of revivals'
378–9
Spotsylvania, Va., 94–6
Spotsylvania Church, removed to
Kentucky 146
Sprague, William B., friendship of
Griffin and Spring 197; on
Griffin's humility 218; on the New
Divinity 280; numbers not necessarily a sign of success 298, 368; on
the SGA 118, 285; on Weeks 291
Spring, Gardiner 194, 196, 338; on
the *1857–58* Revival 345; and L.
Beecher 197, 268; on Finney 250,
288; encouraged by Griffin 197;
humility 218; and Samuel Miller
200; and the New Measures 230n,
231; on Perseverence xvi; preaching and love for Christ 220; and
revival xv, 205–7; on spurious revivals xv, 201; role models 197; on
the SGA 118
Spurgeon, Charles H., on the
1857–58 Revival in New York
406–7; commends John
Macdonald's doctrine 352n; and
inquiry meetings 410&n; importance of preaching 361n; opposition to revivalism xvi, 406–10; on
regeneration 364–5n; on relations
between Britain and the U.S.
xxin; sermons used in New York
344; his students enthusiastic for
New Measures 410; support for
Moody 407, 410–11
Staughton, William, First Baptist
Church of Philadelphia 305